FIRST
WORLD FLIGHT

THE ODYSSEY OF BILLY MITCHELL

SPENCER LANE

U. S. PRESS

Published by

U. S. PRESS

A Division of U. S. Financial Services, Inc.

Standard Address Number SAN 253-8776
www.firstworldflight.com
e-mail: info@firstworldflight.com

Library of Congress Control Number (LCCN) 2001117171

Publisher's Cataloging-in-Publication
Lane, Spencer.
    First world flight : the odyssey of Billy Mitchell /
Spencer Lane. — 1st ed.
    p. cm.
    Includes bibliographical references and index.
    ISBN: 0-9710110-0-1
    1. Mitchell, William, 1879–1936. 2. Air pilots—
United States—Biography. 3. Generals—United States—
Biography. 4. Aeronautics—United States—History.
5. Flights around the world. I. Title.

UG626.2.M57L36 2001   358.4'0092
                 QBI01-200419

ISBN 0-9710110-0-1

PRINTED IN THE UNITED STATES OF AMERICA

Cover design and interior by John Wincek,
Aerocraft Charter Art Service (aerocrafter@home.com)

To our grandchildren; Lily, Rachel, Sarah, Elliott and those to come.
May they be blessed with a better world than the one we leave them.

Lowell Smith

Erik H. Nelson

Leigh Wade

Leslie P. Arnold

Henry H. Ogden

John Harding Jr.

Contents

Acknowledgments

Few books about aviation history are written without assistance and valuable input from dedicated aviation enthusiasts, historians, creative professionals, family and friends. This book is no exception.

I am grateful to Lowell Thomas who, within days of the World Flight's conclusion, faithfully preserved the original diaries and recorded the reminisces of the airmen who participated in it.

I am most appreciative of the efforts of Charles Schwartz and George Kirkman, enthusiastic and dedicated archival historians of the Museum of Flying at the Santa Monica Airport, formerly Clover Field, from where the flight started and returned. They shared with me their treasured collection of original notes, drawings, letters, photographs, and a unique day by day compilation of several years of newspaper coverage of both American and foreign world flights, as well as related domestic events.

I thank the very talented writer, William Hoffman, whose enthusiasm for the adventures in this book, storyteller's soul, and uncompromising content editor's intellect gently prodded me into the seemingly endless rewrites which have made a good book better.

I am grateful to Naomi Shulman who, in her last months as an expectant mother, has taken the time and effort to edit the text, and to John and Rhonda Wincek of Aerocraft Charter Art Service whose enormously creative design talents are evident in the book you hold.

I deeply appreciate the efforts of Paul H. Poberezny, the legendary honored airman and founder of the E.A.A., who reviewed the completed text for technical and historical accuracy.

Most of all I am grateful to my wife, Dee, who has encouraged me to persevere and guided me through the difficult periods when the task seemed endless and the rewards small. Without her support it is doubtful if this book would have ever been completed.

JOIN THE
ARMY AIR SERVICE
BE AN AMERICAN EAGLE !
CONSULT YOUR LOCAL DRAFT BOARD. READ THE ILLUSTRATED
BOOKLET AT ANY RECRUITING OFFICE, OR WRITE TO THE CHIEF
SIGNAL OFFICER OF THE ARMY, WASHINGTON, D.C.

B illy Mitchell's lone voice, fearless and heroic as his efforts were, could not withstand the assault of the anti-aviation forces arrayed against it . . . and the country paid a dear price. American general aviation survives today as the sole remaining base of vigorous, robust, and affordable general aviation activity only through the organizational efforts of a few far-sighted individuals. Joining with their fellow airmen, they formed a brotherhood of those who believe the freedom of America's skies belong to all Americans. It is largely through the continuing efforts of two American aviation organizations that access to the nation's heritage of flight has been preserved.

On May 15, 1939 a small group of airmen founded the Aircraft Owners and Pilots Association, which dedicated itself to keeping general aviation safe, affordable, and fun for all Americans. It was the civilian pilot training programs of AOPA that supplied many of the early pilots and flight instructors when the Second World War began. These brave men held the line in the air against the enemy until government trainees became available.

On January 1, 1991, Phil Boyer succeeded John Baker to become the third President of the A.O.P.A. Phil has flown well over 6,000 hours in single and multi-engine propeller and jet aircraft. Formerly a senior Vice President with ABC TV, he brought to AOPA communication skills which have proved invaluable in empowering and achieving the organization's objectives. On February 13, 1992 Phil was elected President of the International Council of Aircraft Owner and Pilot Associations representing fifty-five national AOPA organizations and over 420,000 pilots around the world.

With boundless energy, Phil started frequent "Pilot Town Meetings" in 1992. They take him through virtually every center of general aviation activity listening to member's opinions, aspirations, and local problems, and bringing the resources of A.O.P.A. to find solutions.

AOPA monitors all aviation legislation and Phil has made numerous appearances before Congress vigorously protecting his member's interests. With AOPA's Air Safety Foundation efforts, general aviation has achieved a greatly improved safety record. Through Phil Boyer's leadership AOPA has grown to over 370,000 members, representing over half of the licensed pilots in the United States.

Foreword

by PHIL BOYER, PRESIDENT
AIRCRAFT OWNERS AND PILOTS ASSOCIATION

I t's easy enough to recount the exploits of heroes, but Spencer Lane has accomplished a far more difficult feat. He has made his hero come alive for the reader—alive in all the complexity of the hero's character and the challenges, both brutal and subtle, that were thrown against him.

This is an exciting and inspiring story. It should serve as inspiration to all involved in aviation and particularly to those of us in general aviation. We, too, must often fight to defend our right to fly in freedom. Like Billy Mitchell, we find selfish economic and political interests nearly as formidable as wartime opponents.

In the 1980s, for example, the great piston-engine segment of general aviation was almost destroyed by outrageous judgments against aircraft manufacturers. Many of them were simply forced to shut down production lines. The resulting lack of new aircraft and even of parts to repair the aging fleet made this a consumer issue, hurting pilots and small operators as well as the manufacturers. It took a full decade of intense advocacy by the Aircraft Owners and Pilots Association and others to get Congress to set reasonable limitations on aviation product liability suits. The bill is rightly known as the General Aviation Revitalization Act. Our struggle was long and tough, but like Billy Mitchell, we never gave up and, in the end, we were justified.

For many years, successive administrations kept the Aviation Trust Fund locked, refusing to spend the aviation tax revenues it held in surplus in order to make the federal deficit appear smaller. General aviation suffered along with other sectors of civil aviation, but we never gave up. Finally, in 2000, the 106th Congress accepted the justice of our argument and passed AIR-21, the Aviation Investment and Reform Act, which unlocked the trust fund and set more reasonable standards for funding the national air transport system.

General aviation has also been party to a substantial number of major technological advances over the years, from AOPA's lead role in the campaign for the Global Positioning System to the current cooperative effort with the FAA to develop the Capstone program which will provide traffic, terrain and weather information on a multifunction display in general aviation cockpits.

As we take satisfaction from these advances, we must also recognize that the future will raise obstacles for general aviation. We face attacks from those who want to replace airports with malls for their own profit, ignoring the airports' social and economic benefits to their communities. Others seek to divert aviation revenues to private interests instead of the aviation infrastructure improvements for which they were intended. Politicians courting favor with anti-noise activists try to unreasonably restrict airport operations—or even abolish the airport!

But we shall continue to defend the nation's air transport system, of which general aviation is the bedrock. We shall continue to enlighten the ignorant, motivate the apathetic, and mobilize those who understand the great contribution general aviation makes to our country's economy, security and social welfare.

In reinterpreting Billy Mitchell's story, Spencer Lane has given us inspiration for the work and the achievements that lie ahead.

To honor its most cherished pioneering airman, the State of Wisconsin renamed their airport in Milwaukee, "General Mitchell Field," and their Milwaukee airmen became the "Billy Mitchell Squadron." In January of 1957 The State Air Force Association awarded its prestigious "General Billy Mitchell Award" to Paul Poberezny as the person making the most outstanding contribution to aviation. The sister of Billy Mitchell personally made the presentation calling Paul "a tireless worker in the development of experimental aircraft," and praised his efforts "in forming the Experimental Aircraft Association with the objective of aiding flying enthusiasts who were interested in flying their own airplanes . . . Nothing could have pleased my brother more than having this squadron named in his honor, and he would have been happy to know that a person of such high caliber as Paul Poberezny received this plaque." [*]

Paul was not always an aviation enthusiast. It seemed to come on him gradually sometime between the age of two, when the First World Flight returned to a triumphant "Welcome Home", and five years old, when Lindbergh completed his successful solo Atlantic crossing. By his own admission, from the age of five, not a single day has passed in which he has not spoken the word "airplane."

With his lifelong belief that, "America *can* become a better place through aviation," Paul Poberezny picked up the fallen torch of Billy Mitchell, keeping the flame alive and inspiring new generations of young Americans to pursue their dreams and achieve their goals. In an age of few heroes, Paul stands with the tallest.

Flying virtually everything with wings, his aviation achievements are legion and legendary and he has received numerous awards and accolades. But the legacy he created, with his very capable wife, Audrey, in founding the Experimental Aircraft Association in early 1953 is indeed the achievement of a lifetime.

Each year 850,000 aviation enthusiasts, the young in body and the young in spirit, visit the E.A.A. Exposition at Oshkosh nurturing their passion for building and flying experimental, historic, aerobatic, and highly advanced aircraft. After fifty years of spectacular growth and leadership, Paul and Audrey have much to be proud of . . . and the rest of us much to be thankful for.

*Page 324, Poberezny, *The Story Begins.* . . . Red One Publishing, LLC, Oshkosh, WI.

Foreword

by PAUL H. POBEREZNY
FOUNDER AND CHAIRMAN OF THE BOARD
EXPERIMENTAL AIRCRAFT ASSOCIATION, INC.

Billy Mitchell is a name familiar to those in aviation, but few realize that he was far more than just a strong advocate of air power and the champion of an independent air force which, to many early in the twentieth century, seemed unnecessary.

Most are not familiar with his early life and his keen foresight during World War I in recognizing and bringing to the forefront in France such illustrious pilots such as Hap Arnold, Eddie Rickenbacker and the famous balloon-buster, Frank Luke.

Mitchell faced many challenges and strong opposition from General Pershing, President Coolidge and the political factions who believed a Second World War impossible. At a time when the Navy believed battleships could not be sunk by bombs dropped from the air, he defied his superiors by warning of the coming war with Japan and its inevitable attack on the naval fleet at Pearl Harbor which he concluded was ill equipped to defend itself.

Would there have been a successful Douglas Aircraft Company or a strong base of U.S. aircraft manufacturers without Mitchell's insistence that U.S. Army planes enter the race to accomplish the unbelievable task of an around the world flight to demonstrate U. S. aviation leadership?

Spencer Lane has written a book that tells far more about our country's historic challenges than just the first world flight. It should be required reading for all high school and college students as well as all others who would then realize there is far more to the making of a great country than just the technical challenges of aviation milestones.

Few had Billy Mitchell's foresight.

Introduction

Tuesday, September 23, 1924 was a momentous day for the city of Los Angeles. Most schools had closed and many businesses had given their employees the day off to join in the festivities. Even before the sun came up that morning, automobiles and trucks clogged the roads leading to Clover Field in Santa Monica. Despite the valiant efforts on the part of the city to provide public transportation using buses and horse drawn carts, the steep ten-cent fare discouraged many potential riders.

By eight A.M., the crowd at the airfield numbered into the thousands. By ten A.M. it had swollen into the tens of thousands, and by noon hundreds of thousands of spectators covered the entire periphery of the airfield, spilling over onto hangar rooftops, onto every branch of every tree, onto the roof of every car and truck, and still they came.

Traffic surrounding the airport had ground to a stop. The cacophony of blowing horns and the fist-shaking frustration of the hapless drivers had finally ceased. Resignedly, many had left their vehicles in the stalled traffic to complete the journey on foot. Many of their companions had left the roads and were driving over the hills toward the airfield. The thickening carpet of dark specks looked like hordes of invading ants. The spinning wheels of the cars threw plumes of sand high in the air. The drivers raced to join the fortunate multitudes who had already arrived to claim the best place to watch the historic event unfold.

Thousands of U.S. Army soldiers, bayonets fixed to their rifles, combined with the local police forces in an increasingly difficult struggle to keep the burgeoning crowds from spilling onto the center of the airfield and into the reserved VIP seats of huge, recently erected reviewing stands.

To honor this unprecedented day, *The Los Angeles Times* printed five hundred thousand copies of a four page "World Flight" souvenir edition to be distributed without charge. A continuous stream of Boy Scouts filed past the trucks parked toward the center of the airfield, each taking a handful of the hundreds of tons of flowers provided for the celebration by all the communities of Southern California.

Six brass marching bands, each in its own splendid regalia, and led by its own high-stepping, baton-throwing leader, competed with one another to be heard. The increasing din of the huge crowds slowly drowned out the patriotic martial music until only the *oom-pah-pah* and the low-pitched boom of the bass drum survived.

Hundreds of bucking broncos galloped and pranced while their rodeo-riding, lasso-throwing cowboys roped and hog-tied elusive calves. Others, with drawn six-shooters firing white puffs of smoke, chased willing, bareback-riding, tribal-costumed Indians in mock battle.

Resourceful vendors seemed to be everywhere, hawking their endless supply of high-priced hot dogs and soda pop. Dan Toby, the stentorian-voiced announcer, projected his amplified message from the many pole-mounted speakers to the crowd. His earlier role of stirring enthusiasm for the day's events had now changed to one of calming the assembled multitudes, urging patience and discipline, his voice reflecting increasing despair as crowd control threatened to move from tenuous to impossible.

By one P.M. that afternoon, the reviewing stands were filled. All the government officials, mothers, fathers, brothers, sisters, sons, daughters, uncles, aunts, and miscellaneous relatives were in place, chatting amiably with the top brass of the military, the high-placed and high-born, the mayors and councilmen, the rich and the famous, actors, actresses—they were all there . . . waiting.

At one-thirty final arrangements were completed. An armored truck, accompanied by machine-gun carrying armed guards and soldiers, drove up to the front of the reviewing stand. Locked inside were six cloth bags filled with gold, a gift donated by the grateful citizens of California to be given to each of their returning heroes.

By two P.M., the crowd grew increasingly restless. Every eye scanned the horizon. Occasionally, an arm pointed excitedly, and thousands of heads turned, squinting to see the object. After long minutes, the pounding pulses slowed. The adrenaline rush subsided. Another false hope was dashed.

By two-thirty the crowd became hushed and anxious. The brass bands stood silently waiting, poised and ready to explode into a cacophony of sound. The cowboys and Indians stood together, expectantly holding the reins of their mounts. The Boy Scouts nervously picked at bouquets of flowers just starting to wither in the hot Southern California sun. Even the raucous hot dog and soda pop vendors quietly scanned the horizon for some sign that the waiting was about to end.

At 2:32 P.M., a young man's keen eyes picked up the first sign. Three tiny specks on the horizon, and growing larger. As if by an unseen signal, all heads turned south and a murmur blanketed the crowd. First one arm pointed, then others, then still more, then all at once, to the southern horizon. A thunderous, spontaneous cheer filled the air. They made it. They were finally here!

At 2:46 P.M., one hundred thousand balloons were released. The brightly colored balls cut off the afternoon sun, rising high into the heavens. Bombs and rockets exploded. An orgasm of color and light and sound filled the sky. *Boom-boom-boom* reverberated the city. Sirens and automobile horns blew. Six brass bands played the martial music of "Stars and Stripes Forever". The crowds waved silk American flags high over their heads. Grownups cheered and cried at the same time. Hearts burst with national pride and patriotism and love for the returning young Americans.

At 2:47 P.M., the wheels of Lowell Smith's airplane rolled onto the grassy runway. In rapid succession, the two planes accompanying him also landed, followed by fifteen escort ships. Hundreds of Boy Scouts ran to greet the fliers, throwing bouquets of flowers. The crowd overwhelmed the police and soldiers. Tens of thousands surged onto the airport to greet the fliers. Chaos reigned, but the first world flight had been completed. Each person in that crowd knew that at that moment, in that place, history was made—the world would never be the same.

To the residents of Los Angeles, it couldn't get any better. The flight started and finished there. The airplanes were designed and built there. The flight had even been led to victory by one of their own. The flight's completion made newspaper headlines in virtually every city of the world and carried with it unprecedented prestige and respect for the United States.

Less than twenty years after the Wright brothers made their first tentative twelve-second flight of 120 feet on December 17, 1903, a flight around the world seemed impossible. The pundits of the time called it a flight of fancy, a Jules Verne science fiction story, a useless waste of effort, an impossible dream. But General Billy Mitchell called it an inevitable necessity. The flight was his legacy to those who would follow.

Billy Mitchell planned the flight in exquisite detail. He designed its pioneering route and chose the few airmen with the skill, courage, and determination to complete it. He found the obscure young genius who could build the aircraft to survive the ordeal. It was Billy Mitchell who proposed it, agitated for it, schemed, cajoled, threatened, begged, and eventually sacrificed his career and his life for it.

The first world flight was, by any standard, the greatest aviation achievement of the twentieth century. The support requirements were daunting. Worldwide resources of the Army, Navy, Coast Guard, Fisheries Research Board, State Department and a host of private U.S. companies were coordinated into one seamless endeavor, involving 250,000 people worldwide. It was the largest logistical peacetime effort of the century, far larger in manpower and scope than even the first moon landing, which followed forty-five years later.

The stakes for the flight were high. For the military, 1924 started another year of devastating budget cuts and continuing losses of personnel and resources. The dwindling U. S. Army and Navy were competing with each other for the meager scraps of diminishing funds thrown to them by an indifferent Congress and a penurious new President.

Commercial aviation in the United States was virtually nonexistent. For the tiny Army Air Service, things were very bad and getting worse. From a wartime peak of twenty thousand airmen, only 232 remained. Accident rates of 30 percent annually threatened to decimate what was left. Enlistments faltered. Even an impoverished

England spent 350 million dollars annually on the Royal Air Force, while an indifferent U.S. Congress allocated only twenty-five million to its air service. A successful world flight, with its attendant publicity and prestige, would be an undeniable demonstration of the future military and commercial potential of aviation. Mitchell believed it was also the last hope for its salvation.

General Billy Mitchell, then the Assistant Chief of the Air Service and strongest advocate of aviation, had been trying unsuccessfully for years to get permission for the flight. His military objectives were considered unnecessary for a country at peace. Politicians believed new weapons made another World War unthinkable. Unmoved by the fact that many other nations were making their own preparations for the flight to capture the power and prestige it would bring, the President and War Department repeatedly denied authorization. It was considered far too costly, too hazardous, and with too little chance of success.

Mitchell saw his world flight as the last, best chance to save the Air Service from total destruction. To the aging cavalry-trained Army staff and the battleship admirals mired in the outmoded, obsolete military concepts of the last century, his advocacy of aviation was insubordinate, opinionated, and irrational. Both branches considered the tiny Air Service to be an expensive and unnecessary indulgence. To the presidents, cabinet officials, politicians, and military leaders whose views he challenged, he was an egotistical maverick, an uncontrollable loose cannon that had to be stopped. His laboriously written, highly detailed reports supporting his views and proposals were all relegated unread to the "flying trash pile" reserved just for that purpose.

To the American public, however, he was a courageous war hero. To foreign Heads of State, he was the most significant American of the time—feted, honored, and awarded their highest medals. To historians, he later became . . . a prophet.

Billy Mitchell had powerful enemies. They chastised him, disciplined him, tried to jail him and even commit him to an insane asylum. When that didn't work, they exiled him, court martialed him, broke him in rank, and suspended him from salary and duties. Then they quietly swept his first world flight into the closed dustbin of history.

It was not until World War II was well underway, and long after his death, that Mitchell's dusty, musty, unread flying trash pile dating from 1919 to 1925 was finally reopened. Like some latter-day, incredibly accurate Nostradamus, it all came tumbling out. The resurgence of German military power and spirit, the threat their Luftwaffe would present in the future, their jet engines, their V-2 rockets that would rain on England—it was all there.

The reports covering the Pacific regions were even more incredible. The Japanese attack on Pearl Harbor occurred within ten minutes of the time Mitchell predicted it would back in 1924. The number of aircraft carriers that would be used, the direction from which they would come, the number and types of planes and the munitions they would use, the ships and men that would be lost—it was all right there. Similarly, the attacks on Clark Field in the Philippines—the devastation they wrought on U. S. defenses, even the precise time of the attack—was all there. The battles of Iwo Jima, the Solomon Islands, Guadalcanal, Wake Island, Guam, Singapore—all were described exactly as they would happen . . . seventeen years later. Included with each report were detailed recommendations and proposals by Mitchell that would prevent each of the attacks he described from ever occurring. They were all ignored. On August 8, 1946, President Harry S. Truman posthumously awarded Billy Mitchell the Medal of Honor. Early in the year 2000, the U.S. government honored his memory with a new postage stamp.

In 1936, shortly before his death, a visitor asked Billy Mitchell if he had any regrets. "Only one," he said. "I've never been given credit for my greatest accomplishment, my first world flight." In 1953, Ruth Mitchell, Billy's sister and confidante, expressed his wish in his biography, *My Brother Bill.* She wrote, "on September 22, 1924, came the greatest record of them all: the great pioneer flight around the world, prepared by Bill and carried out by his men, for which . . . under the displeasure of his superiors he was never accorded recognition."

This is Billy's story, the untold history of the first world flight, and the forgotten heroes who made it happen.

Billy

CHAPTER 1

FRIDAY, MAY 9, 1898
6:28 P.M.
U.S. ARMY BASE, WASHINGTON, D.C.

T he orderlies had just started clearing the dinner dishes in the officer's mess hall when Colonel Johnson entered. He stood with his hands on his hips surveying the latest crop of newly appointed second lieutenants. It took a full ten seconds before one of them thought to interrupt their meaningless chatter long enough to notice him. "Aaa-tenn-shun!" someone finally called from the back of the room. They stood too slowly, pushing their chairs noisily away from the table with the backs of their knees. *Another sorry lot of spoiled college brats*, Johnson thought to himself. *We'll soon see how badly they want to play soldier.*

The colonel took one of the sturdy chairs and, facing its back to the young men, stepped up onto the seat. "Now listen, you men," he said, raising his voice so they could all hear. "I've just gotten a call from the Washington police for help. We've got seventy-five enlisted men tearing up a bar downtown and terrorizing the locals. They jumped off the train coming through here when your fellow "Lieutenants" forgot to feed them for the past three days. They're madder than hornets, heavily armed, and drunk as skunks. They've already shot up the place and threatened to do the same to anyone who comes into the bar to stop them. The

1

police won't go near the place and have called us. They're our men and we have to go get them. I need a volunteer to lead a detachment to bring them back."

As he knew they would, the young lieutenants shuffled from side to side looking down in silence, avoiding eye contact with him as he scanned the group. The orderlies had stopped clearing the dishes. The silence was deafening and unbroken. Ten long seconds passed, then twenty, then thirty. Finally a voice from the back of the room: "I'll do it, sir."

Colonel Johnson observed the lean young man making his way toward him through the crowd. Standing at his feet, with clear, determined eyes returning his skeptical look, the young officer looked too young to be out of school. "How old are you, son?" asked the Colonel. "I'm eighteen, sir," replied the young man. "I can do it, sir."

"Eighteen!" he said contemptuously. "Sure you can. At eighteen you can do anything. That's why we don't take them at eighteen. Are you Senator Mitchell's kid?" The young man nodded assent. "Gentlemen, when we send our young Lieutenant Mitchell back home in a pine box to his daddy, please note that he volunteered for this assignment. You all heard him volunteer, didn't you?" Mitchell's fellow officers smiled smugly at each other, relieved that reprieve had come from the youngest among them. In one voice they replied loudly, "Yes, sir."

7:48 P.M.
CRAZY HORSE SALOON
WASHINGTON, D.C.

Second Lieutenant Billy Mitchell looked out from the alley across the street at the Crazy Horse Saloon. Behind him were twelve enlisted men he had hand-picked to accompany him. They nervously fingered their rifles, to which they had affixed their bayonets. They were clearly outnumbered and outgunned. Each new chair, bottle, and body that came through the shattered plate-glass window increased their apprehension. The occasional shots and boisterous laughter coming from within were not reassuring. The young lieutenant leading them seemed no match against the rough, tough hoodlum soldiers inside. *What was this inexperienced child going to do? He was going to get them all killed.*

Lt. Billy Mitchell observed the drunken revels of the soldiers for fully twenty minutes. He had considered all his options. His raiding party could break in suddenly and surprise them. With ninety armed men shooting at each other in a small space, casualties would be very high; a lot of soldiers would die. He could wait them out, but they had sufficient food and drink for weeks. The fistfights among them were becoming more frequent. These would soon escalate to knives and then guns; again, a lot of casualties, a lot of deaths. Time was against him. Daylight was fading, darkness was descending. His options had been considered. He had to act—now.

Billy released the cocked hammer of his revolver and checked its fall until it rested harmlessly against the cold steel frame. He holstered the weapon and unbuckled the gun belt, folding it carefully before handing it to the soldier behind him. He pointed silently toward Sergeant Horn and Private Kowalski, indicating they were to do the same. Reluctantly they gave their rifles and pistols to the other men.

Horn and Kowalski had been specially chosen by Mitchell because they were the largest and strongest men in the company. Sergeant Horn stood six feet, six inches tall and weighed a muscular three hundred pounds. Mitchell had seen him once take an enlisted man who had slept past reveille and throw him fifty feet through the barracks. He'd seen Sergeant Horn lift a four hundred-pound cannon and place it on the back of a supply truck as if it were a fifty-pound sack of potatoes. Just an angry look from Sergeant Horn was enough to petrify a man with fear. No one gave any lip to Sergeant Horn. No one alive, anyway.

Private Kowalski was the wrestling champion of the company. His massive arms bulged with muscles, and no army shirt could be found to contain his huge barrel chest. Mitchell had seen him wrestle as many as five men at one time. He would lift each one high over his head before setting them down gently, unhurt, in a pile of limbs and torsos on the ground. Everyone loved going out with Kowalski and basking in the respect they would receive from other men who would cross the street to avoid him. They didn't know the gentle giant Kowalski wouldn't hurt a fly. And neither did the seventy-five armed soldiers tearing up the Crazy Horse Saloon.

The ten soldiers remaining huddled together in the alley. They gripped their weapons tightly and watched, fascinated, as Lieutenant Mitchell, flanked by Sergeant Horn and Private Kowalski, walked unarmed across the street toward the Crazy Horse Saloon. At five feet, eleven inches and a trim 160 pounds, Billy looked every bit the small child sandwiched between the huge adults towering above him on either side.

Mitchell flung open the door of the Crazy Horse Saloon. The three men stood in the doorway, waiting to be noticed. The action in front of them continued unabated. Two soldiers were stripped to the waist and circling each other warily, their fists held high in a boxing stance. A circle of spectating soldiers picked up one and then the other as their rubber legs buckled, succumbing to the alcohol, and they ducked as their wild swings swooshed overhead.

On the floor in the corners of the saloon, other soldiers had passed out, tightly clutching liquor bottles oozing their contents onto their disheveled uniforms. Still others had obviously not been able to contain the unaccustomed liquid intake and were snoring loudly, oblivious to their soiled uniform pants. One large drunken soldier was crawling on his hands and knees carrying two others singing "Yankee Doodle Dandy" on his back. Another drunken soldier swung from the chandelier singing bawdy sea chanteys off-key. *He's got to be in the wrong service*, thought Mitchell.

Mitchell and the other two soldiers looked at one another and were suddenly laughing uncontrollably. With great effort, Mitchell composed himself and walked briskly to the center of the room, flanked by his large escorts. He pulled himself up to his full height, took a deep breath, and at the top of his lungs yelled, "Aaa-tenn-shun!" He had figured correctly that this was the one thing that even the most drunken soldier would respond to.

The effect was immediate. The soldiers came groggily to their feet and stood stiffly. With no further protest, they fell sheepishly into the marching order Sergeant Horn indicated. Private Kowalski lifted the stragglers off the floor, holding them up by the backs of their collars. They were marched outside to join Sergeant Horn's growing column of men. A few well placed kicks to their butts had everyone marching in step to Horn's cadence count. The ten concealed soldiers emerged bravely from the alley and took flanking escort positions with rifles and bayonets. With Mitchell leading, the rapidly sobering company completed the three-mile march in double time. An incredulous Colonel Johnson instructed the sentry to raise the entry gate for them.

Wednesday, January 2, 1899
Havana, Cuba

My dearest Mother,

Thank you so much for the presents. My nineteenth birthday was most enjoyable, thanks to your generosity. To my surprise, I find life in the army to be most agreeable. Unfortunately, the war with Spain lasted only eight months and concluded before my arrival and participation.

You know I love Father dearly, but I can no longer support his pacifist views or his rejection of the imperialism required to achieve our goals. Earlier today I witnessed the lowering of the Spanish Flag over Havana and its replacement by the Stars and Stripes. This event, undoubtedly the most important in the history of our country since the surrender at Yorktown, has stamped itself on my mind and on the minds of everyone else that was there.

It marks the beginning of a new policy on the part of the United States, that of territorial expansion and showing itself to the world as one of the greatest of nations. During this last year, Roosevelt's doctrine of Manifest Destiny has given us control over Puerto Rico, Guam, the West Indies, Hawaii, and the Philippines. The achievement and expansion of our Manifest Destiny seems to me, even if not to Father, an honorable and worthy goal.

Your loving son,

Billy

Monday, March 31, 1899
Havana, Cuba

My dearest Mother,

The time goes slowly here in Cuba, but I have made some progress. The insurgents we armed to help us defeat the Spanish now roam the cities, freely killing and robbing the remaining Spaniards and local inhabitants alike.

I was given the task when I arrived of completing 138 miles of telegraph wire throughout the province of Santiago. My company of forty soldiers faced over three thousand armed Cubans. It was only through the use of cunning, deceit, and brutality, which I found most distasteful and shall not amplify for you, that I was able to complete my mission, to the surprise and satisfaction of my superiors.

I was the only officer in the Signal Corps able to complete his telegraph network and have been promoted to Assistant Chief Signal Officer. With the war over and our pacification program starting, there are no further challenges for me in this country. We are planning to leave Cuba soon and return the government to the Cubans. I am certain that someday we will live to regret this decision. Despite my personal progress here, I dearly wish to leave this dreary land.

Emilio Aguinaldo, our former ally in the Philippines in the war with Spain, has started an insurgent war against us upon learning of our plans to bring democracy to these troubled islands. I hope to participate in the war against him. I long desperately to face battle with an actual enemy. Dearest Mother, you don't know how much I want to go to the Philippines. Can't something be done to get me assigned there?

As always, your loving son,

Billy

Friday, April 18, 1899
Washington, D.C.

My dearest Billy,

I understand your feelings and have discussed them at great length with your father. As you must know, the matter of a senator interceding on behalf of his son with the War Department is a most delicate situation. We could not ask to have any assignment for you, as it seems to disgust them at the War Department to have favors asked. We beg your indulgence and patience in this matter.

Your loving mother

Tuesday, June 24, 1899
Havana, Cuba

Dear Dad,

Please respond to my letters. I understand your position as senator places a special burden of integrity and appropriateness on your actions. I further understand that we have very different views of the world, the role of our army, and the morality of imposing our way of life and democratic traditions upon other nations. I love you and I know you love me. Let us agree to disagree upon the correct role that destiny defines for us as a nation.

As a child, I believed in and defended your position of opposing war in any form and for any purpose to be moral and correct. I have gladly suffered the childhood bruises and cuts to fight the bullies who called you "coward" and worse. To me, you are the rock—the strong, brave, and courageous defender of principles and honor.

I have long ago committed myself to following your shining example. Throughout my life, I too will never compromise my principles in exchange for favors. I know you are not happy with my role as a soldier and therefore make you this promise. If I can only get out there before this business is over with in the Philippines, if you want me to resign after that, I will.

Your loving son,

Billy

Wednesday, October 15, 1899
Washington, D.C.

My dear son Billy,

Do you realize you've sent me twenty-six letters during the past seven months all with the same request for transfer to the Philippines so you can go fight a war? You've even got your mother giving me the silent treatment these days until I give in to you, although why she should want to send you someplace to get your fool head blown off is beyond me. You never could take no for an answer.

Billy, you've plumb worn me down. I've asked General Greely to pass your request on to my old friend, General Arthur MacArthur, much against my better judgment. His son Douglas is now at West Point and wants to be a general someday just like his father. He's only four weeks younger than you are, but always looked up to you as an older brother. Arthur still remembers you as Douglas's best friend when the two of you were both little tykes playing war together in Milwaukee.

General MacArthur's running the show now in the Philippines, and got word to me that he can use a good assistant chief signal officer. He'll request your transfer from Cuba to his unit next week. Mother's talking to me again like I've done some sort of good thing for you. I don't feel I have.

Try not to get yourself killed or she'll stop talking to me again.

I love you, Billy

Dad

Friday, October 31, 1899
Mayalang, Philippines

Dear Dad,

I just arrived today in Mayalang. It's great here. We're under heavy fire constantly from Aguinaldo's forces. Very exciting. I can't thank you enough for helping with the transfer. Have to run now. Give Mom a big kiss for me.

Your loving son,

Billy

WEDNESDAY, NOVEMBER 5, 1899
7:10 P.M.
MAYALANG, PHILIPPINES

Chief Signal Officer Captain Carr sat at the large packing box that substituted for a desk in the deteriorating field tent. The mosquitoes entered freely through the wide rips and tears in the ancient fabric. He penned a few lines of his daily report before slapping at the unseen insects sucking the blood from his exposed sweating arms. He cursed under his breath at the elusive pests. They always seemed to take flight before he could strike. Still no progress to report. Another month of failure and frustration.

How could they expect him to construct a telegraph line through seventy-five miles of enemy-held jungle without supplies? Yes, of course it was important! If General MacArthur could only communicate with General Lawton's forces on the other side of the island, they could coordinate their attacks and defenses against the elusive Aguinaldo and dominate the island. Without supplies and the means to move them though, it was impossible.

A loud voice interrupted his journal transcriptions. "Permission to enter, sir".

He recognized the voice of young Billy. *Been here only five days. Probably wants to leave already. Can't blame him. Nothing to be done*, he thought. He answered, "Permission granted!"

Billy Mitchell saluted smartly. Captain Carr had resigned himself to grant the request for transfer. *Can't fool around with a Senator's kid.*

I've developed a plan, sir. I can do it."

"Do what, Billy?"

"Run the line, sir. You know, to General Lawton."

Captain Carr stared at Billy incredulously. *He must be crazy. No, this must be some sick joke.* Captain Carr waited, smiling, for the punch line. Billy looked serious. Carr started laughing at the obvious joke.

"I'm serious, sir. I can do it," Billy repeated.

Carr stopped smiling. In icy tones he said, "Lieutenant, we have no wire. We have no insulators. We have no poles. We have no batteries. Even if we did, we have no mules or horses to carry them through the jungle. Even if we had all of that, which we emphatically do not, it would take an entire army to get through seventy-five miles of jungle held by the enemy. Even if Aguinaldo's forces weren't there, which they most certainly are, it would take boats to get across the rivers and climbing equipment to get over the mountains. Lieutenant, you're either a lunatic or an idiot. This conversation is ended. You are dismissed." Captain Carr returned to his report.

Billy stood his ground and took a notepad from his pocket. "Please, sir, I've spent the last five days working out the details. At least let me show you. I know I can do it."

Captain Carr put down his pen and stared intently at Billy. *He's the Senator's kid, and the Senator is good friends with the General. Maybe I should humor him.* He said sarcastically "Okay, Lieutenant. Show me!"

Billy came over to Carr's side of the packing case, and excitedly started going through his extensive notes. "We've got two sources for the wire. We can strip the barbed wire from the fenceposts surrounding our compound. That will get us the first thirty-one miles. The Spanish cannons use wire-wound barrels. I've found almost two hundred cannon barrels. If we unwind the wire from the barrels, that will get us the remaining distance. I've found several groves of large bamboo. That will give us the poles we need to support the wire. Our garbage dump is filled with glass bottles. We can break them and use the broken glass for insulators. This village has twenty water buffalo. We can make pack saddles for them using dried banana leaves and hemp. I've tried it already. It works."

Captain Carr was now listening attentively. He was amazed at the work and effort that Billy had put into this incredible plan. "Okay, now you've got the supplies and transport. How do you get your army across the rivers and mountains?"

Billy was warmed by the change of tone. "That's the part that stumped me too, until the solution came to me earlier today. We don't take an army. Only twenty men. Without weapons. We tell them we are just the advance scouts and a large army is just behind us. If any harm comes to any of us, or if our wire is broken, the army following us will kill everyone in their village and burn it to the ground. The natives would never believe twenty unarmed soldiers would enter the jungle without an army behind them. It's got to work."

Captain Carr pushed himself back from his improvised desk and whistled in amazement at the bold plan. "And to get across the mountains and rivers, I suppose you all turn yourselves into birds and fly across, right?"

Billy continued, ignoring the sarcasm. "Almost. I've designed giant kites made of bamboo and cloth, which are easily carried. We attach our wire to the kites and fly them across all the obstacles. Well, what do you think?"

Carr let out a long sigh and shook his head in disbelief. "I think that's the craziest plan I've ever heard. What do you do for batteries?"

Billy nodded. "Batteries are a problem. Hopefully we will find some discarded, old Spanish batteries on the other side of the island. If I can locate some sal ammoniac, I can revive them."

"And if not?" asked Carr.

"If not, we can use a trick I learned as a child. Table salt in water will produce a weak current. By keeping one hand in wet mud and touching the wire with the tip of my tongue, I can read the dots and dashes of the Morse code. It's not elegant, but it will work. What do you think?" Billy repeated.

"I think your plan has a very slim chance of working, but it's the only one I've got," said Carr. If you can find twenty other men bent on suicide, I'll let you try it."

Billy's face broke into a broad grin as he saluted. With an enthusiastic "Thank you, sir, we'll make it," he left the tent and rounded up his volunteers.

October 26, 1900
Mayalang, Philippines

Dearest Mother,

Next week will mark a full year for me in the Philippines. Being able now to speak fluently in the local Tagalog language, I have developed a most useful network of loyal spies and local informers. I also secretly monitor insurgent activities by taking photographs from high in the air using cameras mounted on large kites of my own design. Using this "aerial reconnaissance," we have won every battle with the insurgents. I'm certain it will be improved and widely used by the Army in the future.

Using such unconventional methods, I have completed stringing sixteen thousand miles of telegraph wire throughout the Philippines with the lowest casualty rate of any unit. General MacArthur has often praised my efforts. Unfortunately, my relations with my fellow officers have become increasingly hostile. Many of these lazy dolts resent my success in inventing methods for creating supply, transport, and communications. They deride each new idea I propose and represent my competence as arrogance to my superiors. They seem more interested in gambling and pursuing the native women than in capturing Aguinaldo who, not sur-

*prisingly, eludes them. The loudest criticism comes from the most stupid
and cowardly among them. I have taken it upon myself to teach those
with the biggest mouths a lesson in fisticuffs they will not soon forget.
General MacArthur has more concern for these nincompoops than I do.
He has ordered me to leave for a few months to allow tempers to cool. I
will be traveling through Japan, China, and India to observe and report
on military activities in those regions. With Germany and Russia challenging Britain and France in Asia, we must determine if any Asian
power could confront the Europeans in the future. Intelligence and communication are essential to military success, so I have eagerly embraced
this new assignment although my return to the Philippines remains in
doubt. General MacArthur has given me permission to meet with Papa
in Egypt and accompany him to Paris as he has requested. My only regret
is that you will not be there to share my twenty-first birthday with us.*

As always, with love,

Your Billy

This exploratory trip confirmed Mitchell's belief that Germany
and Russia would be America's greatest antagonists in the twentieth century. It also convinced him that the United States had
totally underestimated the technical and military capacity of the highly
educated Japanese. He returned with the belief that Japan had both the
will and ability to contest the western power's dominance of Asia.

Anxious for new challenges and good hunting grounds, Mitchell
requested assignment to Alaska to expedite the construction of 2,200
miles of telegraph wire to connect the interior of Alaska with the
coastal settlements. The project had made little progress over the past
thirty-five years. With temperatures of minus 70 degrees, deep snows,
and blizzards, winters were considered too harsh for working, and the
melting snows and deep mud of the summer months made roads
impassable and the transport of construction material impossible.

Mitchell spent his first winter in Alaska developing a plan to sur-
mount the formidable obstacles. Developing his skill with a dog
team and sled, he surveyed the required route while hunting moose,
caribou, bears, and birds. He planned to transport and cache mate-

rial during the winter using dog teams over the frozen roads. Mules could then transport lightly laden laborers over muddy roads to dig holes for the cached poles and to string the wires during the summer months. The Army, however, resisted replacing trucks and automobiles with mules and dog teams.

To convince his superiors of the efficiency of winter dog-team travel, Mitchell became proficient at driving dog sleds. He then left the head of Good Pasture River at three o'clock in the morning and arrived at Fort Egbert, 150 miles away, at two o'clock the next morning. He beat the best time made by motorcar over the rough roads and set a new long-distance dog-sled record that would stand for more than fifty years.

With Congress slow to provide funding for his plans, Mitchell placed orders for material, salaries, and services totaling $45,000 without waiting for approval. General Greely saved him from court martial and criminal charges with a personal appeal to Congress for a supplementary appropriation to pay for the prematurely ordered supplies. This helped establish Mitchell's lifelong pattern of proceeding first and relying on forgiveness when permission was not forthcoming.

Mitchell led the working parties through the exceptionally hard winters of 1901 and 1902, often seizing an axe to fell trees and blaze the trail ahead. On June 27, 1903, a triumphant Mitchell would write his father, "I made the last connection of the Alaska system myself. . . . From Nome on the Bering Sea, clear through to New York and Washington, the electric current transmitted our messages with the speed of light. . . . America's last frontier had been roped and hog-tied."

With Mitchell's success, the Army Signal Corps basked in the reflected glory and favorable publicity. This gave him considerable stature among the General Staff, but also created additional enemies, jealous and highly critical of his unorthodox methods. He paid little attention to the criticism and looked for other new challenges.

Billy's father, Senator John Lendrum Mitchell, was a close friend of General Adolphus Greely, Chief of the Signal Corps and a famous Arctic explorer. Billy admired General Greely and his adventuresome spirit; Greely became his mentor and idol. It was Greely who first appointed young Billy an officer in the

Signal Corps, and it was Greely who interceded on Mitchell's behalf numerous times. Greely and Theodore Roosevelt, then Assistant Secretary of the Navy, were the strongest supporters of Samuel P. Langley, Secretary of the Smithsonian Institution, in his early experiments with manned flight.

Langley had made several successful albeit uncontrolled flights. In early 1898, at the insistence of Roosevelt and Greely, a joint Army-Navy board was established to investigate flying machines and, if feasible, construct one. The chairman of this board, Commander C. H. Davis, recommended a flying machine be constructed as soon as possible, concluding that ". . . in military operations it would be revolutionary in questions of strategy and offensive warfare."

Unfortunately Roosevelt left for battle in Cuba shortly thereafter and Greely, now officially recognized as the officer in charge of military aeronautics, was left the lone supporter of aviation in the government.

On May 25 of 1898, Greely requested the Secretary of War provide funds for Langley to continue his experiments with flying machines, considering "the great importance of such a machine for warfare and the great good that would result to the world at large should a flying machine be made practicable."

With funding available and at the urging of Greely, Langley reluctantly continued his risky and often frustrating aeronautical experiments. He eventually built an "aerodrome" capable of carrying a person aloft. It was the impeccable scientific credentials and excellent reputation of Langley and the Smithsonian that legitimized the quest for manned flight. Several years later, the Wright brothers acknowledged that it was Langley's belief in manned flight and his assistance that made their success possible.

With his newly developed interest in using kites for aerial reconnaissance, and now sharing Greely's enthusiasm, Mitchell spent almost all his free time in Alaska studying Langley's experiments in aeronautics, researching gliders, kites, balloons, and powered aircraft. He returned from Alaska a passionate convert to aviation and a true believer in its future. With success came promotion, and Mitchell became the youngest Captain in the army.

Mitchell remained extremely close to his mother. While he was in Alaska, he became engaged to Caroline Stoddard. Mitchell's and

Caroline's mothers were roommates and best friends during their boarding school days. Both resolved that if they had eligible children, they would make certain they wed each other. Billy and Caroline's childhood friendship was encouraged by both mothers, and on December 2, 1903, Mitchell fulfilled their childhood promise. Two weeks after they were married, on December 17, the Wright brothers made their first successful flight.

The first flight lasted only twelve seconds and covered 120 feet. Within the next two years, these flights had extended to thirty-eight minutes and covered twenty-four miles. The U.S. government saw little commercial or military application for these fragile "motorized kites," and refused to support further development. Private funding sources demanded patent protection, so further flights were curtailed for the next two and a half years awaiting the granting of patents.

During this period the French made intensive efforts to catch up with the Wright brothers. On November 12, 1906, the Brazilian Santos-Dumont, based in France, flew 720 feet. On July 6, 1908, the French Voisin brothers extended this distance to twelve miles. With little support available at home, and French enthusiasm for flight growing, the Wright brothers sailed for France. On December 31, 1908, they capped a series of 104 demonstration flights with their two-seater Model A, covering an incredible seventy-seven miles.

Meanwhile, the British also experimented with flight. Early enthusiasts formed the Royal Aeronautical Society. Following the Wright's seventy-seven-mile flight, Major B. F. S. Baden-Powell, the previous president of that society, wrote of the Wright brothers, "That Wilbur Wright is in possession of a power which controls the fate of nations is beyond dispute."

Unwilling to jeopardize scant resources, most of the Wrights' demonstration flights were made by circling over the fields from which they took off, thus keeping the aircraft within sight of observers and within gliding distance of a safe landing. They scoffed at suggestions that the flights would have more dramatic impact if they flew in a straight line and crossed the channel from France to England. To their scientific minds, these applications of flight were so obvious that demonstrations were unnecessarily risky. They were, after all, "engineers and not stunt men."

The Wright brothers' reluctance for dramatic aerial demonstrations cleared the way for the French to capture the public's imagination. On October 30, 1908, France's Henry Farman flew sixteen miles from Chalons to Reims. On July 25, 1909, Louis Bleriot flew from the French cliff tops near Calais across the twenty-two miles of the English Channel to land on an English hilltop in Dover.

With this crossing came worldwide publicity and a recognition of the military and commercial potential of aviation by the leading European nations. The London *Daily Telegraph* predicted, "Air power will become as vital to us as sea power has ever been." Thanks to the publicity garnered by this flight, Louis Bleriot had few problems raising the necessary funds to start France's first aircraft factory.

The Wrights belatedly realized that the drama and publicity of new aeronautical records created the public support essential for aeronautical progress. This lesson was not lost on Billy Mitchell.

Dispatched to the Philippines in 1909 as chief signal officer for Luzon, Mitchell undertook a mission to spy on the growing Japanese military communications installations on the islands off the coast of Formosa. Disguised as a naturalist, in 1911 he traveled to China, Korea, and Japan photographing and reporting on their growing air force, army maneuvers, military installations, and organization.

In 1912, at the age of thirty-two, Mitchell became the youngest appointee ever on the general staff as Chief of Military Intelligence. With his growing interest in aviation, he frequently visited the army's new flying school at College Park, Maryland, where Lieutenant Henry H. (Hap) Arnold was trying to develop the airplane into a military weapon. Arnold had just earned his military aviator rating from Orville Wright. Seemingly always jolly, Hap was given his nickname by his fellow students at West Point. He rose to the position of General of the Army Air Forces during World War II, and remained a lifelong loyal friend of Billy Mitchell's.

The Drums of War

On June 28, 1914, a Serb terrorist assassinated Archduke Francis Ferdinand, heir to the Austrian-Hungarian throne, in Sarajevo, Bosnia. Austria accused Serbia of complicity, refused international attempts to mediate the dispute, and declared war on Serbia on July 28. Russia came to the aid of Serbia and Germany came to the aid of Austria as the Balkan conflict overflowed into the neighboring countries.

Within the next few months bloody battles erupted, pitting Austria, Hungary, Germany, Turkey, and Bulgaria against an Allied force of Serbia, Russia, France, Britain, Poland, Belgium, Australia, New Zealand, Canada, Italy, Greece, Romania, Galicia and, eventually, the United States and Japan.

As Chief of Military Intelligence, Mitchell informed Congress on a daily basis of the progress of the war. He expressed his alarm to them at the growing investment the Europeans were making in aviation. By 1915, twenty-six nations had spent a total of one hundred million dollars on aviation. The United States had spent only $435,000; the Europeans were spending two hundred times more than the United States on aviation. Worldwide, 2,400 pilots had been licensed but fewer than fifty were in the United States, and only seven were in the U.S military air service.

America's combined army and navy air strength was six airplanes, while Japan had fourteen and France boasted 1,200. Mitchell's insatiable quest for aviation knowledge led to extensive discussions with aviation pioneers on the future military applications of this new science. He became convinced that air power would dominate all future conflicts.

The use of aircraft, tanks, submarines, machine guns, poison gas, accurate long-range artillery, and mortars produced millions of casualties. Domestic sentiment was strong to avoid U.S. involvement. Britain and Germany announced a naval blockade against each other. Both countries violated the rights of neutral ships in international waters. U-boat attacks on U.S. flagged, unarmed merchant ships bringing supplies to England made neutrality increasingly difficult to sustain.

America turned the other cheek when the American tanker *Gulflight* was torpedoed by a German U-Boat on May 1, 1915, killing three Americans, and again on May 7 when the luxury liner *Lusitania* was sunk, killing 1,198, of which 124 were Americans. On August 19, the British liner *Arabic* was sunk with four additional American deaths. President Wilson's protests secured an offer by Germany to halt U-boat sinkings of unarmed merchant vessels and lift the blockade if Britain did the same. Britain refused. On March 24, 1916, the *Sussex* was torpedoed, and three additional Americans died.

In late 1916, President Wilson was reelected on the Democratic party slogan, "He kept us out of war." Mitchell, now thirty-six, scoffed at these efforts and urged the U.S. military to prepare for battle. He publicly predicted our entry into the war would come within the next year. Shortly thereafter, Mitchell started taking flying lessons at the Curtiss Company flying school. He paid most of the $1,470 bill from his own personal funds since the army could not reimburse more than $500 to a civilian agency.

After only four days, and overly confident in his flying abilities, Mitchell insisted Walter Lees, his instructor, let him take his first solo flight. On landing, he didn't compensate with sufficient rudder input to counteract a gusty crosswind. A wingtip dug into the ground and the biplane cartwheeled onto its back, a total loss. Mitchell emerged unhurt but chastened. The flying was easy; the landing was not. That crash, he felt, was the most instructive and valuable lesson of his entire flying career.

Mitchell's enthusiasm for aviation soon earned him the position as head of the Army's aviation section, with promotion to the rank of Major. With the passion of a newly converted zealot, Mitchell threw himself totally into aviation. He studied domestic and foreign aviation books and experimented with aeronautics.

Convinced that war was inevitable, Mitchell devoted himself to raising funds for aviation. Using threats, cajoling, arm twisting, promises, and an alliance with the governors of the Aero Club, Mitchell leaked stories to the press illustrating the "Aviation Gap" developing between the United States and the rest of the world. Under increasing public pressure generated by an alarmist press, Congress appropriated $13 million for aviation, of which $9 million was to go to the National Guard and the Aero Club.

With the money now allocated, Mitchell felt no further need for his alliance with the Aero Club or National Guard, whose policies and officers he had little respect for.

Mitchell insisted the Army be the sole recipient of the funding, remarking publicly: "To hell with the National Guard. It will never amount to anything." A bitter feud followed.

Secretary of War Baker was called on to intercede in the growing dispute and eventually sided with Mitchell. He used the funds to set up aerial training centers and establish a reserve of five hundred aviators authorized by President Wilson.

In 1916, with the war growing daily, Mitchell requested transfer to Europe to gather intelligence. These requests were denied. Late in the year his lengthy report, "Our Faulty Military Policy," written in July 1915 for the Army War College, leaked into newspapers. This report, highly critical of U.S. policy, advocated combining the Army and Navy into a single, coordinated Department of Defense. He wrote, "Without preparation in time of peace, no nation has the remotest chance of defending itself against a world power in time of war." This contrary report was considered an insubordinate and self-serving justification for increased aviation funding.

Mitchell was cautioned to clear all written or oral statements to the press with the War Department before release. This hardly slowed him down. He continued his criticism by writing articles for newspapers and magazine under a fictitious name and as an anonymous source. Now under attack from numerous politicians, including President Wilson and most of the War Department, Mitchell was exiled, for a second time, to Europe as an "aeronautical observer" . . . just as he had originally requested. It was felt he could do no harm there, and the strong feelings against him could, once again, be allowed to cool.

Mitchell knew U.S. entry into the war in Europe was imminent, and he was eager to be at the scene of the fighting. He felt the politicians and the War Department would soon realize his warnings were correct. Weak militarily, the United States ranked with Denmark, Holland, and Chile. The tiny Air Corps then had only fifty-five obsolete aircraft without any fighters or bombers. The U. S. army of 127,000, led by six thousand officers, was woefully inadequate. The French and English had lost most of the five million men they had fielded, and casualty rates were increasing daily.

Before leaving, Mitchell, now a fledgling flier, decided to make a flight into Mexico where a young, idealistic American aviator had been helping Pancho Villa evade capture by maintaining continuous aerial surveillance on the mercenaries and Regular Army recruits led by General Pershing, who had pursued him for the past year.

Pershing wanted the young aviator shot. Mitchell had other plans for him.

FEBRUARY 4, 1917
CHIHUAHUA, MEXICO

Major Billy Mitchell pushed the nose of the Curtiss JN-4 biplane down to counteract the rising flow of air coming from the upwind side of the mountain ridges. The wheels of the Jenny passed scant feet over the reaching rock faces. The early morning sun had made him vulnerable to rifle fire, and he didn't want to give any errant Mexican bandit an easy target. The white truce pennant fluttering on the staff behind his head gave him scant comfort against the "shoot first and ask questions later" mentality of the rebel bands.

He knew he shouldn't be there. Of his forty flights, only a few had been lengthy and none over mountainous terrain. His fifteen hours of instruction did not include the type of flying he was now attempting, but he was a voracious reader of flying books and had enormous self confidence.

The Jenny he flew was the last one left of the eight sent to assist General Pershing in his pursuit of Pancho Villa. One by one the JN-4s had succumbed to the harsh desert heat and the high mountains. Throttled back to reduce the engine noise the airspeed indictor hovered between fifty and sixty miles per hour, twenty slower than his usual cruising speed, and an easy target for a good marksman.

As the Jenny cleared the highest of the ridges, Mitchell spotted what he had been looking for: three dilapidated but flyable aircraft that constituted Pancho Villa's Air Force. He brought the Jenny's engine back to idle and silently glided down for a landing, slipping the aircraft to lose altitude as his instructor had taught him.

The Jenny bounced three times on the hard, packed sand before coasting to a stop. As he climbed from the cockpit, lifting his flying goggles onto his leather helmet, Mitchell was surrounded by six Mexicans pointing their rifles menacingly at him. He fought off the impulse to reach for the revolver in his belt holster, raised his arms in the universal sign of surrender, and pointed at the white pennant of truce that fluttered in the light breeze behind the rear cockpit.

The apparent leader of the group poked and pushed his rifle barrel into Mitchell's' back as he climbed out of the cockpit and onto the wing of the airplane.

"Hey, loco gringo, you wanna die?" he said. Mitchell didn't answer as he stepped down from the wing. Before he could turn around, the barrel of the rifle was pushed painfully into his back again. "You wanna die? Okay, I help you."

Without turning around, Mitchell reached behind and in one continuous motion grabbed the rifle barrel, moving it swiftly to his right side and pulling it forward. The man behind was pulled against his back and Mitchell, reaching behind with his right foot, hooked the man's leg and leaned back. The heavy weight of the crossed ammunition belts across the guard's chest accelerated his fall, and Mitchell turned and fell heavily on top of him. As Mitchell fell, he grabbed his revolver from its holster. Before they both hit the ground, the barrel of Mitchell's gun was between the Mexican's teeth, and his thumb held the hammer back.

The man's eyes widened in surprise and fear at this sudden turn. Mitchell heard the bolts of half a dozen rifles pulled back as they sighted on him. Without looking up, Mitchell spoke quietly to the wide-eyed leader of the band. "If they shoot, my finger will slip off the hammer and the top of your head will be blown off. Do you understand that?" The man quickly nodded his understanding. "I've come in peace with a flag of truce and mean you no harm. Do you understand?" asked Mitchell. Again the man nodded. "Then please ask your companions to lower their rifles." The man waved an arm in the air, motioning for the rifles be lowered.

Mitchell smiled and carefully closed the hammer of his revolver. Before removing the barrel from the man's mouth, he leaned over and whispered into his ear, "If you poke me again, I'll shove your rifle so far up your ass it will come out your throat. Do you understand?" The Mexican nodded again. Mitchell rose and brushed the sand from his uniform while the man muttered under his breath, "Muy loco gringo."

Turning to Mitchell, the Mexican asked defiantly, "Why should I not shoot you?"

Mitchell calmly replied, "Because if I return safely today, General Pershing will pull his troops out of Mexico tomorrow and the hunt for Pancho Villa, and all of you men, will end. If I do not return, General Pershing will double the number of soldiers hunting for you. They will hunt you down and kill you and every member of your family."

The Mexican looked into Mitchell's penetrating, icy cold blue eyes and felt a shiver up his back. Mitchell's unyielding expression radiated self confidence, determination, and a total lack of fear. Mitchell's posture was erect. Almost six feet tall, his trim figure towered above the Mexican's.

The Mexican shifted nervously from foot to foot as he looked up into Mitchell's implacable face. "Okay, gringo, why you come here?"

"I've come to speak with Lowell Smith," replied Mitchell. The Mexican turned to glance at the slender young man leaning on the lower wing of one of the airplanes, quietly observing the proceedings.

Mitchell followed the Mexican's glance and called to the young man, "Are you Lowell Smith?"

"Yup," replied the young man.

Mitchell approached him. "Can we talk?" he asked. The young man nodded assent. Mitchell took his arm and led him behind the parked airplanes, away from the group of Mexicans.

Mitchell saw the defiance in the eyes of the twenty-four-year-old Lowell Smith. For the past two years Smith had been a one-man air force, constantly patching up and flying his dilapidated and ancient aircraft. He had easily outflown every U.S. Army pilot sent to pursue him and kept his own planes flying long after the army's had been relegated to the scrap heap. His reconnaissance flights had kept Pancho Villa knowing the location of General Pershing's entire army at all times and made capture impossible. He and Villa had escaped every trap laid for them, frustrating a pursuing army many times their size.

Mitchell, unsure how to start the conversation, said, "You're a good pilot, Lowell. I've seen you fly." Smith carefully took in every aspect of Mitchell—the polished riding boots, the spotless uniform neatly pressed, the cherished wings and insignia of rank, the new leather flying helmet, clean goggles, and gloves that protected his carefully manicured hands and clean fingernails.

This was a world he had left. His world consisted of greasy, threadbare overalls, broken goggles, and cracked, torn leather helmets. A world with no spare parts, a file in place of a machine shop, airplanes held together with countless stitches, baling wire, tape, and glue with the last vestiges of paint clinging to the sun-baked, rotting fabric.

Lowell finally replied sarcastically, "You're not. I've seen you land."

Mitchell, momentarily taken aback by the comment, recalled his three bounces on landing. With self-deprecating humor he replied, smiling, "All three landings felt pretty good to me. I've made worse."

Lowell considered his reply carefully, then nodded agreeably. "I'm sure they did and I'm sure you have. Go back and get some more lessons, Major," said Lowell derisively. "You're jockeying the elevator too much in the flare and you're holding too much throttle in. Pull back on the throttle and the stick all the way and just hold it. The airplane will do the rest."

Mitchell felt irritated to get a lecture on flying from the younger man. The fact that he was absolutely right made it even worse. "Look, kid," replied Mitchell, "I'm not here for a flying lesson. I'm here to save your sorry ass."

"My sorry ass doesn't need saving, and you can call me Smitty," said Lowell defiantly.

"Okay, Smitty," said Mitchell gently. "You're terrific as a mechanic and a pilot, but you're going to get yourself killed for no good reason. Your mom asked me if I could get you into the U.S. Air Service. They want you home. Your family misses you. They don't want to see you dead."

Lowell replied quietly, "I've told her. Pancho Villa needs me. He'd never make it against your army without my airplanes, and he's Mexico's last hope. I can't just walk out on him."

"He killed eighteen Americans at Columbus last year," replied Mitchell.

Lowell's defiant look returned. "Right. And ninety-two Mexicans died also. What do you know about Pancho Villa?" Without waiting for a reply, he continued, the emotion rising in his voice. "This man is Doroteo Aranga. His family were slaves. When he was fifteen, he killed the man who was raping his sister. For that they hunted him like an animal for fifteen years. This man wants nothing for himself. He doesn't drink. He doesn't smoke. He devoted his whole life to freeing the Mexican people from slavery and corruption. President Wilson called him the George Washington of Mexico and promised to help him become president."

The Mexicans, unaccustomed to hearing Lowell so animated, were staring at them suspiciously. Lowell continued, "And what did our country do when he finally toppled the dictator? We stopped the shipments of the weapons he had already paid for and handed the country to that jackal, Carranza. Villa raided Columbus only to get what he paid for. He never wanted anyone to die."

Mitchell felt frustrated and put his arm around Lowell. "Look, kid—I mean Smitty, we supported Pancho until the new government took over. They're a lot friendlier to us now. Don't get yourself involved in Mexican politics. It's a no-win situation. Pershing is pulling out soon anyway. You really aren't needed here anymore."

Lowell looked skeptical. "Why is Pershing leaving? Did he find his conscience?"

"We're heading into war, Smitty," Mitchell replied. "The Germans have started sinking our ships again with their damn U-boats and offered the Mexicans, Texas, Arizona, and New Mexico if they would join with the Japanese and attack the United States." Lowell Smith's expression changed from defiance to incredulity.

Mitchell continued, "President Wilson's kept us out of this thing for the past three years but now he has no choice. Even Congress won't let them get away with starting a war with Mexico. In a month or two we're going to be in this hook, line, and sinker, and it couldn't come at a worse time. We've got no army to speak of, no fighting airplanes, and damn few pilots. Pershing is being pulled out of Mexico to help. We're going to declare victory and pull out of Mexico. I'm leaving myself to go over to Europe next month. We're going to need every pilot we can get our hands on, including you."

Lowell replied with a sneer, "How can I help? I'm not even in your army."

Mitchell nodded slowly. "I can fix that. If you're intent on killing yourself, do it for your own country. The Air Service needs you, Smitty. We need your training and your skills." Mitchell took a folded typewritten letter from his pocket and handed it to Lowell.

"Look, think about it. If you want to help your own country for a change, take this to any recruitment office. I'll pass the word along to give you clear sailing. I'll see you over there, kid—uh, I mean Smitty."

Mitchell gave him the letter of recommendation and extended his hand. Lowell looked at it for several seconds before extending his own, tentatively at first, and then firmly and with conviction. Mitchell's grip was strong, and his eyes remained locked on Lowell's. Despite himself, Lowell realized he liked Billy. No bull. Not the usual military bureaucratic windbag. A fellow aviator.

Lowell watched Billy walk to the waiting Jenny, swing the wooden propeller to start the engine, and quickly climb onto the wing and into the cockpit. Lowell called after him loudly to make himself heard above the noise of the engine, "Take off to the south, Major, the hills are lower there, and don't forget to keep the ailerons into the wind." Mitchell smiled at the last bit of unsolicited advice from the young man as he pushed the throttle control fully open. The engine roared loudly. The propeller became an invisible blur. The biplane moved forward, slowly at first, and then faster.

I can sure use that boy. Hope he joins up, thought Mitchell. The biplane continued its takeoff roll, the tail skid coming up quickly in the brisk wind. Suddenly its wheels lifted free and it was in flight.

The Jenny clawed its way through the thin air, slowly gaining precious altitude to rise beyond the grasp of the mountain peaks reaching toward it. Finally the biplane disappeared from view behind the hostile rising terrain. *I like that guy,* thought Lowell. *Maybe I will join up. Maybe I'll even teach him to fly someday.*

FEB. 5, 1917
MIAMI, FLORIDA

This was it, payday at last. Erik Nelson and his cousin, Bill, sat waiting in the old wooden hangar that housed their "Viking Automobile and Airplane Repairs." Erik had meticulously maintained the red biplane for the pilot for the past four months without being paid. He had disassembled and repaired the engine five times, had recovered the fuselage and the wings, meticulously adjusted the tension of the flying wires, changed wheels and tires and replaced most of the nuts and bolts that had corroded in the damp salt-laden air of Southern Florida. "Captain Floyd, the Fabulous Flyer" had flown away at 8:00 A.M. with the latest repairs completed on the Biplane, promising to return by noontime with the cash that would finally settle up his bill with them and buy them both lunch for their patience. And so they waited.

Born on June 12, 1888, in Stockholm, Sweden, life had not been easy for Erik since he had left home at the age of sixteen to become a sailor. The next five years were spent first on Swedish training ships, then on sailing schooners that plied the oceans on endless voyages, exchanging holds filled with lumber from South America for machinery in England to be exchanged yet again for barrels of oil from the Middle East and Russia.

Finally he'd had enough of heaving decks, mountainous waves, storms, ice-encrusted rigging, and listless days stalled in the doldrums of the Pacific. Shortly before his twenty-first birthday, Erik booked passage on a steamship from Hamburg and arrived in Hoboken, New Jersey, in the spring of 1909 seeking the opportunity for fame and fortune that relatives told him awaited in the New World of America.

It was more difficult than he had expected. The streets were not paved with gold after all, and good jobs were hard to come by for a young immigrant whose skills lay mainly at sea, and whose knowledge of American customs and language was very limited.

Erik had always been fascinated by machinery and tried getting a job as a machinist's assistant or as a mechanic, but his lack of experience prevented that.

After a few months of fruitless searching, Erik turned again to the sea, getting a job as a rigger of sailing yachts at a shipyard in Greenwich, Connecticut. His excellence in tuning the sleek yachts to achieve maximum speed led to an offer by a wealthy yacht owner to serve as captain of his sailing yacht during that summer's sailboat races on Long Island Sound.

With the fall came the end of the racing season, and young Erik was back wandering the streets of New York looking for a job. He secured a position as swimming instructor at Fleischmann's Turkish Baths on 42nd Street, but after ten days, the heat resulted in him losing twelve pounds. He quit and again started walking the streets for another job.

Erik then took a job as a bit player in the Oscar Hammerstein musical "Salome," but he felt the low pay hardly compensated for the self consciousness he felt appearing each evening in front of audiences costumed as a Roman Centurion, holding a wooden sword and shield, while Salome's seven veils fluttered across his shiny helmet.

Being free in the mornings, Erik again started searching for a new job. The firm of A.T. Demarist, an importer of foreign automobiles, had a sign posted looking for a handyman. Erik applied and got the job. His innate skills with engines developed rapidly repairing the troublesome English and Italian motors. By 1911, he realized his opportunity to progress beyond handyman was limited by the jealousy of the older mechanics to whom he reported, and Erik decided he'd better move on.

In 1911, he returned to the Greenwich area and took a summer job with the Indian Harbor Yacht Club as dockmaster responsible for the launches and garage areas of the Yacht Club. Working winters as a technician for the Lancia Car Company, Erik developed extensive mechanical expertise. During the summer of 1914, Erik got a job as captain of a 75-foot Motor Yacht, further developing his mechanical, navigational and meteorological skills.

The winter of 1914 saw 26-year-old Erik again unemployed and feeling rootless in his adopted country. He turned to his cousin, Bill, to invest their savings in a new business. With Erik's mechanical skills and Bill's business acumen, they relocated to Miami, Florida, and opened an automobile repair shop, trying to make their fortunes with the rapid growth in the land of eternal sunshine.

The business stumbled along with customers few and far between. Their pitifully small savings did not cover the high rentals of the decent locations available, and they settled on a decrepit and inexpensive hangar on a small grass airfield hoping the small sign they had erected on the road would lure drivers to them. It didn't.

With few automobiles to service, they were delighted when the swash buckling and (by his own admission) world famous aviator and barnstormer, "Captain Floyd, the Fabulous Flyer," pulled up in front of their hangar in his faded red biplane, his coughing and sputtering engine obviously needing repairs.

Before the engine could be shut down, Bill signaled Erik to pretend they were very busy, and they both leaned over a junked engine that adorned their workbench. Studiously ignoring the handlebar mustachioed aviator in his dirty white scarf and torn leather jacket, Bill eventually looked up, as if suddenly interrupted from his heavy workload.

"Do you repair aircraft engines?" asked the airman. Before Erik could reply, Bill said, "Repair them! Why, this man here practically designed and developed them." Bill ignored Erik's open mouthed-surprise and his stern glance.

Knowing full well what the answer would be, Bill continued, "Of course, we are pretty busy. When do you need the repairs?"

"I'd sure appreciate it if you could get her running right by tomorrow morning. I've got a flock of customers going to be mighty disappointed if I can't take them up tomorrow." said Fabulous Floyd.

"Tomorrow? You actually mean tomorrow? Boy . . . I just don't know, we're swamped with work. Let me check our schedule," said Bill as he went over to a blank notebook and pretended to thumb through many entries page by page. Erik stifled a chuckle and reflected that Bill should have been on the stage instead of himself. He watched to see if Bill's nose grew longer.

Shaking his head and looking concerned, Bill turned to Erik, "Can you work late tonight and finish up all your other work so we can help this poor man out? I'll pay you overtime." Erik nodded, restraining himself from laughing at Bill's performance.

"OK, Captain. If Erik doesn't mind the overtime, we'll have it for you first thing in the morning. What time did you want to come by?"

"Seven A.M. would be perfect." said the airman. "I sure do appreciate that, Gentlemen. Let me take you for an airplane ride sometime to reciprocate. Of course . . . you've probably had loads of those. I mean, with all your aviation experience and that."

Before Bill could reply, Erik blurted out, "I'll get you fixed up, Captain, and I'd sure like that ride." Erik had always wanted to ride in an airplane, but could never afford it. Now it looked like it might happen at last. He smiled at Bill's reproachful expression as Captain Floyd threw them a quick military salute and left the hangar.

Erik's first aircraft engine repair proved easier than he thought. The cowling of the engine came off easily and their was far more room to work than the automobile engines that he was familiar with. The wiring was simpler, with a more primitive electrical system without generator, lights, battery or any accessories. By dinnertime he had located and replaced the badly corroded magneto wire to the spark plug that had caused the problem.

Since they had moved into the airfield hangar, Erik had watched as airmen started their engines. He tied down the tail skid of the airplane so that it wouldn't move and instructed Bill on how to rotate the propeller by hand to start the engine for testing.

Erik then climbed onto the lower wing of the biplane and into the cockpit, lowering himself down into the seat. The labels on the controls were well worn but still readable. The starting sequence was obvious to him. He leaned over to call to Bill as he had heard the airmen do, "Fuel off. Mixture off. Switches off. Throttle closed. OK, Bill, rotate prop." Bill pulled and then pushed down on the wooden propeller with a rapid motion. The engine made a sucking, swishing noise as the engine rotation filled the cylinder chambers with air. "OK, Bill, be careful now. Fuel on. Mixture on. Switches on. Throttle open. Ready to start. Pull!"

With a roar which surprised them, the engine came suddenly to life and Eric quickly reduced the throttle as he felt the airplane strain against the line holding it earthbound, as if eager to return to the heavens from whence it came. With the reduced throttle, the engine ticked over smoothly, the rhythmic explosions deep within the heart of the engine popping from the exposed exhaust stacks.

Eric felt deeply moved. There was a magic sitting there, the rotating propeller's slipstream creating its own windstorm.

Erik put his hand around the wooden control wheel and watched as the control surfaces on the wings and tail moved in response to his movements. He couldn't see the ground in front of him over the high nose of the biplane looming above his head. With the clouds in front of him against the darkening sky, the propeller blowing the cool evening wind through his hair, it was easy to believe he was flying. He was Captain Erik Nelson, ace pursuit pilot of the Lafayette Escadrille, fighting the Huns with the rest of the American volunteer pilots for God and Country, ready to save Europe from the dark forces that threatened to engulf them. This was his airplane and he flew high over the front lines of France swooping and diving through the thickening clouds, his blazing machine guns ready to defend the forces of freedom.

Bill's banging on the side of the fuselage woke Erik from his reveries, and he was suddenly on the ground again. "How's the engine?" shouted Bill. Erik scanned the engine instruments, "Looks good." he shouted. "Stand back and I'll rev it up." The engine revs increased smoothly, climbing to a crescendo, and then down again.

Oil pressure and oil temperature looked normal. The engine ran smoothly throughout its range. Satisfied, Erik methodically shut down the engine, bringing the spinning propeller to a sudden stop. He was reluctant to leave the cockpit, reluctant to leave Captain Erik Nelson of the Lafayette Escadrille, reluctant to end the dream.

Again Bill called from the hangar. "Hey, Erik, I'm hungry. Let's go to dinner." He climbed out and Bill helped him push the biplane into the hangar for the night. Erik slowly closed the hangar door taking one last look at the creation of wood and wire, fabric and engine, which took on a life of its own, silently beckoning him with its siren's call. He found it difficult to finally lock the door and turn away.

"Boys, you and I are going to do a lot of business together, and I'm going to send all my pilot friends directly to you as soon as they come down next month," said Captain Floyd earnestly. "Forget automobiles. You're both going to be doing a land office business in airplanes."

Captain Floyd was good as his word. He came by almost every evening and Erik worked on his airplane, spending their scant resources to buy parts. Each of the many repairs made to the engine, airframe, propeller and landing gear was dutifully recorded to his account by Bill. Each of the requests for payment made with the weekly presentation of their bills was met with a hurt, "Don't you trust me?" facial expression and a weekly offer of a flight, eagerly accepted by Erik. Somehow Captain Floyd always had a plausible reason why he was short of cash that month, but would be rolling in it the next.

Erik had become hooked on flying. He was willing to sacrifice anything for his lessons to continue. The money for food, clothing and shelter wanted by Bill seemed less important to Erik. Erik was learning to fly. Floyd had taught him how to take off, and how to land, how to loop and roll the airplane, how to fly through the clouds without losing control, how to put the airplane into a spin and then recover without crashing, how to cut the engine and glide silently to a safe landing. As with most flying students, Captain Floyd, the Fabulous Flyer, had become an exalted being to Erik, just a short step down from the Almighty. He believed Floyd would pay them as he promised.

And so they sat and waited for Floyd, the Fabulous Flyer, to return for lunch with their money. And they waited, and they waited. By dinner time they could deny the truth no longer. The Fabulous Flyer had flown the coop.

There would be no money, only the mountain of debt they had accumulated during the past few months. Bill turned to Erik and emptied his pockets. He had 14 cents. "How much you got, Erik?" Erik searched all the pockets of his coveralls. He came up with 8 cents.

"Well, we've only got 22 cents left, Erik. What do we do now?"

"Only one thing we can do, Bill. Let's hitch a ride out of here and join up as pilots with the Lafayette Escadrille. I hear they are accepting recruits in California."

The Lafayette Escadrille turned down Erik and Bill, as did the United States Air Service and the Royal Air Force. Bill gave up the dream of flying and joined the Artillery which promptly accepted him and sent him off to France to fight in the newly declared war.

Erik couldn't give up his dream of flying. He kept trying and finally, with the need for pilots growing and the standards being lowered, convinced a receptive enlistment officer that his existing knowledge of flying overcame his being over the acceptable age limit. Within a few months, he was in pilot training as a bomber pilot in Texas.

To insure secrecy and his safety, Mitchell departed from Key West by ship to Cuba where he boarded a Spanish ship, the *Alfonso XIII*, bound for Corunna, Spain, and hopefully out of the paths of the U-boats.

Despite the *Lusitania* sinking two years earlier and powerful economic interests lying more with the British, there was little pressure from the American public to involve the United States in the World War in 1916. The blockades by both Germany and England violated international laws, however, and Germany had resumed U-boat attacks on U.S. flag vessels.

In early 1917, Germany calculated that with the three hundred new U-boats recently added to her fleet, Britain would be forced to surrender within five months. U.S. entry would therefore have no effect on the outcome. On February 1, 1917, Germany delivered a declaration of unrestricted warfare to the U.S. State Department. On March 2, the *U.S.S. Algonquin* was sunk, quickly followed by three other U.S. ships.

To cover their bet on American impotence, the German ambassador sent a coded message to the Mexicans offering them Texas, Arizona, and New Mexico if they would declare war on the United States. This infamous "Zimmermann telegram" was intercepted by British intelligence and sent to President Wilson. Wilson now felt he had no choice. On April 2, 1917, he requested Congress issue a declaration of war against Germany. Discussions in Congress over the next four days were filled with far more heat than light. The central issue was whether the dual challenges and affronts by Germany to U.S. national sovereignty on the high seas and the mischief intended by the Zimmermann telegram were of sufficient magnitude to warrant a declaration of war. Conspicuously absent was a reasoned, careful analysis of the military situation that existed at the time, or the resources that would be required to win this war.

On April 6, 1917, the U.S. Congress declared war on Germany. France and England believed, with Germany, that U.S. participation would be of little significance. A single week's war casualties exceeded the size of the entire American army. The U.S. military was poorly armed and ill equipped. Artillery pieces were ancient and obsolete. Only 1,500 machine guns of four different types with a total of nine hours of ammunition were in inventory. Not a single fighting airplane or combat-ready division existed. The American Merchant Marine, still decimated by their Civil War losses, depended upon a motley collection of chartered, leased, and rented vessels. Many were obsolete derelicts.

President Wilson, Congress and the U.S. military were unsure of the next steps. Within the first three weeks of the declaration, no funding for the war had been appropriated and fewer than five thousand volunteers enlisted. The military had drawn no plans for the transfer of men or materials to Europe. Wilson looked for someone to lead the U.S. military effort. Of the five senior U.S. generals, four were in their sixties and considered too old and too committed to the warfare methods of the previous century for consideration. Secretary of War Newton Baker, the army, influential politicians, and the public called for the immediate appointment of General Leonard Wood.

Wood had served previously as Chief of Staff. He was outspoken and admired by both the officers and enlisted men who served under him. He strongly supported Billy Mitchell's warnings of the lack of U.S. military preparedness and, aligning himself with Republican Theodore Roosevelt, made that a campaign issue in 1916. Wilson changed his Democratic party platform to include increased military expenditures.

Wilson, stung by Wood's earlier criticism, told Newton Baker he would not approve Wood's nomination to lead the American forces, but instead wanted General John Pershing to assume that position. Pershing was less senior in rank, experience, and qualifications. At fifty-seven, he was older than Wood and not much younger than the other, more senior generals ruled out earlier.

Pershing's career was unremarkable. Although a West Point man, by the age of forty-five he had not risen above the rank of Captain. His most recent year-long campaign to capture Pancho Villa was unsuccessful. Pershing was a strict by-the-book disciplinarian, often more concerned with form than substance. He was austere, graceless, and minutely exacting. He was incapable of inspiring affection from those under him and exacted their compliance through stern but fair discipline.

Although ambitious, he was diplomatic and cautious never to challenge his superiors. He carried out his assigned orders without complaint or modification. Pershing was the controllable military bureaucrat Wilson wanted.

Pershing had lost his wife, Frances, and three young daughters in a fire as they slept in their bungalow at the Presidio in San Francisco on August 26, 1915. Pershing knew this would be his last opportunity to convert an easily forgotten career into immortality. He was anxious to secure the assignment. His old friend Major General J. Franklin Bell reassured Wilson that Pershing could do the job. Pershing assured Wilson he met all the requirements, including fluency in the French language. Secretary Baker was forced to withdraw General Wood's name from consideration using the lame excuse that his limp, sustained in an old injury, made him ineligible.

CHAPTER 3

The Yanks Are Coming

April 30, 1917
Paris, France

My dearest Mother,

Forgive me for not writing sooner but the days fly by for me in a great blur. I've not slept more than three hours in a single night since my arrival and my knees, elbows, and shoulders are up to their usual rheumatic tricks. I'm afraid the bitter cold of those Alaskan winters have left an indelible impression upon my body.

Caroline has not written for several weeks now. I'm not certain if my wife is still angry at me for leaving her or simply too busy with the child. It is comforting for me to know that, with the Stoddard family funds available to her, she is not dependent in the least upon my meager army major's stipend. But let me bring you up to date with my own activities.

You will be pleased to know that since arriving in Paris scarcely six weeks ago, my childhood French has completely returned. I now speak better French than most Parisians, although that is not saying as much as you might think.

It is hard to believe we have been at war with Germany for the past three weeks. Major James Logan, his three assistant officers, and I are the only five Americans in military uniform in all of France. We have three pistols between us and no other arms. We have no desks or chairs, nor even the space to put them. We have no communication equipment, airplanes, trucks, or even automobiles. The most offensive weapons we have are our unchanged undergarments, and even those are in short supply.

The American Radiator Company has offered us some temporary office space, which we desperately need. We have no funds to make any purchases whatsoever. I have been using my own personal funds plus the contributions of some patriotic American tourists.

When I cabled Washington for $50,000 last week, General Squier replied it was not "customary" to send so much money to a junior officer. I had Lieutenant Miller cable him back to remind him that it was not "customary" to have a world war. Our army staff seems firmly rooted in the obsolete military concepts of the last century.

I've continued with my flight lessons over here under the instruction of Victor Fumat, the best pursuit pilot in the French air force. It has been most illuminating. The Spads, Breguets, and Nieuports I have been flying under his direction are truly greyhounds of the air. They are twice as fast as the animated kites I've flown back home. We have no choice now but to purchase the airplanes we need from the French. I have been telling the Army for years, if you haven't kept up with your enemies in time of peace, you will certainly not catch up with them in time of war. I wonder if there is a man among them who has the gumption to say, "Perhaps Billy was right."

I doubt it!

Last week, under the examination of Major Harmon, I flew an eighty-horsepower Nieuport from LeBourget airport in Paris on a triangular flight of over three hundred miles in six hours, using only a map and compass, to Chateâuroux. Today I flew sixty-four miles in fifty minutes and demonstrated the full range of aerial maneuvers, including flying through cloud and making an excellent landing within a one hundred-foot circle. This completed my final examination. Major Harmon personally pinned on my wings. You alone know how much this means to me. Your son is now an official junior military aviator.

Another matter may give you some pride. On April 22, they finally let me visit the trenches on the front lines. We were over one hundred men strong and being held captive by a single German machine gun and mortar emplacement of fewer than a dozen men. One by one they were picking off the French troops as the days went on. I saw this technique used by the insurgents in the Philippines. It was inevitable they would eventually all be lost.

After a sleepless night of constant shelling and sniper fire, I threatened to shoot any of them with my pistol that did not follow me over the wall. Just before daybreak and under cover of a moonless night, I led a mass attack against the Huns and within a few minutes the threat was ended. Frankly, my motivation was self preservation. The French confused this with courage and have awarded me their highest decoration, the Croix de Guerre, as the first American to come under fire. They tell me I'm the youngest since Napoleon to receive this honor. In the interests of Franco-American relations, I've reluctantly accepted it.

My time in the trenches has given me a new perspective on this strange war. Each side sits, separated often only by yards, for years. Men die in great abundance on both sides to move a few blades of grass to and fro across the battle lines. Overhead, airplanes cross these same lines with impunity at will. In but a few minutes, an airplane can fly from the rear of its own lines through the front and into the rear of its enemy's. Surely this war, and perhaps all future wars, will be settled in the air. Modern warfare has rendered ground armies impotent and insignificant.

Love to all of you.

Your new junior military aviator, and loving son,

Billy

I n early May, French and British missions arrived in Washington to discuss the war. The French mission was headed by Marshall Joseph Joffre, a war hero. The British mission was headed Arthur Balfour, the Foreign Secretary of Lloyd George.

Both missions agreed that "The United States could not possibly raise, train, and transport an army of sufficient size to have any effect in the European theater, but . . . perhaps a token force might be sent to cheer our people."

Both countries were spending over $300 million per month and were on the verge of bankruptcy. They requested and received from President Wilson low-cost loans of $218 million per month each, a total of $16 billion at 3.5 percent interest payable over twenty-five years.

General Pershing was put in charge of creating and leading an American expeditionary force. Pershing selected Major James G. Harbord as his Chief of Staff, who had come up the ranks from private. He was a brilliant choice with all the precise qualities needed. They concluded victory would require an army of four million men led by two hundred thousand officers—a forty-fold increase within one year. The President and Congress were stunned; never had they even considered such a vast undertaking. These goals seemed totally unobtainable. They were scoffed at by friends and foes alike who also questioned the quality, resolve, and will of a nation of immigrants to fight and die on foreign soil for a cause few held dear or even understood.

Congress passed a compulsory draft law on May 18, 1917. Liberty bond drives brought in $4.6 billion. The necessary funds were appropriated to expand the Army to forty-two divisions totaling three million men, and increase the Navy to eight hundred thousand men. Uncle Sam was off to war. In one giant leap, American soldiers, whose most recent adversaries were hostile Indians armed with bows and arrows or Mexican bandits with ancient single shot rifles, would have to face weapons more terrible and more lethal than they could ever imagine.

On May 28, General Pershing sailed with his staff of 190 officers and enlisted men for Liverpool on the transport ship *Baltic*. For safety and security from U-boat attack, a secret, low-key departure was planned. Civilian clothes were to be worn in place of military uniforms. Apparently, the message didn't get to everybody; Pershing showed up in civilian attire. Most of his entourage did not. Mountains of boxes on the pier were clearly labeled "General Pershing's Staff," and were in full view of the reporters who suddenly appeared.

As the *Baltic* cleared the harbor, a twenty-one-gun salute was fired and formations of aircraft flew overhead. The departure was so blatantly obvious that German intelligence was certain this was an Allied ruse to cover his real departure by another means. Sending U-boats in pursuit of an obvious decoy would have little value. The Allies knew better and were surprised by the lack of discretion. After meeting with the British Military Staff in London, Pershing planned to arrive in Paris on June 13, 1917.

Early in the war, aircraft flew over enemy trenches dropping numerous deadly six-inch steel darts called "flechettes." Accelerating downward from several thousand feet, these darts easily ripped through flesh and bone. They killed any hapless soldiers or horses they struck. The darts soon gave way to exploding artillery shells, then stabilizing fins were added. The newly designed aerial bombs grew larger and more destructive as the months went on. They eventually grew to 1,680 pounds.

Aircraft also observed enemy troop movements and frustrated concealment. They directed artillery and infantry fire. Aircraft could not be stopped by barbed wire, trenches, concrete abutments, or masses of troops. "No doubt about it," Mitchell wrote, "war will be won by the side with superior air power, without which the infantry will be rendered impotent."

Within three weeks of his arrival, Mitchell had worked out a plan with several French officers to establish an air branch of the American Expeditionary Force. Detailed plans requesting five-thousand planes on the front lines and twenty thousand total within a year with 38,500 mechanics to service them, training and support facilities, and procedures were sent to the War Department repeatedly by Mitchell with no reply.

By May, Billy Mitchell had thoroughly endeared himself to the French. He was the entire U.S. Air Force, flying daily reconnaissance missions over enemy lines. His extensive aerial observations were made from the cockpit of the single Nieuport loaned to him by the French. His daily briefings, most often in fluent French, included notes, reports, and carefully drawn maps of enemy troop movements, construction of fortifications, weaknesses, strengths, and the most recent German deployments.

Perceptions of Billy Mitchell in Paris and Washington were polar opposites. Washington pretty much ignored Mitchell and his suggestions, pleadings, and reports, while the French hung on every word. He was invited everywhere, loved by the rich and famous, sought after by royalty. Billy Mitchell was the talk of Paris. The French saw him as incredibly hard working, courageous, highly intelligent, and the de facto leader of American, if not Allied, air power. At French insistence, Pershing promoted Mitchell to Lieutenant Colonel in May with the new title of Air Officer.

Mitchell expected rapid deliveries of new aircraft, pilots, and aviation resources. He became increasingly insistent with Pershing that the needed U.S. aviation resources be expedited.

Frustrated by the lack of a response, on May 24th he drafted a cable requesting the aviation resources he wanted, and convinced Premier Ribot of France to send it out over his signature directly to President Wilson. This bogus cable got immediate action from Wilson and promises of compliance from the U.S. War Department, which had no idea Mitchell was behind it. Wilson held emergency meetings with congressional leaders that very day and, on the strength of Ribot's signature, promptly allocated $650 million for aviation expenditures plus the immediate implementation of new engine and aircraft building initiatives under top wartime priority conditions.

This represented the largest expenditure for a single purpose ever made by the United States. Ignoring Mitchell's suggestions to copy and mass produce the latest French Nieuport fighters and engines, a far more ambitious plan developed.

The only aircraft manufactured in quantity in the United States when it entered the war were the JN-4s or "Jennies," the Thomas-Morse "Scout," and the Standard E1. All had engines of less than one hundred horsepower and, while suitable for training or barnstorming, were not suitable for war.

Allied European aircraft engine factories produced more than sixty different engine models. These ranged from the small Clerget at 130 horsepower through the Rolls Royce at 275 horsepower. Bugatti made a monster five hundred-horsepower engine. With production divided among so many different models, unit costs were high, spare parts inventory was low, and throughput of completed engines was painfully slow.

The U.S. government, invoking war emergency powers, seized the use of all aviation patents that had been filed by private individuals and companies. Use of these patents was given to a newly formed aviation trust, which included many of the largest and most powerful U.S. manufacturing companies. Most were large automobile companies.

During World War I, this monopoly eventually controlled $1,650,000 of aviation funding. Its exclusive and aggressive use of these basic aviation patents continued decades after the war ended, bankrupting numerous smaller American aircraft manufacturers. Using the same methods employed by its domestic automobile industry to mass produce cars, one hundred thousand aircraft, with a target of 22,625 airplanes and 45,250 engines within the first year, were planned. All they needed was an airplane and an engine.

Against the advice of Billy Mitchell, the aviation trust chose the English DeHaviland DH-4. The choice was a strange one. The DH-4 was too large and cumbersome to be a good pursuit plane, and too small to be a decent bomber. Those few that finally arrived in Europe had to be used strictly as reconnaissance aircraft where enemy fighters couldn't challenge them. The DH-4 had a vulnerable fuel tank in the fuselage between the two crew cockpits. Crews were often incinerated with a single well-placed bullet or hard landing. This soon earned them the nickname "flaming coffins" by the pilots. Modified DH-4s were to be supplied by England until sufficient domestic production became available in the U.S.

For the engine, the War Department turned to Elbert John Hall and Jesse G. Vincent. Hall, a Californian, had designed and built the Comet automobile. With his partner, Bert C. Scott, the Hall-Scott Motor Car Company was building railway locomotives, coaches, and engines for automobiles and aircraft. Vincent was Vice President of the Packard Motor Car Company and a brilliant engineer. Both had made the mistake of visiting the War Department on the same day and at the same time to sell their companies respective products to Colonel E. A. Deeds, chairman of the newly formed aircraft production board.

MAY 28, 1917, 3:35 P.M.
AIRCRAFT PRODUCTION BOARD WAITING ROOM,
WASHINGTON, D.C.

Colonel Deeds was late for his appointments. He was detained by an urgent meeting and request from his board members. They needed a new aircraft engine. A big one. Fast. Preferably yesterday. Deeds had no idea where or how he was going to get it . . . until he walked into his waiting room. There they were: Hall and Vincent.

Engine designers. This is too good to be true. "Gentlemen," he said, "So glad to see you both. I have an urgent new assignment for the two of you."

For the Liberty engine that would make the first flight around the world seven years later, this was the moment of conception. Their assignment was simple. Build a new, more powerful aircraft engine than has ever been made before in the United States. And, by the way, let's make it a whole new family of engines. Modular, if you please. That way we can use the same parts for engines from four to twelve cylinders, from one-fifty through four hundred-horsepower. Makes production and inventory of spare parts much simpler, you know. Also, no fancy tooling, if you please. Takes too long to make.

"Oh, and about the time. Forget the usual twelve months for design and eighteen additional months for tooling and production. We can give you only one week for design, and it must be running within one month."

Colonel Deeds shook their hands and left. Hall and Vincent looked at each other in astonishment. "Was he serious?" they both asked the secretary as they left. "You bet he was," she said. "I'd get started right now if I were you." They were too stunned to say no. The task seemed impossible.

MAY 29, 1917
THE WILLARD HOTEL
WASHINGTON, D.C.

Their wives were suspicious. Some other women, perhaps? Why else would they leave home for a week? Without saying where or why they were going? Top secret, they said. A likely story. The desk clerk was suspicious also. "Don't disturb us for any reason," they said. "Unless the hotel is in imminent danger of collapse," one added.

No room service. No maid service. For a whole week. Very suspicious. And all that paraphernalia. Looked like a drafting table. And chairs. Tons of pads and paper. Strange drawing tools. Even brought their own food. Both signed in as "Mr. Smith." Very suspicious. "Maybe they're

German spies," the desk clerk whispered to the bellman. "I say very suspicious."

On June 4 Vincent and Hall, weary from lack of sleep and endless cups of coffee, checked out of the Willard Hotel. In their briefcase they carried the design of a new modular line of aircraft engines which could be built as V-4s, V-6s, V-8s, or V-12s. The V-8 should produce three hundred horsepower, and the V-12 more than four hundred horsepower.

Within one month, the first prototype engine, a V-8, was tested. A V-12 was completed shortly thereafter and carried to the top of Pikes Peak in Colorado. On July 3, 1917, at an altitude of 14,109 feet, the engine thundered to life, proving it would run in the rarefied air of flight. Despite their rapid gestation, all the early tests went very well. The 1,649 cubic inch V-12 developed over four-hundred horsepower at sea level and weighed only 790 pounds.

Packard, Lincoln, General Motors, and Marmon factories attempted to mass-produce Liberty engines using hastily trained workers. Few ran at all. Even fewer were assembled correctly. Production of airplanes and engines was far more difficult and slower than originally thought. Newly trained workers lacked the necessary skills, and hastily introduced training programs proved inadequate. The lack of time to prepare tooling to make a proper die-cast engine block for the Liberty engine required that an intricately welded assembly of water-cooled cylinders be combined with a crude sand-cast crankcase. The twelve separate cylinder assemblies vibrated heavily in flight. Constant oil and water leaks caused premature engine failures. Poor quality of workmanship and hasty assembly resulted in deficient mechanical tolerances and reduced reliability. Many Liberty engines had to be painstakingly taken apart and reassembled before it could be certain they would run at all.

Of the orders for one hundred thousand V-12 Liberty engines, only 20,478 were built before the war ended. Most of those proved defective and required rebuilding. Few Liberty engines lasted fifty hours. A saving grace, however, was that they could be repaired relatively easily and continue to run even with multiple cylinder, piston, and connecting-rod failures. Vincent and Hall could not have imagined these characteristics would prove invaluable to the crew of the first flight around the world, seven years in the future.

Of the one hundred thousand aircraft promised to Pershing by the aircraft production board, only 196 of these aircraft would arrive before the war ended. Unfortunately for the Allies, word of the new American plans were a poorly kept secret. Newspaper headlines, quoting army sources, boasted, "100,000 U.S. planes will soon blacken the sky over Germany." Germany took the boasts seriously. They developed the "Amerikann Programme," which greatly increased their own aircraft output to match the expected flood of airplanes from America.

JUNE 4, 1917, 9:00 A.M.
BRITISH AIR BASE, COMMANDER'S OFFICE
PARIS, FRANCE

The knock on the glass door panel was loud and insistent. Sir Hugh Trenchard had no time for visitors. He was leaving at that precise moment for an inspection tour of his facilities. The new SE-5 fighters had just arrived from England, and he was anxious to see them. He carefully placed his starched uniform cap on his head, picked up his riding crop, and turned toward the door. The rude knock came again. The visitor entered without permission. *Has this dolt no manners at all.* he thought. The unwelcome visitor smiled at him. He glared back in return.

"Young man, have you forgotten your manners? I didn't give you permission to enter. Please leave immediately."

His orderly stumbled in apologetically behind the intruder. "I'm terribly sorry, General Trenchard. I told the colonel you could not be disturbed, but he barged right past me. Shall I have him escorted out, sir?"

The intruder was tall, almost as tall as he, but younger. He looked thirty but the lines around the steely blue amused eyes indicated he was older, forty perhaps. His lips curled into a grin. Trenchard noticed the wings on his chest. *Damn,* he thought. *I can't throw out a fellow airman. Especially an American colonel.*

"Who are you, young man?" he said sternly.

"Name's Mitchell, General. Colonel William Mitchell. My friends call me Billy."

General Trenchard's scowl softened into a half smile of recognition.

"So you're Billy Mitchell. Been hearing a lot about you, young man. Like to talk, but I really must fly now. Call me. I'll set you up with an appointment."

Mitchell wasn't so easily dissuaded. "Mind if I tag along? I've always admired the fantastic job you've done building the RAF," he said.

Trenchard laughed. "I can see they were right. You can't take *no* for an answer, can you?" Billy returned the laugh without replying. "Very well then, Billy. Let's go."

B illy Mitchell spent the next three days with General Hugh Trenchard. Trenchard recalled the incident years later: "His questions were penetrating and indicated a knowledge of aviation which was enormous in scope and depth. His intelligence came through without him making any effort to assert it. His suggestions and predictions for aviation's future was spot-on. I learned as much as he during his visit. No visitor has ever impressed me as much, before or since. If only he can break his habit of trying to convert his opponents by killing them, he'll go far."

Billy Mitchell met General Pershing within hours of Pershing's arrival in Paris on June 13, 1917, demanding to know the status of his numerous unanswered requests for aviation resources. Pershing deplored this breach of etiquette. He considered Mitchell rude and insubordinate with unreasonable demands. All his needed war materials were in short supply. To Pershing, the lack of tanks, artillery, trucks, rifles, and ammunition had an infinitely higher priority. Airplanes had proven totally ineffective when he tried using them to capture Pancho Villa, and he didn't expect much from them during this new war. Pershing installed himself and his entourage in one of the most expensive and opulent hotel suites in Paris, and he made it plain to Billy Mitchell that aircraft were not his first priority, nor were they even close to the top of his long list. He also resolved to put Mitchell under supervision and close control. On July 4, a disappointed Mitchell wrote in his diary, "Our entire air force consists of one Nieuport plane which I use myself, and that is all."

Relations between Pershing and the French soon deteriorated. Within a few days of his arrival, the aging Pershing started a love affair with Micheline Resco, a young French artist, more than thirty years his junior. France was losing the war and in danger of being overrun by Germany. The French, normally tolerant of affairs, became increasingly resentful of its intrusion upon Pershing's duties at a time of imminent national disaster. Pershing's response was to vehemently deny the affair, and maintained that position decades after the war ended, even through his secret marriage to Micheline shortly before his death. The French viewed Pershing's affair as evidence of his flawed judgment, and his clumsy denials as deceitful.

Throughout Pershing's life, he was chronically late. Obsessive with the smallest details, he often delayed meetings or inspections for hours while he shined the tips of his shoes or polished his belt buckle. During his tenure as a cadet at West Point, the consequences were numerous demerits. Arriving often at midnight for high-level dinner meetings scheduled for 6:00 P.M. with French commander General Petain and Premier Georges Clemenceau, the consequences were far more severe, further damaging his relationships with the French. The fluency in French that Pershing had assured Wilson of also proved illusory. Pershing insisted all meetings be conducted in English, another irritant to the French.

Pershing demanded the same obsession for detail and discipline that he had of all the American troops. On October 4, 1917, he issued these orders: "The standards for the American army will be those of West Point. The rigid attention, the upright bearing, attention to detail, uncomplaining obedience to instruction required of the cadet will be required of every officer and soldier of our armies in France."

The citizen soldiers arriving from America resented the severe military discipline and make-work projects Pershing had ordered. The French also fumed at Pershing's obsession with minutia, claiming his micromanagement of insignificant details contributed to his inability to make war decisions in a timely manner.

In contrast to Billy Mitchell, Pershing was not a trench warrior. He had no wish to evaluate the front lines, lead by example, or energize his troops with personal visits. Most of his time was spent in splendid luxury close to Micheline's home in Paris. He occupied a three-story palace with magnificent gardens built by Napoleon at 73 rue de Varenne. The dining room had a single-slab marble table that would seat one hundred guests. Ornate tapestries adorned marble floors and walls; the ceilings were intricately carved with frescoes of prominent artists. Dozens of opulent guest rooms boasted their own solid-gold bathroom fixtures. Giant crystal chandeliers hung from the high ceilings.

The most contentious point between the French and English was the disposition of the American troops who started to arrive in July. The war was going poorly for the Allies; millions of Allied troops had died. General Foch, the Supreme Allied Commander, wanted to use Americans to bolster the decimated French and English units as replacements. Pershing insisted on keeping the American forces intact and under his command. The role of American troops in the conflict remained a bone of contention among the Allies for over a year.

British Prime Minister David Lloyd George and French Premier Georges Clemenceau started going around Pershing, writing directly to Washington and imploring President Wilson to give them the help that Pershing would not. By December, Clemenceau, with the assent of Lloyd George, pleaded with Wilson to replace Pershing, preferably with General Leonard Wood. Wilson declined, but Pershing found out. He confronted Clemenceau, and both Allies resigned themselves to continuing, albeit reluctantly, with Pershing.

Meanwhile, Admiral William S. Sims headed the effort to break the stranglehold of German U-boats that had effectively cut off all U.S. troops and supplies from reaching Allied ports. Over the objections of the English, he organized U.S. ships into convoys escorted by fast destroyers and cruisers. On November 17, 1917, depth charges dropped by American destroyers damaged the navigational systems on the German submarine U-58. Captain Amberger's U-boat was forced to the surface and he surrendered his ship and its crew to the American destroyers *Fanning* and *Nicholson* rather than suffer through any more of their depth charges. Sim's controversial strategy which effectively countered the U-boat menace, was vindicated.

On the Eastern front, the sacrifices forced upon the Russians to aid Serbia were extremely unpopular. Uprisings forced Czar Nicholas II to abdicate the Russian throne. The new Kerensky government fared little better, losing its civil war to a pacifist Bolshevik regime led by Lenin and Trotsky and secretly aided by Germany. On November 7, the Bolsheviks took over the Russian government, promising "land, peace, and bread."

Soon thereafter, on November 26, 1917, Russia abandoned the war effort. A truce with Germany was signed on December 15. Two hundred-fifty thousand German soldiers were now freed to fight the French, and the Germans gained access to huge reserves of food and war materials in the Ukraine, Finland, Georgia, Poland, the Baltic states, and Russia itself.

On March 15, the first American airplane was shipped to Europe from Hoboken, New Jersey. That same month, the Germans broke through the French lines. The situation looked grave for the Allies. Many French civilians, fearing the worst, were trying desperately to escape. Most of their war heroes were dead. After years of relatively static positions, a new German offensive pushed forty miles through France, separating the two Allied armies and causing massive French and British casualties.

The Germans had perfected enormous cannons that hurled shells into the heart of Paris from secure positions seventy-five miles away. Invented by Dr. von Eberhardt and built by the Krupps factory, these monster guns had barrels more than one hundred feet long, weighed more than 150 tons, and hurled 250-pound shells to an altitude of twenty-five miles above the earth. They were nicknamed "Big Bertha" by the Allies after the head of the Krupp family, Frau Bertha von Bohlen. On Good Friday, 1918, these guns destroyed the Church of St. Gervais, killing eighty and seriously wounding an additional sixty-eight religious worshipers. The French government tried to avert panic by claiming this shelling was aircraft bombardment and would soon be stopped by antiaircraft fire, but the relentless shelling continued night and day. The French public soon discovered they lacked any defense against the death that rained down on them from the heavens. Morale plummeted.

On March 21, 1918, the Germans launched Operation Michael, intending to annihilate the remains of the British forces. With the defeat of the Italians at Caporetto and the Russians surrendering, 265 German and forty-five Austrian redeployed divisions broke through the line of British trenches to claim 1,250 square miles of French territory. Two hundred thousand British troops were killed, wounded, or captured.

One week later, on March 27, U.S. Secretary of War Baker was visiting Paris and saw the hordes of Parisians fleeing in panic. The next day, under Baker's orders, Pershing lent the French five American divisions to be used in a quiet area, freeing up ten French divisions to reinforce the British. Additional American divisions were loaned during April to fight at Cantigny, Chateau-Thierry, Belleau Wood, and the Marne. As valuable as they were, these troops represented only a small portion of the five hundred thousand American troops in France by the end of May.

It was an agonizing time for Billy Mitchell. When the United States entered the war, it had fewer than twenty-four combat-trained pilots. The eager recruits being hastily trained at the Issoudon flight training center, 125 miles south of Paris, were no match for the well trained and disciplined German veteran pilots. Often the Americans were sent into combat with fewer than twelve hours of combat flight training.

Mitchell often breakfasted with the fledgling airmen and felt the compassion of an elder brother for each one. Reviewing the latest German aerial combat tactics with his instructors, he often walked alone to the Center's graveyard after dinner to bid a tearful good-bye to the young fliers who were being buried daily.

American casualties grew, and many high-profile deaths threatened to demoralize the troops and the American public back home. The sons of ex-President Roosevelt fared particularly badly. Quentin died when his Nieuport fighter plane was shot down in flames, and his brothers Archibald and Theodore were badly wounded. Sergeant Joyce Kilmer, the gentle, beloved poet of "Trees," died of a single gunshot to his head, leaving a wife and three young children.

Billy Mitchell's own younger brother, John Lendrum Jr., thirteen years his junior, died in the crash of his airplane during his first aerial engagement with the enemy. Billy had pleaded with him not to volunteer for the Air Service, but the lure of emulating the older brother he idolized was too strong for John to resist. Mitchell took John's death very hard, never fully recovering from it.

After months of battling with General Pershing for the promised U.S. airplanes, Mitchell finally realized his cause was hopeless and changed his strategy. With the Amerika Programme in full swing, Germany had built up a numerical superiority in total airplanes. Their squadrons flew in larger formations than the Allies; as a result, they were inflicting greater casualties.

Mitchell believed the key to winning the air war, and thus the ground battles under it, was to use all the aircraft in massive formations under a unified command—which he wanted to lead. French, English, and Italian squadron leaders, reluctant to surrender command to Mitchell, complained of the risks involved in putting all their eggs in one basket. "Large formations would make easy targets for ground fire. They'll all get shot down," critics said. The Allies, with fewer aircraft, could afford air losses far less than the Germans. Mitchell remained convinced the bold plan would work. Mitchell's flamboyant and irreverent style, with his custom-made flying suits, pink breeches and patch pockets, irritated the highly traditional Pershing and many of his staff. Pershing would not lend support to his plans.

At Mitchell's request, the French gave him the fastest car in France, a Mercedes that had won the race to Lyon in 1914. Mitchell loved to drive fast. His chauffeurs became terrorized passengers as Mitchell careened past other traffic at top speeds, often over the narrow, curving switchback mountain roads whose sheer drops he loved to challenge. None of the chauffeurs lasted very long; they all begged for transfer to another assignment, any other assignment. Mitchell became a familiar sight racing at top speeds along the French roads, the car sliding, often on two wheels, scattering livestock and pedestrians alike.

Mitchell had the uncanny ability to recognize competence or incompetence after only the briefest of meetings. One day, driving at his fastest, he noticed a car behind his had little trouble following him, even at his breakneck speeds. It was obvious to Mitchell, watching in the rearview mirror, that the unknown driver was driving more smoothly than he was and just as quickly—in a much slower car.

Mitchell's engine suddenly started misfiring and he pulled over to the side of the road. The talented driver behind him stopped to help, and explained to an admiring Mitchell that he had been a champion race-car driver in the United States before the war. He had trained himself to think fast but react slowly, smoothly, and deliberately. The young stranger diagnosed Mitchell's engine problem immediately and repaired it within a few minutes. Mitchell asked, "Ever flown an airplane, son?" The chauffeur replied, "No sir, I tried to, but they said I was too old and too uneducated to learn." Mitchell said, "You'll make one hell of a good pilot. I'll see that you learn to fly."

It took a long while for that chauffeur to be accepted by his fellow pilots. His name clearly revealed his German origin despite his attempt to Anglicize the spelling. During a 1916 trip to England, the championship race-car driver and holder of the world land speed record of 134 miles per hour, was detained and strip searched by Scotland Yard, who suspected he was a German spy.

He was earning $35,000 per year when rejected for entry into the air service on the basis of his not completing grammar school and, at twenty-seven, being too old to learn to fly. With Mitchell's help, he was soon in the newly formed 94th Aero Squadron, which was getting off to a slow start. The Nieuport pursuit planes, newly purchased from the French, were grounded, waiting for machine guns to arrive.

The squadron's restless, college-educated young men, reeking of good breeding and manners, resented his fame and his gruff tough-guy manner of speaking. He earned his wings in just seventeen days, and had as little regard for his fellow pilots and the silver spoons they were born with as they did for him and his blue-collar past; a past that had required him to work full-time from the age of twelve to support his family.

When finally armed, his first kill almost became his last. In the heat of air battle, and contrary to warnings by his instructors, he had followed a German Albatross into a fast dive. As his bullets struck the enemy pilot, he heard a loud crack as his Nieuport's top right wing collapsed, the torn fabric trailing in the slipstream.

The War in the Air

To control the irrepressible Colonel Mitchell, Pershing appointed several more senior officers to supervise his activities. None were successful until General Mason Patrick was brought in as chief of the air services. Patrick was sixteen years older and, although a nonflier, felt secure enough in his own abilities not to feel threatened or overwhelmed by Mitchell. Steeped in army tradition, Patrick remained open to logical, objective analysis of the many recommendations he made. Initial animosity between the two men soon gave way to mutual respect. Patrick's seniority, diplomacy, and discipline proved invaluable to Mitchell in convincing the Allies to implement many of his radical and untested theories of aerial warfare. Mitchell rapidly became the de facto leader of all Allied air power.

Lieutenant Leigh Wade, flight instructor and test pilot for the Army Air Service, was finally living up to the nickname that had followed him since childhood, "Happy". After a full year of instructing novice airmen in the fine art of aerial combat in Texas, the army had finally agreed to his transfer to France. For the first time, he could put into practice the techniques he had been teaching.

Pacing up and down anxiously on the deck of the troopship carrying him and several of his student pilots, Leigh couldn't wait to at last engage the enemy. He would soon know how good he really was. Oh, they were good, those German pilots. He knew that. Many of his students, whom he had come to love, had returned in pine boxes.

Now, at last, he could wreak his revenge—for the parents, the wives, the girlfriends who would never see their handsome airmen again.

L eigh's mother's ancestors were of the old, well-bred English aristocracy and had crossed the ocean on the Mayflower seeking a new home and a new life. His father's family was from Canada; rough and tough, they survived countless cold, cruel Northern winters eking out subsistence from the unyielding soil of their farms. Leigh always marveled that these two families, from such different backgrounds, found mutual love in each other's hearts.

Leigh was born February 2, 1897, on his parent's farm three miles from the small town of Cassopolis, Michigan, which lay forty miles southwest—and a world away—from the urban sprawl of Kalamazoo. From the age of five, he walked the two miles each day to the little red wooden schoolhouse in whose single room a middle-aged and kindly teacher sought to fill the heads of a dozen or so students of different ages with book learning. He enjoyed mathematics, with its orderly precision and unambiguous solutions, but felt little interest in all the other subjects.

It was high school that broadened his horizons and excited his imagination with visions of faraway places and exotic adventures. He disliked farming. When he was sixteen, a lovely damsel declined his invitation to elope with him until he proved his manliness and independence. A young Leigh Wade, very much in love, then left a note for his parents, packed his few belongings and his meager savings, and left his home under cover of darkness for a life of adventure out west.

He got as far as the badlands of North Dakota, where he found work repairing fences and farm implements on a Dakota ranch. After a full season of work new adventures beckoned, and Leigh, now cured of his youthful infatuation, joined the First North Dakota Infantry. He was sent to the Mexican border to help General Pershing in his pursuit of the elusive Pancho Villa.

Leigh came to admire the young man who kept Pancho Villa's airplanes flying while the American planes crashed or were grounded by poor maintenance and poorer flying. If Lowell Smith, only four years older than he was, could fly so well, then surely he could too. Leigh went on a relentless campaign to get himself transferred to the air service. His superiors, growing weary of his continuous requests for transfer, finally agreed, and he was sent to Toronto for training with the Royal Air Force.

Leigh took to flying as naturally as a bird. He amazed his instructors by soloing expertly within a few hours, making perfect takeoffs and landings within a few days, and performing complex aerial maneuvers better than they could within a few weeks. Within a few months, Leigh was instructing new students and testing new airplanes. His cautious analytical and mathematical approach to each new challenge of flight and his extensive notes were enormously valuable to other pilots who had to face similar problems.

Leigh always seemed to make the best of a bad situation and was unerringly cheerful, upbeat, and smiling. His happy face soon wiped away the gloom of his students' errors, and he restored their confidence by minimizing their failings and maximizing the few things they did right. He seldom took control of the aircraft from them unless it was absolutely necessary, preferring to surreptitiously add small, unnoticed control correction inputs from his remote cockpit. He laughed off the many bounced or hard landings of his students with humor, which restored their bruised egos and made a new and better attempt possible.

Now, on the upper deck of the troopship, Leigh turned up the woolen collar of his army overcoat against the cold night wind of the north Atlantic Ocean and leaned over the rail. The dark profile of the destroyer guarding them from the ever-present U-boats stood out starkly against the sky, illuminated by the full moon. He could see the spray thrown up by the bow of the destroyer as it sliced through the ten-foot seas, rising and falling as the waves broke over its bow. The other ships in the convoy, silhouetted against the lightening sky, stretched for miles all around him.

Even without any lights showing, he knew that on each ship, alert sailors peered anxiously through high-power binoculars for the telltale periscope of the submarines that hunted them. Under the full moon that night, he knew concealment was impossible. Even darkened, they were sitting ducks. It was only the threat of the rolling thunder and death that would stream down on them from the destroyers that protected them. Leigh looked up toward the lightening sky in silent prayer. *Please, God, don't let them get me now. Not until I have done battle with them. Not until I have repaid the debt I owe to my comrades of the sky.*

Leigh didn't notice the muscular young man who had silently joined him at the rail until he felt his strong left arm around his shoulders. His reveries suddenly broken, Leigh turned to face Les Arnold, his best—and worst—student. You couldn't look at Les without laughing. Les was the class clown, the buffoon, always wearing the same mischievous grin that said, *You'll never guess what I've just done!*

Les was the incorrigible child. Always late. Always in trouble. Always involved with some outrageous nefarious scheme, some oversexed damsel in distress. Always on the verge of being expelled—from class, from school, from the service, from his job. But put an airplane in his hands, and the clown metamorphosed into the grandmaster, the impresario, the conductor of a symphony orchestra in the sky. And what music he could play! The airplane took on a life of its own, climbing and diving and zooming, painting impossible patterns on the canvas of the sky. Only his consummate flying skills kept the army, again and again, from throwing Les out.

L eslie Arnold was born in New Haven, Connecticut, on August 28, 1894. His father, Frank, was a railroad man. His grandfather had manned the great sailing ships of New Bedford, as had his father and grandfather before him. Frank missed his seagoing family heritage and moved young Les and the family from New Haven to New London, where he and his son could make better contact with their roots in the sea.

As a youngster, Les was constantly in trouble with the stern schoolmasters of the day, who failed to appreciate his sense of humor or the practical jokes he would play on them. He was the most-whipped boy in the school, and soon earned his reputation as the class clown. To his parent's frustration, he had little regard for authority and a high tolerance for the pain of punishment that resulted.

In high school, football was Les's favorite sport. His square, muscular physique easily drove the ball through the opposing team unless his opponents teamed up in groups of four or five to bring him to the ground. Even then he would often rise and carry them on his back across the goal line. Les particularly enjoyed making the most unexpected plays with the highest risk—a propensity which his coach did not admire, so he kept him on the bench to be used only as a last resort to even the score when all else had failed.

As a teenager, Les was constantly attracted to the opposite sex, who usually reciprocated with great abundance. Blessed or cursed, depending on one's viewpoint, with more than his share of raging hormones, Les quickly gained his reputation as a ladies' man and was the envy of his fellow students. One summer was spent selling pianos to lonesome farmers' wives, who often insisted on personal demonstrations in the privacy of their bedrooms. A close shotgun blast from an irate farmer brought the risk of his escapades too close to home. Several seasons as a player in summer stock followed, which provided many of the same rewards with considerably reduced risk.

Another summer, Les, now fully grown with an exceptionally powerful physique, landed a well-paying job as a member of a team of linesmen traveling from town to town installing telephone and telegraph lines and poles. He could dig the hole into which the pole was inserted in less than half the time of the other men, who marveled at his strength. In one town, their team was assaulted by the town bully, who demanded that they leave. Les was sent to reason with him. The bully threw several punches, which Les easily avoided. Les turned to leave and the man kicked him in the back with a sharply pointed boot. In pain, Les faced the man and knocked him out cold with a single punch, lifting him off his feet and flinging him several yards down the street and into the mud, to the astonishment and applause of his coworkers.

From then on, they arranged for Les to challenge the strongest man in each town they visited, placing substantial bets on Les winning the contest. Soon the profits they were all making on Les's prowess exceeded their wages, since Les never lost a match.

When war became likely, Les joined the air service studying aerodynamics, meteorology, engine mechanics, and navigation at Princeton University before being sent to Waco to complete his flight training. He found Leigh Wade to be an incredibly good instructor and progressed rapidly, although not without conflict with his superiors. They, as their predecessors, did not appreciate his humor, practical jokes, or frequent disregard of curfews. This earned him numerous AWOL citations and the threat of dismissal from the service, despite his obviously superior flying skills. Les Arnold and Leigh Wade were the only pilots at Waco who could faultlessly perform the most complex aerial stunts, amazing their fellow pilots.

O n deck, Leigh simply nodded to Les and turned again toward the shadowy profile of the destroyer. Les started to say something funny but saw that Leigh was lost in thought and didn't want to intrude. He gave Leigh's shoulder an affectionate squeeze, turned and walked away.

Much of the success the Germans were having in the air war was directly attributable to the fertile mind of Anthony Fokker. He was a superb Dutch pilot who had turned his fascination and talent for aviation into a lucrative business. From the new manufacturing plant he established in Germany, Fokker perfected the synchronizing mechanism for aircraft machine guns. This mechanism prevented bullets from striking the firing aircraft's propeller blades by using a cam-actuated pushrod interrupter device driven from the engine's oil pump. This gave the Germans an enormous advantage over the bullet-deflecting, heavy steel propeller plates required on Allied planes.

Fokker's Eindeckers (single wing monoplanes) were the first aircraft to place the gun-firing buttons on the control stick. This allowed the German pilots to accurately maintain the nose of the plane, and their gun sights, on enemy planes while firing. During 1915 the Eindeckers were virtually invincible. The first German aces, Oswald Boelcke and Max Immelmann, flew Fokker Eindeckers to numerous victories.

By 1916, the maneuverability of English DeHaviland DH-2 and RAF FE-2b biplanes put an end to the Eindecker's supremacy, but Germany's immediate introduction of the Albatros D1 model again gave them the advantages of greater firepower, more maneuverability, and a faster climb rate. Fokker also countered with his own D-series biplanes. The D1 through D4 models were mediocre, but the D5 and D6 were both very good aircraft and equal to the best combat aircraft then flying. The improved Albatros D2, introduced at the same time, again gave Germany the advantage.

Fokker's Dr.1 (Dreidecker or three-wing) triplane, introduced in August of 1917, followed and apparently copied the English Sopwith triplane introduced earlier in February of 1917. The Dr.1 was flown by Manfred von Richthofen, the famous Red Baron. The Dr.1's three short wings gave the aircraft increased maneuverability and lift, which Richthofen made maximum use of to increase his score of Allied pilot kills.

Although both sides were rapidly improving their airplane designs, German aircraft performance remained superior to the Allies during the last two years of the war. The Albatros D3 model further extended the advantages of the D1 and D2, and was the best fighter plane in 1917 until the introduction of the Fokker D7 early in 1918. Even the huge German Gotha bombers had advantages of maneuverability, climb rate, and firepower over the English Handley Page and Italian Caproni bombers.

The D7 had maneuverability almost equal to the Dr.1, which it replaced, but was more strongly built. With its 185 horsepower Mercedes engine, it was also faster, reaching 128 miles per hour. It could climb at a faster rate and to a higher altitude than any Allied aircraft. Fokker's increasing production rate produced sufficient quantities of the D7 to rapidly equip most front-line squadrons. Fokker built more than eight thousand airplanes during the war.

The German Fokker D7s, unfortunately for the Allies, had few weaknesses that could be exploited in aerial combat. It was an easy airplane to fly, and its strong construction could withstand the abuse of even the most heavy-handed novice aviators. It could be maneuvered rapidly, without breaking, and could climb faster than Allied types.

This ability to fly safely at the extreme outer edges of the performance envelope is what gave the Fokker D7 its winning advantage. The superiority of the D7 was acknowledged at the conclusion of the war. It was the only aircraft the Allies demanded be turned over to them as a requirement of the Armistice.

In early 1918, the Allies were losing the air war. Germany had five times the number of aircraft than did the allies, and they were generally superior in performance as well. The Allies could prevail only by radical new tactics, innovation, and cunning. Before Bloody April of 1918 ended, the British had lost over one thousand aircraft. The huge Allied losses continued through May. Major R. Lufbery, the heroic leader of the Lafayette Escadrille, and later the equally famous 94th Aero Squadron, was lost. Casualties in the squadron had so decimated the pilots that with the death of Lufbery, not a single original member of the squadron remained. Eddie Rickenbacker was eventually given command of the 94th, now called the "hat in the ring" squadron after their well-known fuselage insignia.

During this period, Manfred von Richthofen, the top ace of the war with eighty confirmed kills, was also shot down. Command of his famous Flying Circus, named after the brightly painted planes that traveled by rail to outlying bases, passed on to Hermann Goering— the man who would lead the Luftwaffe in the next war. By the late summer, eight hundred D7s had been delivered to forty of the top German squadrons. These units were challenged by only a few of the first new Spad 13s, whose production had just started. The Allies were losing five times the number of pilots than were the Germans and realized that they must change their air strategy to survive.

The war was going poorly for the Allies on the ground as well. Critical shortages of materials, resources, and manpower caused major battles to be lost. After three years of little movement, in March 1918 the Germans broke through the Allied lines and advanced fourteen miles for the largest gains of the war. The British Fifth Army was crushed on the Somme. German production of munitions and aircraft reached their highest output levels, surpassing even the maximum levels of World War II. German reinforcements and supplies were arriving unimpeded from the east. The situation looked very grave.

U nder Allied pressure to face the reality of Mitchell's uniquely talented leadership, Pershing reluctantly confirmed him as the Chief of Air Service, and both were finally given permission by the Allies to use their own tactics and strategies. General Foch, the French Supreme Allied Commander, allowed General Pershing to form the separate American army he had been requesting, which became official on August 10, 1918, with headquarters at Neufchateau, south of St. Mihiel. Foch gave Mitchell, who was flying daily reconnaissance, direct command of ninety-eight French, American, British, and Italian air squadrons, totaling fifteen hundred aircraft and four hundred large bombers. Six hundred of the planes were to be flown by Americans. For the first time, Mitchell was free to employ all of the Allied air forces as he believed best. Now he could put his own controversial theories of air power to the ultimate test.

Many of Mitchell's most experienced pilots had been lost to enemy gunfire, mechanical failures, bad weather, or just bad luck. The replacements coming from the United States had few flight hours. They were unfamiliar with the techniques of aerial combat and incapable of the accurate gunfire required to survive encounters with the new Fokker D7s and the disciplined German pilots who flew them.

The Germans were following Allied planes home to their base at night and then, unseen, bombing the air bases. Mitchell set up well-lighted dummy air bases. The Allied pilots returning at night would flash a secret signal, and the real air base runway would be momentarily lighted, then darkened again. The German bombs landed with little effect on the dummy base.

September 1918, was a crucial month for the Allies. Hundreds of thousands of German troop reinforcements had been sent to the Western Front after Russia capitulated. Captured Russian factories and farms were coming on line with rapidly increasing shipments of weapons and foodstuffs, potentially surpassing the Allied shipments. German control of railroad lines and key roads gave them far greater supply mobility than the Allies. They could rapidly and efficiently supply war material to their front lines in France.

Mitchell had seen, on numerous occasions, small groups of Allied planes fall victim to equal or larger groups of superior German planes. To him, the lesson was clear. The existing strategy of employing many small air squadrons over a wide area was futile and counterproductive, since losses exceeded any likely damage inflicted on the enemy. Mitchell believed air superiority required massive quantities of Allied aircraft, flying in close formations and making simultaneous air strikes.

To coordinate the air activities of Great Britain and end the unproductive competition between the Royal Flying Corps and the Royal Naval Air Services, Mitchell suggested they be combined into a single entity. The new Royal Air Force or RAF was placed under the command of Major General Hugh Trenchard. Similar entreaties by Mitchell that the United States do the same went unheeded.

Few knew exactly where or when the strike would be made, but most knew this would be the largest aviation operation ever, and the outcome of the war might depend upon its success. This was Mitchell's ultimate test, and he would need every aircraft and pilot he could muster to meet the challenge.

Opponents of his bold plans forecast the destruction of the Allied air fleet. The large formations would become easy targets for ground fire and midair collisions would occur, they said. Misplaced friendly fire by panicked gunners would shoot down Allied planes. Coordination of air forces that large would be impossible. Attacking German fighter pilots would have a field day, a turkey shoot. Never put all your eggs in one basket, they warned. Mitchell, convinced they were wrong, continued to implement his plans. He knew the fate of the war hung in the balance.

Many of the best U.S. pilots were being used back home to train twenty-three thousand new aviators and a similar number of aircraft mechanics. Ground schools lasting two to three months were established on eight college campuses. The largest of these were at the Universities of Texas and California. Pilot trainees were then sent to newly constructed domestic military airfields for flight training, and finally on to European training centers for ten to thirty hours of combat training. With the huge pilot losses of the earlier months and the pressing need for qualified replacements, Mitchell ordered all available trainees and instructor pilots sent to Europe. Among those pilots were Erik Nelson, Leigh Wade, and Les Arnold. Lowell Smith was felt to be too valuable in his position as chief flight instructor, and his repeated requests for transfer into combat were deferred. When he finally stepped off the troop ship in London he found the day had been declared a national holiday: Armistice Day. His trial by fire lay several years in the future.

The Germans had held a salient or large bulge into France since 1914, through which they freely resupplied their armies. All efforts to dislodge them had failed. Pershing decided that on September 12, 1918, his newly formed American army of over a million troops, supported by the world's greatest aviation offensive, would crush the German salient at St. Mihiel.

President Wilson had grave reservations about launching a huge-scale attack on a heavily fortified and entrenched enemy using American troops untested in battle, even when supported by almost all of the remaining Allied aircraft. If the St. Mihiel offensive failed, the losses of trained pilots, aircraft, artillery, and infantry would be disastrous. He feared a catastrophic defeat against the reinforced German lines would cost them the war. He requested both General Pershing and Commander-in-Chief Foch to reconsider the offensive, but left the final decision in their hands.

The other Allied commanders had little confidence that this newly formed, improvised army of farmers and cowboys, bankers and businessmen, students and teachers would be an effective independent fighting force. They had no common culture to bind them, no history of military discipline to guide them, no generations of attachment to the land upon which they fought. This was, after all, not their war. Where would their motivation come from? Surely the highly disciplined, well-trained, and battle-hardened German troops, fighting from defensive positions, prepared and reinforced with years of effort, would quickly dispatch these brash neophytes.

Foch had confidence in Mitchell and was comfortable with his decision to place all Allied air forces under his command. Mitchell had won his admiration by repeatedly demonstrating his bravery and dedication. He had personally observed many of Mitchell's daily flights over enemy guns, often alone and unprotected, to report the enemy's movements to Allied pilots and infantry forces. He knew Mitchell to be dedicated and his judgment to be sound.

Foch had far less confidence in Pershing, though, and had second thoughts on allowing the operation to proceed. Foch summoned Pershing for an emergency meeting shortly before the St. Mihiel offensive was to begin. He informed him, in light of his own and President Wilson's reservations, that he had reconsidered and wanted to call off the assault. Instead, he would split up the recently unified American forces and use them in conjunction with other Allied forces in separate, smaller campaigns in other areas.

Pershing was stunned. This was the opportunity he had been waiting for. To have finally gained control of the American army and now to suddenly lose it was a devastating blow. It took a while for Pershing to collect himself sufficiently to respond.

Pershing begged Foch to relent. With little time left before the campaign began, he argued, it would be impossible to recall all of his forces. Those that went would be annihilated without support. He promised he would reduce the number of his men used in the attack on St. Mihiel, leaving sufficient strength to accomplish Foch's other objective, an attack in the Meuse River–Argonne Forest region. He knew that waging war in two separate campaigns, forty miles apart, had never been successful. With reduced forces in each, far larger numbers of American casualties could be expected.

Foch had a difficult decision before him. He knew Pershing would lose face if he countermanded his authority, and an open breach might gravely effect American morale. He also knew the devastating effect it would have on Pershing's career. Reluctantly, Foch accepted the compromise, but warned Pershing that participation by French ground forces would be minimal. The St. Mihiel campaign would proceed with American ground forces carrying the brunt of the fighting for the first time.

SEPTEMBER 12, 1918
5:15 A.M.
OVER THE ENGLISH CHANNEL

The predawn September sky was still dark. Lieutenant Erik Nelson used his small flashlight to record the readings of his watch, compass, altimeter, and airspeed indicator on the pad tied to his leg. Flying over the water from England toward the coast of France in the darkness, with the horizon almost invisible and no lights except those of an occasional fishing trawler, was difficult and required constant attention.

He didn't like the aircraft he was flying, but he wasn't given a choice when they assigned him to bomber-pilot training in Texas, nor afterward, when they kept him at the school instructing pilots and mechanics. They told him that, at twenty-nine, he was too old, too mature, too slow to react, and too cautious for the rough-and-tumble tactics and hair-trigger responses required of the young pursuit-plane pilots.

The Handley-Page Model 0/400 that he was now flying was certainly no pursuit plane. It was huge, larger than any airplane he had ever seen. Its wings stretched over one hundred feet, and sitting on its ungainly double sets of landing gear it dwarfed all the other airplanes concealed in its shadow. The two 360-horsepower Rolls Royce Eagle 8 Engines could lift over a ton of bombs and fly them over 750 miles at almost one hundred miles per hour from air bases in Great Britain to targets deep within Germany. It was easy to see why the Brits called it the Bloody Paralyzer.

Flying the Handley-Page reminded Erik of the largest ships he had steered before arriving in the United States. You turned the control wheel and waited; eventually the behemoth would reluctantly change direction. It seemed to Erik that no matter how early or vigorous his control inputs were, the aircraft would respond too little and too late. You didn't fly this monster, you guided it, eventually coaxing a response from it. In smooth air it was very stable, but in turbulence the huge wings flapped and wobbled, and the fuselage twisted and flexed with alarming cracking and groaning noises that could be heard above the roar of the 720 horses powering it.

Erik was in a loose formation of forty Handley-Page bombers. Each carried a single, newly developed 1,650-pound bomb. The bombers had been delivered only the previous month, and each pilot had the task of finding and purging the gremlins that accompanied every new aircraft. The fuel system had been particularly troublesome. The heavy steel fuel tanks lying behind the armored engine nacelles restricted the flow of fuel and had to be relocated to the fuselage and lightened.

Two additional fuel tanks were added to the upper wing center section, fed by wind-driven fuel pumps to increase the endurance and range of its thirsty engines. Erik disliked the burdensome complexity of the fuel system and its close proximity to the crew. He took little comfort that, in the event of a crash, their own bombs would kill them before any fire caused by leaking fuel could get started.

A squadron of twenty BE-2 dual cockpit biplanes, mounting a single Lewis machine gun awkwardly behind the front cockpit, escorted them across the choppy waters of the English channel. The BE-2s, slow and cumbersome, had long ago been relegated to reconnaissance use only. They required full throttle to stay with the newer, faster bombers. Erik knew they would have little chance of defending his formation against attack by any of the agile German Fokker or Albatros fighter planes. More likely the bomber's guns would have to defend them. He felt no sadness when they reached the limits of their short fuel range and waved a cheery salute as, one by one, they turned back toward home.

Until the appointed rendezvous with the sleek Spads of the 94th Aero Squadron deep within France, their defense now lay in the hands of their gunners in the front and rear cockpits, each controlling two Lewis machine guns. Erik liked the .303-caliber Lewis guns, designed by an American and built in Britain. They couldn't match the power, nor the eight hundred-rounds-per-minute firing rate, of the newer Vickers guns; but they were lightweight and reliable, and their emptied rotary magazines were easily exchanged with full ones.

Erik was surprised by the youth of his crew. They looked barely old enough to be in high school, and their eager smiles betrayed a lack of understanding of the carnage that awaited. Would they hold their position and return fire accurately through a lethal hail of German bullets, or panic into impotence when the onslaught started? He would know soon enough. He put the doubts from his mind and concentrated on flying the heavily laden, wallowing airplane, and holding his position in the formation.

As the bombers reached the coastline of France, the beauty of the sunrise seemed incongruous with the lethal cargo of death and destruction he carried. In the cockpit of the bomber, Erik could now check his map without using his flashlight. Their target: the key German railroad and supply centers at Metz and Sedan. The flight leading pathfinder plane was right on track. One more hour to go.

SEPT. 12, 1918
6:10 A.M.
U.S. ARMY BASE NEAR ST. MIHIEL, FRANCE

In the clammy, cold predawn hours, Captain George C. Marshall—the future American Army Chief of Staff during World War II—paced back and forth restlessly, checking and rechecking that his elements of the First American Army were in readiness. He had been one of the first Americans to arrive in France, and spent what seemed to him an eternity waiting for supplies that were constantly being delayed or lost.

Captain Harry S. Truman—the future U.S. President—reported to him that ammunition missing the day before had been located and his howitzer, mortar, and cannon crews now had sufficient munitions for the long hours of firing that would herald the attack. Marshall noted with relief that each gun emplacement had reported their readiness. The telegraph circuits connecting his courageous hidden spotters were alive, and signals had already been exchanged and tested. Marshall looked up and offered a silent prayer of thanks after completing his final checklist.

Several miles away, squatting half-hidden in the tall wet grass, lay the armored tanks of Colonel George S. Patton. Patton had fought with Pershing in Mexico, and had taken up the challenge the year before of establishing the first American tank corps. The relationship between the two men had become strained after Pershing's infatuation with Micheline Resco caused him to break off his engagement to marry Patton's sister. Starting with two tanks custom built in Washington from French blueprints, Patton now had 174 of the metal monsters poised to lead the infantry in the battle of St. Mihiel. He would have far more under his command in the next war.

Tanks had been developed by the British early in the war. The British concealed the military purpose of the early armored containers from prying eyes by calling them, innocuously, "tanks." The name stuck. The French requested the Americans use their designs to simplify maintenance and repairs. At this stage they were all slow, ponderous, unreliable, incredibly noisy, and highly vulnerable. Before the day ended only seventy would make it to the German lines; 104 would fall victim to German guns, mechanical breakdowns, or simply run out of gas. Even with this high attrition rate, tanks were still very useful. They brought companies of infantrymen, protected by their cannon and armor, safely through the barbed wire, and hails of rifle and machine gun bullets, into the enemy trenches. The Germans considered tanks too unreliable, and built very few.

In the predawn darkness, Patton chatted amiably in muted tones with Mitchell's childhood friend, Colonel Douglas MacArthur.

MacArthur was commander of the 84th Brigade. After the artillery completed their shelling, his men would follow Patton's tanks in the assault. They laughed and joked and spoke of home, family and friends. Anything but the hell the dawn would bring.

Most of the half million American troops were facing battle for the first time, and they were apprehensive. Unspoken fears ran through their heads. *Will I shamefully panic and run when the bullets coming at me are for real? Will I let my buddies down? Will I get hit? Will it hurt?* Most lay awake, alone with their own thoughts and fears in the predawn darkness until the call came: "Everyone up and ready. Check rifles and bayonets. Check ammo and cartridge belts." The letters they had written to loved ones were collected by the chaplains who also blessed them as they knelt in groups with bowed heads bare, their helmets clutched in their hands.

The training these troops received had been controversial. The British and French were taught the art of defense, holding a position, reinforcing it, and defending it. Americans learned the art of offense: getting through the barbed wire, the minefields, the machine-gun fire, the poison gas, and even the newly developed German flamethrowers—which could toast a man before he could get within fifty feet.

Americans practiced the art of hand-to-hand combat, the use of the bayonet to gut an enemy before he could fire his pistol. They were taught the use of the dagger, the choke hold, how to use their hips and arms to sweep the enemy off his feet and onto his back where a well-placed heel boot could crush the bones of his throat. They learned about the vulnerability of the temple area and the eye sockets.

SEPT. 12, 1918
6:25 A.M.
U.S. 94TH AERO SQUADRON AIRBASE, FRANCE

Several miles to the west, the early morning wake-up call at the 94th Aero Squadron was hardly necessary. Most of the airmen were already up and dressed. Many had written letters and left them discreetly on the mantle of the fireplace in the rustic dining room. Most of the envelopes were inscribed, "In the event of my death . . . " Some contained small memorabilia from far-off encounters, reminders of a happier time, to be passed on to those who waited at home, anxiously, for the day of their return. Most of the new men hadn't slept well. They looked tired and worried. They knew today was the big one. They'd all be up. No more practice. This one's for real.

Eddie Rickenbacker watched them file into the dining room. His seasoned pilots looked unconcerned. They always slept well. They'd been through it before and survived. Worrying didn't help. They left their worries with their letters on the mantle.

Within the squadron, the new replacements were called *vultures*, since they had no planes of their own until a more seasoned pilot became a casualty. When that happened, the vulture had to down a liter of Champagne while singing the squadron's song of battle. The vulture than became a *buzzard* and received his own Spad. When the buzzard logged his first kill, he became a *goofer* and, if he lived to make it to the exalted position of flight leader or squadron commander, he became a *guimper*, which to the new recruits ranked only a short step down from God.

Among the newest temporary replacements, Lieutenants Leigh Wade and Les Arnold were vultures. They had no planes of their own but would fly the oldest and most obsolete of the aircraft, the ones grounded long ago as being too shot up or otherwise unfit for flight. These airplanes had been cannibalized for the few good spare parts remaining in the lifeless carcass of a fuselage, an instrument panel, or an engine. These were the aircraft no one else wanted to fly. The mechanics had, under orders, reluctantly resurrected the dead for them. Mitchell demanded that, on this day, "everything but the cookstove" was to be in the air and on target.

To the veteran fliers, this provided a source of great humor. To protect their rear ends from constant ground fire, they had dismantled numerous cookstoves, fitting the heavy metal parts under their seats as bullet shields. The quartermaster never could understand the frequent demands for stove replacement parts from aircraft squadrons. Rickenbacker assured Mitchell that in the 94th Aero Squadron, even the cookstoves would be in the air and on target.

The resurrected airplanes included a Nieuport 17 and a Spad 7. The Nieuports were powered by the 110-horsepower LeRhone rotary engines. While less powerful than the 130 horsepower versions reserved for French aviators, their light gross weight of 1,235 pounds gave them excellent climb rates and a 109 miles-per-hour speed in level flight. The short wingspan of less than twenty-seven feet yielded rapid turning rates, making them highly maneuverable. The Nieuports featured both a forward-firing Lewis machine gun on the upper wing and a synchronized Vickers gun mounted on the cowl. William Avery Bishop, the second highest British ace, scored seventy-two kills flying a Nieuport 17 with the British 60th Air Squadron and won the coveted Victoria Cross, but the Nieuport 17's tendency to shed wings in high speed steep dives made it unpopular with American aviators.

The Spad 7 was an earlier version of the Spad 13s flown by most of the squadron. Stronger and heavier than the Nieuports at a gross weight of 1,554 pounds, its more powerful 175-horsepower Hispano-Suiza engine gave it a faster top speed of 119 mph. With its robust construction, it could safely dive at high speeds. A single Vickers machine gun was mounted on the cowl.

To vultures Wade and Arnold, the aircraft they were being given didn't look all that bad. By European standards of rapidly evolving war planes, they were ancient, but still light years ahead of the crates flown back home by the air service. Les Arnold assured the apologetic mechanics he had flown many planes with far less performance and in even worse condition. The mechanics seemed skeptical but nonetheless relieved. Leigh Wade extended his hand holding two wooden matches. The concealed shortened match stick represented the Nieuport, and Les Arnold drew it.

As a flight leader, Eddie Rickenbacker had been a guimper for some time. Today, his first day as the new squadron leader of the 94th, required him to protect the fleet of forty Handley-Page bombers coming across the Channel to bomb the German railroad yards, warehouses, and ammunition depots at Metz and Sedan.

The 94th Aero Squadron had started with Nieuports before switching to Spads. Many pilots had been lost when the fragile Nieuports shed their wings. The German pilots had parachutes and could jump to safety; the Allied pilots did not. When their airplanes lost a wing or had a stabilizer fail, or flamed as the enemy's bullets punctured their fuel tanks, they died.

The Spads were a welcome change. They stayed together. Spad 13 deliveries started in May of 1917 with 200-horsepower Hispano-

Suiza Be engines, and later with 235-horsepower H-S 8B engines. The French received the new Spad 13s first, and then the Italians, the Belgians, and finally those Americans who survived their aerial encounters with the Germans in their obsolete Spad 7s. The Spad 13s were fast at 138 mph, and nothing could outdive them until the Fokker D7s came along in April of 1918.

The D7s proved a nightmare for the Allies. They could outclimb, outdive, and outmaneuver almost every Allied aircraft. They had no known weaknesses for the Allied pilots to exploit. Rickenbacker knew his boys would be tangling with the D7s that day. Would Mitchell's theory of massive air power translate into massive losses for them or their enemies? In a few hours, he would know the answer.

M itchell finished his fourth cup of coffee as he sat at the large planning table in the sandbag-reinforced command bunker in the predawn hours. He had left nothing to chance. He knew how much depended upon this day. He'd drawn the air battle plan dozens of times over the last year. He'd stroked it, massaged it, perfected it. He anticipated what could go wrong, listed it, considered it, and came up with an alternate plan if the first should not work. He knew the assigned position and the exact time over target of every one of the fifteen hundred aircraft under his command. He knew the names of each squadron leader, their records, their strengths, their weaknesses. He knew the characteristics of each aircraft flown. Each assignment was made with careful consideration of each pilot and the aircraft he flew. He was ready. His adrenalin mixed with the caffeine in the coffee he'd consumed and kept him fully alert. The sleep denied him over the past forty-eight hours seemed of no consequence.

Weather information from Allied air bases was updated hourly. Unlighted reconnaissance planes, flying high through the dark night with muffled engines and concealed exhausts, were returning with the latest weather over the target areas. Temperatures and winds aloft, cloud coverage, ceilings, and visibility were sent by coded telegraphic transmission back to the Allied air bases. Teams of meteorologists evaluated the incoming data and predicted the likelihood of ground fog, rain, and turbulence. Teams of navigational officers evaluated wind patterns to determine the precise takeoff time of each air squadron. For the mass bombardment to have maximum effect, timing was critical. It was essential that each aircraft arrive over their target area at the precise time required. The lethal hail of bombs and bullets raining down on the enemy all at once would cause maximum confusion and casualties. They would panic and run, unable to hide or retaliate.

For Pershing, Mitchell, and the half million Americans serving under them, September 12, 1918, was their date with destiny. For the first time in the war, and at one of its most critical moments, the Americans were in charge of a major battle. Before the sun went down that day, all would be tested. Many would sacrifice their limbs, their lives, their souls. Whatever the outcome, the events of this day and this place would never be forgotten by any of them. Here the future of air power would be decided for generations to come.

SEPT. 12, 1918
7:10 A.M.
JAGDGESCHWADER 1 AIRBASE, FRANCE

To the German airmen who flew the fifty aircraft of the Flying Circus, the distant booms of artillery in the inky blackness before the dawn were of little surprise. The heightened activity at the Allied air bases and front lines had been reported to them over the past few days. They knew an attack was imminent and Jagdgeschwader 1 would be called upon, yet again, to climb into their cockpits and defend the advances their comrades in the infantry had made into the Allied lines. Most of the new recruits were already wide awake, apprehensive but eager to prove their manhood in the battle to come. The snoring of the veterans were punctuated by curses and grumbling. The unwanted intrusion of the mortars and long-range Allied guns, which could be more felt than heard that morning, was disturbing their sleep, and they didn't like that at all.

In soft tones shielded from the new initiates, the veterans expressed their intense dislike of their new squadron commander. Their leader, their beloved Red Baron, had perished. They were grateful to the honor guard of high-ranking English aviators who had lovingly buried him with full military honors and a twenty-one-gun salute. On his grave, a huge wreath of flowers from British head-quarters honored "our gallant and worthy foe."

To the veteran German pilots, such a code of honor and chivalry among airmen was common and expected. Manfred von Richthofen, with eighty air victories, would never fire on a helpless enemy, nor would Ernst Udet with sixty-two, or Erich Loewenhardt with 53, nor would any of the Allied aces. They had seen Rickenbacker wave and break off his attack against several young German airmen who, paralyzed by panic, could not respond. They had smiled knowingly at each other, listening to the young novices claim they had outflown the great Eddie Rickenbacker, ungrateful for the lives he could have taken anytime with the push of a button.

With the death of Richthofen, the Flying Circus was not the same. Their soft-spoken, gentle teacher and hero was gone, and in his place was a strutting, bellowing, intolerant martinet who had little respect for them or their code of honor. His mission was self promotion and his methods were fear and brutality. His name: Hermann Goering, and he would survive to become the leader of Hitler's Luftwaffe.

When the wake-up call came, the veteran pilots of Jagdgeschwader 1 rose sleepily from their bunks. The young novices had slept little and were already showered and dressed. The older ones knew there was no hurry. Their Fokker D7s could only stay aloft for ninety minutes, and the Allied planes would not be flying before daylight, before their pilots could see where to bomb and strafe. They had plenty of time to eat their breakfast of cheese and sausages, time for coffee and bread, time to check the weather, time to load the guns.

As the stragglers came for breakfast, Goering wrote their names on the yellow pad he carried. There would be no breakfast for them today and no leave this weekend. Tonight they would wash dishes, clean latrines, scrub floors. If they were late again, their mail privileges would be canceled—forever! Goering despised the lack of discipline displayed by the charismatic air aces who formerly led the Flying Circus. Under his watch, there would be no more open collars, no more unshined buttons, no more unpolished boots. His airmen would sit ramrod straight in the mess hall. They would address each other by rank and last name only. They would snap to attention with eyes straight ahead and salute any superior officer.

They would forget that they happened to be pilots and would become German officers, just as he was.

Goering gathered his flock in the ready room just after dawn. He told them that that day would be the most important of the war. Each man would be expected to act heroically and without hesitation. Any pilot exhibiting cowardice would be shot upon his return. This new tone erased all concealed hopes that their new leader would, in time, mellow into the gentle and protective father that Richthofen had been.

SEPT 12, 1918
7:30 A.M.
OVER THE COASTLINE OF CALAIS, FRANCE

Erik Nelson's squadron of bombers had turned south upon reaching the coastline. The low clouds and drizzle obscured most of the ground below them, but occasionally the clouds opened and they could see surprised French farmers excitedly point skyward toward the flock of monsters lumbering noisily overhead.

When they reached the Somme River, the formation turned twenty degrees east to stay in the protected airspace of the Allied air bases. Activity was everywhere. Airplanes were departing in huge numbers from bases at Bertangles, Amiens, Cachy, and Mondidier, turning toward the east and the rear of the German lines. Erik had never seen anything like it. The skies were alive with aircraft, an awesome sight, the scale unimaginable.

Through the breaking clouds, they saw the large air base at Chateâu-Thierry. The pathfinder bomber made its final course change directly toward the primary targets at Metz. Erik returned the waves of airbase mechanics who stood in front of the deserted hangars and cheered. He smiled at the open mouths and wide eyes of his young gunners, disbelieving the images they were seeing. Were there really that many airplanes in the world? It seemed impossible, even to Erik. Suddenly the U.S. air service he had known and loved back home seemed tiny, puny, and insignificant.

As the bomber flight started its climb to clear the rising terrain under them, Erik noted the outside temperature gauge. The needle had fallen into the freezing zone. He knew what that meant in the wet clouds they were flying through. He watched apprehensively as ice started forming on the leading edges of the wings and on the barrels of the machine guns. His bomber's engines were now at full throttle but the airspeed and climb rate continued to decay. His young gunners knew the thickening ice spreading backward over the wings boded no good. Erik met their worried looks with a thumbs-up, which concealed his own concern. Reassured, the gunners removed their gloves and continued scraping the rapidly forming ice from the barrels of their weapons.

Ice is the bogeyman of flying. It does many things to an airplane, all of them bad. Ice changes the shape of the wings and thus destroys the lifting forces generated by the carefully cambered shape. Ice forming on the propeller reduces the forward thrust generated by the precisely sculpted spinning blades. Ice blocks the throats of the carburetors, leaving the engine gasping for air and reducing its power. Ice adds weight to the airplane, pulling it inexorably downward and adding to the engine's burden just when it is most vulnerable. Ice blocks the airflow to the sensitive instruments needed by the pilot to maintain control of his aircraft and gives him false information that, if acted upon, can cause the airplane to crash. Uncontrolled icing, even to the bravest, most experienced pilot flying the most modern aircraft, is terrifying.

Erik watched his airspeed indicator slowly fall as the huge Handley-Page struggled to lift its great weight into the thinning air. If it fell 10 percent further, the airplane would cease flying and plunge into the rocks below. The terrain was rising. Through breaks in the clouds, mountain peaks seemed to be at or very close to his altitude. Most of the formation had also stopped climbing, but still the airspeed fell. Was the indicator still accurate or was its ice-blocked air inlet giving false readings?

He had no way of knowing, or how long the heavy bomber would continue to fly with its increasing burden. Erik considered his options. Descent to warmer air was not possible. The terrain was too high, barely below his present altitude. The only option: to lighten the aircraft, but the only significant weights not structurally attached were the crew, the guns and ammunition, and the huge, 1,650-pound bomb he carried.

The crew was out. Without guns or ammunition, they would probably be killed by the Germans. Only the bomb remained. He lightly fingered the bomb release. If he released the bomb, his mission would be a failure. They were too low over the terrain anyway. The resulting explosion just below his plane would hurl it high into the sky above, breaking it into small pieces and probably taking several nearby planes with him into oblivion. In fact, he had no options.

Erik flew grimly on, resolving not to look at the falling airspeed indicator or the thickening ice. On his knee pad, he started calculating the rate at which the fuel he burned lightened the aircraft. The twin 360-horsepower Rolls Royce Eagle engines were burning forty gallons of aviation fuel each hour. That meant for each minute he could stay in the air, they would be four pounds lighter. It seemed a pitifully small percentage of their total gross weight of 13,350 pounds, but at least it was getting lighter.

The Handley-Page flying just off his wing started sinking under its ice burden. Erik watched helplessly as it struggled in vain to hold its altitude. He estimated it had dropped fifty feet below the formation when its forward gunner reached over the front of his cockpit and, using the wrench he carried to free up a jammed gun, pounded at the thick ice covering the nose of the bomber. Erik watched as chunks of ice released their hold and fell onto the snow-covered rocks below. This modest success seemed to arrest the sink rate and, within a few minutes, all the other gunners followed his example. Erik noted with satisfaction that his airspeed indicator had stabilized, just above the stalling speed.

His relief was short-lived. A small but insistent, growing vibration shook the bomber. He knew that propeller icing was making its unwelcome presence felt. The unbalanced accumulations of ice on the four massive wooden propeller blades would increase until the violent shaking tore the engine from its mounts and destroyed the aircraft. It had to be stopped.

Eric remembered a trick his first flight instructor, Captain Floyd, had shown him when they inadvertently flew through the severe icing conditions of a Florida thunderstorm. He removed the heavy leather glove on his right hand and pushed aside the metal guards covering the magneto switches controlling the ignition on each of the engines. He hesitated, knowing that if this didn't work, they would crash. With a silent prayer, he shut off the magneto switch of his right engine and started counting.

The airplane immediately yawed to the right and into the dead engine as it started to descend. The silenced exhaust stacks and windmilling propeller frightened the gunners, and they turned questioningly toward Erik Nelson who was silently counting, "One thousand . . . Two thousand . . . Three thousand . . . Magneto switch on."

With a huge backfire and a cloud of dark smoke from its exhausts, the Rolls Royce engine protested the over-rich mixture of fuel and air and barked back into life. It ran smoothly with increased power and decreased vibration. The backfire had blown out the offending ice from the carburetor, and the explosive impact of the engine start loosened the grip of the ice on the wooden blades of the propeller. Sounding like a gunshot, the centrifugal force flung the ice harmlessly into the side of the fuselage.

With a thankful prayer to God and Captain Floyd, Erik did the same to the left engine, with similar results. The other nearby pilots, observing the curious events and the increased speed and climb rate of Erik's airplane, performed the same unorthodox maneuver.

As the bombers continued eastbound toward Metz, clouds dissipated and the terrain flattened. Descending into warmer air, the ice broke off, departing noisily in great chunks. As they approached their rendezvous point with the fighters waiting to escort them, the gunners happily fired a few rounds to test their guns. After their miraculous survival against the forces of nature, battle with the Huns suddenly seemed less intimidating.

Erik's forward gunner, perched in the overhanging nose and peering through his binoculars, spotted them first. Flying far above them and appearing intermittently through the layer of clouds separating them were two groups of fighters. *This must be the 94th Aero Squadron*, Erik thought, *sent to escort us to Metz . . . but they are too high . . . eight thousand, possibly even ten thousand feet above us. Why are they flying so high?* Erik's gunner pointed at the approaching formation. It was hard to make them out clearly, silhouetted against the rising sun.

The lead pilot of the formation removed his gloves and, holding the control wheel with his legs, squinted through his own binoculars. These planes were not flying in the loose gaggles of the 94th. They

were flying in the precise close finger formations of four ship elements favored by the Germans. These were not the Spads of the Aero
Squadron. These were Fokker D7s and Albatroses. These were the
enemy. The lead pilot circled his arm high above his head. All the
other pilots did the same: the signal to form a defensive circle.

With the huge bombs they carried, evasive maneuvers with these
lumbering giants were out of the question. Instead, like the pioneers
who arranged their wagons in defensive circles, they would do the
same. Raoul Lufbery, the charismatic former leader of the 94th Aero
Squadron, had shown them this technique shortly before his death.
They had practiced it many times, forming and reforming the
Lufbery Circle.

Hermann Goering's wingman spotted the bombers first. They
were far below. He pointed them out excitedly to his leader. From his
angle of observation, Goering had first thought they were German
Gotha bombers but, as they got closer, he could see they had the
three vertical fins and dual horizontal stabilizers characteristic of the
British Handley-Page bombers. Pointing and holding up an appropriate number of fingers, he indicated to his lead pilots, exactly how
the attack would be made. He would lead the first six elements of four
planes each. They would dive through the bomber squadron at high
speeds with machine guns blazing, then turn and come up at them
again from the rear and under their vulnerable tail section.

The Germans would have the slow-moving, huge horizontal surface areas of the bombers as targets, while the British gunners, blinded
by the sun, would have only the fast-moving, tiny frontal areas of the
much-smaller fighters to shoot at. A similar assault by the second wave
of fighters would follow immediately and keep the British gunners
engaged while the first group made its second attack, finishing off the
bombers from their vulnerable underbellies with little risk.

The gunner cockpits on the Gotha and the Handley-Page were in
the same positions, in the extended nose, and just behind the rear wing.
The pilot sat between the two. The Gotha had a tunnel through the
center of the fuselage which allowed the rear gunner to shoot down
through it and to the rear, protecting its lower abdomen. The Handley-
Page did not, and was powerless to protect itself from that quarter.

Goering signaled and lowered the nose of his D7 to lead the
attack. His altimeter hand spun downward as the airspeed indicator

approached its maximum permissible speed. He pulled the throttle back slightly to stay within the prescribed limits and felt secure that the strength of the D7 would carry him safely through any excesses. The bombers rearranged themselves, completing their circle. Goering hadn't seen this pattern before. The wind whistled loudly through the perforated cooling jackets of his twin Spandau machine guns. *Why did they do this?* His mind was racing. He had just a few seconds to reevaluate the attack.

With the impact of a lightning flash, it suddenly became chillingly clear. When they dove through the center of the circular formation, eighty machine guns would be focused on the single point in space from which they were coming. Even if they were bad shots, with so many lines of fire converging, some were bound to find them. There would be losses, maybe even heavy losses. *This will not work.* Goering frantically signaled his wingman to break off the attack and pull up out of range of the bomber's guns, some of which were already belching fire at them.

In the diving attack, Erik could see the red noses and brightly painted airplanes of the Flying Circus. He knew these pilots were good—very good. He knew what they were thinking when they broke off the attack. The price they were about to pay was simply too high—and he knew their next move. They would stay out of range of the bomber's guns, dive under them, and attack from the rear. If they could descend and fly just above the trees, the Jagdstaffel couldn't get to their soft, unprotected bellies.

Erik's mind raced. They were at six thousand feet. The Handley-Page had low-speed structural limits. They had to descend slowly or risk tearing the airplane apart. It would take at least six minutes. They didn't *have* six minutes. Goering was already leading his squadron in a high-speed dive just out of range of their guns and to their rear. In two minutes, they would bring the noses of their D7s safely within a few yards of their underbellies. Streams of carefully aimed bullets from their rapid-firing Spandau machine guns would rip into their exposed undersides, and their was nothing they could do about it. A single word went through Erik's mind: *Checkmate!*

Goering had led his squadron into the precise position he wanted. They flew only two hundred feet over the ground; from that low altitude they could not see the rear gunner, and he could not see them or fire at them. This would be easy and free of risk. The Jagdstaffel pushed their throttles forward to close on their prey and climb at a rate just over the speed of the bombers. Goering pointed to each of the bombers and then to the pilot who would make the kill. Each Jagdstaffel member maneuvered into position carefully behind his chosen victim, closing the last thousand yards and focusing totally on the target. If they missed these huge wallowing whales growing in their gunsights, they would be the butt of jokes on their triumphant return to base. The Jagdstaffel was so focused on their imminent kill, they failed to see the Spads of the 94th Aero Squadron diving at them from the precise spot out of the sun they had vacated moments before.

Erik was overjoyed when he saw the bulldog profiles of the Spads in a high-speed dive directly in front of the bombers. As they flashed by with a cheerful wave, the gunners stood up in their cockpits applauding their rescuers with Uncle Sam's stovepipe hat in the red ring emblazoned on their fuselage. The hat-in-the-ring squadron flew under the lead bombers and headed directly toward the pursuing groups of German fighters. The D7s, silhouetted low and slow against the ground, made an easy target.

Just as the Handley-Page filled his bull's-eye gunsight, and before he could fire, Hermann Goering's wingman cut in front of him frantically pointing out the squadron of Spads now traveling at twice their speed and closing fast from out of the sun at twelve o'clock. The Spads had all the advantages: they had speed, precious altitude, they were partially concealed in the rising sun, and they would have covering fire from the bomber's guns above them.

The D-7s broke formation and scrambled in all directions at once. With engines now at full throttle, they were making frantic zigzagging climbing turns, desperately trying to avoid the hail of bullets coming at them from the Vickers machine guns. At their low altitude and slow airspeed in the climb, they were at a huge disadvantage—and they knew it!

The hunters had suddenly become the prey. Even the outstanding climb rate of the Fokkers could not make up the dual deficits of speed and altitude. Eddie Rickenbacker closed rapidly on the slow-moving D7 that had come into his sights. The German pilot rolled his wings violently from side to side attempting to fly out of the small target circle defining the killing zone of the Vickers.

Rickenbacker fingered the firing trigger, anticipating the Fokker pilot's next move. As he expected, the target moved out of center of his gunsight. When he saw the D7s ailerons go to full opposite lock, he was ready. He squeezed the trigger an instant before the D7 again flew across the gunsight's center. He saw the bullets streaming into the side of the fabric fuselage and then march across the cockpit.

The German pilot slumped over the instrument panel with blood gushing from his mouth. The D7s nose dropped and the machine rolled onto its back before exploding into a ball of fire, impacting the ground with a *whoomp* that chilled him.

In Rickenbacker's peripheral vision, he saw Leigh Wade's older Spad scant feet away, still flying in tight formation with him. Protectively, he insisted the newest recruits stay close to him. Few had been able to do that through the high speeds and abrupt turns of an attack. He gave Wade the familiar thumbs-up salute and marveled that the new recruit had shown sufficient skill to protect him, the master.

He pointed ahead and immediately both of them were behind a trio of D7s jinking violently to avoid their guns. Each fired at the same time, raking the D7s tails with bullets. With his rudder shot away, one D7 pilot pointed his nose into the sky, attempting to gain sufficient altitude to use his parachute. Wade felt relieved when the German pilot's parachute blossomed, setting him firmly but unhurt onto the earth. Gathering the shrouds, the German looked up, smiling, and threw a snappy salute at Wade that clearly said, *see you later.*

Around Leigh Wade, chaos reigned. D7s and Spads were maneuvering wildly, each trying for the fatal positional advantage. The pilots of several D7s, trailing dense black smoke, attempted to nurse their stricken craft to safety. An Albatros and several D7s had come within range of the bomber's guns and had taken numerous hits.

Goering reevaluated the situation. His Jagdstaffel had brought down several bombers and Spads, but had paid a heavy price. They were clearly outnumbered and outgunned. The combined strength of the bomber guns and the 94th Aero Squadron threatened to decimate the Flying Circus. Better to save the squadron to fight another day. Goering turned northwest, signaling his squadron to break off and follow him into the safety of the German lines.

Les Arnold, flying the lone Nieuport cautiously through the diving maneuvers, was the last to arrive. He saw the German squadron retreating from the scene and immediately gave chase, expecting his squadron to follow. Rickenbacker, satisfied with his squadron's latest conquests and eager to complete his mission at Metz, joined up with the bombers heading east.

Les Arnold cocked his machine guns and turned to pursue the retreating Jagdstaffel. With the advantage of altitude, he rapidly closed the distance. When he got within firing range, he shot a burst at the last four D7s flying in close formation. The startled Fokker pilots turned to face their unexpected new opponent. Les waved his arm to signal his squadron behind him to join his attack. The only problem: there was no squadron behind him. They had joined up with Rickenbacker to escort the bombers to Metz.

Not getting the expected response, and with the four D7s bearing down on him, Les was shocked to find himself alone. Les put the Nieuport into a sixty-degree bank, pulling two Gs in a tight turn to escape the pursuing Fokkers.

The German element leader, surprised to see the lone Nieuport that challenged them, could taste the easy victory that lay in front of him. He closed on the fleeing Nieuport. Les felt the dull thudding impact of the German's bullets ripping through the fabric covering. He put the Nieuport into a steep climb and checked his six o'clock position. They were outclimbing him and still closing. A thick cloud left over from the morning rains lay ahead. He entered the cloud to the accompaniment of numerous bullets whizzing by his head.

Flying inside the cloud was like being inside a huge cotton ball: no up, no down, no horizon to level his wings with, no sky, no ground, just milky white all over. Had they followed him into the cloud? He couldn't tell, but he knew in a few more seconds, without outside references, he would lose control and crash.

The pilot's inner ear accepts the centrifugal forces of the banking airplane as the pull of gravity. His brain tells him he is upright and in level flight. The death spiral intensifies and the airspeed increases until the overstressed wings break away, and the cloud spits out the airplane as small pieces of torn fabric and splinters. He'd seen it before, but desperate times called for desperate measures.

Les closed the throttle of the Nieuport and pulled the control stick into his stomach. With its nose pointing skywards, the propeller slowed and the airspeed needle dropped below the stalling speed. The wings shook in protest. Les stepped hard on the left side of the wooden rudder bar. The left wing dropped immediately and the nose fell as the Nieuport went into a spin.

He was now a passenger in a falling object. The airspeed indicator hung lifelessly as the altimeter unwound . . . Four thousand feet . . . three thousand feet . . . the spin tightened pinning him against the right side of the cockpit . . . two thousand feet . . . he pulled hard to keep the stick into his stomach until the right moment came. . . . Fifteen hundred feet . . . he prayed he would come out of the cloud before the Nieuport smashed itself into the ground . . . twelve hundred feet . . . he was still in the clouds . . . eleven hundred feet . . . clouds . . . one thousand feet . . . clouds . . . nine hundred . . . finally, ground!

A large grove of trees spun rapidly in front of him. Was it too late? Would the spinning Nieuport recover? Les pushed the control stick full forward and trounced on the right side of the wooden rudder bar. For what seemed an eternity, the grove of trees continued to spin, growing ever larger in his tiny windscreen. Eight hundred . . . seven hundred . . . six hundred . . . Suddenly the spinning stopped. Les centered the rudder and ailerons, still pushing forward on the control stick to get the little Nieuport flying again. He checked his airspeed indicator.

The needle had come alive and raced across the dial toward the red line marked *never exceed*. The ground rushed up to meet him at an accelerating rate. He coaxed the stick further back, raising the nose of the Nieuport. This was the tricky part. Pull too hard and you tear the wings off; pull too little and you smash into the ground.

The spruce wing spars made cracking noises as the fabric ripped and the four wings deflected upward, yielding to the overload. The normal 1,235 pounds of the airplane, its pilot, and its fuel momentarily soared to ten thousand pounds under the stress of pulling eight Gs. He prayed the spars would hold as the trees filled his windscreen. The altimeter hand slowed . . . two hundred . . . 150 . . . 125 . . . one hundred . . . reflexively, Les covered his eyes with his left arm and waited for the impact. He felt his wheels striking the uppermost branches of the trees.

He lowered his arm. Miraculously, the Nieuport still flew. Leaves and small branches were entangled in the wheel's axle, but it still flew.

His wings were level and his airspeed settled back down into normal cruising range of one hundred miles per hour. Other than a few rips in the fabric covering and some additional bullet holes, the diminutive Nieuport brought him safely through the ordeal. He looked anxiously around, scanning the sky for the Fokkers. They were gone.

Les smiled at the story the German pilots were sure to tell around dinner that evening, of the crazy lone American who attacked their entire Jagdstaffel in an obsolete Nieuport, and how they had quickly dispatched him to his maker. Suddenly he felt the great joy of being alive and planted a wet kiss on the leather cockpit coaming of the little plane that had held together and saved him. Still grinning, he pushed the throttle in, climbed, and turned to pursue his vanishing squadron. He'd have a dinner story to tell tonight also.

The destruction of Metz—its strategic railroad lines, stations, warehouses filled with supplies, and armories bristling with weapons— was almost total. The rising dense black clouds of smoke and raging fires were all that remained of the former fortress. Waves of Allied planes had dropped the largest bombs ever used in the war on the city, and the Bloody Paralyzers had lived up to their name. Squadrons of Allied fighters strafed loaded buses, trains, and trucks. The hospitals overflowed with the dead and wounded. The antiaircraft fire had taken a toll on the Allied aircraft, but was powerless to impede the destruction.

T hree Allied fleets of five hundred aircraft each simultaneously attacked the rear of the German lines, cutting off their supplies and blocking their retreat. Their frontline positions were bombarded for hours by artillery before the skies over them filled with wave after wave of Allied aircraft, bombing and strafing at will.

Despite having far more total aircraft than the Allies and a higher production rate, the German air forces were widely spread out and operated under separate command authority. Each individual squadron maintained air superiority over Allied air forces operating within its area. This system had worked successfully all through the war. The Germans never expected the Allies to combine all of their air forces, and therefore no defense had been planned. During the massive Allied raids, they were able to send up only 295 planes into the air at the same time to counter the offensive. Outnumbered five to one, they could do little to blunt the onslaught. For the first time in the war, German air losses exceeded the Allies.

With Mitchell's display of massive air power overhead, a half million American soldiers assisted by one hundred thousand French troops attacked the entrenched German forces head on. The German line had highly fortified positions painstakingly built and reinforced over the past three years. Much of the fighting was hand-to-hand combat. Often the first assault waves sacrificed themselves to make the success of the following waves possible.

That afternoon, an exuberant Billy Mitchell flew his airplane over the scene of the battle for a personal inspection. The results exceeded even his high expectations. The Germans were in complete retreat, some dragging artillery behind them. Many of them, terrified by the death raining down from the skies, discarded their weapons and ran toward the rear of their lines or surrendered. Mitchell located his old friends Douglas MacArthur and George Patton to fly over with a jubilant waving salute from the cockpit. At last he had been able to show the world the huge military advantage of overwhelming air power, and how to employ it.

Before the battle of St. Mihiel ended, the Americans had achieved all of their objectives, crushed the "invulnerable" German salient, captured sixteen thousand Germans, and turned back the vaunted German air forces. They paid a heavy price, suffering seven thousand casualties, but won the respect and admiration of not only the European Allies but the enemy as well. A formerly skeptical General Foch described the performance of the American forces on the ground and in the air as magnificent, and, with a new respect, sent his own staff for training in the American techniques of assault and battle.

As Pershing promised Foch, on September 26 the Meuse-Argonne offensive started using the five hundred thousand American troops originally intended to be used at St. Mihiel. Four of the nine American Divisions had no previous experience in combat. The few days between campaigns and the bad weather made it impossible to move much of the heavy equipment, artillery, and seasoned troops who normally would have been used.

Under pressure from the French air squadron leaders, Foch withdrew the French Squadrons from Mitchell's command. Mitchell used the remaining aircraft to support the offensive, with many aircraft flying low over the American troops, shielding them from attack by German aircraft and lifting morale. Even at reduced strength, the two hundred to eight hundred planes used on each strike overwhelmed the Germans, downing three enemy planes for each one they lost. Coincident with the new American offensive, British troops broke through the Hindenberg Line in Belgium. These battles involved massive casualties on both sides, but in both the Allies were victorious in capturing tens of thousands of German soldiers.

Incredibly, within a single month, the tide had turned massively against the Germans. Allied forces had ten thousand aircraft, and Mitchell's air strategies succeeded beyond his most optimistic estimates. German air power had been neutralized. Two million fresh American troops were in Europe with another two million available at home. The U-boat threat had completely collapsed, and a million tons of supplies from the United States were arriving in Europe monthly. Mutinies had started in both the German Army and Navy. Devastated Russian factories and farms could not produce the anticipated weapons and food. Famine was pervasive in Germany, sparking a revolution that threatened to overthrow the German government, and a growing epidemic of influenza caused massive deaths among German soldiers and civilians at home.

On November 9, 1918, the dispirited German government resigned, and a new Socialist government came to power. A few days later, at five A.M. on November 11, 1918, Germany's new government signed a surrender agreement. At eleven A.M. all hostilities ceased. After thirty million casualties, World War I was over.

At the end of the war, Mitchell was the most decorated American war hero, receiving numerous medals from all of the Allies. He was the only American ever to receive America's two highest decorations, the Distinguished Service Cross and the Distinguished Service Medal "for repeated acts of extraordinary heroism in action" and "for displaying bravery far beyond that required by his position." Pershing acknowledged that it was Mitchell's daily aerial reconnaissance, flying his own airplane over enemy lines under constant hostile fire, that led to the successful strategic placement of Allied air and ground forces. Mitchell was awarded the temporary rank of Brigadier General and feted by Heads of State. In the last six months of the war, he had never gotten more than three hours of sleep in a single night. He visited most of the battlefields, and then sailed for home on the *Aquitania*.

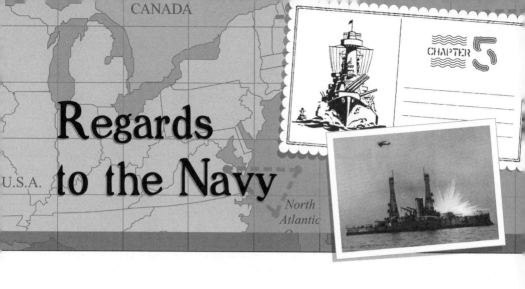

Regards to the Navy

Mitchell received a hero's welcome when he arrived back home. Newspapers throughout the world doted on his wartime exploits. He emerged from the conflict with name recognition usually reserved for heads of state.

The buoyant and jubilant Brigadier General Billy Mitchell who proudly stepped off the *Aquitania* in New York fully expected to receive command of the Army Air Service, now well funded with its $650 million wartime appropriation and staffed with 170,000 officers and men.

Mitchell made extensive plans on his ocean voyage from France. The war convinced him aircraft would be the decisive military weapon of the future. With the resources now available, he looked forward to building a unified air command that would make the United States invincible. He would lead the greatest military air power on earth. Through training programs and robust civil and commercial development, aviation would take its rightful position of dominance over the army and the navy—or so he thought.

His dream was short-lived. Despite Mitchell's objections, General Menoher, a nonflier, was put in charge of the Army Air Service with Mitchell relegated to his assistant. Officers and men were being discharged in huge numbers, and orders for undelivered aircraft and engines were being canceled.

The years following the war were filled with disappointments for Mitchell. His long absences and preoccupation with the Air Service had left his relations with his wife and child in tatters. His frequent accusations of incompetency against those who disagreed with his opinions, which were most of the nonflying officers, created many enemies. Enthusiastic support came only from fellow airmen, and their number had been reduced from twenty thousand to fewer than thirteen hundred as 1919 began. With his dreams turning into nightmares, Mitchell's frustration grew as his efforts redoubled. The Air Service was being dismantled before it could prove its value. He believed he had a mission to save it.

As assistant to General Menoher, Mitchell prepared reports concluding that aircraft could sink surface ships, a view challenged by the Navy as unsubstantiated and a gross exaggeration of air power. During the war, only one obscure Greek aircraft had actually dropped bombs on a surface ship, causing minor damage—certainly a long way from sinking the ship. Mitchell insisted that military prudence demanded he have the opportunity to demonstrate his theory. In April 1919, in order to blunt Mitchell's flurry of written reports and memos, Admiral Winterhalter agreed to a meeting at which Mitchell could present his case to fourteen naval air officers.

The morning meetings went very well. Mitchell's views of air power seemed to complement the Navy's plans for future expansion of naval aviation. Lunch was a cordial affair with General Menoher relieved that his assistant had not, after all, added to the simmering competition and turf warfare that had characterized Army and Navy relationships since the services began.

The afternoon meetings proved otherwise. Mitchell went into the details of his vision of future U.S. military defense. He dismissed naval aircraft, slow and ponderous, encumbered by bulky pontoons or clumsy amphibian designs, as useless. Needed were the sleek, aerodynamic, speedy army airplanes which would quickly dispatch any opposing aircraft. Furthermore, only land-based bombers could lift the heavy bomb loads against which sea or land defenses would be completely helpless.

As usual, Mitchell came prepared with convincing facts and figures. In three years of gunnery practice, land-based guns struck targets towed by planes only one in ten thousand shots, while guns fired from the heaving deck of a ship were even less successful. For the cost of one battleship a thousand aircraft could be built, and perform one hundred times more effectively. Mitchell concluded that surface ships were obsolete and that an independent navy must be subjugated to a unified defense command under the supremacy of land-based air power.

A stony silence followed his presentation. The naval officers couldn't believe what they were hearing. General Menoher sank down in his chair as if to slide unnoticed under the table. Admiral Winterhalter slowly rose and in icy tones thanked the Army for its presentation—and advised them the meeting was over.

The naval delegation filed out of the room in silence. In their minds, Mitchell had transitioned from a minor annoyance to a mortal enemy. He would never again be invited to speak before their general board. Menoher sat slumped in his chair, too shocked to rise until assisted by Mitchell. Mitchell left more resolved than ever to prove, through a bombing demonstration, that everything he had just said was not only true, but militarily inevitable.

Mitchell knew traditions die hard, and unless he could bring external pressure to bear, bureaucratic inertia and the entrenched comforts would perpetuate the military tactics of the past. In May 1919, he wrote the first of many magazine articles in an effort to arouse the general public, and through them the political establishment, of the efficacy of air power.

The articles found a receptive audience, including Congressman Fiorello H. La Guardia, himself an Allied combat pilot on the Italian front during the war. As chairman of the subcommittee on aviation he invited Mitchell to testify, and became one of his staunchest supporters within the government. Mitchell convinced progressive elements within the government that a separate and independent air force was essential for the United States to develop air superiority. The Army and Navy, meanwhile, joined forces to vigorously oppose its creation.

To blunt Mitchell's criticism of naval air power, in May 1919, the Navy launched three newly designed Curtiss seaplanes from Newfoundland to the Azores in an effort to be the first aircraft to cross the Atlantic ocean. Two of the aircraft didn't make it, but the remaining Curtiss did. Lieutenant Commander Albert C. Read flew into history making the 1,380-mile flight to the Azores and continuing on to Portugal and England.

Mitchell responded by entering Army aircraft into international air races, winning many of them, and setting new records for speed, range, and altitude. Mitchell himself flew many of the record setting flights, seeing his competition as not only the larger air forces of England, France, Italy, and Argentina, but the U.S. Navy as well.

The Navy's successful flight lifted morale considerably and increased requests for an expanded air program. Admiral Charles Benson, Chief of Naval Operations, saw the flight as having little military significance and as a further threat to his beloved battleships. He took immediate steps to thwart the growing perception that aviation had greater significance than he believed. In August 1919, Admiral Benson issued a secret order for the "Discontinuance of Aviation Division," commenting, "I cannot conceive of any use the U.S. fleet will ever have for aircraft. The Navy doesn't need airplanes. Aviation is just a lot of noise."

This order was concealed from the Assistant Secretary of the Navy at the time, Franklin Delano Roosevelt. Naval pilots, seeing Mitchell as a sympathetic fellow airman, leaked a copy of the order to Mitchell before he testified before Chairman Wadsworth of the senate subcommittee on military affairs. Mitchell testified, "Our army aviation is shot to pieces, and our naval aviation does not exist as an arm under their new organization." When challenged by Roosevelt to retract his "ridiculous" statement, Mitchell triumphantly presented him with a copy of the Benson order, which then became public record.

For an army man to have access to documents that the assistant naval secretary did not proved a shocking embarrassment, and one which did not endear Mitchell to the future President. Behind the scenes, Benson quietly withdrew the order.

M itchell traveled constantly, usually flying or driving himself at breakneck speeds. He seemed to be everywhere, and rumors circulated saying he never slept. Despite his Herculean efforts to promote aviation, by September 1919 more than six thousand fliers had been discharged, leaving only 232 air officers. Mitchell had scaled his budget request to a paltry $83 million—of which Congress appropriated only $25 million, unmoved that even an impoverished England had allocated $350 million to their Royal Air Force.

Mitchell's war-hero image, the loyalty of fellow pilots, and his friends in high places protected the maverick aviator from much of the political and military wrath directed against him. When he wasn't testifying before Congress, writing newspaper articles, or researching new aircraft developments, Billy spent 1919 developing the first airway system across the United States by installing an interconnected series of landing fields with radio communications, mechanics, aviation fuel, spare parts, night lighting systems, and weather reporting stations stretching from New York to San Francisco. He helped the airmail service expand from eleven thousand miles flown in April 1919 to 127,000 miles in December 1920.

Mitchell worked with aeronautical engineers on the design of a huge superplane, which he envisioned equipped with six engines designed to give it a speed of three hundred miles per hour, a range of thirteen hundred miles, and carrying fifty passengers or a pair of four thousand-pound bombs—wings ten feet thick and propellers twenty-seven feet in diameter. His detractors called this impossible science fiction, and made certain his ideas went no further.

In late 1919 Mitchell received permission from the War Department to purchase a large airship from Germany, and he sent a delegation to the manufacturer to negotiate the purchase. When the Navy heard about this, they used congressional influence to transfer all lighter-than-air ships to naval jurisdiction. Within a few years, the crash of one these airships on what Mitchell believed to be a foolish and dangerous mission resulted in the death of its commander—and one of Mitchell's closest friends. This caused him to launch a crusade against ineptitude at the highest levels of government, and ignited a raging fire from which even he could not escape.

Mitchell sponsored the first aerial forest fire patrol. Colonel Hap Arnold, a combat pilot, was assigned the task of organizing it. Flying fabric-covered biplanes through the heat and smoke of infernos was dangerous, demanding work. Hap Arnold chose Lowell Smith to head the new unit. Through his service with Pancho Villa before the war, Smith had developed a reputation for being able to keep airplanes flying when all others had failed, even in the intense heat of Mexico.

Smith had an uncanny sixth sense for navigation, a trait believed to have been passed on from his famous relative, Daniel Boone.

Smith's Forestry Air Service became hugely successful, and soon grew to twenty planes covering sixteen million square miles. Smith invariably led his patrols safely back to base through fog, smoke, rain, blizzards, and other "impossible" flying conditions. At a time when high casualty rates and frequent breakdowns were accepted as the norm, he did not lose a single airplane or pilot during the three years of highly dangerous flying. He maintained continuous dispatch reliability by personally overhauling engines and airframes. Always modest and unassuming, he never dreamed that in a few short years, he would hold the future of United States aviation in his hands while facing unimaginable adversity.

M itchell remained consumed with the ultimate aviation challenge, which, if overcome, would once and for all silence all those critics who felt aviation "was just a bunch of noise." In December of 1919, Mitchell received permission from the Army to attempt the first flight from New York City to Nome, Alaska. He confided to his old friend Hap Arnold that if they made it to Alaska, they would continue the flight around the world. Mitchell secretly laid in caches of supplies, fuel, and spare parts far beyond the approved flight route for the Alaskan flight. Advance parties waited to lend support at strategic locations known only to Mitchell and his most trusted confidants.

Lieutenant St. Clair Streett commanded the flight of four open cockpit biplanes. Lieutenant Erik Nelson, chief engineering officer, had the responsibility to prepare, service, and pull the airplanes safely through the harsh arctic conditions. Erik had recently completed leading a flight of four aircraft through almost every state, recruiting for and promoting the Army Air Service in thirty-two cities. In 1920 preparations were completed and the "nine thousand-mile exploratory and mapping flight to Alaska" departed.

The entire flight arrived successfully in Nome, Alaska, and awaited further clearance to continue the flight across the Bering Sea and on to Japan. With no hope for immediate permission from the War

Department, Mitchell pleaded for presidential approval. The State Department, fearful of confrontation with Russia and Japan, denied permission for the flight to continue. Mitchell was ordered to instruct the flight to return immediately. His goal for the United States to make the first world flight would have to be postponed—for now.

On January 20, 1920, Mitchell's wife, Caroline, gave birth to their second child, whom he named John Lendrum after his brother, who had been killed in the air during the war. Mitchell spent little time, however, with his wife and children. He left shortly after the birth to address the West Point cadets at the invitation of his friend Douglas MacArthur.

Mitchell received a long standing ovation from the young enthusiastic cadets, who were deeply moved and sympathetic to his reminisces and the strong role aviation would play in future military engagements. Among them were Maxwell Taylor, who would later become Chairman of the Joint Chiefs of Staff, Lyman Lemnitzer, the future Supreme Allied Commander, and Hoyt Vandenberg, future Chief of Staff of the Air Force.

With his plans canceled by the State Department and an unsympathetic president, Mitchell changed strategy. Admiral Benson had publicly stated he could see little military application for aviation. Mitchell confided to his friend Hap Arnold, "I'll make him choke on those words. I'm going to sink every type of ship they've got, including their floating palaces that masquerade as battleships."

The Navy remained adamant in opposing Mitchell's demonstration requests. To head off growing momentum for tests, Admiral Charles J. Badger, head of the naval board, scheduled their own aerial bomb tests during the week of October 28 to November 3, 1920, on the obsolete battleship U.S.S. *Indiana*. The week of presidential elections was carefully chosen knowing that reporters would be too absorbed in the contest between Cox and Harding to cover the tests listed as "routine naval training exercises." The Navy carefully rigged the demonstration, using dummy bombs to minimize the effect of aerial bombs.

Captain Chester Nimitz took charge of implementing the rigged tests. Nimitz was a brilliant tactician who would rise to become supreme commander of the United States fleet in the war to come. He knew that aviation was vital to the navy's future and resented the efforts of Admiral Badger to prove otherwise. In an effort to level at least part of the playing field for aviation, Nimitz called in Captain C. H. M. Roberts, the leading air armament specialist from the army's Air Ordnance Corps. Robert's assignment called for him to explore the structure of the battleship and plant small charges in areas where bombs might strike. The size of these charges was left up to Roberts. Admiral Badger intended to do little damage to the ship, have all or most of the "bombs" miss their target, and prove the inability of aircraft to sink a battleship. Captain Nimitz had other ideas.

Clumsy naval seaplanes, poorly suited to accurate bombing, were chosen and made to fly high over the target at an altitude of four thousand feet. They lacked bombsights and the stabilizing fins of their bombs had been cut off so they would drop haphazardly. The bombs further had all explosive material removed and replaced by sand. The naval pilots, despite all the encumbrances, placed the bombs much more accurately than forecast, with 11 percent striking the battleship and 40 percent within a sixty-foot lethal kill zone.

After the airplanes made their drops, Roberts set off a 214-pound charge that he had planted in the area he found most vulnerable, thirty feet underwater and twenty-five feet from the stern. This relatively small charge bent the shaft and rudder, disabling the ship completely and caused massive flooding of the hull. To the high-ranking naval observers on the observation ship it appeared that little damage had been done, and they smiled broadly. When the second of Roberts's charges was detonated their smiles quickly vanished.

Roberts's charge of five hundred pounds, simulating an actual bomb that would likely be used and placed on the deck of the ship, exploded with tremendous force. The entire superstructure of the ship, including the command bridge and the heavily armored gun turrets, were instantly turned into molten, twisted ruins. The ship was a shambles, totally disabled and sinking rapidly. Badger turned an ashen face to his staff. "These results, gentlemen, will be kept in absolute secrecy."

Nimitz turned away, smiled, and winked at his staff officer. On the decks below, Captain Roberts gathered his extensive notes and the photographic plates of the bomb damage he had made. Stepping into the waiting naval launch, he departed.

O n November 2, 1920, Warren Harding celebrated his fifty-fifth birthday by winning the presidency for the Republicans on a platform of returning the country to normalcy: "America's present need is not heroics but healing." Mitchell strongly supported Cox and the Democratic party, and was chastised for so doing by many in the military as well as some Republican congressmen.

On December 11, scarcely two weeks after the secret naval tests, the prestigious London *Times* published an article by Admiral Sir Percy Scott. He and Admiral Fisher had designed and developed the modern battleship and were among the most highly respected naval authorities in England. The headline quoted Scott: WHAT IS THE USE OF A BATTLESHIP? The article reported Scott's opinion that the day of the battleship had ended. It had no further useful role as a naval weapon.

On that same day, the London *Illustrated News* published two "secret" photographs showing the effect of aerial bombs exploded on a battleship. There for the world to see sat the once proud U.S.S. *Indiana*, her huge decks torn up, her gun turrets and superstructure heavily damaged from bow to stern.

Six weeks later *The New York Tribune* published a lengthy article on the tests, as well as the navy's attempts to conceal the results. The article contained seven photographs of the *Indiana* in ruins. The paper asked, "Is this not ample evidence that a full-scale evaluation be conducted without delay to determine the effect of aerial bombardment on surface ships?"

Admiral Badger, during a subsequent congressional inquiry, accused Mitchell of stealing the photographs from secret Naval files and releasing them to the press. Mitchell denied stealing anything. Many Congressmen were incensed that the Navy withheld the results of their tests from them. Naval statements had concluded that the tests proved aviation was ineffective against ships, when the photographs clearly proved otherwise.

Mitchell testified to an increasingly interested Congress about the great effort the Navy expended to make the results come out the way it wanted. He requested authorization to proceed with his own, more realistic public demonstrations of actual attacks on battleships.

Germany, as a condition of its surrender, had to turn over all its warships to the Allies. Mitchell intended to bomb and sink these warships to demonstrate the effectiveness of air power against surface vessels. In an article written in the *Review of Reviews* in October 1920, Mitchell wrote, "The solution of control of the sea lanes is not in a great battleship and its accessories, but in the provision of a suitable air force and its accessory airplane carriers."

Several months earlier, after studying the writings of Hermann Goering, ace pilot in the war and father of the Luftwaffe, Mitchell had written, "Germany sees in the air her means of controlling the seas and her principal weapon of offense. The Air Force, therefore, will take the place of Germany's destroyed Navy not only as a means of defense on land and sea, but as her great offensive weapon."

The naval tests and the investigation that followed propelled Mitchell into the national spotlight. He wrote and spoke frankly, if not eloquently. Unlike most politicians and military leaders, he didn't fear speaking his mind, criticizing incompetence at all levels, and courting controversy. He was therefore enormously popular with reporters and often quoted.

Secretary of the Navy Daniels consistently counterattacked Mitchell, becoming the target of satire after offering to stand on the bridge of a flagship attacked by Mitchell's pilots, where he would feel perfectly safe. This statement was often published next to a photograph of the twisted carcass of the *Indiana* and, much to his displeasure, he became the laughingstock in many newspapers throughout the country. Although Secretary Daniels and Admiral Badger remained firmly opposed to air power, their support among high-ranking naval officers was quite thin. Daniels had no naval experience and knew nothing of boats or the sea. A North Carolina newspaper editor, his main qualifications for his appointment by Woodrow Wilson were his friendship and support of the president.

An ardent temperance advocate, he had immediately abolished the Navy's traditional grog ration. In his first inspection of a naval ship, he evoked derisive snickers from the crew when he revealed his ignorance of ship's construction. On seeing crewmen emerge from below decks, he remarked to the captain, "My God, it's hollow." Unfamiliar and confused by naval terms, he demanded his assistant secretary, Franklin Roosevelt, issue an order barring the use of "port" and "starboard" by naval personnel and substituting "left" and "right." Career naval officers resented his appointment and his obvious lack of qualifications and experience for the position.

One of Mitchell's unlikely allies was the outspoken Admiral William S. Sims, Chief of the Naval War College. The Wright brothers themselves, in 1910, felt that aircraft would have little military significance and bombs dropped from them would seldom, if ever, strike the intended target. Sims had often quoted the Wright brothers and belittled the naval role that aircraft could play.

Sims, however, helped develop increasingly realistic naval war games at the war college. In the most recent naval exercises using highly accurate scale models and realistic naval engagement scenarios, an all-carrier force was pitted against a naval fleet of mixed battleships, cruisers, destroyers, and carriers. In all engagements, the fleet with the most carriers won the battle using air power.

Sim's analysis of the results of his own war games and the recent naval tests convinced him of the effectiveness of air power in naval engagements. He believed that if the bombs used in the recent naval demonstration were loaded with explosives, rather than sand, they would have destroyed any surface ships they struck. Sims now reversed his long-held belief that aircraft would be unable to drop bombs on ships, and publicly supported Mitchell's view of air power supremacy.

Admiral Sims's conversion was an unexpected coup for Billy Mitchell. Sims had the reputation of being courageous, truthful, and outspoken. Before U.S. entry into the war, he had observed a demonstration of the accuracy of British naval gunners in English waters. He calculated one British ship could outshoot four or five American vessels, and he publicly stated that fact. This almost ended his naval career and inspired a House resolution barring him from stepping foot again on U.S. soil. He refused to retract, however, and was eventually disciplined and allowed to return home.

The public rallied to Sims's defense, recalling his heroic service during the war, which ended the stranglehold of the German U-boats on Allied shipping, and his leadership of the Naval War College. To defuse the issue, Sims was awarded the Distinguished Service Cross by Secretary Daniels. He refused to accept the honor, though, on the basis of its being diminished in stature by its award to others who were, in his opinion, clearly unworthy of its long and honorable tradition.

Sims admired Mitchell as an honest and outspoken opponent of conventional naval doctrine. With his conversion to air-power

enthusiast, and braving the hostility of Secretary Daniels, Sims invited Mitchell to address the naval cadets at his war college. Mitchell
accepted, saying it was ". . . a little like walking into the lion's den."
Sims and Mitchell eventually became close friends.

M itchell had a growing number of converts at his side, and
newspaper editorials and congressmen called for him to be
allowed to hold his bombing demonstrations and settle the
matter once and for all. He never wavered in his belief that eventually he would win.

The obstacles arrayed against him were formidable. No ship had
ever been sunk by an aircraft. All his experienced bombardiers had
left the service. Large bombs were unavailable. Bombsights were
primitive and inaccurate. Army fliers were unfamiliar with navigation
over water. No trained crews existed. Still Mitchell felt confident that
he could and would overcome all the many technical challenges.

To prepare for the inevitable demonstrations, Mitchell created
the First Provisional Air Brigade at Langley Field in Virginia.
Lieutenant Clayton Bissell, winner of the British Distinguished
Flying Cross in the war and a loyal aide, had already started a tacti-
cal air school directed by Lieutenant Tom Milling. This school,
greatly expanded, would produce the highly specialized and trained
airmen, bombardiers, and ground-support crews he needed.

Recruiting every available man and airplane from around the
country, the school grew from seven instructors and eight students
to one thousand men and 250 planes within a few weeks. Lieutenants
Lowell Smith, Leigh Wade, Erik Nelson, and Les Arnold were
among the primary instructors handpicked by Mitchell to lead the
bombing attacks. From dawn to dusk every day, pilots practiced
dropping dummy bombs on the six hundred-foot outline of battleships painted on the ground.

Each day new complaints directed against Mitchell's operation
were delivered to him from the Army finance department, threatening dire consequences. They demanded Mitchell cease all training
activities until formal authorization and funding were approved for
the purpose. Mitchell disregarded the threats. He considered them

the usual bureaucratic harassment—and continued expanding his training program.

As a result of the earlier naval tests and his own experiments and observations, Captain Roberts concluded that two thousand to four thousand-pound bombs would be required to sink a battleship. These were much larger than any bombs ever built. Normally this would take a full year for design, development, and construction, and at least half a million dollars of funding. Mitchell had neither the time, money, nor the authorization to proceed, but advised Roberts, "I'll get you everything you need but time. You've got four months."

Mitchell begged, cajoled, threatened, and called in years of accumulated favors. Sketches were completed in one evening and fins were under construction two days later. He represented their efforts as a top-priority military secret project authorized at the highest levels, and insisted control of the Frankford Arsenal facilities and manpower be turned over to Roberts for development of his secret superbomb. The arsenal assumed that their inability to confirm Mitchell's information was indicative of the extreme secrecy and importance of his project—and gave him complete compliance.

Mitchell next visited George Goddard at his photographic laboratory and studio at McCook Field in Dayton, Ohio. Goddard was the best photographer in the army and one of the best in the world. "George," Mitchell said, "I hate to move you so quickly, but I'm going to bomb some ships, and I need you to form the greatest photographic team the army's ever had—and George, let's keep this as quiet as possible."

Goddard requisitioned the finest cameramen from around the country, mountains of still and movie cameras, film, tripods, eighteen DeHaviland aircraft, and even a small dirigible from the Aberdeen proving grounds, all under the guise of a new, super-secret, top-priority project.

After becoming proficient at land bombing, the pilots moved on to targets at sea. The old hulks of the U.S.S. *Indiana* and U.S.S. *Texas* became targets. Flying out to sea presented new navigational problems for the land-based pilots, especially in fog and mist. Normally, a pilot levels his wings by using the horizon as a reference but if the wings are not level, the aircraft will turn and the accuracy of the bomb drop will suffer. Many days are clouded by poor visibility with an indefinable horizon. A pilot losing sight of the horizon and all ground references invariably loses control and crashes within minutes.

Mitchell followed the inventions of Lawrence Sperry and his newly developed gyroscopes. The rapidly spinning wheels resisted direction changes, and once spinning parallel to the horizon would remain so, even if the support were tilted. Mitchell reasoned that if these gyroscopes were mounted in an airplane, they could be consulted by the pilot to bring the wings level, even if the horizon could not be seen. This marked the first application of the artificial horizon and became the basis for all instrument flying, which today allows pilots to fly safely through darkness or bad weather with no outside visual references.

As the weeks went on, the training intensified. Pilots flew from dawn to dusk and spent nights analyzing the day's results and inventing strategies to improve bombing scores the next day. Each error, no matter how small, was reviewed, and avoidance procedures instituted. Bombing accuracy kept improving.

The pilots hated the new, bulky, uncomfortable headsets they were forced to wear, complaining that constant static drowned out audible clues necessary to their flight, the sounds of the engine, the wind in the wires. Mitchell believed communication essential between the flight elements and ground control. The chronic complainers of faulty radios were sent up repeatedly until their radios worked perfectly.

Funding lagged far behind. Forms, weather reports, batteries, pumps, fuel, film, lights, practice bombs, clocks, fans, and radios were all in short supply. Mitchell resolved that food would be plentiful and sent trucks each morning to pick up supplies from the local food stores, most often with only the promise of future payment. The townspeople felt connected to this band of hard-working young soldiers in pursuit of an unknown, lofty national goal, and did not doubt its importance. They took pride in the small part they were playing in its creation.

The Army General Staff became increasingly angry at Mitchell and critical of what they considered a callous disregard of scarce resources. Funding slowed even more, and already sparse shipments lagged. Continuous requests for the return of men and materials to their original bases came daily. Each needed to be answered and newly justified. Mitchell fumed at this waste of his time and energy. He complained bitterly of the "incompetent bureaucratic nincompoops jealously guarding old fiefdoms in pursuit of an eventual placid retirement."

Tall trees at the end of one runway severely restricted heavily overloaded aircraft, and repeated requests for permission to cut them down went unanswered. Eventually cadets Bowen and Thompson were killed when their airplane, carrying two one hundred-pound bombs, struck the trees and exploded. This was the fourth aircraft lost to the trees, and still permission was denied. Without waiting any longer, a furious Mitchell cut down every tree that affected the flight path of his landing area, and was disciplined for his actions.

Despite setbacks and lack of resources, bombing accuracy continued to improve until well over 90 percent of the bombs dropped were on target, more than enough to sink any battleship. Mitchell turned his attention to the two remaining paths to success; the bombs themselves, and the new bombers promised by Martin Aircraft Company to deliver them.

Roberts planned to make 150 of the two thousand-pound bombs and seventy-five of the four thousand-pound bombs. Bombs this large had never been made before, and would be the record size for the next two decades—into the early part of World War II. Seamless steel tubing of sufficient diameter was made only at a Pittsburgh steel plant for a high priority U.S. naval torpedo program. Mitchell convinced the manufacturer (without the navy's knowledge) that his was a secret naval application that required an even higher priority, and redirected the delivery of previously completed material intended for immediate shipment to the Navy to Captain Roberts at the Frankford Arsenal.

With tubes in hand, special steel noses and tails, onto which the stabilizing fins would be mounted, were made for the tubes. The two thousand-pound bombs were to be filled with one thousand pounds of TNT, and the four thousand-pound bombs with two thousand pounds of TNT. Typical of most bombs, the thick outside casing accounted for half the weight.

The highly explosive TNT had to be carefully melted in steam-jacketed kettles and poured, extremely slowly and carefully, into the bomb casings. No one had attempted to melt such huge quantities of TNT before. Only small quantities could be poured and then allowed to cool and recrystallize before additional quantities could be added. Ice water and electric fans cooled the explosive, but the whole process took much longer than planned.

The first empty bomb cylinders were drop-tested at Aberdeen. They easily penetrated a block of reinforced concrete six feet thick, and then the three feet of gravel beneath, with no damage. The empty casings could be reused several times for testing.

The first two thousand-pound bomb was finally completed and loaded with a 12-gauge shotgun shell acting as a fuse. No one knew how stable such a huge load of TNT would be. Would the airplane's wheels bouncing on the grass runway before takeoff cause the bomb to explode on the ground? Would air turbulence or the vibrations of the engine cause the bomb to explode in midair?

Captain Roberts insisted on accompanying his bomb on its first flight test. Mitchell knew if Roberts was lost, no one else had the knowledge to build additional bombs, and he objected strenuously. The fate of his entire demonstration and thus the future of the air service would be at risk. Roberts was adamant. "I built it. I'll test it."

An old Handley-Page bomber was one of the few airplanes capable of lifting the weight of the massive bomb. Although no one could know it at the time, its sturdiness would be put to the ultimate test. The testing of the bomb had to answer several questions. First, of course, would the bomb survive the rigors of flight? Second, with the newly designed fins and nose, would it drop straight and true? Third, what would be the optimum altitude from which to drop the bomb? Last, but not least, would the new fusing mechanism detonate the bomb, and if so, would it explode cleanly and with sufficient force for its intended purpose?

Mitchell requested volunteers to load the bomb and pilot the bomber for Roberts. He had no shortage of eager young men who passionately believed in his cause. He chose four crewmen and Captain Norbert Carolin as the pilot, as much for his lack of dependents as his flying skills. Roberts took great care to protect the fuse embedded in the nose of the bomb. He knew that if it exploded prematurely, it would destroy much, if not all, of the air base.

Mitchell ordered the area cleared of all but essential personnel, and Roberts, with the four volunteer crewmen, began the process of fastening the bomb in place under the fuselage of the large biplane. The thick steel casing was cold, damp, and slippery. Tiny wet rivulets of morning dew streaked down its sides. The long steel pry bars bent with the great weight, and the wooden cradle groaned and cracked as the bomb was levered up from it. When the bomb lifted clear of its cradle, steel straps were placed under it and secured to the release mechanism. With great care, Roberts stowed the T-shaped activating handle in the aft cockpit he would occupy.

To make the ground roll as short as possible, the biplane had already been brought to the departure end of the grass runway area and turned to face into the wind. Mitchell crossed his fingers and watched as Carolin and Roberts climbed into their respective cockpits and donned their helmets and goggles. Mitchell noted how the Handley-Page, never an attractive airplane, looked particularly ugly and cumbersome with the bomb suspended below it—more like a pregnant toad than a bird.

The loud roar of the two 350-horsepower Liberty 12N engines became a shriek as they were brought to full throttle, and slowly, ever so slowly it seemed, the aircraft with its lethal load started rolling ponderously down the moist grass surface. Mitchell flinched as the heavily loaded wheels bumped on the uneven turf, half expecting a huge explosion.

As the aircraft passed him, he saw the grimly set lips and determination of Captain Carolin focused on the takeoff run ahead. Roberts offered a smile and curt salute as the lumbering biplane bounced down the runway, its wings clutching at the air for lift.

Finally the tail came up, and the biplane's wheels made one last bounce and climbed slowly over the trees. Mitchell realized he'd been holding his breath; with great relief, he expanded his chest to breathe in the clean morning air. He became aware for the first time of the songs of nearby birds. Mitchell watched the biplane grow smaller and turn toward its mission at the vast Aberdeen proving grounds.

In the tight cockpit of the Handley-Page, Norbert Carolin began to relax. He knew how unreliable those two Liberty engines could be, but for now they sounded sweet and ran smoothly. He could see no telltale leaks of oil or water. The sparsely instrumented panel did not show any abnormal readings.

The morning air was so free of any turbulence that even the slight occasional ripple would cause Carolin's grip on the control wheel to tighten involuntarily. Above all, he knew the controls must be moved smoothly and slowly. Turns must be shallow lest the great weight suspended below cause the wings to stall and pull his ship into the earth below. He wondered how a large a crater they would make. *Big, no—huge. Have to stop thinking like this. This is just another flight with some cargo . . . just another trip . . . It's a nice morning . . . when we get back I'll have some coffee . . . maybe a donut . . . eggs, didn't have time for a real breakfast . . . no, when I get back, I'll have lunch.*

Carolin passed a set of railroad tracks, wiped his flying goggles, and pulled out a map to check his position. After what seemed a long time, he made out the familiar landmarks of Aberdeen. A farmer beneath his plane looked up gave a friendly wave to the biplane. He wondered if the farmer would be as friendly if he knew the lethal cargo of death and destruction passing overhead.

The biplane had been flying at one thousand feet. As they approached the drop zone, Carolin pulled the wheel gently back and increased the power to the engines. Roberts had advised him that to be safe from the blast of the bomb, they should drop it from two thousand feet, so Carolin slowly climbed the biplane to what he believed a safe altitude.

As they approached the drop zone, Carolin held up two fingers to indicate they flew at the designated two thousand feet and almost over the target area. Roberts rose in his seat to see better over the high sides of the biplane. When the cross indicating the target center, was fifty yards in front of them, Roberts gave a hard pull to the T-shaped handle of the bomb release.

Relieved of its heavy load, the biplane rose suddenly and Carolin compensated by pushing the wheel forward. Roberts leaned over the cockpit coaming and watched with satisfaction as the bomb fell straight and true toward the target center. It struck the ground, throwing up a tiny plume of earth, and for an instant Roberts had the horrifying thought that it might not explode. Before the thought had fully formed, though, the bomb exploded. For a moment they were surrounded in a maelstrom of black smoke and flames. Huge boulders shot into the sky all around them. Rocks ripped through the fabric covering of the wings and fuselage. Then the biplane was struck from below with an enormous shock wave, throwing it hundreds of feet in the air.

Sounds of fabric tearing, wing ribs and struts breaking, and wires snapping filled their ears. The wings groaned under the enormous stress of the shock wave carrying them violently upward in advance of the fireball rushing up from the ground to meet them. Carolin fought to regain control of the airplane. The roar of the explosion was deafening.

Carolin couldn't believe they still flew. The wings had huge holes and tears, and half of the struts supporting the wings had broken. The flying wires, straight and true an instant before, were now twisted, and several had been torn from their anchorages and trailed in the slipstream below the wings. The fuselage twisted upward toward the rear, and the glass covering most of the panel instruments had shattered. The altimeter showed they had been thrown almost a thousand feet up in the air. Carolin turned around, relieved to find the tail of the airplane still attached. Gently he nursed his wounded craft into a 180-degree turn with a silent prayer of thanks for their survival.

The landing was rough but they were alive and unhurt. Carolin turned toward Roberts, smiling broadly, apparently oblivious to their near brush with disaster. The bomb had exceeded his most optimistic expectations.

Not until early May were the new Martin bombers finally completed in Cleveland and flight testing started at Langley. The first tests were disappointing: the planes would not lift off with the heavy bomb loads required to sink a battleship. Mitchell assigned Lieutenants Carl Cover and Erik Nelson, his best bomber test pilots, to the new Martins.

Cover and Nelson experimented with optimizing carburetor and ignition settings on the engines and different takeoff techniques. Gradually the loads started to increase—sixteen hundred pounds, then seventeen hundred, eighteen hundred, until finally, the heavily laden bomber could be coaxed into the air with the minimum required 2,512 pounds. It would be close, very close. The pilot's flying skill would be all that stood between the crew's surviving or being blown to bits in a huge explosion.

Mitchell was greatly relieved to receive Cover's telegram: "Martin bomber carrying 2,512 pounds live weight this date in addition full gas, oil, and water tank." Mitchell realized the four thousand-pound bombs he had designed could not be used in the demonstrations, and had Roberts concentrate fully on the smaller ones. Roberts designed delayed-action fuses to explode the bombs thirty feet underwater, where his calculations indicated a battleship would be most vulnerable.

Roberts's experience with the earlier naval tests and analysis of wartime sinkings convinced Mitchell that the best way to sink a ship was not by hitting it directly, but by the water-hammer effect of a nearby underwater bomb explosion. The construction of most warships, especially battleships, used the thickest armor on the vertical sides above the waterline, which would be exposed to gunfire. The hull bottoms and areas under the waterline were thinner and more vulnerable. Mitchell planned to have his bombers drop their bombs not on but close by the ships, with delayed fuses for maximum water-hammer effect, pushing in the hull plates and causing massive flooding and rapid sinking.

Mitchell had apparently overcome all obstacles. His final preparation involved organizing a group of the best meteorologists available to provide weather forecasts for the pilots and ground controllers. All stood in readiness. Only the ships were missing. The Navy refused to set a starting date for the tests, hopeful of having them canceled.

Things seemed to improve politically for Mitchell. Although Mitchell, a staunch Democrat, had supported James Cox in his losing battle for the presidency, Warren G. Harding announced his support for a unified service with an independent air force. Harding appointed John Weeks of Massachusetts as Secretary of War and Edwin Denby of Michigan as Secretary of the Navy. Mitchell felt any change in these positions were bound to be an improvement.

Charles F. Curry of California introduced a bill calling for unification of the military with a separate Department of Aviation. An elated Mitchell sent copies to all the major newspapers requesting support for the bill. With things finally going his way and preparations for the tests successfully completed, these were happy times for Mitchell. He published his first book, *Our Air Force*, which he sent to congressmen and powerful private citizens. He made many influential friends, including Babe Ruth and Will Rogers. For the first time since his return from the war, Mitchell had time for doing all the things he loved most—riding in the horse shows, hunting, fishing, and flying. As a handsome, debonair, intelligent raconteur, he found himself a frequent and sought-after guest at numerous Washington social events. The allowance received from his mother's inheritance of her father's large estate, plus his wife's family's wealth, came to considerably more than his army pay and allowed him to keep up with the spending of his affluent friends.

The lack of controversy surrounding Mitchell did not last long. A crash of a large Curtiss Eagle airplane in a storm killed five officers and two civilians. Mitchell held a news conference blaming the crash on a lack of weather-reporting stations and alternate airports to which they could have diverted. "How far do you think the motorcar would have gone if motorists had done without roads or fuel stations?"

Both of Mitchell's superiors, General Menoher and Admiral William A. Moffett, who soon became the new head of the Naval Bureau of Aeronautics, bristled at what they perceived as a blatant attempt by Mitchell to advance his cause, with no justification, over this tragedy. Menoher called Mitchell "a positive detriment" and suggested he resign. Moffett remained an enemy for many years. Complicating matters further, air service films of the bombing of the *Indiana* showed in local theaters. One clip featured an Air Service bomb with the inscription, REGARDS TO THE NAVY.

Mitchell was blamed for military leaks and the animosity he fostered between the services. Naval Secretary Denby was infuriated and demanded Secretary of War Weeks take action. Weeks agreed and forbade Mitchell from making any statements or giving any information on past or future bombing experiments to anyone outside the military, and specifically not to the press. Attempts to muzzle Mitchell continued for the balance of his time in the Air Service. Only his war-hero status and the adoration of the public saved him from dismissal. From this point on, serious confrontations with superiors would follow him throughout his career.

M itchell closely monitored aircraft developments in other countries, and began to grow concerned with the growing aviation strength of the Japanese. From his spying days in the Philippines twenty years prior, he felt they would be a formidable enemy, vastly underrated by western powers.

Although Japan had been an ally of the United States during the war, Mitchell believed western colonization and exploitation of Asia, combined with American laws excluding them from citizenship or land ownership, would inevitably lead to conflict. His investigations revealed the Japanese were purchasing hundreds of the most modern military aircraft from Britain, France, and Italy. In appreciation of the large orders being placed, the British agreed to send Colonel Sempill of their air ministry and thirty military aviators as a civilian delegation to train pilots and help Japan establish a modern and effective air force. Especially worrisome to Mitchell was the completion of the first Japanese aircraft carrier, and the construction in progress of several others. His warnings were dismissed as unjustified and self-serving—an effort to promote more resources for aviation.

With Mitchell ready for the bombing tests and the Navy delaying discussions of the test details, he enlisted the aid of sympathetic congressmen to insist that Secretary Weeks pressure them into moving forward with the tests. Finally, in May 1921, the Navy committed themselves to tests beginning in June or July, and discussions with Mitchell were arranged. The meetings confirmed his fears. The Navy was insisting on procedures that would minimize the effectiveness of the Army Air Corps role in the tests.

The Navy insisted that the purpose of the tests were the evaluation of bomb damage, not the sinking of the ships. Therefore, after each bomb struck, bombing would be halted and a naval team would board the vessel to evaluate damage to its communications, command, control, and defense. Only after a lengthy detailed inspection of decks, hull, turrets, and crew quarters would bombing continue.

The Navy stipulated that the tests be conducted in at least fifty fathoms of water so that sunken ships would not become hazards to navigation. Mitchell chose a point that met that criteria thirty miles east of Cape Hatteras, close to the bomber's base at Langley. The Navy, meanwhile, insisted on a location almost one hundred miles out to sea. Mitchell complained his new, heavily loaded Martin bombers would have insufficient fuel at this range to loiter for cloud coverage, weather delays, and possible naval "inspections" to be completed. He would be forced to drop his bombs only from dirigibles. The Navy was unsympathetic and unyielding, saying in effect, very well then, use dirigibles.

Mitchell requested supplementing his bombs with torpedoes but the Navy refused the request. The Navy would select the vessels to be bombed and would alternate strike days with the Army. The Navy would use their own F-5-L planes carrying 165-pound bombs. Should a second strike be necessary, it would again be made by the Navy using naval Martin bombers followed by marine DeHavilands. Only in the unlikely event that all three strike waves were unsuccessful would Army aircraft be used.

To add insult to injury, General Mitchell would be under the command of Naval Captain Johnson, far more junior than he in rank and experience. With the antipathy aroused against him in the past few weeks, Mitchell knew that complaints for appeal of these terms to his superiors would be futile. General Menoher had already asked for his resignation and was appealing his refusal directly with Secretary Weeks. Naval Secretary Denby was also highly critical of Mitchell, advising Weeks he considered him incapable of being a team player or accepting supervision, highly opinionated, and insolent, if not insubordinate. The gladiator was being thrown to the lions and no reprieve seemed possible. After considering his lack of options, Mitchell grimly nodded his assent to the terms.

The growing feud between Mitchell and the War Department became obvious to reporters and, on June 9, less than two weeks before the bombing tests were to begin, a reporter for *The New York Sun* asked Weeks what action he planned to take. The paper paraphrased, "All precedents of Army discipline and service would probably cause him to accede to the request of General Menoher to remove Mitchell."

The press quickly rallied behind the man they saw as a brave, visionary maverick who would always be truthful with them without regard to political pressure. *The New York Globe* praised "the courage, energy and convictions of General Mitchell," while *The New York Times* described Mitchell as a "brilliant, active, positive, outspoken

officer who is quick to take the initiative and assume responsibility."
The flood of public support for Mitchell, the war hero, caught Weeks
by surprise and he backed off, content to administer a reprimand.

On June 21, the Navy officially opened the bombing test
demonstrations. Admiral Henry B. Wilson presided with Captain A.
W. Johnson as master of ceremonies and referred to by the press as
the ringmaster. Five acts were planned, increasing in drama as the
targets became larger and more significant.

Naval opinion was clearly divided. The older battleship admirals
were hoping the tests confirmed their innate belief that air power
was ineffective against their stout, heavily armored steel fleet, while
the younger officers were anxious to show that naval air power was
quite sufficient to inflict heavy damage on enemy vessels without any
help from the Army.

The naval vessel *Henderson* sailed the day before. Her cargo:
hundreds of reporters, politicians, and foreign dignitaries as well as
official military observers from all branches of the U.S. and foreign
services and allies, including Japan, who had been an ally during the
war. A jovial atmosphere prevailed, with raucous bets being placed
on success and failure. As soon as the ship cleared the three mile
limit, hidden flasks brought aboard despite prohibition were defiantly held aloft to be shared. Loud singing accompanied piano
playing late into the night, making the voyage seem more a carnival
party than a serious scientific experiment.

The first target selected by the Navy was the German submarine
U-117. She measured 267 feet in length and was the most despised
of the warships Germany had been forced to turn over to the Allies
after the war. Naval and merchant marine crews particularly hated
submarines and considered them hidden, sneaky, stealthy, and merciless undersea killers. Their small size and furtive missions
precluded U-boats, giving refuge to the crews they torpedoed. U-
117 had sunk nine defenseless American merchant ships and fishing
vessels off the coast of New England during the war, sending over
one hundred American seamen to a watery grave. The naval airmen
relished the opportunity to wreak retribution on this despised object.

The morning of June 21 dawned with flat seas and clear blue
skies. The *Henderson* rocked gently with her observers crowding the
rails, eager to watch the drama unfolding. Other naval ships, fishing

REGARDS TO THE NAVY

vessels, and private yachts, sensing the unfolding drama, slowly circled the target area. Overhead, George Goddard and his
photographic crew set up several still and motion-picture cameras
out the windows of an army dirigible, focusing them on the U-117
floating serenely on the smooth sea surface. Mitchell's plane, a
DeHaviland DH-4B which he named the *Osprey*, orbited the area
carrying his pennant. It flew in lazy circles around the U-117.

The first wave of three Naval F-5-L seaplanes appeared on the
horizon flying in a V formation, with two other waves close behind.
Mitchell waved at the lead ship, pointing to the submarine below as
if to say, I've got her all lined up for you, now come and finish her
off. With a jaunty salute to Mitchell, the lead pilot signaled for his
wingmen to go into trail formation, nose to tail for the attack. The
pilot descended to eleven hundred feet, the planned bombing altitude. Each aircraft carried two 165-pound bombs. Martin bombers
and Marine Corps DeHavilands stood by if needed, with a total of
112 bombs.

The six bombs of the first wave landed in the water close by both
sides of the submarine. Plumes of spray rose several hundred feet in
the air and could be clearly seen on the *Henderson* before the muffled
"*boom . . . boom . . . boom*" were heard and felt. The bow of the U-117
began to settle. Her decks were awash. The flight leader of the second wave, also in attack formation, released his two bombs. They
fell, as did the two of his wingman closely following, on the decks of
the now stricken ship. Violent explosions threw large chunks of
metal in all directions.

As the last two bombs were dropped by the last aircraft in the
second wave, the submarine was already writhing in her death
throes. With a loud cracking sound clearly heard on the *Henderson*,
the twelfth bomb broke her hull in half. The two sections slipped
beneath the waves. Only a giant bubble marked its grave.

The flight leader of the third wave, incredulous and uncertain,
signaled reluctantly to discontinue the third strike. There was nothing left to bomb but widening ripples where a few moments before
had been a feared underwater killing machine.

Not even Mitchell had expected the demise of the U-boat to
happen so fast. His joy that at last he had proved that aircraft could
sink surface ships was tempered by the loss of his opportunity to

prove the worth of his own squadron—and its months of preparation. The thought that his turn would come made him smile again.

Most observers on the *Henderson* were shocked at the rapid
demise of the U-117, but none more than the old-line naval officers.
On the return voyage, over coffee in the officers' ward room, they
belittled the tests. This was, after all, a submarine, an object of scorn.
"Real sailors don't hide underwater. Submarines are lightweight and
vulnerable. They don't have armor plating. Why, a simple can open-
er will open up their thin hulls. Wait till an aircraft meets up with a
real ship. Mitchell's fly boys will break their teeth trying to chew
those up."

Mitchell lost no time in processing the motion pictures made by
Goddard, distributing copies to many public theaters within the next
two days. The rapid sinking of the U-117 provided the public with
a greatly reinforced image of the efficacy of air power and its ability
to sink surface ships quickly. This counteracted naval assertions that
the tests proved nothing, and resulted in another stern warning from
Menoher for all army personnel to refrain from releasing any test
results to the public or the media.

The second test on June 29 pitted aircraft against a vessel underway in an unknown location within a 25,000-square-mile area. The
target was the old battleship *Iowa*, remotely controlled by the U.S.S.
Ohio steaming five miles astern. As in the very early tests, dummy
bombs filled with sand were to be used. Mitchell's request to use his
bombers was denied. Army participation was limited to two unarmed
dirigibles. Again the *Henderson* took on her load of observers.

The tests were inconclusive. Mitchell took solace that one of the
Army dirigibles was the first to find the *Iowa*, forty-eight minutes
before the naval seaplanes did. Twenty-five of the seaplanes dropped
eighty dummy bombs from four thousand feet. Some weighed up to
five hundred pounds. Only two of these struck the target, and most
observers left believing naval assertions that aircraft would have great
difficulty finding a ship in motion, let alone hitting it and sinking it.

The third test was scheduled for July 13. The observer group
aboard the *Henderson* continued to grow in number and stature as
word of the interesting tests were reported. To counter rumors cir-
culating that Mitchell was being treated unfairly, the Navy finally
gave him permission to use whatever resources he wished and gave

him the G-102, a torpedo destroyer, 312 feet long and thirty feet wide at the beam, built by Krupps and known to be quite seaworthy with substantial armor.

Mitchell's attack started with eighteen SE-5 pursuit fighter planes armed with small bombs and machine guns and attacking at the low level of two hundred feet. Strafing and bombing in three waves of six planes each, the planes first eliminated all defenses. Any crew surviving the machine guns would be cut down by small shrapnel-filled antipersonnel bombs. Mitchell wrote in his diary, "The attack was beautiful to watch. . . . Every bomb went where it was directed. . . . The decks were punctured and swept from end to end."

The next group to attack were DeHaviland light bombers dropping one hundred-pound bombs. The new Martin bombers followed carrying six hundred-pound bombs. These dropped around the entire ship to weaken the hull plates below the waterline. Racked by smoke, flames, and explosions billowing from every aperture of the ship, a final six hundred-pound bomb dropped on the deck. The ship broke into two pieces and slipped beneath the sea, leaving only a spreading oil slick. Observers noted on their watches that the destroyer had been dispatched in twenty minutes. This same attack plan would be copied and repeatedly used in the future war to come.

The fourth test occurred five days later on July 18, a joint test with sixty planes attacking in ten alternating waves of Army, Navy, and Marine bombers. The target, the six-year-old, 5,100-ton German light cruiser *Frankfurt*, was a beautiful ship, heavily armored, with multiple steel watertight compartments.

Mitchell brought his sister Harriet, who was visiting Langley, with him in his DH-4B. Looking down at the *Frankfurt*, Mitchell noted later in his diary, "As she lay in the water, she resembled a swan, so gracefully did she ride the waves. I hated to sink her, as she was far more attractive than any of the seacraft looking on."

The first strikes were, as directed by the Navy, made with one hundred-pound bombs followed by a lengthy naval inspection that revealed the bombs did little but kill the small animals tied to the deck surface. Additional strikes used three hundred-pound bombs followed by another lengthy inspection. The ship still resisted sinking. The Navy ordered Mitchell to signal his six Martin bombers circling overhead with six hundred-pound bombs to cease and return to base. The *Frankfurt* would be sunk by naval gunfire from the U.S.S. *South Dakota*, which was nearby.

Mitchell saw this plan as an attempt to show that aircraft alone could not sink a stout ship that was well designed and heavily armored. As soon as the inspection teams departed on their tender *Shawmut*, Mitchell signaled his bombers to immediately drop their six hundred-pound bombs, in rapid succession, on the *Frankfurt*, and then return to Langley. Amid repeated naval calls to cease bombing, the *Frankfurt* finally succumbed and sank. The Navy was infuriated that Mitchell had broken his promise to abide by naval protocol. Mitchell's lame excuse that the bombs fell too rapidly for him to intercede did little to pacify them.

The German battleship *Ostfriesland*, almost six times larger than the *Frankfurt* at twenty-seven thousand tons, now lay waiting. She was built in 1911, designed by Admiral von Tirpitz to be unsinkable with four hull skins and many watertight compartments. She had taken explosions by Allied mines and torpedoes with little effect. She was the ultimate challenge, and the Navy confidently predicted Mitchell's failure.

This was the ship Mitchell had designed his largest superbombs to sink. The day before the tests, Mitchell flew sixty-five miles out to sea to view his adversary. Flying low, slow circles around the mighty dreadnought, she looked tough and mean. Looking down the huge barrels of her mighty gun turrets, with the tiny shadow of his plane flitting along her broad decks, it seemed impossible, even to him, that such small and insignificant flying machines could challenge this behemoth of the seas. Pulling up the collar of his leather flying jacket against the sudden chill he felt, Mitchell turned toward the setting sun and home.

The morning of July 20 dawned with deteriorating weather. Northeast winds gusting to thirty knots had reduced visibility. Most observers on the *Henderson* were seasick as the ship rolled and pitched in the fifteen-foot seas. White-capped plumes of spray flew over her decks and bridge. Movement on the boat was difficult, and the breakfast served in the mess hall was poorly attended. Most diehard souls that chose to try eating soon relinquished their repasts bent over the side of the ship, tightly clutching the smooth wooden rail.

Observers included the largest number yet assembled of important dignitaries and military leaders. Politicians included three
cabinet officers, Secretaries Weeks (War), Denby (Navy), and
Wallace (Agriculture), as well as Assistant Secretaries, eight
Senators, and twelve Congressmen. From the military came General
Pershing, Fleet Admiral William Fullam, and Marine Commandant
Major General John Lejeune. Almost every major U.S. newspaper as
well as many leading foreign publications had reporters and photographers aboard.

General Pershing basked in the glory of his new appointment.
On July 1, 1921, President Harding appointed General Pershing
Chief of Staff of the U.S. Army, a post he would hold until
September 13, 1924. Pershing remembered all too clearly how Billy
Mitchell upstaged him during the war in France despite all his
efforts to control him and diminish his standing with the Allies.
General Pershing's reputation for wreaking retribution on his ene-
mies had been well established.

Top military leaders of England, Italy, France, Spain, Portugal,
Brazil, and Japan had also been invited. Especially interested were
Captain Nagano, General Katsuda, and General Shibuta of the
Kobe Chamber of Commerce, who brought four cameras and large
supplies of film with them aboard the *Henderson*. None of these men
could know they would be asked to repay the courtesy extended to
them that day by General Mitchell in Kobe, Japan, a few years later,
in a last-ditch effort to save his world flight.

Arrayed in a circle two miles around the *Ostfriesland* was an
armada of other observer vessels, including eight battleships and
numerous destroyers, cruisers, and auxiliary ships. Betting was heavily in favor of the monstrous target surviving any damage the aircraft
were capable of inflicting.

Back at the Langley Air Base, all was in readiness. The Martin
bombers were loaded with their lethal two thousand-pound bombs.
Mechanics and pilots, awake before dawn, were anxiously checking
and rechecking engines and airframes. Preflight checklists were
reviewed again and again as the poor weather delayed their takeoff.

Mitchell finished his third cup of coffee in the radio shack.
Minute by minute he followed the weather reports coming from the
naval fleet. By eight A.M. the ceiling in the target area had risen to

one thousand feet. By nine A.M. it was up to two thousand feet. The bombers required three thousand feet to safely escape the effects of their own bomb blasts, and for the photo observation planes to record the effects. The signal to launch the bombers lay in the hands of the Navy. At the rate the weather was clearing, Mitchell expected to receive his clearance to launch his first strike by ten A.M.

Mitchell's repeated requests for permission to launch were denied with the explanation that the winds, sky, and sea conditions were not yet favorable for aircraft. By noon, the signal had not yet been received. Mitchell was convinced this was a naval plot to represent aircraft as being incapable of operation in windy weather and to prevent him from sinking the battleship.

An impatient and angry Mitchell ordered Lieutenant Streett to get his own aircraft ready for flight, and at one P.M. they both flew out to the target to evaluate the weather with their own eyes. By observing the sea conditions en route, Mitchell and Streett agreed that the winds were not over twenty knots and the ceiling was sufficient to begin bombing. When they were within ten miles of the target, both were shocked to see the entire observer fleet steaming westward, away from the target area and toward home.

In a voice both hostile and commanding, Mitchell radioed Captain Johnson, the naval bombing control officer, advised him the weather was now suitable, and demanded the bombing begin immediately. After a long pause for consultation with his superiors, the Navy capitulated, and Mitchell watched with satisfaction as the observer fleet made a 180-degree turn back toward the *Ostfriesland*.

By 2:30 P.M., naval and marine aircraft started dropping 250-pound bombs on the battleship. Seeing that they had little effect on the target, Mitchell, without waiting for naval authorization, ordered his bombers to depart Langley. At three P.M. bombing ceased, and a naval launch came alongside with the umpires who boarded to evaluate damage. They confirmed what Mitchell could see from the air: the 250-pound bombs had little effect on the *Ostfriesland*.

The Army bombers, led by Lieutenant Clayton Bissell and Erik Nelson, arrived over the *Ostfriesland* with their loads of six hundred-pound bombs before the boarding party had completed their evaluation. The unexpected arrival of the bombers infuriated

Captain Johnson, and he advised them to hold over the area until the evaluation, no matter how lengthy, was completed. After twenty minutes of waiting, Mitchell advised the Navy the bombers' fuel status was becoming critical and bombing must begin soon.

Johnson insisted Mitchell order the bombers to return to base if fuel was becoming critical. Mitchell advised Johnson it would be unsafe to land his bombers with full bomb loads, and issued an ultimatum that they had five minutes to get their evaluation team to safety before the bombs started falling. He emphasized this point by ordering his bombers into attack formation and flying his airplane at deck level while Lieutenant Streett frantically motioned them to clear the ship.

The leader of the evaluation team saw Streett's frantic waving and the bombers circling overhead in attack formation. They scrambled into the waiting launch. At 3:30, just as the launch reached a safe distance from the target, the six hundred-pound bombs dropped in rapid succession. Two fell alongside, sending huge geysers of water thousands of feet into the air, and three struck the deck of the ship.

An approaching storm made further bombing impossible, and all the aircraft headed westward towards land. Even with this fusillade of bombs, the *Ostfriesland* remained floating defiantly, far from being incapacitated, while it was the airmen who would be fighting for their lives, forced to find a safe way through the vicious thunderstorms spawned by the northeast winds.

The *Osprey* could barely be controlled in the severe turbulence. Even the bad weather Mitchell blamed on the Navy, as if they had conspired with the weather gods to wreak vengeance on the fragile craft that challenged them. Fighting the controls each mile of the way back, Mitchell could think only of the fate of the airmen, who would gladly suffer death in their allegiance to him. He was angry at the Navy and himself for putting them in harm's way.

The dirigibles attempted to go around the storm to the north while Mitchell and his crews attempted to escape to the south. They soon became widely separated in the heavy rain, and forward visibility practically disappeared. They were forced lower and lower by the descending clouds until the wheels of the *Osprey* would occasionally brush the topmost branches of the highest trees. Mitchell motioned to Streett he was going to try to land, and Streett nodded his assent.

Luckily, a farmer's field came into view. Mitchell cut the engine and held the stick back into his lap as the aircraft raised its nose, slowed, and descended onto the grass below. Streett helped Mitchell pull back on the control stick so the aircraft wouldn't flip over onto its back in the tall grass. Finally, shrouded in fog, it came to a safe stop and the curious owner ran from his home to investigate the visiting foreign object just fallen from the heavens. Relieved to find it commanded by humans, the farmer offered to hitch up horses and pull it to an area where the grass was shorter and a takeoff possible.

With the worst of the storm having passed, the farmer waved a fond farewell as the *Osprey*, now with a very light fuel load, accelerated on the turf and lifted Mitchell and Streett clear of the trees as they headed back to Langley.

The last vestiges of daylight disappeared before they reached the airfield. Mitchell knew that he and the rest of his pilots must make a risky night landing. The experimental lighting cable he had finally been able to get authorized had ceased functioning just a few days before, when the wires got wet and shorted out. Repairs had not yet been made. They would all have to land using nothing but the faint glow coming from the tin cans filled with gasoline and kerosene. Parked near the landing areas were the Martin bombers with their lethal two thousand-pound bombs. If a landing aircraft were even slightly off course, it could strike a parked bomber, setting off a monstrous chain reaction that would kill every living thing for miles around and leave Langley just a memory surrounding a huge crater in the ground.

Mitchell had flown 660 miles that day, and was emotionally and physically exhausted. He knew that he was in no condition to fly with the precision the night approach required. He wiggled the control stick from side to side and raised both hands to signal the younger Streett that he was giving him control of the *Osprey*. Streett wiggled the control stick, indicating he understood, and flew the *Osprey* lightly onto the wet grass, aligned perfectly between the blazing kerosene lamps.

Several of the strike aircraft had already landed and Mitchell, suddenly feeling rejuvenated among his young airmen, swapped stories about who had the most harrowing flight back. Reporters at Langley, oblivious to the danger of the monster bombs and admiring of their skills, duly recorded each word of the death-defying adventures the pilots recounted, not noticing the occasional winks among the airmen. The dirigible with Captain Roberts made it back that evening and the second, with George Goddard, landed just before dawn with several other aircraft. An angry Goddard emerged to complain to waiting reporters, "The Navy weather boys knew that storm was on the way, and deliberately failed to tell us, hoping to catch the planes up there." Eventually all the airmen made it back safely.

Aboard the observer fleet, to the ill-concealed delight of the high ranking naval officers, Secretary Denby advised reporters of the lack of damage aboard the *Ostfriesland*. Morning newspaper headlines heralded the victorious battleship.

Mitchell wanted to continue the tests, but many of the observers either felt the contest was over or were too seasick to continue observing the next day. The following morning, July 21, brought clearing weather, and by dawn the airmen completed their physical exams and were pronounced fit to fly by the flight surgeon, Captain Strong. Shortly before seven A.M., the *Osprey* followed the Martin bombers now carrying eleven-hundred-pound bombs to the target area.

At the *Ostfriesland*, the tender *Shawmut* was tied alongside with the bombing evaluation team collecting data. The bombers arrived just as the team was finishing its work, and soon the *Shawmut* departed the scene and gave its signal, the display of a red cross on a white background, to the bombing crews to start bombing.

The aircraft formed into the single file, nose-to-tail attack formation led by Lieutenant Bissell, and released the first eleven-hundred-pound bomb at 8:35 A.M. A direct hit on the ship resulted in an enormous explosion. Captain Johnson radioed Mitchell, "Cease firing. Observers going aboard. Acknowledge." Mitchell replied, "Martin bomber number twenty-three will let you know when it's safe to board target." The *Shawmut* approached and signaled for the bombing to stop for evaluation, first by removing the white canvas and then by frantic signals of black smoke, but four additional bombs were dropped with shrapnel and wreckage falling on the approaching boat.

The bombers were eventually ordered back to base with seven unexploded bombs. Since landing was not permitted with bombs of this size, the fliers were ordered to jettison their bombs at sea.

Lieutenant Bissell dropped his far from the naval ships but the other airmen, angered that all their months of practice would be wasted, dropped their bombs within half a mile of the remaining destroyers "to give the boys something to think about." That caused substantial damage to the ships. For these acts of defiance by Mitchell and his airmen, court martial charges were proposed.

Inspectors evaluating this latest damage pronounced the ship badly wounded but not out of action. By ten A.M. that morning, Mitchell returned to Langley for refueling and his last chance to sink the *Ostfriesland*. While briefing his pilots, an urgent message from Captain Johnson advised him the rules were changed. He could now carry only three of his largest bombs to the target.

Mitchell, furious, tore the message into little pieces and threw them contemptuously over his shoulder. The rules he had agreed to permitted two direct hits on the target. He had carefully avoided any restrictions on carried or dropped bombs that were near misses. He ordered Lieutenant Lawson to lead all six of the new Martin bombers and both of the Handley-Pages to the target with their eight two-thousand-pound bombs and instructed them to make six near misses, which he hoped would create a water-hammer effect strong enough to breach the hull before making two direct hits.

He waited until airborne and the flight was beyond recall before answering Johnson's demand via radio, "Martin bomber and Handley-Page formation with two-thousand-pound bombs have taken off. In case of failure to secure two direct hits, subsequent attacks will be made until we have secured the two hits the Army is authorized to make."

The old Handley-Page carrying Captain Roberts suddenly started to trail dense black smoke from its right engine. The crew quickly released the two-thousand-pound bomb and shut down the engine in an effort to save the plane. Heavily laden with fuel, it continued to lose altitude on the single operating engine. Mitchell radioed a nearby naval destroyer, which diverted to pick up the crew. The large biplane continued its inexorable descent into the sea. Mitchell flew circles over the men floating in their life jackets until they were safely onboard, and then signaled that he would continue the flight to the target. The Navy made certain the required rescue of the Army aviators from their turf, and the loss of the aircraft, would not go unnoticed.

Shortly after noon, the lead Martin bomber, piloted by Lieutenant Lawson, dropped the first two-thousand-pound bomb. It fell straight and true, landing within a few feet of the ship's bow. All the observers heard the awesome explosion and watched with open mouths as a giant geyser spewed thirty thousand tons of water three thousand feet into the air. Despite being one to two miles distant from the bomb, the underwater shock wave slammed against the hull of the *Henderson* and the other warships, pushing them over on their sides like some monstrous rogue wave in a violent storm. The violence of the air disturbance and the enormity of the blast shocked even Mitchell, a full mile away.

A second near miss followed with similar results. The third bomb struck squarely on the forecastle bow deck at 12:21, followed closely by another hit from the fourth bomb that effectively tore off the huge stern gun turrets and left a massive hole in the deck. Smoldering debris and structural chunks torn from the hull filled the sky and then splashed into the sea and onto the decks of the spectator fleet.

The ship started sinking rapidly as the fifth bomb fell near the stern, momentarily lifting the entire stern section almost clear of the water. Geysers engulfed the boat in a wall of water. At 12:32, the sixth bomb, which seemed hardly necessary, pushed the great ship over on her port side and, with the bow rising high in the air, the dreadnought, stern first, slipped beneath the sea. By 12:38, all that remained were oily whirlpools where, only a few minutes before, the great "unsinkable" battleship had floated serenely.

The pilot of the aging Handley-Page, knowing he must jettison the final bomb, flew over the whirling slick and, with expert marksmanship, dropped the last remaining bomb in the exact center, as if to speed the great ship to her watery grave. With a triumphant wave of their wings, the bombers joined up in their familiar V formation and, led by a smiling Lieutenant Lawson, headed west toward home.

Mitchell, ecstatic with his success, pointed the *Osprey* toward the *Henderson* and dived as if to hit the ship but, at the last moment, at what seemed like inches from the heads of the observers, threw a final salute and pulled the plane up into a spectacular loop and, rolling upright at the top, followed his pilots westward.

In recounting the event to his sister Ruth years later, Mitchell admitted his eyes were filled with tears. "We wanted to destroy her from the air, but when it was finally accomplished, it was a very serious and awesome sight . . . watching her sink from a few feet above her." When interviewed, Ruth remained firmly convinced that this, out of all his many moments of glory, remained *the* high moment of Mitchell's life.

A board the *Henderson,* observers were strangely silent. They had participated in an experiment that would change the face of not only naval history, strategy, and future designs, but of war itself. They had seen the future, and weren't sure they liked it or the new problems it would bring. The battleship represented the bedrock of their convictions, the solidity of the earth itself, and in just a few moments, their foundations of belief sank beneath the sea with the great ship.

Reporters interviewing the naval and war secretaries found them predictably defensive: "We must carefully analyze the results before reaching conclusions. . . . The ship was sinking anyway even before the bombing. . . . doesn't prove a thing . . . if she were firing back, those planes would never have gotten close. . . ."

Perhaps most concise were the comments by General C. C. Williams, U.S. Army Chief of Ordnance, who said, "A bomb has been fired that will be heard around the world." Most prophetic were the comments quoted in *The Hartford Courant* by Mr. Katsuda of Kobe, Japan: "Very great experiment, profoundly exciting. Our people will cheer your great Mitchell and, you may be sure, will study his experiments. There is much to learn here." Speaking of possible future war with Japan, he continued, "It would be gravely embarrassing to the American people if the ideas of your General Mitchell were more appreciated in Japan than in the United States."

CHAPTER 16

Love, War, and Politics

The bombing tests reinforced Mitchell's image as a national hero. Newspapers and newsreel screens were filled with images of ships ripped apart and sunk by Mitchell's bombs. The Navy resented their role in the bombing being cast as obstructionist.

The New York Times called the tests "an epoch-making performance." *The New York Tribune* wrote, ". . . the Navy will awake to the truth. We must have air forces and submarines.". *The Dayton Journal* wrote, "No single incident since the days of the *Monitor* and the *Merrimac* has had so revolutionary an effect upon warfare."

Admiral Fullam wrote, "It is the greatest revolution in warfare afloat and ashore. Forts are gone, and no nation that has good sense will lay the keel of another battleship." Representative Charles Curry wrote publicly to Mitchell, "You have done more for America in time of peace than any soldier I know. . . . Now we must fight harder than ever for a great American Air Force. . . ."

The editor of *National Geographic* wrote, "You and yours wrote a new page in warfare, Mitchell, and . . . if you weren't blessed with that extra inch of guts, it would not have been written in your day or mine."

Even Captain Johnson, General Menoher, and Secretary Weeks, whom Mitchell saw as his adversaries just days before, publicly congratulated Mitchell on his success. Mitchell reveled in the new perception held by public, and much of the military, of the supremacy and importance of air power and his role as its leader. He was on a roll and not about to let the momentum subside.

On July 29, Mitchell led his heavy bombers on a mock raid from Langley to New York City, and from an altitude of eight thousand feet, they "bombed" the Woolworth building, the Treasury, Customs House, Wall Street and Broadway. Landing at Long Island, he held a press conference to report on the huge damage inflicted by the twenty-one tons of bombs he had rained down on the city. Newspaper headlines the next morning read, CITY IN THEORETICAL RUINS FROM AIR RAID . . . SURVIVORS FLEE. . . . Reports recounted all the bridges, docks, harbors, and buildings destroyed and the thousands of casualties inflicted from bombs and poison gas.

Without prior announcements, Mitchell continued his mock air-raid "attacks" against Philadelphia, Wilmington, Baltimore, the Naval Academy at Annapolis, and the unsuspecting naval fleet anchored at Hampton Roads, blinding them first with the glare of million-candlepower flares he had developed for just such a purpose. Each raid was followed with press conferences, extensive damage reports, and the resulting newspaper headlines.

Mitchell celebrated his victories with a huge party in Washington's Army and Navy Club. Prohibition was the law of the land, but to liven up his party Mitchell had George Goddard bring fifty gallons of the grain alcohol stored at Bolling Field for photographic processing and, with great gusto, Goddard spiked the punch. Hangovers the next morning were in abundance, with little memory of the evening's festivities but the certain knowledge that the participants had the best time of their lives.

The efforts of the Navy to blunt the effects of the sinking of the great battleship *Ostfriesland* were more than academic discussions. There were six large battleships under construction at a cost of $240 million. Congress was becoming increasingly wary of spending that much money on weapons systems that Mitchell had called obsolete. On August 5, Senator Borah introduced a bill that would have delayed or canceled these ships. This was followed with Senator William King, the leading Democrat of the time, recommending the Saratoga, Lexington, and Constellation, all just starting construction, be converted into aircraft carriers.

In defense of their new battleships, on August 20 the Navy released their official report on the bombing results. They prevailed on General Pershing to issue the report over his signature, while omitting any of their own, to add credibility to it. The report concluded the *Ostfriesland* had started sinking before any bombs were dropped, the bombing was less effective than it appeared, and that new battleships were essential to the country's defense.

A furious Mitchell issued his own report a few days later that totally contradicted the naval interpretation of the bombing tests and concluded by listing all the reasons the naval role in U.S. defense should be severely limited and the role of aviation expanded, with all services under a unified command. He insisted his rebuttal report be given the same wide distribution as the naval report. He was frustrated when it became obvious that there was no intention to release his report.

On September 13, without authorization, Mitchell's report mysteriously appeared in *The New York Times*. Menoher was furious and insisted Secretary Weeks discipline Mitchell, threatening to resign if he didn't. That same day, Mitchell sent in his own letter of resignation, citing the incompatibility of his views with his superiors. Weeks accepted Menoher's resignation and Mitchell was asked to remain. Mitchell knew that he would be the logical successor to become Chief of the Air Service and agreed to remain as acting chief while succession was considered. With Menoher gone at last, and in light of his new fame, Mitchell was confident he would be promoted to become permanent Chief of the Air Service.

After consultation with other members of the Harding cabinet, however, Weeks concluded that Mitchell was too much of a loose cannon to succeed as chief. While he did indeed have large numbers of adoring friends in the military and politics, he also had made powerful enemies who hated him deeply. In the end, it was Mitchell's total lack of diplomacy that led Secretary Weeks to choose General Mason M. Patrick, who had served as Chief of the Air Service during the war, to fill Menoher's position. The mature Patrick was one of the few men who had been able to successfully supervise and control Mitchell's activities.

Having served under Patrick during the war, Mitchell knew he had supported a strong role for aviation and considered him an ally.

Although bitterly disappointed, Mitchell rationalized that Patrick was chosen for his well-known diplomatic and administrative skills and his seniority. Mitchell assumed that, in fact, Patrick would be the retiring figurehead and rubber stamp of approval while Mitchell would decide policy, strategy, and future resource requirements and directions.

His first meeting with Patrick in his new post disabused him of those ideas. Patrick made it clear that he and he alone would decide those matters, after considering Mitchell's counsel. Mitchell threatened to resign under those conditions, expecting that Patrick would concede further authority to him rather than risk his loss. He was mistaken. Patrick rose from his desk, put on his hat, and ordered Mitchell to follow him immediately to General Harbord's office so his resignation could be formally accepted.

Fortunately for history and the important role both men would play in its future, this was a Saturday afternoon and General Harbord had left early for the weekend. The meeting had to be postponed until Monday morning. By that time, both men's tempers had cooled. A chastened Mitchell agreed to all of Patrick's terms and withdrew his resignation request. From that point on, Mitchell got on quite well with Patrick.

The two men complemented each other in many ways. Patrick acted as both a filter and shock absorber for Mitchell, pressing for approval where he thought it possible and convincing Mitchell to delay his requests to fund the many changes and technical innovations he knew would be rejected. Although a product of old cavalry officer schooling, Patrick had a sympathetic, open mind to Mitchell's vision of the technical and organizational future of the air service. He was able to implement gradual changes with maturity, wisdom, and diplomacy in a manner that did not challenge or threaten his fellow high-ranking officers. In many ways, the relationship was almost like a gentle but firm father controlling a hot-headed but brilliant son.

With his bombing demonstrations of ships and cities successfully completed, Mitchell threw himself into the technical improvements he knew must occur before aviation came of age. Weather reporting, navigation, and bombing accuracy had to be improved. Mitchell's interest extended to every aspect of aviation. Propellers, improved fuels, de-icing equipment, wing structures, gliders, agricultural applications, improved charts, lighting equipment, catapults, retractable wheels, increased power, speed, altitude—nothing escaped his scrutiny. No detail was too insignificant, no challenge too monumental for Mitchell. He flew his own plane daily to check progress in the field on the projects he initiated. He seemed to be everywhere at once.

On September 19, a young lieutenant named Jimmy Doolittle left his squadron to see what life would be like working under Mitchell at headquarters. Looking back on it many years later he wrote, "I was Mitchell's aide for one day, and on that one day, I've never moved so fast or covered as much country before or since. He was a veritable dynamo of energy." Doolittle returned to the more relaxed pace of his air base, and would become one of the most famous fliers of the next war.

A Russian émigré named Alexander Seversky called on Mitchell one day with a new design for a high-altitude bombsight. Mitchell instantly recognized both the military significance and this man's talents. With this bombsight, his bombers could bomb with impunity at an altitude anti-aircraft guns could not reach. Mitchell made Seversky a consultant and got him together with Sperry, ordering prototypes before receiving approval—despite the high cost of $50,000 each at a time when other sights cast only $2,000. He eventually got his approval, but not without a major battle for the funding.

Meanwhile, Mitchell continued to neglect his home life. He made repeated promises to his wife, Caroline, that things would improve and that he would spend more time with her and his two young children. These promises were never kept. There was always one more war to win, one more battle to fight, one more project to complete.

The hostility between them increased as his absences grew. When almost all of his time and attention was focused on the bombing tests, Caroline felt the tests had become an obsession and pleaded with Mitchell to give them up. Mitchell felt she had turned against him and was "somehow inveigled" by his enemies to try to make him halt the bombing tests on the ships. In his own words, "I was never able to forgive her."

When Caroline found out Mitchell was to make an extended trip to Europe to evaluate new aircraft, she wrote to his superiors to strongly request he not be allowed to go. When the army officers showed reluctance to interfere in his family life, she wrote again, advising them his mental condition was unstable. She demanded they make Secretary of War Weeks aware of this and cancel his trip while he was "nervous and not himself."

Secretary Weeks saw the accusation as plausible, considering the Navy and General Menoher had made similar suggestions. He demanded Mitchell cancel all activities and commit himself to the psychiatric ward of Walter Reed Hospital for evaluation immediately. Mitchell went to Weeks to appeal directly. "Why should I be stigmatized by being placed in a hospital under mental examination," he said, "when I know I can convince any fair-minded person within a few minutes that there is nothing wrong with me?" Weeks relented and ordered Mitchell to be examined in his own quarters by army doctors.

The lengthy examination covered a wide range of actual and theoretical situations that Mitchell had been in or might find himself in the future. Mitchell dazzled the doctors with his incredible intelligence, understanding of the most complex physical processes and accurately recalling reams of statistical data. They found him egotistical and aggressive, but justifiably so. Their extensively detailed written report concluded, "No signs of acute or chronic alcoholism . . . no evidence of mental or physical disease. He is reported as fit for full military duty." Weeks decided this was a domestic matter between the Mitchells, one that did not concern the Army. He cleared him for return to service.

The Limitation of Armaments Conference, whose main subject was the scrapping of large capital ships by the Allies, was starting in Washington, D.C. Mitchell's strong antipathy towards battleships threatened to undermine the naval position at the Conference. At the request of the Navy, General Pershing ordered General Patrick to send Mitchell as far away as possible. General Patrick decided that the safest thing to do with Mitchell was to send him off to Europe on a mission to gather aviation intelligence and evaluate the progress of European allies and the suppliers of their aircraft.

Mitchell knew that this "fact-finding trip" into exile had the ulterior motive of silencing his criticism, but he saw it as an opportunity of promoting his own ulterior motives—the attainment of new and more spectacular aviation records that would promote the cause of aviation and result in larger budgets for the Army Air Service. His own hidden agenda included making an unrefueled, nonstop crossing of the United States followed by another attempt at flying around the world. He knew neither of these would find a sympathetic audience with General Pershing.

A young, self-taught, correspondence-school-educated aircraft designer named Alfred Verville had come to the attention of Mitchell. Verville, despite his lack of a college education, had designed the most advanced planes for Glenn Curtiss and Thomas Morse, and was now considered the leading Air Service expert. Mitchell requested Patrick to release Verville to join him and his longtime aide, Clayton Bissell, on his trip to Europe. Patrick agreed, but only after Mitchell gave his solemn promise that he would not criticize the Washington high command or their air policies during his trip, nor give interviews with members of the press. Mitchell agreed and left in early December 1921.

The French greeted Mitchell as a conquering hero and their savior in the war, returning home. Marshal Foch and Louis Brereton, the most famous French aviation war heroes, entertained him. French women were enormously attracted to the handsome, debonair American hero who spoke their language as well as they did. Each night was another party, with Mitchell the center of attention. He found that aviation in France suffered similarly from being led by nonflying, cavalry-trained officers. Italian aviation progress also did not impress him, despite his warm welcome to Rome by King Victor Emmanuel. He did admire the beauty of Italy's designs and their mechanical abilities, however.

Germany impressed Mitchell the most. Although the Germans were restricted from building military aircraft or flying powered airplanes under the terms of their surrender, they continued to train large numbers of airmen by building and flying highly advanced gliders and airships. The prohibitions forced upon them by the Allies did little to slow German aviation progress.

The newly formed Lufthansa (aviation trust) Company, established despite their depressed economy, received generous funding from the German federal government, states, cities, banks, and their largest companies. Lufthansa efficiently coordinated and disbursed funds for advanced aviation development and manufacturing.

Functioning more as a department of aviation than a commercial enterprise, Lufthansa maintained airports, training, and support facilities. Larger and more efficient commercial transport aircraft, with obvious future military application, were being developed domestically. The trust also helped German aeronautical companies establish "independent" subsidiary factories in Russia, Italy, Denmark, and Sweden. These subsidiaries continued developing military aircraft, which were prohibited on German soil. The host countries, pleased to be the beneficiaries of the aviation progress made by the highly skilled German aeronautical engineers, eagerly provided ample space and facilities.

The German Aero Club gave a luncheon for Mitchell with Ernst Udet, a war ace and Hermann Goering, future head of the Luftwaffe, among his hosts. As the wine flowed, tongues loosened, and Mitchell, who understood German, picked up hints of a new, much more powerful type of aircraft engine and new "flying bombs" under development. He asked Ben Foulois, a fellow aviator and the U.S. air attaché in Berlin, to find the inventor. The next morning, at his hotel, Foulois called Verville: "Tell the General I think I've found his man."

Mitchell immediately visited a obscure wooden building that lay on the outskirts of Berlin. There in a small, dimly lit laboratory, a shabbily dressed scientist proudly pulled out two sets of drawings that he had been working on for several years.

The first set showed a new type of aircraft engine. Using the principle of a continuously rotating high-speed gas turbine, it used cheap and plentiful kerosene as a fuel, weighed less than one-fifth the weight of a Liberty engine, produced two to five times the horsepower, and would outlast at least ten Liberty engines. It would be a decade later before these engines would be rediscovered and "reinvented" by the British. Two decades later, in the next war, Germany produced the world's first jet-powered fighter airplanes. These engines revolutionized military and commercial aviation.

The second set of drawings showed flying bombs powered by liquid oxygen and alcohol. They could fly higher and faster than any airplane and deliver their deadly cargo hundreds of miles away. They were unmanned, unstoppable, and incapable of being intercepted. These drawings were the predecessor to the V1 and V2 rockets. They were the new secret weapon that Germany would use to terrorize England in World War II.

The German inventor confidently predicted that within the next fifteen to twenty years, the development and application of turbine engines and rocket bombs was inevitable. Mitchell—wide eyed, open mouthed, and speechless—nodded his agreement. On his return, his detailed reports of these incredible developments were consigned to the same unread "flying trash pile" that held most of his other reports. It would take another World War and almost twenty years for the United States to recognize the enormous military and commercial applications of these developments—too late to be employed or defended against.

Visiting the Dornier plant in Friedrichshafen, where Zeppelins were formerly built, Mitchell was impressed with the variety and quantity of the newest, most modern aircraft designs he had ever seen. Instead of wood and fabric, all the new aircraft were built using steel spars and duralumin wings, tails, and fuselages. His visit to the Junkers factory in Dessau was equally impressive. Dr. Hugo Junkers proudly showed him their latest airliner, the largest airplane Mitchell had ever seen—a four-engined monoplane behemoth. Vast wings, five feet thick, contained four huge engines. A separate section of the plant was designing and building a great range of engines, small and large, diesel and gas powered, carbureted and fuel injected, normally aspirated and supercharged. Although ostensibly for commercial application, Mitchell recognized how quickly all these new designs could be adapted to military applications, and how far behind the United States had fallen in aviation development.

Anthony Fokker returned from Germany to his native Holland after the war to escape the Allied restrictions. Mitchell was impressed by Fokker's ingenuity in developing the synchronized aircraft machine gun, control stick—mounted firing button, and

superior fighting aircraft such as the Eindeckers (single wing monoplanes) flown by German aces Oswald Boelcke and Max Immelmann;
the later Dr.1 (Dreidecker or three-wing) triplane, flown by Manfred
von Richthofen, the famous Red Baron, and the D7, which was still
considered the finest fighting airplane available. Fokker had left
Germany for Holland with three hundred carloads of tooling, parts,
and assemblies to continue production of the D7s and the newer D8.

With the need for military aircraft diminishing, Fokker designed
a commercial transport using the configuration of his newest D8
fighter aircraft and scaled larger in size to accommodate passengers.
These aircraft, designated the F2, were operated by KLM and
Lufthansa on some of the first air routes between London,
Amsterdam, and Berlin.

When Fokker wrote to Mitchell describing the improvements to
be made in the design of the new upcoming F3, Mitchell prevailed
upon Secretary Weeks for special permission to order from a foreign
company. Mitchell knew he could not order any aircraft from manufacturers based in Germany, since memories of combat were still too
vivid. Fokker was Dutch, however, and making aircraft in Holland,
which gave him the necessary distance from his wartime activities.

In December 1920, Mitchell succeeded in getting the Army to
authorize the purchase of two aircraft, based upon the latest transport
design, and to be powered by 400-horsepower American Liberty
engines, many of which were defective and left over in great abundance from wartime production.

By judiciously dismantling and reassembling each engine, skilled
mechanics could stretch the lifetime to fifty hours—acceptable for
the period. Mitchell shipped several of the remanufactured engines
to Fokker for incorporation into the airplanes being shipped to the
U.S. Army.

The Fokker F3s under development were also single-engine,
high-wing, six seat airliners powered by either 360 horsepower Rolls
Royce, 240 horsepower Armstrong-Siddely, or 250 horsepower
BMW engines. The F3s entered service with KLM in April 1921 on
the routes between London, Amsterdam, Bremen, and Rotterdam.
These and subsequent commercial aircraft were easily militarized by
substituting bomb racks for passenger seats and adding the *M* suffix
to their designation.

Mitchell justified the purchase of the two Fokkers to his superiors on the grounds that they would provide increased endurance and cabin capacity over any domestic aircraft, and could be used for long-range air ambulance, transport, or bomber application. This was only partially true. Both aircraft were modified to accept Liberty engines. With the modifications, these aircraft were designated as F4 models. The Army later changed the designation for the air ambulance version to A-2, and the transport aircraft became the T-2. The T-2 was much more highly modified for an attempt at a new endurance record known only to Mitchell. Mitchell intended using the T-2 to make the first nonstop flight across the United States. He knew that approval and funding for another of his aviation records would not be easy to come by unless he already had the equipment.

To allocate space in the fuselage for sufficient fuel, the front cockpit was moved forward into the engine compartment. Behind the engine lay a second set of flight controls for a second pilot. The copilot had no forward vision and would be forced to fly the airplane looking out the side-facing windows only. The T-2 had greatly increased fuel, oil, and cooling water capacity, as well as strengthened wings and fuselage to support all of that extra weight.

Fokker was a jolly, plump man who kept his pockets filled with chocolates, which he popped into his mouth continuously with great relish. Fokker climbed into his vintage Cadillac and, beaming, drove Mitchell, Bissell, and Verville to inspect the newly completed F4s. Pleased with the evident high quality of the workmanship, Mitchell gave him authorization to crate and ship both airplanes to the U.S. Army.

Mitchell then advised Fokker that he wanted to see his new torpedo planes. This puzzled Fokker. He knew Mitchell characterized torpedo planes, which were usually used by the Navy, as clumsy and almost useless for defense; Mitchell loved speed and maneuverability in both his cars and airplanes. Fokker had also read Mitchell's writings contrasting the advantages of high altitude for bombing ships with little danger to the crew and aircraft versus the peril of flying low-level attack sorties using torpedoes.

Torpedo airplanes were at the bottom rung on the development ladder. Their mission required them to be heavily built and stable, making them slow and less maneuverable. Most pilots considered torpedo planes vulnerable, unexciting, and dangerous to fly in combat. Surely one of the sleek, fast, agile more modern pursuit ships would be of greater interest to Mitchell.

Torpedo planes were slow, ponderous, and cumbersome because they were heavily overbuilt and extensively reinforced. They were required to be extremely strong to survive punishing takeoffs on rough seas, whipped by gale-force winds. Their sturdy pontoons were designed for crashing through walls of water, and their robust construction could withstand the high horsepower required to lift the heavy fuel loads needed for extended range. These were the same characteristics needed for an airplane to survive an around-the-world flight attempt.

The wide range of aircraft Fokker had designed, along with his agreeable nature, made him valuable to Mitchell and the Air Service. With Fokker's resources available to him, new aviation records would be within his grasp. Unfortunately Holland was a long way off, and Mitchell foresaw that communication would be a problem. Aircraft development required the closest contact between test pilots, engineers, designers, and manufacturers. For their mutual benefit, Mitchell proposed that Fokker relocate a part of his facilities in the United States. Mitchell would assist him in the move, provide the new facility with future Army aircraft orders, and allow Fokker the opportunity to enhance his reputation by sponsoring new world aviation record attempts.

Fokker hesitated. He knew he would not be warmly welcomed by the existing American aircraft manufacturers, nor by veteran's groups who remembered that many Americans were lost to Fokker machine guns during the war. Fokker also knew Mitchell had made many powerful enemies within the military, and was uncertain if he retained the authority to place substantial aircraft orders.

To reassure Fokker—and to move his own world flight program along—Mitchell placed additional orders with Fokker for three torpedo planes, which greatly pleased and surprised him. Thanking Mitchell for his new orders, Fokker assured him he would take his suggestion under very careful consideration. This order and subsequent additional orders requiring extensive consultation led Fokker to open manufacturing facilities in Hasbrouck Heights, New Jersey.

Before departing, the Queen of Holland invited Mitchell to a dinner in his honor.

Winston Churchill; Sir Hugh Trenchard, leader of the RAF; Freddie Guest, Minister of Aviation, and the Prince of Wales, whom he had taken flying after the war, entertained Mitchell after he arrived in England on March 9. Mitchell was impressed with their organization and the advancements the British were making in torpedoes, guidance systems, and flight instruments for blind flying. He was far less impressed flying the latest British fighters, which were still of antiquated biplane design.

Before Mitchell left for Europe, General Pershing, now sixty-one, had been dating a beautiful twenty-six-year-old divorcée and heiress to $150 million, Mrs. Louise Cromwell Brooks. Spurning Pershing, she chose instead forty-two-year-old Douglas MacArthur, marrying him in January 1922. That February, Pershing ordered MacArthur to the Philippines. Mrs. MacArthur said, "Jack wanted me to marry him . . . I wouldn't do that. So here I am packing my trunk." During the war, a correspondent had praised the job Mitchell and the Air Corps were doing—and was promptly banished from Europe for the duration by Pershing. Pershing's animosity toward Mitchell would continue through the balance of his service.

Mitchell returned from his European tour in late March 1922. His domestic problems had grown with his recent absence. Their marriage in shambles, the Mitchells soon filed for divorce. The breakup was unpleasant, each party blaming the other for its failure. Caroline received custody of their children. Mitchell became deeply depressed and, uncharacteristically, wrote to his sister Harriet for advice, counsel, and solace.

His mother, hearing of her son's problems, traveled to Washington with his sister Harriet to offer comfort. They remained with him until his mother's death in December 1922, leaving Mitchell an estate that yielded a life income for him of $1,000 per month. With their help, and the diversion provided in analyzing and summarizing his recent trip, Mitchell slowly pulled himself out of his depression.

Verville and Mitchell prepared an exhaustive one thousand-page report in four large volumes complete with photographs, diagrams, copies of blueprints, and lengthy evaluations of all European aviation developments. Numerous recommendations on achieving parity with the latest developments in Europe were made. In addition to providing a technical evaluation of European aviation progress, Mitchell's report warned that the attitude, preparation, and internal political and economic pressures he observed made a future war with Germany very likely.

His report concluded:

> The military spirit of Germany is by no means crushed. It is there just as much as it ever was. It could be seen even in the attitude of all the boys on the streets of every town we visited, and these towns were full of boys who will attain their majorities within a few years. This is in marked contrast to the absence of these young people in France. The German people do not consider that they were whipped on the field of battle, but that they were destroyed by internal dissension and a lack of moral power on the part of the civil population at home.
>
> In Germany, we found a greater confidence in aeronautics probably than in any other country. This is due to two things: (1) that the Germans have so highly developed their lighter-than-air and heavier-than-air construction; and (2) that they know that their aviation can dominate the North Sea and English Channel and can put France out of business providing they have the chance to build. They also know that to defeat England by navies on the surface of the water is practically an impossibility for many generations to come at least, and that aviation can destroy the British sea power very much more cheaply and with a smaller number of men than would be the case with a Navy.

Few people took the time to read Mitchell's detailed and voluminous report, and little came of it. The Washington Arms Limitation Conference ended with agreement to scrap sixty-eight obsolete capital ships. Politicians declared it a huge success. Expensive battleship construction programs would continue; no limitations were placed on aviation. During the balance of 1922, force reductions of the U.S. Air Service continued unabated, and morale continued to sink among the remaining airmen.

Mitchell's wake-up call went unheeded. He wrote articles describing Germany's darkening mood, both in civilian and military life, and the high likelihood of future conflict created by mounting political and economic pressures. Much of the blame for its rapidly growing inflation, deepening recession, and the ineptitude of the Socialist government was placed on the armistice conditions. Germans felt these conditions denied them their rightful colonial interests and resources.

Frustrated, Mitchell returned once again to achieving new air records for the Army. Only through sensational new aviation accomplishments could public enthusiasm for the Air Service be sustained and politicians become sufficiently sympathetic for additional Congressional support.

In 1920, Mitchell had instructed two pilots, Lieutenants Oakley G. Kelly and Muir S. Fairchild, to quietly research a possible non-stop transcontinental air route between New York and San Diego. At that time, all cross-country flights of one hundred miles or more had to be approved by the highest authority, and record flights were not looked upon with great favor or priority by the War Department. Kelly and Fairchild both knew that no airplane they had would be capable of that flight. Mitchell, noting their skepticism, told them, "You prepare the flight, I'll prepare the airplane."

The two Fokker F4s arrived in the United States shortly after Mitchell's return in March 1922 and were shipped to Oakley Kelly at McCook Field. One of the F4s was placed into service as an air ambulance and designated the A-2. The other, heavily modified already by Fokker to accept additional fuel, oil and water, was designated the T-2.

Both aircraft successfully completed their acceptance tests early in June, and payment to Fokker of $60,000 for both aircraft was approved. In July, the wings of the T-2 were removed and sent to Lieutenant Ernest W. Dichman, assistant chief of the structures and airplane section at nearby Wright Field, for maximum static load testing. To Mitchell's delight, the wing proved sufficiently strong to lift the heaviest load of fuel needed for the nonstop transcontinental record attempt.

The aircraft was reassembled and flight tests were started. For the record attempt, the aircraft needed 595 gallons of gasoline, forty gallons of oil, and ten gallons of water. With the crew of two, charts, tools, and instruments, the aircraft had a gross weight of almost eleven thousand pounds—a staggering amount for a single-engine aircraft, far higher than had ever been attempted before. A twin-engine aircraft could do it, but would consume too much fuel to reach its destination.

The flight tests were encouraging but somewhat inconclusive. The aircraft might just make it, but its calculated ability to climb would be almost zero until sufficient fuel were burned off to lighten the load. With perfect conditions, it might fly. Since the airplane already existed, and tests indicated the goal was attainable, Mitchell sought General Patrick's support to get permission from the War Department for his nonstop transcontinental record attempt.

Before leaving for Europe, Mitchell confidentially instructed Major Herbert Dargue to start giving Patrick flight lessons whenever possible. As they flew around the country to visit their bases, and after the aircraft was trimmed for level flight, Dargue coaxed the elder Patrick into holding the controls "just for a moment so I can read the map." These "moments" grew with each flight and, on landing, Dargue would inform the other pilots that Patrick had done most of the flying himself. Self-conscious of his lack of flying skills in his position as Chief of the Air Service, Patrick puffed with pride at being considered a fellow aviator and never denied Dargue's contention.

To live up to his new image as an airman, Patrick became a serious student pilot. At the age of fifty-nine, he earned his rating as the world's oldest junior military aviator. Although the skills and self-confidence for long solo flights eluded him, Patrick's growing enthusiasm for flying lent additional support to Mitchell's requests for authorization of record attempts. On August 10, 1922, the first nonstop transcontinental flight attempt finally received authorization and preparations accelerated.

Mitchell's close friend Major Henry Harley (Hap) Arnold received the aircraft at Rockwell Field in San Diego. It was lightened as much as possible, then dismantled and shipped. The runway was lengthened for the attempt to ten thousand feet, and the aircraft was fueled to a weight of 10,695 pounds. At 5:53 A.M., in the cool of the morning on October 5, 1922, Kelly won the coin toss, slipped into the pilot seat with Macready in the rear, and pushed the throttles forward. The Liberty engine at full throttle strained and pulled at the massive weight without moving, but finally succumbed to the four hundred horsepower and started rolling, slowly at first, and then faster. After more than half of the runway had passed, the airspeed needle started to show signs of life and, inching its way across the dial, barely reached flying speed as the end of the runway approached.

With the choice being flying or dying, Kelly gingerly pulled back on the control column, and at the last possible moment the vibration of the wheels rolling against the ground stopped. He was airborne— but just barely. The aircraft was so overweight that climb was impossible. Requiring the additional lift provided only in ground effect, the aircraft flew inches above the waves of the Pacific Ocean until sufficient fuel was burned off for it to accelerate and climb.

Kelly finally coaxed the ponderous machine up to two hundred feet and started heading eastbound toward New York. The tight pilot's cockpit shared space with the V-12 Liberty engine, and hot oil soon covered his right side. The clattering valves and exhaust explosions created almost unbearable heat and noise.

After fifty miles of nursing the lightening aircraft, Kelly had gotten it up to seventeen hundred feet and entered the foothills of Temecula Pass. Dense morning fog totally obscured the pass. After trying for an hour without success, Kelly realized he would not have sufficient fuel left to make the trip and turned the aircraft back toward Rockwell Field.

Wanting to avoid the hazard of landing an overloaded aircraft with its huge tanks filled with highly explosive aviation gasoline, Kelly made the best of a bad situation and flew the T-2 in lazy circles, staying aloft for thirty-five hours, eighteen minutes and thirty seconds, thus breaking the world endurance record by almost nine hours and proving the T-2 had the endurance to make the record flight distance.

Waiting for better weather and confirmation of a clear pass at Temecula, the pilots' next attempt was made on November 3. This time, encouraged by their experience with the aircraft's benign flying manners and a cooler ground temperature, they took on an additional 155 pounds of fuel to provide a wider reserve cushion against possible unfavorable winds. Once again, at 5:57 A.M., the aircraft, straining against its load of 10,850 pounds, struggled into the air. This time they reached Deming, New Mexico, when they noticed a growing water leak in the Liberty's water cooling jacket. With higher terrain ahead, and downdrafts forcing them within twenty feet of the treetops, they turned south towards lower terrain.

The pilots flew on through the night following railroad tracks and train lights, but the weather deteriorated and forced them lower and lower, to stay under the clouds. The water leak had increased. They knew they had little chance of surviving an engine failure at night. They later recalled this as the longest night of their lives.

As the sky brightened, Lieutenants Kelly and Macready welcomed the dawn. The water still leaked from the engine, but on the plateau beneath them they could begin to pick out possible landing sites if the engine were to stop suddenly. Even the additional cracks in the cylinder jackets, revealed by the rising sun, failed to dampen their rising spirits.

With Terre Haute, Indiana, passing under them, the water stopped leaking from the cooling jacket. Macready, who was flying at the time, knew all too well what that meant. Their ten gallons of cooling water was now gone. The engine would soon overheat and fail. Macready studied his navigational charts in the morning sunlight. Indianapolis lay just a few miles ahead with its familiar army airfield.

The hesitations of the propeller became more frequent as the overheated pistons momentarily seized and then released. Macready knew the Liberty engine would soon die. After twenty-five hours of flying, and covering 2,060 miles, Macready landed at Fort Benjamin Harrison at 9:15 A.M., November 4, 1922, just as the engine stopped. It would be six months before another record attempt, and these two aircraft would become the first and last F4s ever produced.

With the Fokker's failure, Mitchell considered using an alternate airplane. A young man, recently graduated from MIT had started his own aircraft manufacturing business in the rear of a barber shop using six hundred dollars of borrowed money. Knowing of Mitchell's interest in a nonstop transcontinental flight, and eager to prove his abilities, the young man invested most of his scarce resources in the construction of an airplane he was certain could make the trip. He called the airplane, the Cloudster. Mitchell admired his initiative but

. decided that as a new company with no track record, the use of his aircraft would be too risky. When Mitchell's letter of rejection arrived that morning, he was very disappointed. His company was considered too small, too new, and too risky for the Army. Fortunately for him and for history, Donald Douglas had better luck with the Navy.

The fall of 1922 changed Mitchell's life. He had loved horseback riding. Starting as a small boy, he was a gifted equestrian, highly competitive in polo, jumping, and hunting. He published many articles and several books on the art of riding and the requirements and techniques of equestrian excellence.

As summer changed to fall, Mrs. Sidney Miller, a family friend whom he had not seen for many years, invited Mitchell to a horse show on the outskirts of Detroit. She indicated that her daughter also had some interest in riding and he might enjoy meeting her. Mitchell, handsome, cultured, widely respected, and now available, was the epitome of the eligible bachelor. As a single man for the past six months, constant attempts were made to match him with daughters, sisters, cousins, and friends of friends, all of whom were invariably described as being perfect for him, and just as invariably turned out to be of little interest.

Mitchell was inclined to turn down the invitation as he had so many others, but horse shows were among his favorite pastimes, he felt an obligation to humor an old family friend, and a flight through the clear sky of a brisk fall weekend beckoned. To Mitchell, who loved flying above all other activities, an inspection visit to the Army's Selfridge Field, very close to the horse show, became a necessity.

Mitchell landed his biplane and ordered his fuel tanks filled late that afternoon. He disliked leaving full fuel tanks baking in the sun. The heated, expanding fuel would be forced out the tank's air vent holes. Major Carl "Tooey" Spaatz, commander of Selfridge and a close personal friend of Mitchell's, took him through an inspection tour of the airbase, then loaned him his personal car, a Stutz Bearcat.

Arriving at the horse show from Selfridge Field, Mitchell decided to linger in the excitement of the paddock stables rather than hurry to meet another boring blind date. A beautiful and graceful young lady expertly handling a very impressive horse caught his eye. Her dark eyes and easy smile radiated intelligence and self-confidence as she sized up the stranger in uniform watching her. He praised her horse and the way she rode him. They spoke, first of horses, then of the military, politics, and the world of the future. Their words were overshadowed by the subliminal, primal message of mutual attraction radiating from their eyes. All thoughts of his appointment with Mrs. Miller were forgotten.

Before Mitchell could learn her name, she left for her performance. As suddenly as she appeared, she was gone. Mitchell recalled his appointment with Mrs. Miller, and reluctantly left to join her in her box.

He heard little of the small talk from Mrs. Miller, being still under the spell of his recent anonymous companion. Mitchell, usually dispassionate and analytical of new acquaintances, felt more strongly attracted to the strange girl than to anyone before. Several times he borrowed Mrs. Miller's binoculars, ostensibly to examine more closely an exceptional example of horsemanship, but actually furtively scanning the arena, hoping in vain to catch a glimpse of his lost goddess.

Mrs. Miller apologized for the delay of her daughter, but Mitchell, relieved, hoped that she wouldn't come at all. This would spare him the necessity of using his usual excuse of duty calling to explain his early departure and escape the boredom the introduction would likely bring.

Returning the binoculars reluctantly to Mrs. Miller, Mitchell couldn't believe his eyes. His lost lady love came into Mrs. Miller's box. Mitchell rose joyfully to greet the new guest, unable to believe or understand his incredible luck. The slender young woman, as surprised as he, smiled knowingly. Their eyes locked. Mrs. Miller observed their intent gazes. In place of her daughter's usual expression of boredom and superiority that invariably greeted new men, Mrs. Miller now saw approval and admiration. Mitchell's joy was obvious. At first confused by the tableau into which they had frozen, Mrs. Miller suddenly understood. Looking at the eyes of one and then the other, she realized that, at last, her quest for a suitable suitor had ended. With a satisfied smile, Mrs. Miller turned to Mitchell: "Ah, General Mitchell, I see you've met my daughter."

Sitting next to Elizabeth Miller, the horse show droned on end-lessly. Mitchell was restless. He wanted to be alone with her. After a very long hour, he leaned over and whispered into Betty's ear, "Please come flying with me." Betty pondered this for a moment, then turned to her mother. "Would you excuse us?" With her moth-er smiling approval, Betty rose, took Billy Mitchell's hand, and drove with him to the airport.

B etty Miller had never been up in an airplane before, but the opportunity to be with the first man in a long time whom she did not find boring seemed well worth the risk. She was extremely bright, inquisitive, and adventurous; during the war she had served at a field hospital close to the front lines in France. Arriving at the airport with Betty, Mitchell was obviously distracted. Anxious to share the magic of flight with her, he borrowed a leather jacket, helmet, and goggles from one of his airmen. She eagerly put them on and let him help her into the rear cockpit.

Betty Miller heard the engine rev up to a loud roar. She felt the rush of acceleration, the tail came up, and suddenly the ground was falling away under her. She was flying. Sitting in the front cockpit, Mitchell could see the reflection of Betty's face in the small mirror mounted on the upper wing. He moved the controls slowly and deliberately so as not to alarm her with any sudden movements.

She was in his world now, fascinated at the panorama passing under their wings. That was good—no panic, no hysterics. She looked poised and comfortable, as if she had ridden this horse before. She trusted him to return her safely to earth. He would earn her trust on this flight—hoping, no, knowing there would be many more to come. Her hair streamed out from under the helmet and back in the wind. Mitchell knew that his search had ended.

Cumulus clouds rose all around them. The engine droned on at full power. The biplane bumped and rocked its way through the clouds. On top, all would be serene, peaceful, and smooth. They climbed through six thousand feet, then seven thousand feet. Mitchell watched Betty close the collar around her neck as the air temperature fell.

Suddenly the clouds fell away under them. All was smooth and quiet as they passed through ten thousand feet—too quiet. The propeller continued to turn in the slipstream, but the airspeed indicator and tachometer had started to fall. The engine noise had ceased. Instinctively, Mitchell lowered the nose of the biplane to maintain flying speed, and worked the wobble pump to give the engine more fuel. It caught for a few moments but then stopped again. For the first time he checked the float enclosed in the glass tube suspended under the fuel tank in the upper wing. The float lay lifeless and inert at the bottom of the tube. *Damn, stupid idiot*, he thought, *you didn't check your fuel.*

He remembered that he had instructed his mechanic not to fill the fuel tanks until the late afternoon. He had departed without being fueled. *Dumb . . . dumb . . . dumb*, he thought, *and now, of all times. Even if I'm lucky enough to land this thing undamaged, she'll probably never fly with me again.*

He checked the mirror again, expecting to see some sign of panic. There was none, just a casual look, as if nothing unusual had happened. *So that's what pilots do*, she thought. *They climb very high and then glide down to land, like sailing. It's like a bird, just the rush of air and solitude. How peaceful . . . and quiet. It's very nice.*

The mechanics at Selfridge Field saw the biplane side-slipping toward the grass landing area. It was coming in quietly—too quietly! They could tell even before they saw the stopped propeller that the engine had quit. "My God," one of them shouted, "That's General Mitchell's plane."

Mitchell kicked the rudder to align the airplane for landing, lowered his left wing into the crosswind, and made a perfect landing, first on one wheel and then the other. Finally, the tail skid gently brushed against the grass and the biplane came to rest. Taking a moment to thank the unseen hand that guided his plane to safety through the clouds, Mitchell rose from the cockpit, raised his goggles, and turned to his placid passenger, saying calmly, "Well, Betty, how did you like your first airplane ride? "Betty pulled up her goggles, revealing her lovely dark eyes. "I enjoyed that, Billy. Thank you for sharing it with me."

Three mechanics ran through the grass, reaching them as they climbed from the cockpit. The expressions of fear and concern on their faces were evident. Betty looked at them, then at Mitchell. *Maybe this wasn't supposed to be like sailing after all*, she thought.

Selfridge Field was near Detroit and the Grosse Pointe home of Betty Miller. Mitchell's "official inspections" of Selfridge grew in frequency as his relationship with Betty deepened. Major Spaatz remained a good friend, always covering for Mitchell and going along with the facade. Flying to Selfridge on one visit, Mitchell's engine failed and he landed in the Ohio River. Arriving soaking wet and several hours late, Spaatz wryly praised his diligence and, with a wink and a nod, the high priority Mitchell gave to these "inspections."

Mitchell's sister Ruth recounted years later that Mitchell had fallen irretrievably in love with Betty from that first flight with her. Although Betty's interest in flying was never as intense as Billy's, she flew with him whenever he asked her to. They shared many other interests as well, and were happily engaged within six months.

Mitchell never outgrew his addiction to the adrenaline rush that came from pushing the envelope. His wingmen often told of a mischievous Mitchell challenging them to follow him under low bridges, or leaving a wake with his wheels on the water, or flying circles within inches of monuments and buildings, or landing on narrow cow paths and railroad tracks.

Typical of a reporter's description of Mitchell was this in a Philadelphia newspaper, during his address to the National Geographic Society: "General Mitchell has speed written all over him. He talks, thinks and practices speed. His very person is streamlined in real-man fashion. Just short of six feet in height, weight about 180 pounds, looking about ten years younger than his actual 42, the most competent and intrepid pilot in America is as trim as a college halfback . . . His dark hair parted over his high brow, his strong stern face and compelling eye, his entire person has speed, intelligence and pride written all over it."

Although Mitchell appeared to everyone to be in perfect health, actually he was not. He suffered from a rheumatic condition originating from his days in Alaska that often left him bedridden in great pain and with chronic fatigue. Slowly this condition took its toll on his heart and made it increasingly difficult to pass his flight physicals.

Often he had to plead, cajole, and beg the flight surgeon to pass him "just this once."

Led by Mitchell, the shrinking group of U.S. Army pilots were challenging the world's aviation records, entering and often winning international air races. On October 18, 1922, Mitchell himself flew to a new world record of 224.38 miles per hour, officially becoming the world's fastest human being.

Despite the apparent impatience and appearance of recklessness many saw in Mitchell, he was actually extremely methodical and analytical. Daredevil stunts were actually carefully calculated and evaluated. Only if he believed the goal worthy would he put his life on the line without hesitation or regrets.

I n contrast with General Pershing, Mitchell seldom was concerned with the appearance of things, but he was totally uncompromising with the substance. During his inspections, he relentlessly quizzed mechanics on the details of the engines they maintained, and woe to the one who couldn't accurately recite valve clearances, timing adjustments, backlash tolerances, and torque settings for every nut and bolt in the engine. New mechanics were stunned to find a General who actually knew these details for every model of every engine in the Air Service. "You don't fool ol' Billy," the older ones snickered. "Better go back to the books, son."

N ineteen twenty-two had special political significance for the United States: that was when the details of the most serious political scandal of the century started to emerge. The Republican National Convention, acrimonious, turbulent, and deadlocked in its efforts to agree on one of several prominent and qualified nominees for the Presidency in 1920, compromised on Warren Gamaliel Harding. Persistent rumors of graft and corruption surrounding his political career were ignored or dismissed as being unproven. He won the election with Calvin Coolidge, Governor of Massachusetts, as his running mate. Harding promptly filled his cabinet with his cronies, "the Ohio gang," as the newspapers called them.

On April 16, 1922, the U.S. Senate opened its investigation of charges that Secretary of the Interior Albert B. Fall, had accepted large "personal loans" from oilmen Edward L. Doheny and Harry Sinclair to lease them drilling rights on the oil-rich naval reserve fields in California and Wyoming. When asked about these serious charges brought against his cabinet appointee, Harding replied, "If Fall isn't an honest man, then I'm not fit to be President." The scandal that grew was named for the shape of the oil-rich Wyoming fields, "Teapot Dome."

As the Senate investigation expanded, Fall could not explain how he could spend $170,000 for improvements on his ranch in New Mexico with an annual salary of only $12,000. With pressure mounting, Secretary Fall resigned on March 4, 1923. During the widening investigation of his cabinet, and before he could be questioned by the Senate, President Harding left Washington on a transcontinental trip during which he suddenly died of "apoplexy," providing conspiracy theorists with plausible material still debated to this day.

The Senate investigation continued for the next several years under the newly confirmed presidency of Calvin Coolidge, who said, "Let the chips fall where they may." As the Teapot Dome scandal widened, it became apparent that Harding appointees Navy Secretary Edwin Denby and Attorney General Harry M. Daugherty had assisted Fall in his misuse of the public lands.

Eventually Fall was indicted, found guilty of bribery, fined $100,000, and sentenced to one year in prison. Secretary Denby resigned in shame. Coolidge demanded and received Dougherty's resignation. Sinclair and Doheny were both indicted on bribery and conspiracy charges. This growing scandal and its potential effect on the reelection of the President in 1924 became an important factor in consideration and approval of the first world flight.

CHAPTER 7

Preparations Begin

For most Americans, 1923 dawned with great promise. America was at peace. The Industrial Revolution had spread its wealth of new products and high wages down to the grassroots level.

Prohibition was the law of the land. Babe Ruth belted out home runs for the New York Yankees. People ate Kellogg's Corn Flakes for breakfast and washed it down with Maxwell House Coffee, which Teddy Roosevelt told them was "good to the last drop." Frigidaires replaced ice chests, and rayon hosiery from DuPont replaced silk stockings.

Empowered by winning the right to vote three years earlier, emancipated flappers shocked the public by binding their breasts and wearing lipstick, rouge, short hair, and knee-length skirts that exposed their legs while they publicly drank and smoked with the "smart set" in fashionable speakeasies.

Dancing marathons became a national craze. Weary, sleepless couples clung to each other for support as they swayed to music for up to one hundred hours until exhaustion and even death stilled the rhythm.

The affluent consumer had unprecedented choice. Motorcars from Cadillac, Packard, Peerless, Pierce-Arrow, Rolls Royce, Stutz, and Mercedes were available. Model-T Fords, Chevrolets, and Chalmer-Franklins put the less affluent on wheels.

Magnificent operas sung by Enrico Caruso and Nellie Melba played on the Victrola. Those less cultured listened to the first broadcast of a heavyweight title boxing match between Jack Dempsey and Georges Carpentier. An enterprising radio announcer gave the first play-by-play account of a World Series baseball game. Just tune in station WJZ and there it was, the Yankees locked into a titanic struggle with the Giants in New York City. It was almost as good as being there, and getting better.

Russian-born inventor Vladimir Zworykin, working at the University of Pittsburgh, unveiled his latest invention, the iconoscope, which used a cathode ray tube to display moving images. The fantastic promise of future radios displaying moving pictures and electronic microscopes that could probe the secrets of molecular biology lay just ahead.

In 1920, fewer than two thousand American homes had radios. By 1923 that number had exploded to over two-and-a-half million. A humble, folksy humorist named Will Rogers made everyone laugh. Flaunting his poor Oklahoma Cherokee ancestry, he poked fun at the pretentious. "My folks didn't come over on the Mayflower, but they did meet the boat" and politicians: "Congress writes most of my funniest jokes".

Created originally in African-American saloons, the upbeat foot-tapping rhythm of jazz spread into the mainstream, led by Scott Joplin, Benny Moten, and pianist Eubie Blake as Dixieland and Ragtime. Despite Prohibition and jails filled with violators, alcohol could be easily found in many crowded speakeasies doing a hugely lucrative and illegal business.

To the general public, 1923 promised to be a great year and another giant step away from the deprivation of the World War. For the military, however, 1923 marked another year of disastrous budget cuts and the continuing loss of its most able young men. The Army Air Service, depleted by annual casualty rates of 35 percent of its pilots and diminishing enlistment enthusiasm, was particularly hard hit.

With an unsympathetic president and superiors too concerned about the budget axe falling on them to champion his cause, General Billy Mitchell tried to keep the flame of enthusiasm for aviation alive the only way he could—through appeals over the heads of superiors and directly to the general public, through sensational record flights and aerial demonstrations.

Commercial aviation thrived in Europe, aided by government funds in England, France, Italy, Russia, and Germany. By 1923 most large cities of Europe were connected by scheduled airline service. In the United States, there were no scheduled airline passenger services—only airmail-carrying flights.

Mitchell had two main goals in 1923. The first was his elusive nonstop crossing of the United States after two failed attempts the previous year. Transcontinental flights across the United States always made newspaper headlines.

The first transcontinental flight was made in 1911 by Cal Rodgers in a spindly wood and fabric biplane built by the Wright brothers. Rodgers received his pilot's license on August 7, 1911, after ninety minutes of flight instruction and a solo flight at the Wright school in Dayton, Ohio. He combined $11,000 he had won in a Chicago flying contest sponsored by Hearst newspapers with the sponsorship of J. Ogden Armour, the meat-packing tycoon eager to publicize his Vin Fiz grape soft drink.

Rodgers bought a new Wright Model EX airplane. He followed a three-car railroad train carrying spare parts and mechanics across the United States and received $5.00 per mile from Armour. The *Vin Fiz* lifted off on September 17, 1911, from the Sheepshead Bay racetrack in Long Island, New York. After numerous mechanical failures, crashes, broken bones, and hospitalizations, and with only the rudder and two wing struts of the original plane remaining, the wheels of the aircraft ceremoniously rolled into the Pacific Ocean on December 10, 1911, after almost three months.

In October 1919, Lieutenant Belvin Maynard made the flight from Mineola, New York, to San Francisco in an Army DeHaviland DH-4 in three days, eight hours, and forty-one minutes, and in 1922 Jimmy Doolittle had reduced the crossing time to less than a single day.

On May 2, 1923, the T-2, using the heavier landing gear of the Martin MB-1 bomber to support its takeoff weight of 10,800 pounds, departed westbound from Roosevelt Field on Long Island, New York. Having burned off considerable fuel, it was better able to climb when it reached the western mountains, and prevail over storms, headwinds and mechanical problems. It landed successfully in San Diego after traveling 2,470 nonstop miles in twenty-six hours and fifty minutes.

Mitchell was now eager to challenge the other nations attempting the first world flight. This time he prepared a much more detailed plan employing eight specially built, rugged biplanes that would travel a new route westbound, against the prevailing winds, for meteorological considerations. His route would take him where no airplane had ever flown, over the frozen northern areas of the Pacific and Atlantic oceans.

The flight would have extensive logistical support from land bases established for this purpose and from ships at sea. The aircraft would be changed from wheels to pontoons as required. He calculated that of the eight aircraft, four to six would be lost, but the chances were good that two would complete the trip. In the summer of 1922, Major Herbert Dargue, chief of the war plans section for the Air Service, presented Mitchell's plan to General Pershing. The plan was immediately rejected as too risky and too costly.

In October 1922, a frustrated Mitchell scaled back his requirements and leaked to the newspapers that he was "arranging a flight around the world with a squadron of six airplanes." With publication, the full wrath of General Pershing was brought to bear upon General Patrick, who was thought to have defied his decision. Patrick had not been consulted by Mitchell and knew nothing of the leak. To reassert authority on behalf of both himself and General Pershing over their subordinates, and to avert a potentially explosive confrontation, Patrick issued the following statement: "By *my* direction, one of the divisions in *my* office has been giving study to possible long flights." Patrick was hurt, and resented Mitchell's insubordinate and indiscreet behavior. He called him in and warned him never to do that again. Although chastened temporarily by Patrick's tongue lashing, Mitchell had no intention of dropping his plans for a world flight.

Meanwhile, the three Fokker torpedo planes Mitchell ordered during his European trip arrived in the United States. He planned to modify them discreetly for the long-range world flight. They were flown to McCook Field, where one was disassembled and a long list of modifications was prepared. The modifications would have to include substantial structural changes, which would have to be made in close consultation with Fokker's engineering department back in Holland. Lengthy communication delays were certain, and the scope of the work would require skills that the McCook facility did not have.

Mitchell realized he had underestimated the amount of work necessary to make the Fokkers suitable for a world flight. He also became wary of revealing too many details of his world-flight plans to Fokker. At that time, Fokker was working with several other countries to build world-flight airplanes. They had recently delivered a modified biplane with a 360-horsepower Rolls Royce engine to Commandante Sacadura Cabral, a very experienced aviator from Portugal, for his world-flight attempt.

Mitchell considered requesting that Alfred Verville design a world cruiser. Verville was an aeronautical genius, a brilliant designer filled with new ideas. At Mitchell's request he had designed sleek new record-setting airplanes with many pioneering features, including retractable landing gear and reduced aerodynamic drag. From his fertile mind came designs for commercial and corporate aircraft, highly advanced bombers, pursuit planes, and record-setting racing aircraft.

Verville was on the cutting edge of aerodynamics, but had little experience in the design of sturdy, highly serviceable, long-range aircraft. He had never had to diagnose and repair a failed engine or airframe component a thousand miles from home, alone, with no spare parts and few tools—in the pouring rain. He had never endured the agony of piloting an airplane for twelve hours through a blinding arctic blizzard with one hundred-mile-per-hour winds howling through the cockpit, the icy chill turning the pilot's skin blue and then chalk white as he succumbed to frostbite. He had never wiped the oil streaming from a mortally wounded engine away from his flying goggles, praying that what was left up front would continue to turn the propeller just a few minutes longer until a landing place could be found. He had never sweated through a sleepless night working on that engine, his perspiration mixing with the black, oily grime that permeated every pore, muscles aching with fatigue, dawn coming without relief.

Mitchell knew from previous long-range flights that these would be just a few of the adversities that would face the crew and challenge the construction of a world-flight contender. Sitting at his drafting board with his clean sheets of white paper, it would not be possible for Verville to design an aircraft for conditions that he could not begin to imagine, provide for obstacles he had never faced, or survive challenges that were unknown. Only Erik Nelson had the experience he required.

Within his first two years in the Air Service, Erik had flown seven thousand miles doing recruiting work in every state and major city. He flew the first photographic mission over the Grand Canyon, and was as skilled a mechanic as he was a pilot. Erik was the chief engineering officer and pilot on the difficult and successful flight from New York to Nome, Alaska, and back during the summer of 1920. Erik's preparation, maintenance, and flying ability pulled them all safely through where no man had gone before. It was Erik, working with Mitchell, who prepared the secret, complex logistical plans necessary to continue that flight into Asia and around the world. Erik had the experience required and understood the challenges they faced.

Mitchell assigned Erik to find and work with an alternate source for a world cruiser. Erik had evaluated the Douglas Cloudster in 1921, and considered it a very clever design, superior to the Fokkers. The Cloudster also used the Liberty engine, but its construction was of sturdier steel tubing with welded gussets and crossed tie-rods. The fuselage design used three easily replaceable sections containing the engine, crew compartment, and a rear baggage compartment onto which the tail surfaces bolted. The entire airplane, including the wings and tail surfaces, could be easily disassembled in the event of damage—a certainty on a world flight.

After being rejected by the Army, Douglas had turned to the Navy. The robust, damage-tolerant design of the Cloudster impressed them; they needed that for landing on rough seas and surviving controlled crashes on aircraft carriers. They took a chance on the new company and awarded Douglas Aviation a contract that eventually totaled eighty aircraft. The Cloudster became the prototype of a torpedo plane designated the DT-1. Further modified to meet naval requirements of a more powerful engine, availability of pontoons or wheels, and wings that folded, it became the DT-2.

Building the Cloudster depleted much of Donald Douglas's meager funds. He couldn't afford costly manufacturing space on an airfield, so he moved into the low-cost space of an abandoned movie studio in Santa Monica. To the delight of local children and itinerant movie extras, he pushed completed airplanes, with wings folded, through the city's streets to nearby Clover Airfield (later Santa Monica Airport) for flight testing and delivery.

Nelson advised Mitchell that the DT-2 had many of the characteristics they were looking for in a world cruiser. Douglas Aviation, now filling ongoing naval orders, had sufficient credibility as a source. Mitchell agreed and sent Erik Nelson to Santa Monica in June 1923, to work with Donald Douglas on the design of a world cruiser.

What Donald Douglas lacked in years and experience he more than made up for in vision and brilliance. Douglas knew that to be seen as the equal of the more established manufacturers, his aircraft had to accomplish something new and spectacular. With the failures of the Fokker T-2 in 1922, he wanted to launch his own nonstop flight with the Cloudster, but he didn't have the money to cover the expenses.

Erik Nelson arrived in Santa Monica just a few weeks after the Fokker T-2 had finally completed its successful nonstop flight across the United States. At the movie-studio-turned-aircraft-factory, Douglas enthusiastically embraced the concept of using modified DT-2 torpedo planes for the world flight. The first day's discussion with Nelson went on long into the night. Nelson's specifications required major changes and modifications to the DT-2; with Douglas's meager resources already stretched pretty thin meeting the naval delivery schedules, this would be very difficult.

Mitchell required a guaranteed delivery of a completed prototype aircraft, built to Nelson's specifications, within four months. After the prototype was approved, Douglas had to ship dozens of sets of spare parts, including manufactured subassemblies, pontoons, engines, propellers, and instruments, within sixty days, and completed aircraft within 120 days.

Donald Douglas spent a sleepless night following his meeting with Erik Nelson. He knew the extreme rivalry that existed between the services. If he accepted this new Army order and gave it priority over existing naval orders, he could lose his best customer. Additional orders from the Army were unlikely, and the chances for a successful world flight were very slim. Realistically, the survival of Douglas Aviation would depend upon the success of a world flight.

At 9:00 A.M. EST the next morning, Billy Mitchell received a telephone call from a sleepless Donald Douglas. "General Mitchell, I'm betting the survival of my company on your world flight. Can you at least assure me that all the necessary approvals and funding are firmly in place?"

Mitchell replied, "Of course they are, Mr. Douglas. You can rest assured this flight has been approved at the highest levels with ample funding. Stop worrying. We've got a dozen other countries breathing down our backs. You give me the airplanes on time and I'll give you the record. We'll make Douglas Aviation a household name."

Douglas waited before replying. Did he really want to put his company into jeopardy just when it had finally started showing a profit? Was he really willing to bet everything on the long shot,— fame and glory—or nothing? "Okay, General," he said, "I'll build the airplanes, you build the pilots."

Contrary to Mitchell's assurances, at the time Douglas committed his company neither approval for the flight nor funding had been secured. The delivery schedule Mitchell insisted on would have been very difficult for even the largest aircraft factory. Complicating matters further, as many as fifty Liberty engines, hastily assembled under wartime conditions, would have to be disassembled and rebuilt to assure reliability during the flight. Complex aircraft development projects usually take years, not months. The large sums of money required to meet the ambitious delivery schedule put Douglas Aviation deeply into debt.

Nelson and Douglas worked from early dawn to late into each night. Often groggy and ill tempered by lack of sleep, they had many heated exchanges. Thousands of modifications to the DT-2 were required. The 274-mile range of the DT-2 had to be increased to twenty-two hundred miles. Fortunately, its Cloudster origins included sufficient fuselage strength and space for additional fuel tanks.

After weeks of engineering changes, measuring, calculating, drawing, erasing, modifying, and redrawing, the new Douglas World Cruiser emerged. The fuselage stretched thirty-five feet, 2.5 inches long and stood thirteen feet, 7.25 inches high on wheels. The wings spanned fifty feet and were seven feet, six inches wide from end to end. The straight upper wing had no dihedral angle or sweepback. The lower wing had a dihedral, or upward slant for lateral stability, of two degrees. Both wings had an angle of attack, the angle at which they meet the onrushing air, of three degrees, and were eight feet apart.

All three sections of the fuselage bolted together. The vulnerable tail section could be exchanged simply by removing four bolts. The aluminum engine cowling was divided into quickly removable sections for simplified engine maintenance. The tail skid connected to a steerable rudder bar to simplify taxiing.

The wheels were enlarged to thirty-six inches in diameter and eight inches wide. The distance between them stretched to eleven feet, three inches. The normal axle connecting the wheels was eliminated for safer landings in tall grass or rough fields. Special pontoons were designed with mounting legs easily attached to the fuselage wheel landing gear struts, simplifying field conversion from a land plane to a sea plane and back.

A modified, dual magneto-fired Liberty V-12 engine developing 420-horsepower and employing an electric starting motor was installed with an additional manual starter as backup. This eliminated the difficult and dangerous necessity of rotating the huge wooden bomber propeller, eight feet in diameter, by hand to start the engine. A tank containing thirty gallons of engine oil was fitted to the engine compartment, and a tank holding ten gallons of cooling water was fitted to the upper wing feeding the engine's honeycombed radiator. Special thermostatically controlled shutters adapted it to a wide range of outside temperatures. An additional ten-gallon reserve water tank was installed in the pilot's cockpit for either engine or crew survival.

A 150-gallon fuel tank was installed behind the engine and in front of the pilot, protected by a substantial metal firewall. A second 160-gallon fuel tank was placed under the front pilot's seat, and a third 105-gallon fuel tank was located under the rear mechanic's seat. Two additional 62.5-gallon fuel tanks were carried in the lower wing, at the side of the fuselage. Another emergency fuel tank of sixty gallons in the upper wing permitted the fuel to flow by gravity to the engine in the unlikely event that all three fuel pumps failed. Total fuel capacity increased to six hundred gallons.

A mechanical, engine-driven fuel pump normally supplied the engine. A wind-driven fuel pump served as the primary backup, and a manually driven, rear-cockpit mounted, hand-powered fuel pump provided secondary backup.

An external baggage compartment with a capacity of three hundred pounds, sufficient to hold a life raft, survival rations, rifles, paddles, tool kit, snowshoes, and clothing, was designed into the rear fuselage, with a second, smaller baggage compartment over it. This one would be accessible from the rear compartment in flight to hold maps, charts, small tools, flashlights, and other flight necessities. Night lighting for identification and formation flying were provided, with two white streamlined lights on the upper wing, red and green wingtip lights, and a rear-pointing red light mounted at the top of the vertical fin.

Flight instruments included an airspeed indicator, altimeter, turn-and-bank indicator incorporating two gyroscopes for instrument flying in fog, and a clock. A magnetic and wind-driven earth-inductor compass was installed to provide direction-indicating capability even in the northern polar regions that rendered magnetic compasses useless.

Engine instruments included a tachometer; ammeter; fuel, manifold, and oil pressure gauges; and water-temperature gauges. Mixture, magneto, and priming controls were also available. A large wooden wheel that could be rotated and moved fore and aft controlled the ailerons and elevators. A wooden, floor-mounted, foot-operated bar controlled the rudder.

In contrast to the Fokker T2, the cockpits were large enough to be comfortable during the four hundred hours of flight anticipated. Back and seat cushions were designed to incorporate parachutes for both pilot and mechanic. Below them were Kapok seat cushions with handles that could be used as life preservers. The aircraft weighed 8,180 pounds fully loaded on floats, and 7,200 pounds on wheels. Maximum range on land using wheels stretched to more than 2,200 miles. Water takeoffs required drastically reducing fuel weights and ranges. Maximum cruising speed was one hundred miles per hour while normal cruise speed was eighty to ninety miles per hour.

While Eric Nelson and Donald Douglas were designing the World Cruiser, Lowell Smith was working with Billy Mitchell to develop techniques to refuel aircraft in flight. Detractors had said the idea was impossible. Two aircraft flying through the normal turbulence of hundred-mile-an-hour flight, each rising and falling separately, could never stay in position long enough to transfer highly combustible aviation gasoline from one aircraft to another. The inevitable single drop of gasoline on a heated exhaust would engulf both aircraft in flames.

Smith had risen to the rank of Captain several years before with command over thousands of men. When the budget axe fell on him, he voluntarily agreed to a reduction of salary, rank, and responsibility rather than leave the Air Service. Smith represented the U.S. Army in the 1919 transcontinental speed, reliability, and endurance contest from San Francisco to New York and back. This contest was supposed to promote aviation, but it backfired with numerous crashes and nine fatalities. Smith became the first person ever to reach Chicago by air direct from San Francisco, and the first to complete the return flight. Despite seventy pilots entered, Smith won numerous honors.

During the previous four years, Smith flew 2,400 difficult and dangerous forest fire–fighting missions. He always led his 91st Squadron of twenty forest fire–fighting aircraft safely home without a single fatality. This was an incredible safety record for a service in which one third of its pilots could be expected to die within the first year. Smith agreed with Mitchell that aerial refueling was possible, and they intended to prove it.

On June 27, 1923, Lieutenants Lowell Smith and John Richter departed from Rockwell Field in San Diego in two modified DeHaviland DH4-B biplanes. The upper biplane carefully lowered a rubber hose enclosing a metal sleeve, and successfully transferred a small amount of fuel into the tank of the lower airplane. With the principle proven, on August 27 and 28 they set sixteen new world records for distance, speed, and endurance, flying 3,297 miles over San Diego for thirty-seven hours and fifteen minutes at an average speed of 88.5 miles per hour and refueling sixteen times. This flight covered the distance between the United States and Europe.

The following month they demonstrated the practical application of the new aerial refueling technique. They flew 1,280 miles nonstop from Canada to Mexico, refueling in the air over Washington, Oregon, and California while averaging speeds of over one hundred miles per hour. Mitchell reported that using the new technique, bombers could now depart on long-range missions with lighter fuel and heavier bomb loads. Experimental, advanced, or secret aircraft could be used and concealed from foreign eyes.

Aircraft could be flown from protected home bases to project U.S. air power, with its defensive and offensive potential, anywhere on earth without depending upon other countries to grant landing rights. General Pershing was unimpressed, however, and felt the technique had little practical application for the future.

O n July 5, 1923, Donald Douglas signed a formal proposal. It included a full set of specifications and firm delivery dates for the prototype World Cruiser and four production models, and included all the spare parts, assemblies, and engines needed for the world flight. Douglas, under pressure from the short delivery time, started construction of the prototype aircraft that very day. Erik Nelson, having completed his work at Douglas Aviation, departed with the Douglas proposal and a briefcase filled with drawings, blueprints, and design notes. Extensive meetings with Generals Patrick and Mitchell were held on his return. Specifications were finalized on August 1 and forwarded to General Pershing, requesting his approval and funding.

Contrary to Mitchell's assurances to Douglas Aviation, and despite the successful transcontinental flights earlier, the chances for approval of a world flight looked very poor at that time. Mitchell complained in his writings that summer, "Air power doesn't seem to be getting anywhere at all. The public's interested, but people in Washington who could do something about it aren't." The newly installed, penurious President Coolidge disliked aviation in general and aviators in particular. The U.S. Air Corps, smaller than even the tiny Rumanian Air Corps, was still too large to suit Coolidge. He couldn't understand why the Army needed many airplanes at all. He suggested that they buy just one airplane and let all the pilots take turns flying it. His chief of staff, General Pershing, shared his views.

As the foremost advocate of aviation, Mitchell was particularly disliked by Coolidge, who was quoted in a newspaper interview during that summer: "Now, take those aviators, for instance. There's that Mitchell fellow. Why, he thinks nothing of flying in a government plane to Michigan to visit the girl he's engaged to marry."

Another complicating matter for world flight authorization was the continuing animosity between Mitchell and the naval administration that surfaced again late in the summer of 1923. For two years Army aviators had been trying to get the Navy to supply ships for additional bombing tests, without success. The Navy and General Pershing declared the 1921 tests inconclusive, blaming deficiencies in the vessels for the sinkings rather than the effect of the bombs.

As head of the Army Air Service, General Patrick had been appealing for additional tests without success. In the spring of 1923, he wrote directly to General Pershing: "Repeated requests have been made to the Navy . . . the Navy is simply stalling. I am now told that the Secretary of the Navy will not make these old vessels available until the ratification of the disarmament treaty. This is simply and solely an excuse." Under growing political pressure from Mitchell's allies in Congress, Pershing finally agreed to expedite the tests.

The Navy turned over the *Virginia* and the *New Jersey* both fifteen-thousand-ton vessels. Restrictions were put on Mitchell intended to prevent the bombings from sinking the ships. He could not use the new four thousand-pound bomb he had recently developed, but must use bombs left over from the 1921 tests. The ships would be anchored rather than put into motion, as Mitchell had requested.

The Navy, with agreement from General Pershing, waited until August 31—just four days before the tests were to begin, and presumably too late for Mitchell to prepare counter measures—to put additional restrictions on the bombing. The bombs had to be dropped from an altitude above ten thousand feet rather than the earlier lower levels. The Navy knew that no bomber in the Army fleet could even reach this altitude with its bomb load, let alone hit anything from such a vast height.

Fully expecting the anchored ships to easily survive these restrictions, Admiral Shoemaker, an opponent of expanded air power who wanted to cut flight pay for pilots to ten percent of base pay, arranged for a large group of blue ribbon spectators. The navy's transport ship, *St. Mihiel*, came down from Washington with three hundred dignitaries, including Acting Secretary of War Dwight Davis, General Pershing, Glenn Curtiss, Vincent Astor, congressmen, numerous reporters, and foreign military leaders.

What the Navy did not know was that Mitchell had anticipated these restrictions. Several months earlier he enlisted the aid of

Sanford Moss, who had recently invented the supercharger, to modify the Martin bomber's engines for high-altitude flight with a full
bomb load. Over the past two years, Mitchell worked with engineers
at the Sperry plant to improve the precision of their gyroscopes for
instrument flying. Alexander Seversky, the Russian war ace and now
Sperry's inventive aircraft engineer, combined these gyroscopes with
one of the world's first computers into a new type of more accurate,
high-altitude bombsight that he completed a few days before the latest bombing tests were to begin.

Working that Sunday and Labor Day, Mitchell and Seversky
used a hatchet and hacksaw to install a prototype of the new bombsight into a Martin bomber. This bombsight became one of
America's most valuable, top-secret weapons during World War II.
Seversky later wrote, "As a result of the energy and foresight of this
great man, Billy Mitchell, America today leads the world in instrument flying."

Mitchell worked through most of the nights before the bombing
tests, directing and orchestrating the thousands of technical details
required. At four A.M. the morning of the bomb tests, he climbed
into his DH-4, the *Osprey*, and flew out to check conditions at the
target ships and direct the bombing. Using the new superchargers
and bombsight, the *Virginia* and the *New Jersey*, were ravaged and
torn from end to end. They both sank within twenty-six minutes.

The incredulous naval officers made an immediate attempt to
conceal the results with the imposition of a huge fee of $170 per
thousand words for use of the ship's radio room. Only *The New York
Times* could afford to pay. All the other newspapers were forced to
run Pershing's tepid remarks, which had been written for him by the
Navy. Major Lester Gardner, publisher of *Aviation* magazine, wrote
his eyewitness description of the damage done by the bombing's
accuracy and was forced to give it to Admiral Shoemaker for
approval. Shoemaker read it and then tore it to pieces saying, "It's
true, every bit of it, but by God, we can't let this get out or it would
ruin the Navy."

Faced with every argument from "national security" to "naval
morale," along with a good deal of arm twisting and not-so-veiled
threats of loss of access, the newspapers cooperated with the Navy.
The New York Times reported, PERSHING PRAISES AIR BOMBERS'

AIM—BUT TESTS DO NOT PROVE MODERN WARSHIPS CAN BE SUNK, HE SAYS.

Mitchell was infuriated at seeing the same misrepresentations that accompanied the 1921 bombing tests, and he tried to correct them. To the public, the tests were seen as a repeat of old news simply being rehashed. Pershing ordered Mitchell to leave the naval conclusions unchallenged.

Mitchell's latest tests did not endear him to either the Navy or the old-line Army officers. He never was one of them. He didn't graduate from West Point, as almost all officers of similar rank had. He started military life as a lowly private and was not from military stock, as most of the other generals were. He was a Democrat in a Republican administration, and his self-righteous, uncompromising, and argumentative ways offended and often embarrassed his superiors. The Navy characterized his use of new engine developments and bombsights as cheating. He was using alien and unfair technologies, of which they were unaware, against them.

Relations with Mitchell deteriorated even further when the Navy found out that, in collusion with Donald Douglas, he had "stolen" the technology of their own naval torpedo plane, the DT-2, and was now trying to steal their glory by making a world flight over "their" oceans. Desperate to block the Army flight, they requested the Chief of the Naval Bureau of Aeronautics, Rear Admiral W. A. Moffett, to create a naval world flight and seek immediate authorization.

Moffett's plan envisioned twenty-one station ships departing on February 1, 1924, along a flight route stretching from California to Hawaii, Wake Island, and Guam, then continuing in a global circle. As justification, he wrote, "We think we shall be able to operate aircraft with the fleet anywhere in the world by the time the next war comes along, but we haven't proved it. It's high time we started to prove it, before we go too far in placing reliance on aircraft. Maybe we are placing too much faith in aircraft; maybe we aren't placing enough."

The naval chiefs were ambivalent. On the one hand they were against an expanded role for aviation, which the world flight would almost certainly bring. On the other hand they were infinitely more opposed to the Army making the flight and Mitchell using it as justification for a separate air force. Within the Navy, other ideas began to surface.

A growing enthusiasm for lighter-than-air ships had created a rival aeronautic service. It was the Navy that had full responsibility for the operation of all dirigibles. Curiously, the most vocal opponents of airplanes within the Navy displayed a tolerance, if not outright enthusiasm, for their own proprietary airship program. Airships, imposing and majestic, presented no threat to their surface ships, and created enthusiastic and receptive audiences wherever they appeared. Many high-ranking naval officers confidently predicted that it was only a matter of time before these airborne behemoths, operating as an adjunct to an expanded Navy, were carrying thousands of passengers smoothly, safely, and in great luxury over the turbulent oceans of the world. An alternate plan to send the naval airship *Shenandoah* over the North Pole and beyond was proposed and began receiving increasing support.

Both naval plans were presented to Edwin Denby, Secretary of the Navy, with the request for funding and approval. Denby, embroiled in the expanding Teapot Dome senate investigation and pending criminal charges, showed little enthusiasm for promoting either plan to a hostile Congress and president. Patrick, however, strongly supported the Army's world flight and appealed to General Pershing for assistance. Pershing held Patrick in high regard, admiring the maturity and diplomacy he had shown in coordinating Allied air operations during the war. They agreed that Coolidge, who had often said, "The business of America is business," was unlikely to be moved by justifying the flight on the basis of military advantage. Coolidge believed a future war highly unlikely, and intended to continue the reductions of military expenditures and personnel.

The Army flight would have to be justified as a world demonstration of the peaceful applications and objectives of the U.S. Armed Services in the exploration and development of future routes of commerce and industry. If successful, it would showcase American ingenuity and counteract the enlarging stain on U.S. national honor inflicted by the Teapot Dome scandal. With elections coming up, it might just work.

Patrick listed objectives for the flight that he felt would be most palatable to President Coolidge, carefully excluding any military purpose. They were:

1. To determine the feasibility of establishing aerial communication with all the countries of the world

2. To determine the practicability of travel by air through regions where surface transportation does not exist or at least is slow, tedious, and uncertain

3. To prove the ability of modern aircraft to operate under all climatic conditions

4. To stimulate the adaptation of aircraft to the needs of commerce

5. To show the people of the world the excellence of American produced aircraft and thus stimulate American aircraft industry, and lastly

6. To bring to the United States, the birthplace of aeronautics, the honor of being the first to fly around the world

Mitchell was considered an insurmountable impediment to getting approval for the flight. His penchant for using aviation records to garner public and congressional support, coupled with the animosity of the president, General Pershing, cabinet officers, and the Navy, made authorization impossible. The flight would require the closest cooperation and logistical support from the Navy. They could only get it by removing Mitchell and any belief that the Army flight attempted to achieve military advantage over the Navy.

Pershing's 1923 evaluation of Mitchell read, "This officer is an exceptionally able one, enthusiastic, energetic, and full of initiative. . . . an expert flier . . . He is fond of publicity, more or less indiscreet as to speech, and rather difficult to control as a subordinate."

Patrick's 1923 evaluation similarly noted that Mitchell had shown "considerable improvement" in the last year but "it is difficult for him to subordinate his own views and opinions to those of others. He is somewhat erratic and changeable. I cannot always rely upon either his opinions or his judgment. His enthusiasm sometimes carries him away."

Pershing and Patrick agreed that if the U.S. world flight were to receive approval, Mitchell had to go as far away as possible and have nothing to do with it. Pershing left the details to General Patrick.

Patrick felt great sympathy for Mitchell. He knew, far better than most, that Mitchell's strong views and intemperate speech and actions were not motivated by personal aggrandizement but by firmly held convictions that he acted in the best interests of his country.

Undoubtedly he was a zealot, but a patriotic one, and therefore worthy of respect and compassion.

Patrick also felt sympathy for Mitchell's personal problems. His previous family life and relationship with his young children lay in shambles. His mother, with whom he had lived and was very close to, had recently died. Many of his young pilots, for whom he felt responsible, had been killed in air crashes. Patrick had seen the usually stoic General Mitchell weeping uncontrollably at the recent funeral of Captain Tiny Lawson, who had replaced his lost younger brother, John, in his heart.

Mitchell's engagement to Betty Miller provided Patrick with a seemingly benign plan that would meet everyone's objective. He would send Mitchell on an extensive fact-finding mission to the Pacific to evaluate air defenses at remote locations and report on aviation advances of potential adversaries. He could take his new wife with him and make it a relaxing honeymoon. Before leaving, Mitchell would turn over the plans he had developed for the world flight and his recommendations for the pilots most qualified to fly the aircraft. If funding were received, Patrick would implement his plans.

Mitchell was forbidden to speak with any reporters he might encounter on the trip, or have any further contact with the world flight. This would be simply a well-earned, pleasant vacation devoid of controversy for the Mitchells—or so he thought.

On October 11, 1923, a dozen airplanes from Selfridge Field flew in tight formation over Betty Miller and Billy Mitchell's wedding reception at Grosse Pointe, Michigan. Fawning over the event, the society columns of the local newspapers described the beautiful and charming bride and the handsome war hero, his uniform adorned with medals, "the youngest man in the legion of honor since Napoleon."

The next day the couple left for San Francisco to board the *Cambrai*, and sail to Hawaii. As he had done on his first honeymoon, Mitchell took time away from his new bride to continue military affairs. He sent a detailed report to Patrick of his evaluation of the air maneuvers performed for him by the west coast air reserve squadrons and listed the improvements they must make during his absence. He also informed Patrick that he would expand the scope of his own mission, saying, "In addition to the regular inspections, I shall study the whole Pacific problem from both an offensive and defense standpoint." Patrick approved the expansion.

Meanwhile, the situation at the Douglas Aircraft Company grew critical. Donald Douglas had put thousands of man hours into the design of the World Cruiser. Despite assurances from General Mitchell, he had still not received any compensation or even a purchase order to cover the prototype now nearing completion. He had been thoroughly chastised by the Navy for giving the Army "their" designs. His future looked very grim.

With Mitchell exiled to the Pacific, General Pershing assured the Navy of an equal role with equal credit going to both branches. He stressed the historical importance of the United States capturing aviation's greatest prize and the enormous commercial benefits that would accrue for the balance of the century. Patriotism prevailed over rivalry, and the Navy withdrew its opposition. Liaison officers of both branches promised their full cooperation to the flight.

In Mitchell's original plans for the flight, naval support vessels played a relatively minor role. Most supplies were to be cached on land bases as Mitchell had planned for the Alaskan flight. Passages over water were shortened as much as possible. Only when they exceeded the aircraft's considerable range would they be supplied by commercial and government ships of the Bureau of Fisheries and the U.S. Coast Guard.

Mitchell's reluctance to rely on naval vessels was due as much to past experience as animosity. On May 16, 1919, three U.S. naval flying boats set off on the first flight from Newfoundland across the Atlantic to Europe through the Azores. The Navy stationed twenty-four warships at fifty-mile intervals to assist in rescue and navigation. Despite the ships' firing flares and making smoke, clouds, rain, and fog obscured many of them from the view of the pilots. One of the planes, the NC-4, succeeded, becoming the first to cross the Atlantic Ocean, winning a close race with the British.

Mitchell thought the flight would provide salvation for his shrinking Army Air Service by demonstrating the feasibility and military significance of establishing air routes to Japan and the Pacific region. He believed air forces based in Alaska, Labrador, Greenland, and Iceland would contain any potential future aggressors, and support for the world flight would provide a plausible reason to establish these bases.

No aircraft had ever flown over this route. The flight depended upon advance parties laying in food, fuel, supplies, tools, engines, and spare parts in advance of the aircraft at newly created air bases. In anticipation of the flight, Mitchell formed an Army World Flight Committee before he left for Hawaii. Members of the committee included Lieutenant Robert J. Brown, chairman; Captain Lorenzo L. Snow, foreign relations; and Captain William Volandt, finance.

The flight route was divided into seven sections and each assigned to a committee officer. They had the responsibility of completing all the logistical support arrangements within their division as the flight proceeded west. The first division, from Seattle, Washington, through Alaska to Attu Island, was headed by Lieutenant Clayton L. Bissell; the second, from the Russian Komandorski Islands through Japan, was led by Lieutenant Clifford C. Nutt; the third, from China through Calcutta, India, was headed by Lieutenant Malcolm S. Lawton. Lieutenant Harry A. Halverson led the fourth, from Allahabad, India, through Constantinople, Turkey, and the fifth, from Bucharest, Rumania, through London, England, was headed by Major Carlyle H. Wash. Lieutenants Clarence E. Crumrine, LeClaire Shultz, and Clayton Bissell shared the sixth from Brough, England, to Boston, Massachusetts. The seventh, from Mitchell Field on Long Island, New York, to Seattle, Washington, was headed by Capt. Burdette Wright.

With Mitchell's departure, the role of the Navy increased substantially. Naval warships became primarily responsible for support of the flight. They would be supported by other ships only where naval ships were lacking. Land-based supply depots would be used only in the few areas ships could not reach. For maximum naval access, the flight's route was modified to pass over coastal areas wherever possible.

Overflight and landing permits had to be obtained from dozens of countries, many unfriendly or even hostile to the United States. General Pershing, always diplomatic and politically astute, insisted there be no further mention, either within or outside of the United States, of any military purposes for the flight, nor any desire to gain any advantage over another country by beating them in the race to be first to fly around the world.

Captain Volandt, finance officer, came up with estimates of $257,882 for the flight expenses, $50,000 for contingencies, and

$192,684 for purchasing the aircraft. When he presented the estimates to President Coolidge, the president said he would not spend half a million dollars of taxpayer money on a risky venture with little chance of success, unknown benefits, and a high likelihood of fatalities.

The Senate Teapot Dome investigations taking place at the same time threatened to continue through the upcoming elections. The scandal was growing, and Coolidge faced the prospect of losing. He could be forced to leave office without the legitimacy of being elected and a legacy of leading his Republican party into defeat.

Pershing had sought the Republican party nomination during the last party primary and was politically savvy. Meeting with Coolidge, he convinced him that a U.S. attempt at a world flight had the unique ability to divert public attention and create positive newspaper headlines during the upcoming election season. As a loyal Republican, he asked Coolidge to reconsider—for the benefit of the party.

THURSDAY, NOVEMBER 1, 1923
9:00 A.M.
HONOLULU, HAWAII

Billy and Betty Mitchell were still unpacking their large steamer trunks when the knock on the door came. Billy checked his watch. His new orderly was right on time. That was good. He had given Betty the full week he had promised during the voyage. No Army. No Air Corps. No fights with the Navy. Just a happy honeymooning couple dancing the night away. Now it was time to get back to business—Air Corps business.

Billy opened the door. The army lieutenant standing outside saluted, and Billy motioned him inside. The lieutenant saluted again and stood stiffly as he introduced himself. "Good morning, General Mitchell. Welcome to Hawaii. I'm Lieutenant Johnson. General Summerall has assigned Sergeant Palmer and I to escort you and Mrs. Mitchell while you're in Hawaii, sir."

Mitchell casually went back to his unpacking. "At ease, lieutenant. What did General Summerall have in mind for us?"

Lieutenant Johnson relaxed slightly before replying, "Sir, General Summerall thought you might enjoy a visit to our gardens at the country club and a round of golf this afternoon. I've also brought a guidebook for Mrs. Mitchell, sir. We could drive you anywhere you wish. General Summerall wants your stay in Hawaii to be as pleasant as possible, sir. He's planned a welcome party for you and Mrs. Mitchell this evening at the Officer's Club, sir."

Mitchell's face clearly showed he was not happy. Betty caught the look and cautioned him with a quick glance to be nice. "I certainly appreciate the General's hospitality, but I'm here to evaluate Hawaiian defenses. An airplane for reconnaissance would be a lot more useful than a golf game. Also, I prefer to do my own driving, so if you can leave me a car, preferably a fast one, that will do nicely."

Johnson nodded his understanding. "Yes sir, General Mitchell. I'll send Sergeant Palmer to make those arrangements right now, sir. Will you need a pilot, sir?"

Mitchell replied scornfully, "Johnson, I *am* a pilot. Go do it. I'll be down shortly."

Johnson saluted smartly and left the room. This was not going to be as easy as all those other visiting bigwig assignments. He sent Sergeant Palmer on ahead to the airfield to make the arrangements for Mitchell's flight. As Mitchell approached the waiting staff car, Johnson dived out to open the right rear door at the curb for him. Mitchell walked around the back of the car, opened the driver's door, and sat down. "I'll drive. You navigate," he said.

The sentry at Luke Field was reading a magazine in the small gatehouse as Mitchell's car pulled up. Without looking up, he motioned for the car to continue through the open gate. Mitchell stopped the car and started timing. It took twenty-six seconds for the sentry to take his feet down from the desk and turn curiously toward the stopped car. It took another four seconds for the startled sentry to recognize the fluttering flags of rank on the fenders of the car, run outside, snap to attention, salute General Mitchell and, wide-eyed with the shock of being caught, wave him through the gate. Johnson gave him an exasperated look as they passed.

Mitchell looked over the obsolete biplanes responsible for Hawaii's defense. He selected the newest of the aging group, a Thomas Morse Scout. The Scout was based loosely on a European design. It was faster and more maneuverable than the large DeHaviland DH-4 next to it but inherently unstable. If you took your hands off the controls, even for an instant, the Scout would bank sharply. If you didn't correct quickly, it would turn over onto its back and drop its nose into an inverted high-speed dive toward the ground. If you survived your flight, on landing it would take another bite at you. Unless you were quick—really quick, with the correct rudder inputs at the exact moment they were needed—the little Scout would ground loop, the tail would come around, a wingtip would dig into the grass, and it would cartwheel onto its back. If it didn't kill you, it would sure leave you looking like a ham-handed dunce to your fellow aviators.

The nimble Scout was loved by only the most skillful aviators, the ones who could master it. Mitchell confidently climbed into the cockpit, carefully folded the borrowed map, and strapped it and the small notebook he always carried to his leg. He buttoned his worn leather jacket before pulling his goggles down over his eyes. After starting the engine he checked the wind sock, put in the appropriate aileron and then rudder inputs, and lifted off into a freshening southern breeze.

Flying low over the many naval ships anchored at Pearl Harbor, Mitchell returned the friendly waves of the sailors on the decks below him—then recorded the type and exact location of each ship in his notebook. Continuing his low flight around the island, he marked on his map the exact location of Wheeler Airfield, its hangars, defensive gun emplacements, bunkers, fuel depots, armories, barracks, and communication facilities.

Mitchell went to full throttle on the Scout and pointed the nose upward. He climbed one thousand . . . two thousand . . . three thousand . . . four thousand feet, then leveled off and flew in large slow circles, mentally formulating a theoretical air attack on the island. *How easy it would be*, he thought. He drew the lines of attack on his map. He would strike early on a Sunday morning, when they would be least prepared. One hundred attacking airplanes would reduce Pearl Harbor to a watery naval graveyard in minutes. The few coastal gun positions and antiquated U.S. airplanes would be no match against a determined, better equipped foe.

On landing, Mitchell was required to present his pilot's license and medical certificate for recording in the airbase's logbooks. His medical had expired, so he reported to the resident flight surgeon,

Dr. David Myers, for renewal. The examination was more thorough than Mitchell would have liked. Dr. Myers duly recorded the numerous old fractures and dislocations from his early days of riding and jumping and his punctured eardrum from the rapid descent he had made over France to escape enemy fire. Listening to Mitchell's heart and taking his blood pressure, Dr. Myers shook his head. He didn't like what he heard and saw. *High blood pressure* and *increased arterial tension* were noted on his chart. This could disqualify him for a medical certificate.

Mitchell blanched noticeably. He feared the loss of his pilot's license more than anything else on earth. Quietly he explained to Dr. Myers what that would mean to him. Myers understood. He noted on Mitchell's chart that the readings might have been the result of extensive travel, the loss of recent sleep, and a transitory gastrointestinal upset. He recommended a follow-up examination but signed him off as being fit for flight. Immensely relieved, Mitchell carefully placed his renewed medical certificate with his pilot's license in his wallet and left a happy man. He could fly for another year.

Betty and Billy Mitchell enjoyed the next six weeks in Hawaii. They went horseback riding, hunting, swimming, sailing, fishing, hiking in the mountains, attended numerous parties in their honor, visited every island in the group except Lehua, and attended plays, polo matches, and sumo wrestling.

General Charles P. Summerall, commander of the Army's Hawaiian Department, was the consummate host, graciously acceding to Mitchell's every request and making certain he and Betty were always well provided for. Even his former Chief and adversary, General Menoher, now happily stationed in Hawaii's Schofield Barracks, warmly welcomed him with an honor guard.

Mitchell flew almost every day in the Scouts, DeHavilands, and Sopwith biplanes of Luke and Wheeler Airfields. He inspected almost every military installation on Hawaii and participated in all the maneuvers and training exercises. Each night he made copious notes, often working into the dawn hours to prepare the most extensive report ever made on Hawaiian defenses and the improvements he deemed necessary.

Before sailing to Guam and on to the Philippines on the old Army transport ship the *Thomas*, Mitchell completed a scathing one hundred-page preliminary report that severely criticized Hawaii's defenses and the complete lack of communication and coordination between Army and Navy commanders. As with most of his reports, this one was open, impersonal, unsparing, and critical of almost every command function.

He cited the lack of adequate air power, gun emplacements, poor training of personnel, lack of proficiency, inadequate weapons, inefficient deployment, and a high degree of vulnerability to even the smallest attack from the air. He concluded that the supply system was chaotic, the islands lacked airways or even weather reporting and no command communication with defenses existed. He reported General Summerall as hopelessly unprepared for war.

After showing his report to headquarters at Schofield Barracks, Mitchell sent it to General Patrick for forwarding to the War Department. General Summerall felt Mitchell had betrayed him, stabbed him in the back. He derided the report as an academic exercise with little practical application. Mitchell's assumption that an enemy force might someday attack Pearl Harbor was, he felt, ludicrous and unrealistic. Summerall believed Hawaii's defenses were completely adequate and capable of repelling any attack with minimal damage. Summerall complained bitterly to General Patrick of Mitchell's unwelcome and undeserved criticism. Although Patrick wrote at great length to Summerall apologizing for Mitchell's evaluation, calling it a theoretical exercise, Summerall joined the long and growing list of Mitchell's lifelong enemies.

O n November 23, 1923, a greatly relieved Donald Douglas finally received his purchase order for $192,684 to cover immediate delivery of one prototype and four World Cruisers plus spare parts to be delivered in March 1924. With re-election looming, the antiaviation president reversed course and gave his approval to the first world flight.

CHAPTER 8

The Chosen

A s 1924 dawned, America's largest movie studios had been established in Hollywood and a virtual torrent of films were being made and exported throughout the world. Through these films, America's way of life—its hopes, dreams, and aspirations, even its political, legal, and judicial systems—were being exported to Europe and Asia.

Calvin Coolidge, who had become president upon the death of Warren Harding, promised to continue the return to normalcy that started after the end of the Great War five years before. Despite the discordant tones of the growing Teapot Dome scandal, 1924 looked like a good year for most Americans—unless they were in the military.

For the military, 1924 started as another year of devastating budget cuts and continuing losses of personnel and resources. The dwindling Army and Navy competed with each other for the meager scraps of diminishing funds thrown to them by a diffident Congress and a penurious new president.

In Europe and Japan, aviation flourished, awash in generous government funding. They had seen the future during the war and knew it lay in aviation. Foreign factories worked overtime to produce advanced engine and airframe designs while the United States stagnated, content to consume the surplus antiquated, defective aviation remnants left over from the war.

The factors arrayed against the world flight's success were awesome. Scarcely twenty years after the Wright brothers' first flight, most countries had never seen an airplane. With only a few exceptions along the flight route, there were no airports, no aircraft fuel, no spare parts, no outside help or tools of any kind. Available engines were notoriously unreliable and airframes fragile. Navigational aids were primitive at best.

The crew would have to fight their way through the blinding blizzards of Alaska, the typhoons of Japan and China, the monsoons of Burma and India, and the sandstorms of the deserts. If they survived all that, lying in wait were the monstrous icebergs of the North Atlantic, many rising unseen thousands of feet into the sky shrouded in the impenetrable fog of the arctic regions.

Pilots would have to face these elements in open cockpits with only their leather flying suits and their indomitable will to survive protecting them against the ravages of nature. Headwinds on their westbound flight route would slow their lumbering aircraft and make forward progress agonizingly slow. Their route had never been attempted before. No aircraft had ever crossed the Pacific Ocean, nor the North Atlantic. Many countries such as Iceland and Greenland had never been visited by aircraft. Many didn't think it possible. Just to start the flight, the planners needed overflight and landing permits from thirty different foreign countries. Strong resistance or even denial was to be expected from some countries.

To make it over the great oceans, the crew would have to locate and land next to ships that would be tiny specks often hidden under clouds, immersed in rain, or shrouded in fog on turbulent seas. The naval ships were their sole source of sustenance. Unless they found each and every waiting ship, they would have no fuel, no food, no spare parts, and no way to continue on to safety. If they missed a single ship, they would all perish. Previous experience provided little encouragement. In the first crossing of the Atlantic in 1919, naval pilots missed seeing many of the twenty-four beacon ships through the typical clouds, fog, and rain. The northern Pacific promised to be even more hostile.

The poor reliability and short life of the Liberty engines required each aircraft to make as many as six engine changes during the trip. Engine failures were almost certain. Ocean crossings required heavy pontoons. Sensitivity to weight meant that much of the needed survival equipment could not be carried. All previous attempts at this flight by other countries had failed; most pilots succumbed to air crashes or were simply lost forever. Gamblers extended odds of ten to one that this attempt would meet the same fate.

TUESDAY, JAN. 1, 1924,
5:15 P.M
LANGLEY ARMY AIR BASE, HAMPTON, VIRGINIA

The taxicab slowed, its narrow tires sliding on the fresh evening snow, and finally stopped a few feet beyond the entrance gate guarding Langley Air Base. A uniformed guard, rifle at the ready, peered through the rear window at the handsome, lean figure in the leather flying jacket. The airman reached into his pocket to display his identification papers and the crumpled telegram with his orders:

DEC 21 1923 STOP LIEUTENANT LOWELL SMITH STOP YOU
ARE HEREBY DIRECTED TO REPORT TO LANGLEY AIR BASE
NO LATER THAN 0600 HOURS JAN 2 1924 STOP SIGNED
GENERAL MASON PATRICK CHIEF U S ARMY AIR SERVICE
STOP

Satisfied with his credentials, the guard gave the lieutenant a crisp salute and stood aside, motioning for the taxi to enter. The crunching of the wheels on the wet snow continued on to the officer quarters. Lowell Smith leaned over, paid the driver, and left the cab, hoisting his duffel bag on his shoulders. Heading to the entrance, he noticed the doors of a nearby large hangar standing open. Curious, he put down his duffel and walked over.

An electric ceiling lamp illuminated a huge, single-engined biplane. The large radiator perched above the wooden propeller looked like some ungainly proboscis. Six exhaust stacks protruded through each side of the engine cowling, enclosing the 420-horsepower of its V-12 Liberty engine. Through the open hangar door, it reminded Smith more of a tank than an airplane.

Close by, it was even larger than it appeared at a distance. The wheels were waist-high. The lower wing was at shoulder height, and the upper wing barely fit under the ceiling of the hangar. Everything about this airplane was oversized. Smith had never seen a single-engined airplane this big. Circling it warily, he wondered if it would be his adversary or his friend. As a pilot, he knew all airplanes had a soul. The good ones looked after you, protected you, rode the storms and the winds with level wings and stable cockpits. The bad ones tried to kill you, flopping and churning in the slightest turbulence, their wings stalling without warning. Which would this one be?

The robust, sturdy construction typical of naval torpedo biplanes revealed its roots. This airplane was big—everything on it was heavy, overbuilt—the airplane was painted in the olive drab of the army. He smiled at the familiar growing puddle of oil and water under the Liberty V-12 engine. Developing over four hundred-horsepower from its 1,649 cubic inches, it was the largest and most powerful American aircraft engine that existed at the time. Hastily assembled under wartime conditions, most would not run well unless taken apart and rebuilt properly. New, more modern and efficient engines could not be purchased by the military until the ample supply of old Libertys were exhausted. Since they were modular, they would often continue to run after losing several cylinders, but few if any lasted beyond fifty hours, and all leaked copious amounts of oil and water.

As Lowell inspected the airplane, he could almost feel its massive palpable presence. It towered above the DeHaviland DH-4 biplane next to it. His first thought was that it was the ugliest aircraft he had ever seen. With its bloated, stubby fuselage, bulldog radiator nose, and thick wings stretching to fifty feet, it looked too ungainly to fly.

Slowly, the robust construction of the aircraft mellowed his initial impression. All the many things that had broken during his thousands of hours of flying airplanes were reinforced. They were larger, thicker, and more solid on this aircraft. A flying elephant—

slow and ponderous, but unstoppable. He shook his head, wondering if he could coax this reluctant pachyderm around the entire planet.

"Well, Lowell, what do you think?" said a voice from the shadows. He wasn't alone after all. He turned toward a young man in civilian clothes, half hidden in the shadows, leaning against one of the hangar's supporting posts. He seemed to know him. Who was that? Lowell squinted, trying to attach a name to the voice.

"Well, *what do you think?*" the voice insisted. Lowell recognized Donald Douglas as he stepped from the shadows, smiling. The two had met at Rockwell Field after Lowell's successful demonstration of aerial refueling.

"It's not very pretty, but it sure is big," said Lowell. "Does it fly?"

"Beauty is as beauty does. Of course she's big . . . big and strong. She has to be to take the gaff," said Douglas. "Lieutenant Ernest Dichman's been flying her out of McCook Field in Dayton. He'll tell you she's one hell of a strong airplane, strong enough to take all of you around the world—and get you back safely."

"We'll soon find out," replied Lowell.

"You treat her right and she'll make it," said Douglas.

Lowell stared at Douglas, nodding silently before replying, "We'll see."

TUESDAY, JANUARY 1, 1924
5:30 P.M.
CHANUTE FIELD, ILLINOIS

New Year's Day in the home of Major Frederick Martin was not a happy event. His wife had been pleading with him since the telegram had intruded on their Christmas festivities.

"Please," she begged him. "You're too old, Frederick. You catch colds easily. Let those young men freeze in their open cockpits. Let them sacrifice themselves. Your son needs you. I need you. If you go, I'm afraid you'll never come back to me. None of you may ever come back. Please don't go. Please don't. Please."

Despite his wife's pleadings, he was determined to leave that day for training as leader of the first world flight. Martin understood the risks very well and feared his flying abilities might not be up to the task. He seriously considered refusing the assignment in deference to his wife and young son but rejected the idea, knowing he would be tarred with the brush of cowardice. With the entire world watching, his fear of failure overshadowed his fear of death. His wife had been crying herself to sleep each night. Now, sobbing quietly but resigned, she was helping him pack, folding his underwear and uniforms neatly into the family's large suitcase.

Hap Arnold had recommended that Lowell Smith lead the flight. Smith had skill and seniority, having stepped down in rank from captain to avoid the budget axe. Patrick, though, believed he was too young. Patrick chose tall, distinguished looking Martin mainly for his diplomatic skills and the favorable impression his maturity, rank, and stature would make on the high-ranking foreign leaders he was certain to encounter.

Martin had graduated from Purdue University as a mechanical engineer and been with the Army for sixteen years. He had learned to fly at the advanced age of thirty-nine in 1921. Now, at forty-two, he was the oldest of the crew. Only General Patrick himself, who became the world's oldest junior aviator at sixty, had learned later in life. Martin was the only one married, and with a mere seven hundred hours of flight time was the least experienced. Before he was chosen, his wife had felt relieved that his latest position as head of the Air Service Technical School often kept him bound to the safety of a desk.

"Can I come with you, Dad? I could help you fly."

Hugging his son, Martin replied, "You're the man of the house now, John. You've got to look after your mother."

The *Ahooga* horn signaled the arrival of the waiting taxi. Martin embraced his wife and kissed her cheek with a forced smile. He picked up his small boy in his arms and held him tightly in a bear hug that concealed tears. Setting him down, he chucked him on the chin. The small boy saluted his father as he picked up his suitcase and left for Langley. When safely out of sight, Major Frederick Martin wiped the moisture from his eyes.

JANUARY 2, 1924
7:45 A.M.
LANGLEY AIR BASE CLASSROOM

L owell Smith sat with the other new crew members, quietly
waiting for the session to begin. Almost half the pilots in the
Air Service had volunteered for the flight. Although most
were very good, some were not. He knew his life and the flight itself
would depend entirely on the skills of the crew. He was relieved by
the choices.

To his right sat Lieutenant Erik Nelson, thirty-five years old and
born in Sweden. Only Erik's mechanical genius with engines exceeded his skill in flying. Erik had worked day and night for weeks with
Donald Douglas to hammer out the final performance specifications
and the myriad detailed modifications of what would become the
Douglas World Cruiser. Erik also worked with Billy Mitchell to lay
out the flight's route. Erik, as Lowell, always brought his crews safely back home.

To Lowell's left sat Lieutenant Leigh Wade, only twenty-seven
but already a grizzled veteran test pilot and flight instructor. Leigh
had flown everything with wings, surviving countless engine, propeller, and control-system failures. He had dived, swooped, and
zoomed new designs until the airframes broke and then, somehow,
gotten them back on the ground and walked away. Leigh had set a
new world altitude record, coaxing his open cockpit airplane up to
27,120 feet, suffering severe frostbite in the process.

Sitting to the right of Erik Nelson were Lieutenants Leslie
Arnold and LeClaire Schultz, winner of the recent Pulitzer air races.
As alternate pilots, they would go through the entire six weeks of
intensive training to be available if a primary crew member became
incapacitated.

Lowell knew the pilots there were highly skilled and experienced. They had all been hand-picked by Billy Mitchell to learn the
difficult art of precision bombing far out at sea. After months of flying wingtip to wingtip within inches of one another, often carrying
bombs in tight formation, they had no hesitation in trusting their
lives to their flying skills. When the time finally came, they followed Mitchell out to sea and dropped their bombs with such

precision that even the most unsinkable of the battleships succumbed. Together they had forever changed the face of warfare at
sea. Lowell knew that they, like himself, were the best of the best.
They were the A-team.

Les Arnold, twenty-nine, charismatic class clown, and cutup,
chatted nonstop as usual. Frustrated by his frequent AWOL status
and stunt flying, the Army finally capitulated and made him their
official exhibition pilot, recruiting at county fairs throughout the
Midwest. Lowell knew that behind the amiable nonchalance lay a
passionately dedicated pilot.

Sitting one row back from Smith were ten potential mechanics,
the best mechanics in the Air Service, waiting to go through the
same course with them. After the four pilots had the opportunity to
interact with them, four mechanics would be selected to accompany
the crew on the flight.

At precisely eight A.M., to the call of *Atten-shun* and the required
standing salute, Major Frederick Martin entered the room with the
members of the World Flight Committee. Lieutenant Robert J.
Brown, its head, was an organizational genius well known throughout the Air Service. He introduced Captain Lorenzo Snow, who had
the unenviable task of securing overflight and landing permits from
thirty different countries.

William Volandt headed the finance committee and obtained the
half million dollars of funding for the flight. The World Flight committee divided the flight route into seven divisions and assigned an
individual advance officer to each. The advance officer had to recon-
noiter each area and provide strategically located caches of tools,
spare parts, repair facilities, local labor, and everything else the flight
would need for safe passage through their sector, as well as any
emergencies that might arise.

The U.S. Navy, Coast Guard, Bureau of Fisheries, State
Department, and many U.S. companies operating abroad had
pledged their complete support to the flight. The extensive facilities
of Standard Oil Company would prove extremely useful. Lowell
was amazed at the huge scale and extent of the resources that would
be employed.

Lieutenant Brown had succeeded in marshaling most of the
available resources of the Army and Navy in support of this flight.

He had enlisted the aid of almost all the other government agencies, and he had whipped up the management of U.S. companies doing business around the world into a patriotic fervor and pledges of support. At that very moment, as they sat in the classroom at Langley Air Base, members of his World Flight Committee were enlisting the aid of private and government facilities throughout the world that were anywhere near the flight route. No detail of support was too small to be considered, no possible adverse event too unlikely to be provided for.

Before the flight came to an end, the supporting cast would grow to 250,000. The thoroughness and scale of the world flight would remain the largest peacetime undertaking for the rest of the twentieth century.

During their six weeks at Langley, the committee had to cover a formidable amount of material. Their instructors were the top men in each field. Subjects included meteorology, marine law, navigation, medicine, engine and airframe repairs, welding, riveting, recovering, water takeoffs and landing, survival skills, and even boat handling. Calisthenics, tennis, basketball, weight lifting, and endless miles of daily roadwork completed their daily routine. Evenings were consumed with homework and tests covering the day's instruction.

Before the end of the six-week course at Langley, each of the pilots selected their mechanics. Lowell picked Sergeant Arthur Turner, whose abilities he knew from years before when Turner helped him keep his forest fire–fighting aircraft flying. Major Martin selected Sergeant Alva Harvey, a twenty-three-year-old five-year Army veteran, modest, skilled and powerfully built. It would be Harvey's strength and resolve that would save Martin's life during the ordeal to come. Leigh Wade chose Sergeant Henry Ogden, twenty-three, born on his family's large plantation in Woodville, Mississippi. As a small boy, Henry enjoyed tinkering with machinery and maintained most of it in his father's factory. When he turned nineteen, he joined the Army Air Service and attended training courses in aircraft repair. Within a few months he earned a reputation for diagnosing "impossible" engine problems, the nickname "Houdini," an instructor's rating, and the rank of staff sergeant. After discovering aviation, Ogden quickly came under its spell and spent all his working and leisure hours flying, fixing, and wingwalking on friends' aircraft. He described the date he was chosen for the world flight as "the happiest day of my life."

General Patrick gave Erik Nelson special permission to take an officer of equal rank with him as his mechanic "if that was what the entire flight wanted." All the pilots agreed there was no finer mechanic in the Air Service than "Smilin' Jack" Harding. Lieutenant Jack Harding was the fourth generation born on his family's famous five thousand-acre plantation near Nashville, Belle Meade, on June 2, 1896. Shortly after learning to crawl, Jack delighted in systematically dismantling mechanical devices to see how they worked. By the age of five, he had filled the woodshed with parts from his mother's sewing machines, clocks, and watches. By ten, the family buggy and those of several neighbors had been added to his collection. He escaped punishment by eventually reassembling the machines better than ever. His father, a prolific inventor and chemical engineer, often tried to shield young Jack from the wrath of his mother claiming that Jack had inherited his compulsion to dismantle mechanical objects from his genes.

The Harding dynasty had come to an abrupt end following the Civil War. Jack put himself through school working as a locksmith, garage mechanic, and engine assembly specialist for the Chalmers and Dodge Motor Car companies. As a growing adolescent he juggled engines weighing several hundred pounds, building powerful muscles and enormous upper-body strength. His strength would be severely tested against an Arctic blizzard that threatened to destroy his aircraft during the flight to come.

With his extraordinary talents at engine building, Jack enlisted as a private in the Air Service to work on airplanes as soon as war was declared in 1917. The army assigned him to many months of kitchen duties and, when he rebelled, many additional months of digging ditches. It was only through the chance breakdown of an officer's motorcar that no one seemed capable of repairing that Jack was "discovered" as being able to perform the duties he had claimed to all along.

Desperate for aircraft mechanics, Jack was sent to the Aviation Mechanics School in St. Paul, Minnesota. Within days, they realized Jack knew more than the instructors. They made him a sergeant with ratings of Master Signal Electrician and Aviation Mechanician.

Smilin' Jack was considered an engine genius. He made his reputation by getting engines to run after all other mechanics had given up hope.

Lieutenant "Tiny" Harmon and Colonel Hartz chose him as their mechanic on the record-setting "Round-the-Rim" flight of 1919 in a Martin Bomber that circumnavigated the United States for the first time. They flew from Washington, D.C. north to Maine, west to Puget Sound, south to Mexico, east to Florida and then returned north again to Washington, D.C. Harding's pleasant smile always persisted. Even in the face of adversity Harding was always jovial, although painfully shy with strangers and the opposite sex.

Finally recognized as a mechanical genius, Jack soon held the rank of lieutenant and the position of assistant chief of airplane and engine maintenance for the Air Service. He logged more than five hundred hours participating in and saving various record-setting flights from imminent mechanical disasters.

Les Arnold often recounted his first meeting with Smilin' Jack Harding. Les was ferrying a Martin twin engine bomber from Dayton, Ohio, to Washington, D.C. He had just sat down in the pilot's seat when Jack, in civilian clothes, came up from behind and tapped him on the shoulder. Jack asked if he could ride with him in the rear of the empty airplane. Les replied that this was an Army flight and did not take passengers. Harding explained he had recently joined the service and had an officer's permission. Nelson reluctantly agreed and told him to just sit quietly in back of the plane and not disturb him. While over the mountains of West Virginia, and with no safe place to land, the right engine started misfiring and lost power. The airplane was losing altitude. Without parachutes, a high-speed crash into the face of the mountain seemed inevitable.

At less than one hundred feet from destruction, the engine suddenly regained power and the descent slowed. Greatly relieved at this unexpected and timely deliverance, Arnold started easing the airplane back into the sky. Glancing at his right wing, Les couldn't believe what he saw. His "civilian" passenger had crawled out of the fuselage and onto the wing. Holding on with one hand against the one hundred-mile-an-hour windstorm and the turbulence of the propeller backwash, Harding had reached into the cowling and reconnected an ignition wire to bypass a short circuit in the electrical system.

Arnold made an emergency landing for repairs at a nearby Army flying field. Three mechanics were unable to fix the problem after four hours of work. Harding asked to try his hand. He fixed the problem in less than thirty minutes, and they continued on.

MONDAY, FEB. 18, 1924
10:00 A.M.
THE WHITE HOUSE, WASHINGTON D.C.

After six weeks of intensive training, the crew received two weeks leave to "put their affairs in order." They knew there was little chance all would return safely. Before traveling to California and reporting to the Douglas factory for additional training and the start of their flight, General Patrick wanted them to meet Secretary of War John Weeks and President Calvin Coolidge to receive encouragement and well wishes.

Patrick had made the arrangements weeks before, and carefully reconfirmed them before they arrived. Now he sat with Major Martin and his seven other crew members in the waiting room outside Secretary Weeks' office. As the time for their appointment came and went without acknowledgment, Patrick grew angry and increasingly embarrassed. After almost an hour had gone by, Secretary Weeks left his office and hurried through the waiting room, oblivious to the waiting airmen.

Patrick rose and hurried after Weeks, catching him as he was about to leave, and pointed at the eight waiting airmen now standing at attention in their dress uniforms. Weeks looked at the group and turned to Patrick. "Who are those men?"

Patrick patiently explained they were the crew of the world flight, and that his appointment had been confirmed several times. With his hand on the doorknob, poised to leave, Weeks turned to them, said, "I see. Good luck and good day, gentlemen," and he left his office.

Greatly disappointed at the war secretary's cavalier attitude, Patrick took them next to the office of President Coolidge, which was filled with visitors. He had painstakingly provided a complete written briefing on the personal life and military achievements of each man in the crew so Coolidge could personalize the meeting.

Patrick and Martin took the available seats while the others stood. The time for this appointment, too, came and went. Periodically, each of the other visiting groups would rise when called and enter the president's office. It was many hours later, after every other visitor had been seen, that they were escorted to the front lawn of the White House and made to pose as a group for a waiting photographer. After another thirty minutes had passed, Coolidge hurried over to the opening left for him in the center, smiled, and the photograph was taken. The president then hurried away. The only words spoken to the group by Coolidge were, "Hurry up, hurry up!"

Leigh Wade was the most charitable of their day at the White House, saying, "At least we got a smile out of him."

MONDAY, MARCH 3, 1924
7:50 A.M.
DOUGLAS AVIATION, SANTA MONICA, CALIFORNIA

Lowell Smith leaned low over the handlebars of his 1915 Indian TT motorcycle, weaving at high speed through the slow-moving traffic that increased as he approached Santa Monica. He had just passed an unsuspecting, plodding motorist, flashing by on a sharp curve, the bike leaned over, his knees just touching the road surface and his chin on the handlebars.

Lowell had been a carnival motorcyclist before learning to fly. Stunt riding was his specialty but with the years and the loss of many friends, his riding style had mellowed—at least a little—with the realization that immortality did not exist after all. Squinting through his flying goggles at more than eighty miles per hour, the adrenaline rush carried him to new heights far above the mere mortals confined in their four-wheeled boxes, oblivious to the dual pleasures of danger and speed. His white scarf trailed like a pennant in the breeze, giving a backhanded salute to surprised motorists and concealing his mirror, which displaying the angry fists shaking at him through the driver's open windows.

The trip from San Diego had been exhilarating. Smith's Tourist Trophy Road Racer could leave almost any automobile in its dust. The shortened stiff leaf springs in the front and rear fed back to him every nuance of the road's surface. Though almost nine years old, the highly desirable TT model was more than he could afford. His mother diligently mailed in the payments of twenty-five cents per week to the dealer, and Smith reimbursed her periodically from his meager army pay.

He slowed when the converted movie studio, the home of Douglas Aviation, came into view. He drove his machine through the entrance gate, where a few short years ago uniformed guards welcomed the famous idols of the screen and kept out the riffraff. The surrounding studio buildings still made movies but this one had failed, and Douglas leased the property at a very attractive price. A side benefit for Douglas employees were the scantily clad nubile beauties strolling through the narrow streets during the luncheon shooting breaks.

They looked gorgeous in their revealing costumes. Heavy make-up gave them dark eyes and sensuous red lips. Their sexy, mincing walks, high heels clicking on the concrete, radiated confidence that fame and fortune lay just around the corner. Always in groups, they giggled and basked in the ogling of the male Douglas engineers and production workers, ignoring the disapproving, reproachful expressions on the faces of Douglas's female workers.

Lowell dismounted the Indian and put it on its stand. He checked his watch, noting with satisfaction his timely arrival. He carefully wrapped his flying goggles and helmet in his scarf, then placed them in his saddlebags and walked toward the front door of Douglas Aviation.

The others had just finished their coffee and doughnuts. They were all there—Major Martin, Leigh Wade, Erik Nelson and the two alternate pilots, Les Arnold and LeClaire Shultz. The four mechanics, Harding, Turner, Wade, and Harvey, had already started their work in the assembly area.

They had two weeks to learn every nut, screw, and detail of construction of the Liberty V-12 Engines and the four World Cruisers that were nearing completion. They would have to service their own aircraft. There would be no one to ask, no one to consult, and often no one to help. No one who knew how to fix a recalcitrant engine, no one to rerig the wings, no one to repair a leaky radiator or stop the oil from issuing through expanding fissures. There would be no one to fix the certain damage of landing on turbulent seas, or stop the seawater from flooding into the pontoons. Their would be no one to change engines when they self destructed, no one to change from wheels to pontoons and back again. No one but themselves.

The flight schedule for the trip was simple: rise early, prepare the aircraft, takeoff at dawn, stop flying at dusk. Secure the aircraft. Complete repairs and maintenance during the night. If all went well, they might get some sleep before the cycle began again.

There is, arguably, no more exhausting and punishing flying than from the open cockpit of a heavy biplane. The windscreens do little to stop the cold one hundred-mile-an-hour arctic winds from spiraling off the cowling, wings, and propeller tips into the cockpit. After eight hours of muscling a large biplane through turbulence, most pilots are exhausted. Their faces are raw, painfully raked by the winds and burned by the sun. Their shoulder, arm, and leg muscles ache. Their hands are blistered and bleeding from the constant motion of the large wooden control wheel.

Although the pilots would want nothing more than sleep after hours of flying, their work would begin anew through most of the night—fixing, adjusting, cleaning, maintaining. No one knew better than the crew of the world flight the arduous challenges they faced.

By noon of that first day, they had almost filled one of the many blank notebooks each man carried. They were expected to spend their evenings in two-man teams, quizzing each other until they memorized all the details in the many pages of notes each day would bring. That was Major Martin's plan. Les Arnold came up with his own plan.

The crew had left for lunch together, their heads spinning from all the facts, figures, illustrations, and notes. Major Martin led the group two by two, chatting with Lowell Smith. Les Arnold walked with Leigh Wade, doing all the talking as usual. Suddenly he stopped. Wade looked up to see what miracle had caused that. A group of gorgeous dancers walked toward them in their usual brief costumes. Martin sneaked a furtive look and continued walking with Lowell, as did most of the others. Les Arnold, speechless at last, took Leigh Wade's arm and did a quick about-face to follow them.

Major Martin led the remaining crew back from lunch. A large car, its convertible top down, came alongside. Les Arnold drove with one arm on the wheel and the other around the long-legged lovely

sitting on his lap. Two other sequined beauties giggled and poked
playfully at his right side. Leigh Wade sat comfortably ensconced in
the middle of the rear seat, sandwiched tightly between four gorgeous
showgirls. They dangled their curvaceous legs enticingly over the
tops of the rear doors. Arnold stopped and turned to the remaining
crew, now incredulous, wide-eyed, and very interested. "Gentlemen,
I have arranged for each one of you to be assisted in your studies by
my new friends." They all laughed—except Major Martin.

Martin clearly saw that with these distractions nearby, keeping
the crew's attention focused solely on the flight was not going to be
easy. It turned out to be even more difficult than he thought. The
next few weeks flew by, with Martin fighting a losing battle each
evening to keep the crew studying and going to sleep early, alone,
and without distractions. Arnold always found some way to circumvent Martin's curfew and usually took several, only partially
reluctant, crew members with him.

As the word of the world flight spread, the crew was invited to
luncheons, dinners, and numerous parties. At an Optimists Club
luncheon, they received eight stuffed monkeys for luck. Martin and
Harvey named theirs "Jiggs" and "Maggie." Smith and Turner came
up with "Felix" and "Petie." Wade and Ogden took "Mutt" and
"Jeff", and Erik and Jack had "Dodo" and "Bozo." The fliers made
their own large lapel pins, which said simply, LET'S GO.

TUESDAY, MARCH 4, 1924
11:00 P.M.
TOKYO, JAPAN

Frustrated by three weeks of fruitless negotiations with the
Japanese, First Lieutenant Clifford C. Nutt sat exhausted at
the cherrywood desk in his room at the Imperial Hotel
designed by the American architect Frank Lloyd Wright. Again he
had to advise General Patrick that no progress had been made in
securing landing rights for the First World Flight.

Wright's hotel stood almost alone against the devastating earthquake that had leveled Tokyo on September 1, 1923. Despite
Japanese appreciation for the aid sent to them in their hour of need

by compassionate Americans, relations between the two countries remained tense and strained as each struggled to carve out their own sphere of influence in Asia. Increasingly Japan's growing economic and military strength challenged the established colonial interests of the Western powers.

Back home Hearst newspapers fomented anti-Japanese feelings, headlining dire warnings of "the yellow peril." America's Supreme Court upheld the legitimacy of an immigration policy enacted thirty years before that denied the Japanese U.S. citizenship and land and business ownership. Even more restrictive legislation directed against the Japanese lay before Congress. The military on both sides spoke ominously of the inevitability of war between the powers. Japanese newspapers commented continuously on the hatred shown towards them in the United States, the unwelcome intrusions of "the yankee white devils" upon their "noble birthright," and the growing opposition of America to their efforts to form and lead a "co-prosperity sphere" of Asian nations.

Since his arrival on February 6, Major General Yasumitsu, Commander of the Japanese Air Service, had treated Nutt contemptuously. Yasumitsu believed the true objective of the world flight of four military aircraft from Alaska was a thinly veiled attempt by the U.S. military to spy on them, evaluate their military bases, and establish an air route that could later be used for a aerial invasion of their country.

Further complicating matters, Japan's military had established close relations with Britain's Royal Air Force and were receiving increasing numbers of their latest fighter planes and bombers. Under licensing agreements and English technical support, the Japanese built their own aircraft factories and were manufacturing both engines and airframes. Top British pilots, on leave from the RAF and attracted by generous salaries, were actively training and instructing large numbers of Japanese student pilots in the techniques of aerial warfare. The British had already asked for and received the landing rights that were now being denied the Americans.

After long delays between brief and unproductive meetings, Lieutenant Nutt came to realize that, in the inscrutable Oriental hierarchy, sending a lowly lieutenant to negotiate with a general was considered demeaning and insulting. After taking tea and exchanging pleasantries, General Yasumitsu always excused himself with the pretext of "more urgent business." His fourteen army and navy subordinates, armed with the World Cruiser's specifications showing a 2,200 mile range, expressed Yasumitsu's belief that, "considering the advanced state of U.S. aircraft design, landing rights in Japan are unnecessary." All attempts to explain that this range was a theoretical maximum and applied only when on wheels and not on the required pontoons went unheeded. The flight seemed doomed.

Lieutenant Nutt now knew what failure felt like. His assignment had been crucial. Anticipating difficulty in Japan, the world flight committee had painstakingly gone over the route before he left. They had tried countless alternate routes. Each one eventually ended at some point past which the flight could not continue. They might be successful in bypassing Russian territory, but without Japan, the flight must be aborted. Without Japan, U.S. aviation would have no victory, no glory, no salvation.

It was after midnight when Nutt reluctantly wrote out the telegram:

```
TO: CHIEF U.S. ARMY AIR SERVICE GENERAL MASON
PATRICK WASHINGTON DC USA STOP REGRET TO INFORM U
JAPAN WILL NOT REPEAT NOT GRANT WORLD FLIGHT LAND-
ING RIGHTS DESPITE MY BEST EFFORTS STOP NUTT
```

Nutt lay on a low, short bed under heavy covers, insulating himself from the wet cold of Tokyo in February. He couldn't sleep and stared at the wooden ceiling barely visible over his head. He turned over in his mind each of the five meetings he'd had with Yasumitsu over the past three weeks. Was there anything he could have said? Some argument he missed that would have changed their minds?

No, he concluded. Once Yasumitsu left, he was finished. It didn't matter what brilliance emerged after that: the remaining subordinates were not empowered to overrule him or make any decision on their own. In Japan, only the general, the top man, made the decision, and he had closed the door to any further discussion. Nutt recalled all the years of planning, the pilots, the mechanics, the naval crews, the thousands of eager young men depending upon him. He had let them all down.

As the dawn came up, Nutt, still sleepless, arose and stepped into the shower. That was where it hit him. General Billy Mitchell was the solution. Yasumitsu respected Mitchell more than any other American. As a fellow aviator and warrior, Yasumitsu felt a deep kinship with Mitchell. They were professional soldiers and someday they knew they must fight. Of that, there was no question. Until then, each would act in his country's best interests, and each did just that—with neither animosity nor hatred.

It was Mitchell's writings warning of the capability, discipline, and effectiveness of the underrated Japanese military that had given them worldwide respect, for the first time, in the eyes of many world leaders. Mitchell liked them, respected them, and feared them— exactly as they did him. Mitchell invited them to the ship-bombing demonstrations. They had studied all of Mitchell's reports, books and articles. They owed him. If anyone could make them bend, it was Mitchell. Only Mitchell could get Yasumitsu back to the negotiating table. And Mitchell was already in Asia—in the Philippines. If Mitchell could come to Japan, he might be able to get landing rights. Nutt knew that, banned from the world flight or not, only Mitchell could now save it.

Too excited to dry himself and still dripping, he walked to the desk and added a line to his telegram before instructing room service to send it immediately:

```
URGENT U SEND GENERAL MITCHELL TO ASSIST IN
NEGOTIATIONS
```

General Patrick blanched upon receiving Lieutenant Nutt's telegram. He knew the strong role rank and personalities played in negotiations. He readily visualized the insurmountable obstacles facing the junior officer and concurred with his conclusion. No Mitchell, no flight. He went to seek General Pershing's advice.

SUNDAY, MARCH 9, 1924
9:30 P.M.
ARMY SUPPLY DEPOT FAIRFIELD, OHIO

irst Lieutenant Elmer Adler sat down on one of the many packing boxes lying in disarray on the concrete floor of the huge warehouse, each neatly stenciled, TOP PRIORITY—DO

NOT DELAY—WORLD FLIGHT. He'd been working since six A.M.
with three different supply sergeants and their recruits. It was almost
midnight. He hadn't sat down all day. He was exhausted, and started
home to get some sleep.

The train arrived at three A.M. that morning from Douglas
Aviation in California. The sergeant's raucous voice at the other end
of the jingling telephone that woke him sounded excited. His forty
men would have it all unloaded by dawn, and could the lieutenant
report at that time? "Sure," he grumbled. He set the alarm for five
A.M. and went back to sleep.

Washing the sleep from his face, Lieutenant Adler shaved, pulled
on his uniform pants and jacket, and walked the nine blocks to the
depot. The cold of the predawn air chased away the lingering effects
of too little sleep. His pace quickened when he came under the stark
bright lights of the depot. The silent figures of the recruits struggled
as they unloaded their precious cargo from the sidelined boxcars.

When he'd volunteered as supply officer for the World Flight
Committee he'd had no appreciation of the work it entailed. During
the past three months, he had little rest. Nights and weekends blended
indistinguishably with weekdays. His wife complained that his children
missed him, but the cause was noble and the mission essential.

He knew all of the pilots. They were good, damn good! If they
made it, the horn of plenty would be opened to the Air Service. A
bright future beckoned. His present sacrifices seemed well worth the
potential future benefits.

Entering the depot, the sheer number of carefully packed boxes
and crates covering the huge floor were impressive. By dawn, the
men had already neatly separated massive crates containing sixty-
four propellers, forty-two sets of landing gears, thirty-six radiators,
twenty-four spare engines, fourteen sets of pontoons, and thousands
of other vital spare parts to rebuild wings, ailerons, rudders, fuselages, instruments, struts, flying wires, and the tools and instructions
to accomplish each repair.

On the floor lay twenty-four identical large crates built by the
depot's repair shops. They were made of spruce, plywood, and ash,
the same material from which the World Cruisers were constructed.
Even the wood of the boxes could be used as repair material. For the
past sixteen hours, Lieutenant Adler had been receiving and repack-

ing each one of 480 separate parts into the large crates. Each part was in exactly the same location in each crate. Each crewman had a parts-locating list so that, even in total darkness, they could easily locate the exact part they needed.

The supply sergeants and recruits, usually dour and resentful of working on Sundays, were eager and enthusiastic. They were grateful for the small role they were playing in this momentous adventure. In a few hours, the job would be done. The crates would then be loaded on railroad cars for shipment to the Navy. Waiting destroyers would speed them to strategic locations, hoping they would be within reach when needed by the flight.

WEDNESDAY, MARCH 12
9:00 A.M.
ASSOCIATED PRESS, SAN FRANCISCO, CALIFORNIA

In a few minutes, Linton Wells, thirty-two-year-old hotshot reporter for the Associated Press, would be going in to see the chief, his boss, the man who called the shots. Wells loved aviation and airplanes. It had started five years ago, in 1919, when he interviewed Lowell Smith after he flew the first transcontinental air race. Smith didn't talk very much. Getting a narrative from him was like pulling teeth. He wanted to know what Smith felt during the race, what he saw, what he heard. All he got were grunts and monosyllables. Frustrated, he asked Lowell if he would show him what he experienced in his airplane. Lowell nodded and motioned for him to get in the backseat. They taxied out for takeoff. The strange noises of the engine and wind from the propeller frightened Wells. He tried to signal Smith to stop. It was too late. The ground stopped rushing by. The airplane lifted magically into the air. His terror subsided. The alien noises of the engine and the roar of the wind suddenly disappeared. Flight was majestic. They were a feather floating high above the plebeian life on the earth below. They were dancing through the clouds among unseen angels. Wells felt more alive than he had ever felt before. He wished the flight would never end.

Linton never really knew how long they were up. Sometimes it seemed like a moment, sometimes an eternity. From then on he was hooked. He started reading everything he could on aviation. He wanted, more than anything else, to be an aviator.

He applied to the Army Air Corps, but his eyesight wasn't good enough and they said he was too old. A reporter's salary couldn't begin to cover flying lessons. He settled for writing about others' aviation exploits. Soon he was spending all his spare hours hanging around the local airports. Occasionally he'd catch a ride from a sympathetic pilot. It was only the lucky ones who got to drive their magnificent magical machines through the sky.

Before he even walked in through the door, Linton knew the chief would not be sympathetic. He had already said Wells was spending too much time covering aviation and not enough on the bread-and-butter stories most readers wanted. But this was the first flight around the world. Their would never be another first world flight, ever. He was going to beg if necessary, insist, threaten to quit, whatever it took, but he knew he had to, was born—no, destined— to cover this flight. They were leaving in a few days. He couldn't delay any longer.

He stopped first to prepare the chief's morning coffee just the way he liked it. A little groveling subservience never hurt. At 9:03 that morning, Linton Wells summoned up all his courage. *Into the lion's den*, he thought. He knocked on the translucent ground glass of the chief's office, prepared to resign if the answer was no.

MONDAY, MARCH 17
7:00 A.M.
CLOVER FIELD, SANTA MONICA, CALIFORNIA

Major Martin paced back and forth for the second day. Their scheduled departure the day before had to be scrubbed due to bad weather. now the first leg's scheduled takeoff time to Seattle, Washington, had come and gone with zero visibility and zero ceiling. They could not start their flight until the weather improved.

Three of the four World Cruisers were ready to go. The fourth, completed only the previous day, had to be flown first to Rockwell Field in San Diego to have its two compasses calibrated. Each aircraft carried a magnetic compass and a newly developed earth inductor compass.

Magnetic compasses have changed little to the present day. A magnetized needle simply points to the magnetic North Pole. The aviation compass is filled with alcohol to dampen the movement of an otherwise wildly dancing needle. The magnetic compass has annoying errors when used in any aircraft. When the aircraft accelerates, the needle turns more northerly than it should, and when deceleration occurs, it points more southerly. Despite the dampening effect of the alcohol, the slightest ripple or turn, rise or fall, will cause the needle to give a false indication. When flying close to the North Pole, as the World Flight would, its readings are almost useless.

The Earth inductor compass worked on the principle of the generator. That is, an electrical wire cutting across the earth's magnetic field would generate electricity. By measuring the amount of electricity produced with a sensitive meter, it would be possible to determine the direction of travel. This was expected to be more accurate. It was the earth inductor compass that would guide Charles Lindbergh in his solo flight to Paris three years later. Nelson and Harding had to fly to San Diego for compass calibration and catch up with the rest of the flight departing to Seattle later on. But for now, no one was going anywhere.

Martin had other reasons to be apprehensive. Captain Snow had contacted him a few days ago. Requests for overflight and landing permits were not going smoothly. The fact that this was a military flight was complicating the situation enormously. China, with few aircraft of her own and fearful of aerial spying or activities that would foment revolution, would not allow any foreign military flight over its territory. Turkey, still resenting its war losses, refused permission on the basis of not being able to guarantee the safety of any military flight. Without landing rights in Turkey, the flight would have to fly thousands of miles out of the way over dangerous mountains in Greece and Italy. India insisted on a major change of route that would again lengthen the trip and take it far from any hope of assistance.

When the Russian revolutionary government came into power in 1917 and refused to pay the previous government's war debts, the United States withheld recognition. Lacking U.S. recognition, Russia's denial of landing rights was virtually certain. Relations with Japan had deteriorated. The Japanese offered permission only with restrictions that the flight could not possibly meet.

The flight might be able to bypass the Russian-held Komandorski Islands, but landing areas in Japan and its northern islands were essential. The heavy pontoons reduced speed, fuel, and range, making a detour around Japan impossible.

Meanwhile, the European countries stood poised to begin their own flights. Traveling eastbound and using the prevailing tailwinds, most would make faster progress and have a better chance of surviving the worst weather seasons.

Major Stuart MacLaren, the leading British aviator, had just completed testing two of the newest and most highly advanced Vickers Vulture amphibians, built specifically for his world flight. MacLaren had been preparing for this flight for years. Colonel L. E. Broome, heading MacLaren's support team, cached supplies, spare engines, parts, food, and fuel at strategic locations along his flight path. The second Vickers Vulture was crated and shipped to Japan that very week. It would provide a complete, fresh aircraft for MacLaren's use when he arrived. MacLaren scheduled his flight to begin on March 25, only eight days after the U.S. departure from Santa Monica. He challenged General Patrick to make the de facto "race around the world" official. Patrick discreetly declined.

Captain D'Oisy was finishing up his preparations for the French effort and would be starting his flight shortly. Captain Pedro Zanni was preparing Argentina's entry, also using a new Fokker design. Commander Sacadura Cabral, Portugal's leading and highly experienced pilot, had just received a new Fokker aircraft specially built for the world flight using an advanced Rolls-Royce engine. Portugal's team of Majors Brito Pias and Sarmiento Bores stood ready to depart. Benito Mussolini had declared the flight an Italian national goal, and several highly advanced, enclosed twin engine monoplane flying boats were nearing completion under the command of Lieutenant Locatelli.

The Douglas World Cruiser, heavy, boxy, and with high aerodynamic drag, had a cruising speed of ninety miles per hour. Average westbound headwinds would reduce ground speed to seventy or eighty miles per hour for the Americans. The sleeker European entries, lighter, more modern, and with lower drag, had 110- to 130-miles-per-hour cruising speeds. With average eastbound tailwinds added, they could be expected to have ground speeds that were twice as fast as the American entries. It's easy to see why General Patrick declined to call it a race.

By 9:30 that morning of March 17, the sun had burned off most of the fog. The crew, anxiously waiting in their cockpits, started their engines and taxied into position. Within a few minutes, amid rousing cheers from the hundreds of spectators waiting for their departure, Major Martin opened his throttle. The full 420 horses residing in the Liberty V-12 engine came to full gallop. The huge biplane roared down the grass runway. The wings strained and then lifted World Cruiser Number One into the sky. Lowell Smith and Leigh Wade's Cruisers, numbered Two and Three, followed closely.

A fleet of ten escort planes took off just behind them and joined, in loose formation, on the flight to Seattle. In one of the escorts, happily snapping pictures of the flight, was Linton Wells, who was given two of the four months he had asked for to cover the flight for the Associated Press.

Official race or not, every member of the American crew knew the glory would come to only the first to finish. They had the slowest entry. They had to work harder, service the aircraft faster, push through bad weather that might stop the other entries, pray a lot, and hope for incredible luck. There was no other way to win.

Despite General Patrick's reluctance to acknowledge the obvious, everyone knew the race was on. After all those years, and tens of thousands of man hours of planning, the United States had finally begun the race to make the first world flight—on March 17, that St. Patrick's Day in 1924.

Lt. Mitchell at 18 years old (4th from left) was the youngest officer in the Army. He pleaded to be sent into battle and distinguished himself with his bravery and resourcefulness.

During two years of enforced exile spent spying on the Japanese as a "naturalist," Captain Mitchell (seated 2nd from right) visited the Chinese War Lord Chang Tso Lin in Manchuria to warn him of China's future war with Japan. At 32 his insightful reports earned him a position as the youngest member ever on the Army General Staff.

For his outspoken defiance of military policy and publication of "Our Faulty Military Policy," Major Mitchell was again exiled, arriving in France a few weeks before the U.S. entered the World War. Seen here in the French trenches, he became the first American soldier to come under fire. His heroism earned him France's Croix de Guerre, the youngest recipient since Napoleon, as well as numerous other medals. He returned the most decorated hero of the war.

Generals Mitchell and Pershing waiting to welcome the fliers back from Alaska in 1920. Pershing opposed Mitchell's goal of a strong and independent Air Force.

Lieutenant St. Clair Streett who led Billy Mitchell's record setting first flight from New York to Nome, Alaska in 1919, during which Erik Nelson served as Engineering Officer bringing all aircraft safely back. Mitchell had made plans for the flight to continue around the world but was thwarted by the U.S. State Department demanding they proceed no further fearing confrontation from Japan and Russia.

Right: To prove that airplanes could sink ships, Mitchell secretly requisitioned Navy torpedo tubes to the Army's Frankford Arsenal where he created the world's largest bombs weighing up to 4,000 pounds as seen here.

Below: Mitchell supervising Leigh Wade, Erik Nelson, Les Arnold, and his other pilots in his DH-4, the "Osprey," during the bombing tests of 1921. His personal insignia and pennant identify him as flight commander. Defying Army regulations, his sister Harriet often flew with him in the rear cockpit.

The "unsinkable" German battleship *Ostfriesland* taking a direct hit from one of Mitchell's planes. The real damage was done by the water hammer effect of the near miss at lower left which buckled her thick hull plates under the waterline. She sunk minutes later to the astonishment of the Navy observers. Although the U.S. Navy belittled these tests, Germany, Japan, and England believed air power had made surface ships vulnerable and ineffective—if not obsolete.

The wreckage of the *U.S.S. Virginia* after Mitchell's second round of bombing tests in 1923. The Navy again belittled the test results claiming a warship's speed and gunfire would protect them from attack by aircraft.

Mitchell sitting in the back of the Cadillac loaned to him during the Detroit Air races of 1922 with Orville Wright and Admiral W.F. Fullam. They shared his views of the importance of air power. Mitchell delighted in driving this car 90 mph; ordering his terrified chauffeur, cowering in back, to warn him of any police giving chase.

With growing opposition to Mitchell from the President, the War Department, and the Navy, he was ordered into exile as far away as possible, ostensibly for an evaluation of U.S. Pacific Region defenses. In Pearl Harbor on Nov. 11, 1923 Mitchell reviewed flight operations (center left) with the Army's Commander, General Summerall. Battleship row is on the upper left. Mitchell returned with a scathing report calling defenses totally inadequate and predicting an air attack on Pearl Harbor by Japanese planes launched from aircraft carriers at 7:30 A.M. on a Sunday morning. His thousand page report was uncannily accurate in both the time and methods used but languished unread on the "Flying Trash Pile," . . . until December 7, 1941.

Betty and Billy Mitchell in Bangkok with officers of the Siamese Air Force during his tour to the Pacific in 1924. Following Mitchell's advice they had developed into an effective air power. The King of Siam was a great admirer of Mitchell and took them both on a tiger hunt during this trip.

National Archives

Mitchell preparing to depart in his Thomas Morse MB-3 pursuit ship. He was one of the few pilots who enjoyed flying this fast, maneuverable, but highly unstable airplane. Despite its reputation as a difficult airplane to fly, Mitchell set a new world speed record in the Morse and called it, " . . . the best all around fighting single seater in the world," before ordering it into production for the Army against the advice of many other experienced pilots.

The World Flight Committee and its Advance Officers (AO) In the center is Lt. Robert J.Brown, Jr.—Chairman. Clockwise from 12 o'clock at the top; Lt. H.A. Halverson, AO—Southern Asia, Lt. Clayton Bissell, AO—Alaska and Greenland, Lt. LeClaire D. Schultze, AO—Greenland, Capt. Lorenzo L. Snow, Foreign Relations Capt. William Volandt, Finance, Lt. Clifford C. Nutt, AO—Japan Lt. M.S. Lawton, AO—China, Lt. Clarence E. Crumrine, AO - Iceland

Major Frederick Martin (left), 42, ill fated Commander of the World Flight and pilot of the *Seattle*. The oldest and only married crew member and father of a six year old child. A Mechanical Engineering graduate of Purdue University he learned to fly in 1921 and had accumulated 700 flight hours as Chief of the Air Service Technical School at Chanute Field in Illinois when chosen for the flight. He was a distinguished, articulate and highly diplomatic man. Leading the flight, he crashed into a mountain in Alaska during a blizzard. Helped by Harvey, he survived an ordeal of 10 days hiking through waist deep snow with little food.

Museum of Flying, Santa Monica

Sergeant Alva Harvey (right), 23, mechanician of *Seattle*. He maintained Martin's airplane at Chanute Field before being chosen. Raised on a farm in Texas, he was fearless, skilled, sturdy, and strong. His strength and perseverance saved both their lives after the crash when the older Martin weakened.

Lt. Lowell Smith, 32. Born in Santa Barbara, California. pilot and mechanician of the *Chicago* and later, Commander of the World Flight after Martin crashed. Smith's early mechanical aptitude pleased his father, a preacher, mechanical and electrical engineer. A shy, quiet, sensitive idealist, at the age of 20 Smith joined Pancho Villa in Mexico, maintaining his battered fleet of 3 decrepit biplanes and flying reconnaissance flights with several other U.S. pilots. General Pershing hunted Villa unsuccessfully for over 12 months. When America entered the War in 1917 Smith joined the U.S. Air Service and became a flight instructor at Kelly Field before being transferred to Europe.

After the war he commanded the 91st Air Squadron in aerial fire patrols throughout California, Oregon, and Washington. He always led his pilots safely home, often through thick fog, heavy rain, and blinding blizzards. His uncanny navigational abilities were said to be inherited from his famous ancestor, Daniel Boone. During the Great Transcontinental Air Race of 1919 he won more medals than any of the other 70 pilots. With deep budget cuts, he stepped down from his rank as Captain in 1921 to remain a Lieutenant in the U.S. Air Service. He was a veteran with over 2,000 hours of flight experience when selected.

Left: Lieutenant Les Arnold, 29, born in New Haven, Connecticut. Mischievous, extroverted, strong and athletic, he was the class clown, an actor in summer stock, and a champion street fighter. Most ladies found his frequent flirtations and friendly demeanor to be charming and irresistible. He enlisted in the Air Service shortly after the U.S. declared war on Germany. He mastered stunt flying quickly and soon outflew his instructors. Often AWOL and a general nuisance they quickly sent him to France to show other less skilled pilots the aerobatic tricks required in combat flying.

Surviving the war and numerous illicit liaisons with the attractive indigenous females, Arnold returned home flying aerobatics in air shows, circuses and exhibitions while recruiting for the Air Service. Although he had little mechanical aptitude, Mitchell recognized his extraordinary flying abilities and selected him for bomber training. Arnold, along with Leigh Wade and Erik Nelson, participated in Mitchell's bombing demonstrations, sinking ships with pinpoint bombing accuracy far out at sea.

Right: Lieutenant Smith and Lieutenant Arnold.

Left: Lieutenant Arnold and Lieutenant Smith

Below: Lowell Smith developed the equipment and technique required for aerial refueling. On June 27, 1923, Smith and John Richter made the first successful aerial refueling. The following month, they stayed aloft for over 37 hours flying 3,297 miles non-stop and establishing 16 new world records for distance, speed, endurance and range. Using aerial refueling, they made the first non-stop flight from Canada to Mexico, flying 1,280 miles in 12 hours. General Pershing, unimpressed, believed the technique had no future practical military application.

Lieutenant Erik Nelson, 36, pilot of the *New Orleans.* Born in Sweden, he sailed twice around the world before coming to the U.S. in 1909 at age 21. Highly experienced as a young seaman, he captained large racing sailboats and luxurious motor yachts for wealthy Americans and spent 1911 at the Indian Harbor Yacht Club in Greenwich, CT before becoming a swimming instructor in New York City. He became a U.S. citizen in 1914 and traveled to Florida with his cousin to start an automobile and aircraft repair shop which was not successful. After several rejections, he enlisted in the U.S. Air Service upon its entry in the Great War. He was quickly recognized as a brilliant engineer, mechanic, and pilot, and became a bomber flight instructor. As engineering officer on the first successful flight to Alaska in 1919, he had been prepared to continue that flight around the world before it was recalled by the U.S. State Department. Nelson was analytical and logical, with an intuitive practical understanding of the aeronautical requirements of long distance flights.

Lieutenant John Harding, Jr. 28 years old, mechanician of the *New Orleans.* He was shy with women but otherwise eager for adventure and unafraid of danger. His perpetual good humor and easy manner in the face of extreme adversity earned him the nickname of "Smilin' Jack." Harding was the son of an inventor and engineer from a formerly aristocratic and wealthy Virginia family that founded and owned the famous Belle Mead plantation of Nashville, Tennessee. As a child, he spent his entire allowance on copper wires and batteries for his inventive projects and was often disciplined for dismantling and "improving" his family's clocks, sewing machines, tractors, and automobiles. He graduated from Vanderbilt University as a mechanical engineer and worked for the Chalmers and Dodge Motor companies before enlisting as a Private in the Air Service. After completing Aviation Mechanics school, Lt. "Tiny" Harmon selected him as mechanician to keep the engines going on his Martin bomber during its first circumnavigation by air around the perimeter of the U.S. Harding amazed pilots by crawling out on the wings of bombers in flight and lifting the cowling to make engine adjustments and avoid emergency landings. He used this technique during his first flight with Les Arnold when his engine faltered in flight over hostile mountains. His bravery and competence during 500 flight hours quickly earned him his officer's rank.

Lieutenant Erik Nelson (right) and Lieutenant John Harding (left) in front of World Cruiser four, *New Orleans*.

Lieutenant Leigh Wade, 27 years old, pilot of the *Boston,* was born in Cassopolis, Michigan of a family that had come over on the *Mayflower.* As a very bright child, school bored him and he was a poor student excelling only in mathematics, which he found fascinating. Craving adventure, he left home at an early age and joined the National Guard to hunt down Pancho Villa (and Lowell Smith) with General Pershing. Fascinated by Pershing's airplanes, Wade transferred to the Air Service and was sent to the Royal Air Force in Toronto for flight training and then to France where he flew the nimble but somewhat fragile Nieuport fighter planes. He and Les Arnold were recognized as the most skillful and proficient at flying complex aerial combat maneuvers which they passed on to their fellow pilots.

Eventually Wade was given command of the 120th Aero Squadron where he tested and flew every aircraft used by both sides during the war. Upon his return home he became an experimental test pilot. He set a new altitude record of 27,120 feet, suffering severe frostbite in the process. Using his highly developed flying skills, he survived numerous engine and airframe failures. Wade was compulsively neat, orderly, and extremely fastidious earning him the approbation of "The Sheik of Cassopolis" by his fellow crew members.

Sergeant Henry Ogden, 24, mechanician of the *Boston,* grew up on one of the four cotton plantations owned by his father between Natchez and Baton Rouge, Louisiana. Extremely shy and modest but adventuresome and courageous, he was very similar in temperament to Jack Harding who had come from a similar background. Ogden's mechanical aptitude surfaced early when, as a youngster, he repaired his father's farming machinery and equipment. Ogden attended business college in New Orleans but soon left to join the Air Service in 1919. During the six weeks of studying aircraft engines at the repair depot in Montgomery, Alabama, he resurrected many dead engines that no others could bring back to life, earning him the nickname "Houdini," after the legendary magician. Within five months he was promoted to the rank of Sergeant. In his off duty hours he enjoyed wing-walking and jumping from plane to plane in flight. Smith and Nelson chose him after testing as one of the most knowledgeable and skilled mechanicians in the Air Service.

Donald Wills Douglas, born April 6, 1892, designed and manufactured the Douglas World Cruisers. After attending the Naval Academy he registered as the first student of Aeronautics at the Massachusetts Institute of Technology. He graduated in 1914 and went to work designing aircraft for the Glenn L. Martin Company. In 1920 he started his own aircraft company with $600 of borrowed money in back of a barber shop. As a new and unknown company, Douglas believed he had to do something spectacular to establish credibility. Knowing that Mitchell planned an Army non-stop flight across the United States, Douglas designed the *Cloudster*, a rugged biplane carrying huge fuel reserves powered by a 400 H.P. Liberty engine. Mitchell rejected the fledgling Douglas Aircraft proposal preferring to use Fokker, a proven manufacturer with many years of experience and a long history of building outstanding airplanes for Germany during the war. With the Army's rejection and no civilian market, Douglas Aviation turned to the Navy for survival. The *Cloudster* was modified into the DT-1 for use with torpedoes, and eventually into the DT-2 with pontoons—which became very popular as a float plane. With Navy contracts in hand for 80 aircraft, Douglas relocated to an abandoned movie studio in Santa Monica in 1921. Fokker's transcontinental prototype, the T-2 proved barely up to the task and it wasn't until 1923 that the flight was finally completed after several failed attempts. Disappointed with Fokker for designing world flight airplanes for competing countries, Mitchell sent Erik Nelson back to Douglas in 1923 to modify the original *Cloudster* for his world flight attempt. Risking the wrath of the Navy and the loss of all his contracts Douglas agreed to work with Erik Nelson to design and build the World Cruisers for the Army, knowing that the survival of his company would depend upon its success.

Major Martin (officer on left), Inventor Douglas (center in dark suit) and members of the World flight. Douglas is seen holding his hat, with his mother on the right, flanked by the flight crew.

Linton Wells, 32, the intrepid adventurer, aviation enthusiast, and reporter for the Associated Press, who followed and reported on the flight for 15,000 miles. He lost his job when he refused to return home, climbing instead into a World Cruiser's cockpit in Calcutta to share the adventure of flying across India and the Middle East. With Leigh Wade, Wells made the first non-stop record-breaking automobile trip across the United States and then set his own world record time for a trip around the world.

The insignia of the World Flight, designed by a local artist selected by Donald Douglas and emblematic of its peaceful intent, being painted on the *New Orleans*. All references to "Army" sponsorship were omitted to ease its passage through sensitive political areas.

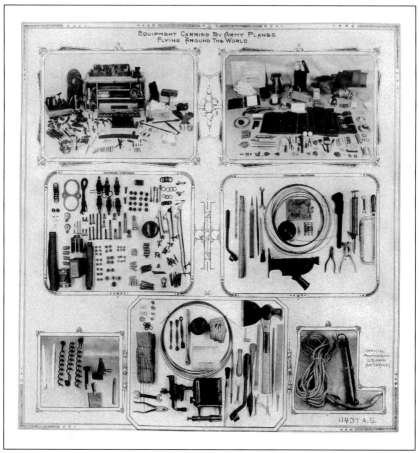

Equipment carried by the World Cruisers. Tests of the World Cruisers on floats proved to be disappointing. They could not lift from the water the original weight intended to be carried without sacrificing precious fuel. After testing, virtually all survival gear had to be left behind—including radios, parachutes, life rafts, life jackets, blankets, extra boots, survival rifles, ammunition, and even changes of clothing and underwear. The photo shows the tools, spare parts, tie downs, and 60 pound anchor which were finally taken aboard. Naval ships stores and cached supplies included additional tools, spare parts, wings, floats, wheels and tires, engines, propellers, fuel and oil The logistical problems of supplying the cruisers as they flew around the world were daunting but extremely well coordinated even in the most remote locations.

The first Douglas World Cruiser is towed, with its wings folded, through the streets of Santa Monica to Clover Field for testing. High rental rates at the airfield made such towing necessary each time an airplane was completed by Douglas.

The World Cruiser stretches her wings for the first time in preparation for its first flight as photographers record the momentous event.

The crew in front of the *Seattle* as it nears completion at the Douglas Aircraft factory in Santa Monica. The crew spent weeks at the factory studying the construction of their cruisers. Left to right: Sgts. Turner, Harvey, Ogden, Lts. Harding, Wade, Smith, and Arnold. The black arm band commemorates the death of former President Woodrow Wilson, who died the week before.

Left to right: Sgts. Harvey, Ogden, Turner, Lt. Schultze (alternate pilot), General Patrick, Chief of Air Service, aide, President Calvin Coolidge, Major Martin, Lts. Smith, Arnold, Nelson, and Wade. Patrick brought the crew to the White House to receive the best wishes of the President. Despite an appointment confirmed weeks in advance, Coolidge made them wait many hours until all other visitors had been seen before rushing through this 10 second "photo-op". His only words to Patrick were, "Who are these men?" The crew was deeply disappointed at Coolidge's lack of even the pretense of wishing them well. Wade was the most charitable saying, "At least he gave us a smile." Their reception indicated the low esteem in which Coolidge held U.S. aviation and contrasted sharply with the warm hospitality, receptions, honors and gifts showered on them by foreign heads of state.

March 16, 1923. Three completed World Cruisers waiting to depart Clover Field for Seattle. With the lure of a large Army air show and heavy advertising that day, 100,000 spectators had come to watch the departure of the World Flight. Heavy fog delayed the flight's departure until the following day when the crowds had thinned considerably.

March 17, 1923, St. Patrick's Day. Actual departure of the three completed world cruisers to Seattle from Clover Field with far fewer spectators. The *New Orleans* was late in its completion requiring Erik Nelson to fly it south to San Diego to adjust its compass before joining the flight. He flew longer legs on the flight to Seattle and arrived within 45 minutes of the other planes.

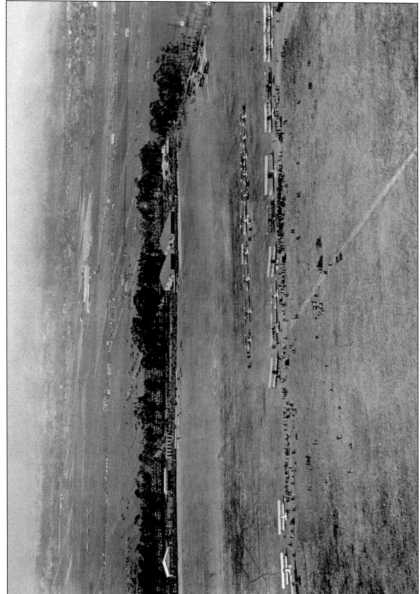

Museum of Flying, Santa Monica

Left to Right: Turner, Ogden, Arnold, Wade, Smith, Martin, and Harvey in their flight suits ready to depart Clover Field towards Seattle. Due to the late completion of the *New Orleans*, Nelson and Harding were in San Diego calibrating their compass at the time of this picture. Turner's poor health required Smith to replace him with Arnold.

Konrach F. Schreier, Jr., County Mesuem of Natural History Photo

March 17, 1923. The three World Cruisers taxi for takeoff from Clover Field as their journey around the world starts.

Lowell Smith (right) and Major Martin (left) watch with Air Service Captain Car Connell as Connell's wife christens the *Chicago* with the waters of Lake Michigan. With prohibition in effect, the local waters of Lake Washington were used in the *Seattle's* christening. The *New Orleans* used the waters of the Mississippi and the *Boston's* came from the Atlantic Ocean in Boston harbor.

The *Seattle* being placed into the waters of Lake Washington by crane after its wheels were removed and pontoons installed. Sgt Harvey stands over the engine to release the crane's cable while Major Martin, on the float, prepares to secure a line to the dock. The heavy cruisers had great difficulty taking off from the water forcing them to jettison additional survival equipment.

The *New Orleans* flying over the lighthouse, harbor, and docks of Puget Sound.

The *Seattle* on route to Prince Rupert, British Columbia. The chop on the water foretold the weather that the flight would meet on route—the worst in ten years—and caused heavy damage to the *Seattle* on landing.

Lt. Clayton Bissell beaching supplies in Alaska for the arrival, weeks later, of the World Flight. The supply officers braved some of the harshest conditions and played a crucial role in the flight's success.

Naval crewmen assist in tying down the *New Orleans* on Resurrection Bay at Seward, Alaska. The engine cowling has been removed to service the engine.

Museum of Flying, Santa Monica

Martin and Harvey monitoring the ice around the stricken *Seattle* at Kanatak where it was towed by the destroyer *U.S. Hull* after losing its engine. The drifting ice floes easily damaged the fragile thin wooden floats of the Cruisers and were a constant problem for the crews through the Arctic regions.

Museum of Flying, Santa Monica

The *Boston* flies over the freighter *S.S. Broodkale* delivering coal to Dutch Harbor.

Will E. Hudson, Pathe News

A Cruiser being assisted in mooring by the Navy at Dutch Harbor, Alaska.

As protection from the "Willie-was," strong winds of up to 100 mph that arose suddenly with no warning from different directions, the Cruisers were pulled up on runways and lashed down on the shores of Dutch Harbor.

Museum of Flying, Santa Monica

The *Boston* being lifted from the water and onto the dock, for engine replacement, at Dutch Harbor by the heavy crane on the freighter *Broodkale.*

The *Chicago* taxis out for takeoff from Dutch Harbor to Chicagoff on Attu Island. Les Arnold stands on the wing watching for ice that could damage the floats.

Martin and Harvey after surviving 10 days in the bitter arctic cold and snow.

Linton Wells, in the black hat, waiting as he did for five weeks for the flight's arrival at Paramushiru. American and Japanese destroyer crews helped each other endure violent gales, freezing cold, thick pack ice, and depleted supplies on Japan's bleak and hostile Northern Kurile Islands. With the flight bogged down in the Aleutians, the sailors learned each other's languages, games, and customs.

The flight finally completed the first aerial crossing to Japan on May 17, 1924. Here we see the *Chicago* being moored by American and Japanese crews at Lake Kasumigaura near Tokyo.

A Japanese Imperial Naval Officer reviews the World Flight's air route with Erik Nelson while a standing interpreter struggles to find just the right word in his dictionary. The Japanese were extremely hospitable, warm, and gracious to the crew—despite the passage of the Japanese Exclusion Act by Congress and President Coolidge—upon their arrival.

The *Boston* flies low over the Yangtze River, with the *New Orleans* not far behind, as they searched for a clear landing area near Shanghai, their entry into China. The *Chicago,* delayed in Japan, arrived the next day.

The Cruisers in Shanghai's harbor surrounded by junks and sampans, their owners curious to get a better view of the strange visitors. Dense water traffic and the high likelihood of collision proved to be a major problem for the flight.

The *Chicago* flying over Indochina (now Vietnam). Lowell Smith's engine failed shortly after this picture was taken.

After a harrowing flight, British airmen help push the oil covered *New Orleans* into a hangar at Karachi where the engine problem can be repaired.

The "New Orleans" is rolled out of the hangar after repair at the Ambala Airfield. England relied heavily upon its air forces to maintain control over its colonies and budgets for the Royal Air Force were far higher than in the U.S.

Their bravery challenged at Ambala, the crew took their first ride on a camel. Of all their aerial adventures in peace and war, they found the camel rides to be the most terrifying.

Sacrificing many nights of sleep, the crew accelerated their schedule to arrive in Paris on the French national holiday of Bastille Day. In the streets, millions of Parisians cheered the flight as it flew over the Eiffel Tower and Arch of Triumph flanked by escorting French military aircraft. They were met by huge crowds on landing at LeBourget airport, as Lindbergh would be three years later.

Lt. Ogden waved the French flag to the tumultuous cheers of the huge crowd.

Wade rubs his hands with glee on hearing from Nelson that the French planned an evening for them at the Follies Bergere. Despite the lovely ladies, all of the Americans fell sound asleep. The next day's French newspapers questioned American masculinity.

The flight crew poses with French and American officials on their arrival in Paris. Nelson and Ogden still wore the shorts given to them by the English airmen in India.

Douglas Aircraft Co., Santa Monica, CA, Public Relations Library

The crew meeting with General Pershing (center in straw hat) outside Foyot's fashionable restaurant in Paris. Pershing made frequent trips to Paris to rendezvous with Micheline Resco. She was an attractive young French female artist he had met in 1917 on the day of his arrival in France to lead the American Expeditionary Forces during the war. Infatuated with her, he broke his engagement to Anne Patton, sister of his aide, George. He secretly married her on Sept. 2, 1946 at the Walter Reed Army Hospital where he remained until his death at 88 on July 15, 1948.

Mrs. MacLaren shakes Smith's hand on their London landing in appreciation of the help the Americans gave to her husband in his round-the-world flight attempt.

Right: Smith, Nelson, and Wade taking a break from their labors converting from wheels to floats. A few minutes after this photo was taken, Smith and Nelson narrowly missed being crushed to death when a chain holding the *Chicago* suspended above their heads suddenly broke.

Below: Left to right: Wade, Arnold, Smith, Ogden, Nelson, and Harding standing in front of the *Chicago* after landing at the Blackburn Airdrome in Brough, England. There they exchanged engines and converted the cruisers from wheels to floats in preparation for the first crossing of the North Atlantic.

The *New Orleans* being launched with its newly installed engine and floats at Brough, England for the first flight to Iceland.

Wade and Ogden spent many hours alone in the North Atlantic waiting for rescue after their engine's oil pump failed on route to Iceland.

The stricken *Boston* being towed by the destroyer *U.S.S. Richmond* after its forced landing. Winds increased to gale force shortly after this photo was taken and heavily damaged the cruiser. Efforts to bring it safely on deck failed when a crane buckled under the strain and crashed down onto the *Boston*.

The *Boston* capsized and had to be cut loose. With eyes full of tears, Wade and Ogden felt as if they had lost a close member of their family.

As the first airplanes ever flown to Iceland, the World Flight was warmly welcomed. Here the *New Orleans* is lifted out of the water in Reykjavik for protection and servicing.

Lt. Antonio Locatelli, leading a crew of four on the Italian World Flight, followed the Americans to Iceland. Premier Mussolini requested permission from President Coolidge to use U.S. Navy support and cached supplies. Their sleek Dornier Wal amphibious monoplane seen here was much faster and more comfortable with enclosed crew quarters and twin engines. Dense fog and huge icebergs required Locatelli to make a precautionary landing on route to Greenland. Turbulent seas damaged the plane, making takeoff impossible. Imprisoned in the most isolated area of the North Atlantic with little to sustain them, after four days they had resigned themselves to death when a miraculous last-minute rescue saved their lives.

The supply ship *Hans Egedi* attempting to break through heavy pack ice.

The supply ship *Gertrude Rask* with Wade and Ogden on board unloading supplies at Fredericksdal. The supply ships found the original harbor 500 miles distant at Angmagsalik closed by heavy pack ice.

After waiting weeks in Iceland with no improvement in the weather, with winter rapidly setting in and President Coolidge preparing to cancel the flight, Smith and Nelson decided to try reaching Fredericksdal—lying 830 miles away, almost 200 miles further than they had ever flown before. After a grueling flight lasting over 11 hours and down to their last drops of fuel, they made it. Here the resupplied *Chicago* dodges floating icebergs and takes off from Fredericksdal for Ivigtut.

Lowell Smith circles over the cruiser *Milwaukee* standing by to assist them with fresh engines and supplies in the harbor of Ivigtut, Greenland. Lying on the sheltered Southwestern side the climate is far more temperate and hospitable.

Museum of Flying, Santa Monica

Lowell Smith steps from the launch of the *U.S.S. Richmond,* anchored behind the cruisers, onto North American soil in Icy Tickle, Labrador after a harrowing flight. The engine-driven fuel pump of the *Chicago* failed and the wind-driven back-up pump lasted only a short time until it too stopped working. Arnold stripped to the waist and exhausted himself cranking an additional manual back-up pump.

In Labrador, Admiral Magruder congratulates the crew upon making the first successful crossing of the North Atlantic Ocean. Left to right: Smith, Arnold, Magruder, Nelson, Harding, and Captain Cotton of the *Richmond.*

Smith and Nelson enjoying their first American breakfast in many months; pancakes and coffee at Mere Point Maine. The prototype cruiser had been renamed the *Boston II* and delivered to Wade and Ogden in Nova Scotia. They flew with them for the balance of the flight.

Billy Mitchell confronts his adversaries, Admiral William Moffett, left, and Assistant Naval Secretary Theodore Roosevelt (in straw hat) after flying to Boston for a welcome reception for his World Flight crew.

On American soil at last, and with all the other competing world flights having crashed or failed, the flight crew relaxed in Boston. The body language says it all. Left to right: Harding, Wade, Nelson, Arnold, Smith, and Ogden.

President Coolidge (left) and Secretary of War John Weeks (right) congratulate Lowell Smith at Bolling Field near Washington. In contrast to his curt send-off, Coolidge waited three hours in the rain for their arrival and then inspected the airplanes at length as waiting photographers snapped photographs.

A White House reception followed the day after the crews' arrival. *Left to right:* Lt. Lowell Smith, Secretary of War John Weeks, General Mason Patrick, General Billy Mitchell, Lt. Erik Nelson, Lt. Leigh Wade. Formerly a Navy officer and Academy graduate, Weeks opposed Mitchell's advocacy of air power. He became the butt of jokes and newspaper cartoons when he boasted he would gladly stand safely on the bridge of any ship Mitchell attempted to bomb from the air. Weeks disliked Mitchell intensely and threatened to resign unless he was terminated.

Lowell Smith being welcomed home to San Diego by his proud parents, Reverend and Mrs. Jasper Smith after the flight landed at Rockwell Field. A banquet at the Hotel Del Coronado followed.

Leigh Wade landing the *Boston II* at Clover Field in Santa Monica.

Sept. 23, 1924. Clover Field as seen from the air. Two of the World Cruisers have taxied through acres of roses to the reviewing stand while the third follows. A formation of biplanes, right, releases smoke to salute the fliers.

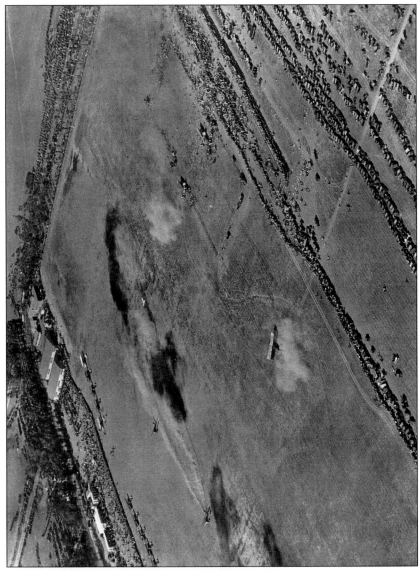

A huge crowd, estimated at 250,000 including tens of thousands of school children, mobbed the fliers upon their return to Santa Monica.

Lowell Smith receives the official kiss of welcome from Miss San Francisco while the others nervously await their turn.

"Smilin' Jack" has good reason to smile as "Miss America of 1924" pins a rose on him in Seattle.

Erik Nelson and Jack Harding checking the oil and water levels while servicing the *New Orleans* before departing from Clover Field for the flight to San Francisco. Throughout the flight, the crew of each plane did their own maintenance and repair.

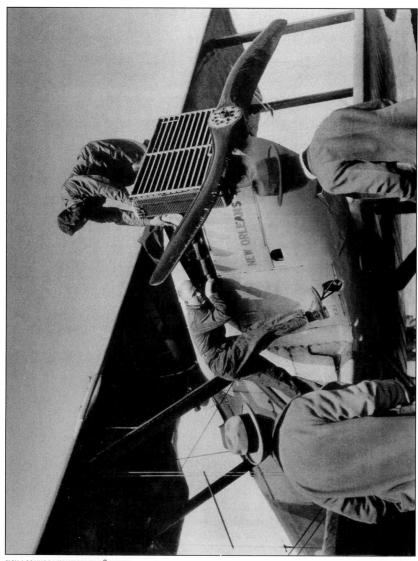

Major Martin greeting Erik Nelson, leaning against the prop of the *Chicago*, upon their return to Seattle. Les Arnold tells one of his many jokes to Leigh Wade and Lowell Smith while Hank Ogden and Jack Harding listen in.

The last picture taken of the crew before they sadly turned over their airplanes to the U.S. government. Lowell Smith stands on the lower wing of the *Chicago* holding her strut. *Left to right standing:* Leigh Wade, Corliss Mosely, Henry Ogden, Les Arnold, Burdette Wright, and Erik Nelson. *Seated in front:* Lowell Thomas, Sergeant Kennedy, and Jack Harding with Frank the Raccoon. Mosely, Wright, Thomas, and Kennedy flew the escorting airplanes.

Back to the real world. The fliers return eastward by train for their new assignments. *Left to right:* Arnold, Ogden, Wade, Smith, Nelson, and Harding. Congress voted all of them the Distinguished Service Medal, never before given except in war. Foreign governments showered them with medals and awards. France made all of them Chevaliers of the Legion of Honor.

The World Cruiser's Liberty Engine, conceived in a single week under war emergency conditions at the Willard Hotel in Washington, D.C. starting on May 29,1917 by Elbert John Hall and Jesse G. Vincent, self-taught correspondence course engineers. A completed engine, ready for testing, came to life only 28 days later—an incredible feat which usually took several years to accomplish. The Liberty was a modular engine which could be made in four, six, eight, or twelve cylinder versions using lightweight steel cylinders with a four-inch bore and seven-inch stroke with water-jacketed intake headers and a two-part box section crankcase. 20,000 Liberty Engines were made during the war by General Motors, Packard, Lincoln, and Marmon. All were hastily assembled under war-time conditions and most required disassembly, reassembly, and parts replacement to run right—including all four of the engines installed by Douglas. Few would last over 50 hours. The World Cruisers used the most powerful V-12s, producing 420 horsepower and weighing less than two pounds per horsepower, very respectable for the era. Although newer, better and more reliable engines were available, the Army had to use up the huge surplus of existing engines before new ones could be purchased. The basic engines were robust, but the water cooling, lubrication, and electrical systems were very troublesome.

The graceful *Shenandoah* cruising majestically along the California coast in 1924.

Part of the wreckage of the *Shenandoah* before crowds looted her and her dead crew for valuables and souvenirs.

Left: Commander of the Shenandoah, Zachary Lansdowne, a close personal friend of Billy Mitchell's. His death, with a dozen other crew members, provoked Mitchell's angry outburst accusing the President and the War Department of "incompetency, criminal . . . and almost treasonable negligence," and made his Court Martial inevitable.

Right: The stern unyielding face of General Robert L. Howze who presided over Mitchell's trial.

Below: Arriving at the Capitol with Mrs. Mitchell and aides for the Special Aviation Board hearing, September 29, 1925.

Billy Mitchell rises to face his accusers as they read the charges against him while his wife listens nervously.

Billy Mitchell with his wife and Lucy the day following the court-martial.

The Mitchells bird hunting at Boxwood, their home in Northern Virginia, two years before his death in 1936. The trial and its consequences aged him considerably. His weakening heart caused the loss of his precious pilot's license. The last years of life were devoted to his children, aviation, and his lifelong love of the outdoors.

The *New Orleans* makes her last flight—in a U.S. Air Force freighter to her birthplace in Santa Monica.

Home at last. *The New Orleans,* the only original and unrestored Douglas World Cruiser on display, with a huge collection of memorabilia from the First World Flight at the Museum of Flying in Santa Monica where it was born, flew for the first time, and started its epic adventure around the world.

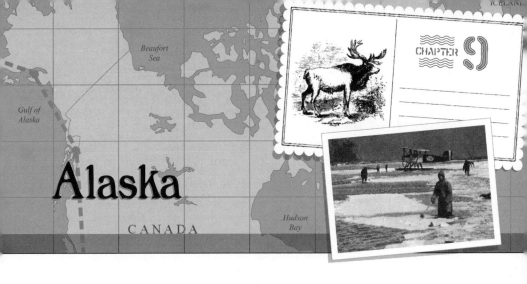

Alaska

CANADA

CHAPTER 9

MONDAY, MARCH 17, 1924
10:25 A.M.
AIRBORNE—NORTH OF SANTA MONICA

Major Martin's World Cruiser Number One led the V shaped formation of three northward toward Sacramento. Lowell Smith flew a few yards behind his left wing with Leigh Wade in the same position on his right. Martin sat bolt upright in his cockpit so that he could see over the top of his small windscreen. The ten escorting airplanes weaved in and out of the V, their pilots determined to maintain close contact while their photographers, oblivious to any danger, happily snapped pictures.

They had been airborne for only a short time and already visibility was deteriorating. Light rain and fog forced the flight and its escorts to fly lower and closer to the ground. Martin's eyes strained to make out the outlines of the terrain now rising ominously all around him. It was becoming more difficult. The mountains, sky, clouds, and ground blended into an amorphous soup with no clear outlines to distinguish one from the other.

Using the chamois sewn onto the back of his flying gloves, Martin wiped the moisture that continuously formed on his goggles and further obscured his vision. Behind him, Sergeant Alva Harvey sat nervously with his head cocked to the right side, trying to see around Martin. Perhaps his younger eyes could make out the signs of danger coming at them a little sooner. He could sound the alarm with a sudden movement of his control wheel and perhaps save the airplane from a collision. Halfway between Santa Monica and Bakersfield, the Tehachapi mountains loomed. At their low altitude, they would have to thread the needle following the narrow pass through the mountains with disaster scant yards off each wing.

Lowell Smith accelerated, bringing his biplane just ahead and into Martin's view. Using hand signals, Lowell indicated he would take the lead. Smith knew every nook and cranny of that pass, every turn, every dogleg. He had flown it thousands of times before leading his squadron of fire-fighting airplanes to safety. Greatly relieved, Martin indicated his compliance and signaled the flight and its escorts to form up into trail formation, nose to tail in single file behind him to follow Smith in cruiser number two. Harvey, also relieved, pulled his head back into the cockpit and behind the small comfort of his windscreen. He had no doubt that Lowell would get them through.

At the northern end of the pass, the fog suddenly ended and the flight broke into the bright sunlight of the San Joaquin Valley. Increasing numbers of oil derricks heralded their approach to Bakersfield. Just past Bakersfield, Martin's cruiser developed an engine vibration. Spotting a convenient farmer's field, Martin signaled to the flight his intention of landing to make repairs.

As Smith and Wade flew slow, lazy circles overhead, Harvey sprang from the rear cockpit as the airplane stopped. Within thirty minutes, he had found the problem and fixed it, and Martin took off again to rejoin the flight. This would be the first of many such unscheduled landings.

Before the sun could slip below the horizon, Sacramento's Mather Field came into view, where a cheering crowd of Lowell Smith's friends presented each of the fliers with a rabbit's foot, four-leaf clover, and a horseshoe. None of these brought much luck.

TUESDAY, MARCH 18, 1924
11:15 A.M.
AIRBORNE—COTTONWOOD, CALIFORNIA

L eigh Wade patted the good-luck charms he carried in his flight suit, hoping they would work. An hour out of Sacramento he noticed an ominous rise in the water temperature of his Liberty Engine. Now the engine sputtered and balked. He had to land, and hoped it was something which could be easily fixed. Cottonwood was a little town near the head waters of the Sacramento River, not likely to have any facilities or mechanics to assist him.

The only field under him looked rough, with plowed furrows and many rocks. Wade signaled his intentions to Martin and Smith, then set up for an approach into the wind. Gliding over a grove of orange trees, he cut the engine and held the nose up to protect the propeller. The tailskid caught in a furrow and he heard it tear from the fuselage. Not wanting the others to risk damage to their planes, he waved them off and indicated they should both go on without him.

They circled hesitatingly, not wanting to leave Wade alone. Linton Wells, orbiting above the scene in his escort plane, saw the developing dilemma and insisted his pilot land immediately to help Wade. With help available, Martin, Smith, and the remaining escorts continued on to Eugene, Oregon, another of Smith's old bases from which his firefighting airplanes flew.

Fortunately the problem was minor. An open drain cock had caused the loss of water. With the help of Linton Wells and a near-by farmer, Henry Ogden refilled the radiator and remounted the tailskid. They flew off again within forty minutes.

FRIDAY, MARCH 21, 1924
4:15 P.M.
SEATTLE, WASHINGTON

They were a day late, but finally they had all made it. Martin, Smith, and Wade should have been there the day before but ran into bad weather one hundred miles north of Portland. The fog forced them down to treetop level. Not even the best efforts of Lowell Smith could get them through. One of the escort planes crashed in the Cascade Mountains and a second plane dropped out. Reluctantly the flight turned back and spent the night in Portland waiting for the weather to clear.

The delay gave Erik Nelson and Jack Harding a chance to catch up. By 4 P.M. all four World Cruisers and their escorts were safely tied down at Sand Point Flying Field. The day's delay in getting to Seattle paled in significance to the rude shocks that awaited them during their stay at Sand Point.

The planners intended Seattle to be the first of several major supply bases along the flight route. They would install new Liberty engines, replace wheels with pontoons, flight test propellers, and determine the capacity of the cruisers to take off with heavy loads before final selection of equipment. When the work started on the aircraft and the Liberty engines were given their final inspection before installation, all were found to be defective. The engines would have to disassembled, remachined, rebalanced, strengthened, carefully reassembled, and retested. Despite the offer of help from the nearby Boeing Aircraft employees, this would take weeks of additional work. Also, the original short list of "to do" items ballooned into ten times its original size. Major Martin called General Patrick with the bad news from Seattle . . . and received the even worse news from Tokyo.

With the lengthy delay in Seattle, and the European flights already started with faster airplanes and tailwinds, Patrick's hope of being first-around-the-world was diminishing rapidly. If not first, perhaps something could be salvaged if they were a faster second—or third—or even fourth. Too much rode on this flight to stop now.

Generals Pershing and Patrick decided to change the starting point of the flight from its original Santa Monica to Seattle. That way they would not be penalized for the delay. They renamed the earlier flights "testing flights." The official beginning would be whenever the flight finally departed Seattle.

Several other unpleasant shocks came in Seattle. While the performance of the World Cruisers on wheels lived up to predictions, the inefficient, leaky, and heavy pontoons impeded water takeoff performance far more than expected and threatened to capsize the airplanes unless carefully monitored. There was insufficient time to replace or redesign them and they would plague the flight throughout the trip.

Radios, considered essential for emergency use, were too heavy to be carried. The life rafts had to be discarded along with the parachutes, life jackets, and most of the survival equipment. Spare parts, first-aid, and tool kits shrank. Warm clothing, sturdy boots, axes, repair manuals, ammunition, and even food rations were discarded to permit the minimum necessary fuel to be carried. They would have little to protect them but their leather flying suits and the .45 caliber automatic pistols they carried.

SUNDAY, APRIL 6, 1924
4:00 A.M.
LAKE WASHINGTON

Major Martin assisted Sgt. Harvey in pulling their World Cruiser to the dock on the quiet lake. The other crews were also preparing for a dawn departure. The truck that brought them dispensed hot coffee and cocoa to fight the early morning chill. The first spectator car was already there waiting for them, the driver pumping their hands and wishing them good luck. He would be joined by other well-wishing residents and friends before they climbed into their cockpits as the sky lightened.

This was their third "official departure date". They were ready on April 4 but the weather had been too foggy. They tried again on April 5 but Major Martin broke his wooden propeller and the piece that had broken off made an ugly gash in one of his pontoons. Assisted by mechanics working at the new Boeing Aircraft factory at Seattle, repairs had taken the entire day. Hopefully, the third try today would be the charmer.

They had gotten a lot done. Cockpit covers had been finished, new engines had been overhauled and installed in all the airplanes, equipment selection had been completed, and the airplanes had been named and christened. They really wanted champagne, but with Prohibition, General Pershing insisted on using water. Their flight represented the entire country so names of distant cities were chosen.

Major Martin's Cruiser Number 1 was named the *Seattle* and christened with the water of Lake Washington by the wife of the head of the local chamber of commerce, Mrs. David Whitcomb. Lowell Smith's Cruiser Number 2 was christened *Chicago* with water from Lake Michigan by the wife of U.S. Army Air Service Captain, Car Connell.

Leigh Wade's Cruiser Number 3 was christened *Boston* with the waters of the Atlantic Ocean by the wife of Army Air Service Major,

M.F. Harmon. Erik Nelson's Cruiser Number 4 had the combined waters of the Mississippi and the Gulf of Mexico anoint it *New Orleans* by the wife of Army Air Service Lieutenant T.J. Koenig.

It was during the christening ceremony that Lowell Smith noticed Sergeant Turner coughing up blood. He knew that cutting him from the crew at this late date would be a crushing disappointment. He had no choice. After the ceremony, he quietly broke the news to him then called Les Arnold into his quarters.

"Still want to go, Les?" Lowell asked.

"Are you kidding Smitty, more than anything else in the world," Les replied.

"Willing to work like a devil, Les?"

"I'd work like a whole flock of devils, Smitty," said Les.

"Okay. Turner can't go, Les. You're going!"

"Are you kidding Smitty? I'm no mechanic."

"I am. You do the simple stuff. I'll do the hard stuff."

Les couldn't believe his good fortune—then was saddened knowing the effect this would have on Turner—then wished he had paid closer attention during classes.

The four World Cruiser's engines split the quiet dawn of Lake Washington and one by one lifted off into the cool, moist dawn of April 6, 1924. That first official day of the world flight presented some challenges. Before Leigh Wade's *Boston* would lift off, he had to get rid of some gear to lighten the ship. Henry Ogden opened the rear baggage compartment and jettisoned a rifle, an eleven pound anchor and a pair of rubber boots.

As they flew toward the Canadian border and the magnificent snow-capped peaks of the last United States sentinel, Mount Rainier, the escort planes came by, one by one and took a final photograph. The pilots saluted, wished them good luck with the familiar "thumbs up," then made a diving turn back toward home. The Indians called Mt. Rainier "Tahoma," "the mountain that was God." As its majesty disappeared into the mist behind them, the name seemed very appropriate. Good-bye America.

They flew in looser formation now, Martin leading, several hundred feet over the lush shoreline, inlets, and water passages of British Columbia. Occasionally, a surprised Indian stopped paddling his canoe long enough to stare and then wave at the strange machines traveling noisily overhead. The light mist turned to a light rain and, as the temperature dropped along their northern route, into a light snow which forced them to fly scant feet over the Discovery and Johnstone Straits.

The tall bridge of a steamer came suddenly out of the snow ahead. The captain, as surprised to see them as they were him, veered sharply, his horn loudly protesting the unwelcome intrusion. Martin pulled up quickly into the fog, barely missing a collision. The squalls changed from sleet to hail, sounding like machine gun bullets striking the fabric-covered wings and fuselage.

At 4:55 P.M., after eight hours and ten minutes of flying time and with the northern light fading fast, they finally completed their six hundred and fifty mile flight to their destination of Prince Rupert. Circling in the now blizzard-like conditions, Lowell Smith located and then led the others to the safety of Seal Cove, shielded from the storm by high wooded hills. Smith and Wade landed without difficulty.

Major Martin's approach was too high. He used cross coupled controls, right rudder and left aileron, slipping to lose altitude. Thirty feet over the water, the heavy airplane stalled and pancaked sideways into the water with a giant splash. The left pontoon was shoved violently under the water. Three vertical flying wires broke in a vain effort to maintain the integrity of the box-like wing structure. With a loud cracking sound the left wing struts broke and the left upper wing section sagged noticeably.

Harvey, disgusted, threw his rabbit's foot as far as he could away from the stricken plane. After Nelson landed, all four cruisers taxied over to the dock where the mayor's delegation waited to greet them in what he described as "the worst day in ten years." Consoling a grief-stricken Martin with the country's highest octane aperitifs, the mayor assured him the skilled workmen of Prince Rupert would have him fixed up and ready to go in a jiffy. Martin wasn't convinced.

Les Arnold commented to the mayor on his British accuracy and conservatism. "Any American would have called today the worst day in forty years—at least." Lowell Smith and Erik Nelson excused themselves and used the rapidly dwindling light to examine the *Seattle*. She was bruised, but not fatally broken. They had spare flying wires and an ample local supply of fine spruce to make new struts.

Before dawn the next morning, the *Seattle* was towed to a near-by boatyard where it was hoisted from the water. The entire crew worked on Martin's airplane, assisted by a local shipbuilder, through the next two days and nights. Only after repairs to the *Seattle* had been completed did they start the job of servicing the other aircraft. Sleet, hail, and freezing rain made the airplanes extremely slippery.

Billy Mitchell's trusted aide, Lt. Clayton Bissell, was responsible for liaison and support of the flight through the frozen and often inaccessible areas of Canada, Alaska, and the Aleutian Islands. He had cached ample supplies of fuel, oil, tools, and spare parts for the flight at Prince Rupert, then continued on in the difficult task of supplying them as they flew northwest into the increasingly hostile wilderness.

Leigh Wade removed the *Boston's* cowl for access to the engine. He laid the large aluminum section on the wing for a moment to reach for a rope which would secure it. Before he could do that, it slipped off the wing and into sixty feet of water. Leigh spent the afternoon fishing for the cowl with no success. A cowling is not the kind of part that would normally be replaced, and no spare was available. Leigh Wade, often called "Beau Brummel" and "The Sheik of Cassopolis," was the most fastidious and superstitious of the pilots. He took the loss very badly.

The next day Lowell Smith took a despondent Leigh Wade to a local coppersmith who fashioned a new copper cowl for the *Boston*. The idea of appearing before the anticipated royalty with a bulbous yellow proboscis depressed him considerably. Contrary to the laughter of the other crew members, he insisted this was a bad omen. As it turned out, he may have been right.

THURSDAY, APRIL 10, 1924
4:15 P.M.

Dear Diary,

Had better weather today. Left Prince Rupert 9:25 A.M. for Sitka.
Over Ketchikan 10:00 A.M. Locals waved.
Over Prince of Wales Island at 11:00 A.M.
Tried shortcut over Christiana Sound. Sumner Strait Okay.

Chatham Strait too foggy. Had to turn back. Low fog.

Had to hug treetops over Cape Decision.

Kuiu Island. More low fog. Forced down to 25 feet.

Boston got too close behind us. Leigh caught in propwash. Almost crashed.

He recovered 5 feet over rocks. Scared us to death. Him too.

12:00 A.M. Fog lifted. Zero wind. Landed Sitka 1:35 P.M. Beautiful harbor. Cold.

Tied ships to Bissell's yellow moorings. Seas calm. Serviced, refueled.

Did 300 miles today. 650 yesterday. 25,500 to go.

Planning to leave early A.M.

Signed, Les Arnold

Alexander Baranof, head of the American-Russian Trading Company, chose picturesque Sitka as the first capital of Alaska in 1804. The locals called the landing area sheltering the four World Cruisers "Three by Three Harbor," since it was three miles wide by three thousand miles long. Open to the sea at one end, the now calm, placid harbor had the capability of changing into a seaman's worst nightmare in a few hours with little warning. The expedition of Vitus Bering and Alexander Chirikov foundered on these same shores two hundred years before when the weather made just such a sudden turn.

After "servicing up," the crew received a warm greeting at the quaint hotel near the old Russian Orthodox Church whose sturdy stained-glass windows overlooked the restless seas. Representatives of the governor of Alaska arranged for an Indian band to play patriotic martial music in keeping with their lofty goals. U.S. Department of Agriculture employees, working at Sitka's isolated experimental station, plucked large bouquets of gladioli from their greenhouse and left them in each of their rooms. The few resident American ladies prepared a delicious dinner which their daughters eagerly served, anxious to meet the history-making airmen.

Late that evening, the *Ranger*, a fifty foot Forestry Service motor vessel, arrived and anchored a safe distance from the four cruisers. The skipper of the *Ranger* had fought forest fires together with

Lowell Smith years before and was anxious to render any assistance his old friend might need. The crew of the *Ranger* joined the crew of the World Flight at the hotel, wished them well, and both crews retired early, planning to depart the next morning.

Leaving the hotel at dawn on April 11, it soon became apparent that the winds, gusting to thirty-five knots, and the seven foot seas which were rolling through Sitka's harbor made departure too dangerous. Until the winds abated, sightseeing would be much safer. During the morning they visited the Alaskan village, taking pictures of each other in front of the brightly painted totem poles before returning to the hotel for lunch.

With the winds increasing that afternoon, Leigh Wade, Les Arnold, Jack Harding, Hank Ogden, and Erik Nelson visited the local photographic shop. They were happily engaged in conversation with the owner when a local Indian walked in. He waited patiently for Les to finish telling his lengthy flying stories to the mesmerized owner. After a good ten minutes had passed, and with the wind increasing, the owner finally turned to the waiting Indian and asked, "Can I help you?" The Indian calmly answered, "Yes sir, I just wanted to let these folks know that one of their planes is adrift."

The five of them dove through the door of the shop at the same time, scattering photographs, books, and supplies in their wake. They sprinted down to the beach bending low in the winds now at gale force. The *Boston* had torn loose from its mooring and was being blown directly toward the *New Orleans*.

Jack and Hank unlashed a beached open longboat and carried it into the water while Leigh and Les did the same with a second longboat. Rowing with all their strength against the rising winds and seas, they set off in pursuit of the *Boston*, while Erik ran back to the hotel for additional ropes, anchors, and assistance.

Frantically gathering what they needed, Lowell and Erik ran back to the beach with the crew of the *Ranger*, launched its tender, and rowed toward it. With the last vestiges of daylight, Erik saw that the *Ranger* also had started to drag anchor and was being pushed toward nearby rocks.

The other two small boats managed to get lines secured to the *Boston*. Pulling with all their strength, they were losing ground to wind and waves as the incoming tide pushed the *Boston* ever closer to the *New Orleans* and toward the large rocks bordering the harbor's entrance.

On reaching the deck of the *Ranger,* Erik grasped with horror the nightmare unfolding and requested the *Ranger's* captain to start the engines immediately and raise anchor. Lowell lifted three hundred feet of three-fourths inch line onto his shoulders and another one hundred feet of three-eighths inch heaving line and ran to the stern of the *Ranger,* slipping and sliding on the teak decks now awash with breaking seas. Several times the heavy weight of line pulled him down onto the deck and perilously close to being washed overboard. The freezing salt spray and hail felt like needles hitting his exposed flesh.

Holding himself in place at the boat's stern, Lowell secured one end of the coiled heavy line to the stern post of the boat before knotting its other end to the heaving line. He stared intently through the darkness and blinding sheets of sea and rain trying to find the *Boston* rising and falling twenty feet in the waves.

With a shudder, the *Ranger's* engines came to life and its spotlight cut through the darkness, illuminating first the *Boston* and then the two small boats straining to tow it to safety. Lowell saw Les outlined in the beam of the boat's searchlight pulling on the oars with every muscle in his body. He signaled to him, waving the heaving line high over his head. He was one hundred yards off the stern, too far to throw the line.

In the *Ranger's* wheelhouse, Erik, no stranger to fighting heavy seas in small boats, expertly manipulated the throttle and rudder, spinning the wooden wheel from side to side, bringing the ship's bow forward onto the anchor rope. The captain went forward to assist his crew struggling with the bow windlass to raise the heavy storm anchor.

When the anchor finally lifted free of the bottom, the cranky underpowered engine required full throttle and rudder to keep the bow into the wind. Erik backed the boat, letting the wind push it toward the shoreline. Slowly the distance closed between the *Ranger* and the two longboats, inexorably losing the battle to keep the *Boston* from being blown onto the *New Orleans.*

As the *Ranger* slipped backward through the huge waves, breaking seas came over the transom. Lowell struggled to keep his footing. The rocks coming out from the shoreline were now only a few yards from the *Ranger's* wooden hull. When the distance to the longboat had closed to fifty yards, the *Boston* was within inches of the *New Orleans*. It was now or never. Lowell steadied himself and divided the heaving line into two coils. With all his strength, he threw the smaller coil with his right arm toward Les.

It was a long throw, but the wind helped carry the line into Les's waiting grasp. Hand over hand, Les pulled the heaving line into the Longboat until the larger line tied to it could be secured to his bow stanchion. He signaled and Erik gave the little engine in the *Ranger* full throttle.

Despite the *Ranger's* best efforts, the intensifying wind and drag of the *Boston* made possible little forward progress. The vessel slewed from side to side, coming closer and closer to the rocks. The *Ranger's* captain signaled Lowell to cut the *Boston's* tow line. Lowell hesitated and looked to Erik. They were running out of options.

From the other longboat, Jack Harding saw the drama unfolding. He jumped into the water and grasping its towline, pulled himself hand over hand onto the Cruiser's pontoons. Fighting seas and wind he managed to remove the Cruiser's engine and front cockpit covers. Scrambling onto the wing, he dove headfirst into the front cockpit.

With shivering and bruised fingers Jack turned on the electrical switches, primed the engine, said a silent prayer, and activated the starter switch. The huge wooden propeller rotated . . . one blade . . . two blades . . . three blades . . . and coughed to life bellowing puffs of black smoke. Cautiously he advanced the throttle and the great plane moved forward. Erik gave Lowell the signal to cut the *Ranger's* towline.

With the *Ranger* now free of the tow, Erik steered it out from the rocky shoreline and into the safety of deeper water. With a greatly relieved captain back on the helm, Erik kept the *Ranger's* spotlight focused on the yellow mooring buoy.

Jack taxied the *Boston* through the breaking seas and wind toward its mooring, towing the two longboats in its wake. Making slow circles around the mooring buoy, Les, Leigh, and Hank scrambled onto the pontoons.

Cautiously avoiding the spinning propeller, they repeatedly tried to secure the cruiser to the mooring without success. Each time a wave carried either the cruiser or its mooring buoy twenty feet into the air and made attachment impossible. After each attempt, Jack had to taxi around in a large circle to come back for another try. Les finally jumped into the water, secured a line to the mooring and, with enormous effort, swam the line back to the *Boston*. For additional safety, sixty-pound storm anchors carried on the pontoons of each cruiser were also used.

The *Ranger* crew reanchored their boat in better holding ground using two anchors before rowing back to shore. It wasn't until after three A.M. that the cold, wet, and exhausted crews of the *Ranger* and the World Flight had the situation under control and returned to the warmth of their hotel rooms.

The next morning, the winds continued unabated gusting to eighty knots. These were the infamous Arctic "Willie-was," fifty to one hundred mph winds which arise with no warning and come at you with constantly differing directions and velocities making countermeasures on land, sea, or in the air almost impossible. That night, a mooring shackle worked itself open in the turbulent seas and the *New Orleans* was suddenly adrift. The sea-going fire drill began anew. The crews concluded that continuous inspections would be required, and they worked in teams, rowing out in the teeth of the storm—checking moorings, shackles, lines, and anchorages. Any illusions that this trip would be easy were snuffed out at Sitka. Tomorrow they would try again to leave.

In an effort to cheer the crew, Leigh Wade said, "Cheer up. Things could be a lot worse." As the next few days were to prove, he was absolutely correct.

SUNDAY, APRIL 13, 1924

Dear Diary:

Weather finally cleared. 325 gallons fuel loaded. Tried to leave Sitka at 6:00 A.M., but couldn't get weather report on radio until 8:00 A.M. 8:45 A.M., off for Cordova, 480 miles. Seward possible as alternate at 610 miles.

Wade led. Good weather over Hayward Strait.

9:45 A.M., 90 miles from Sitka. Fog and snow over Cross Sound. Visibility poor.

In sunlight for 40 miles at Mount Saint Elias. Blizzard at Icy Bay. Visibility zero.

In sunlight again over Prince William Sound. Many wrecked ships and villages.

Many deserted mining towns. Wx good—bypassed Cordova for Seward.

Flew over ship Bissell used, S.S. Star at Latouche. Capt. Johannsen waved.

3:45 P.M.: arrived Resurrection Bay at Seward. Serviced up. Very cold. Filled tanks to 325 gallons. Planning to fly 450 miles to Chignik tomorrow. Now nine days behind schedule. 1,560 miles made good. 24,885 to go.

Signed, Les Arnold

T he residents of Cordova, having planned a sumptuous welcome party for the fliers with decorations, music, and a banquet, were bitterly disappointed when the flight crew bypassed them. On April 14 the flight crew awoke hopeful of departing Seward for Chignik. Blizzards and high winds forced them to again delay their plans. The burly fishermen of Seward's halibut and salmon fleet helped them to add 250-pound storm anchors to each cruiser's mooring. As the fliers struggled to get through the Arctic conditions, another drama was being played out for them on the other side of the world in Japan.

TUESDAY, APRIL 15, 1924 8:50 A.M.
HEADQUARTERS OF MAJOR GENERAL YASUMITSU
COMMANDER OF THE JAPANESE AIR SERVICE, KOBE, JAPAN

G eneral Billy Mitchell sat waiting in the overstuffed chair in General Yasumitsu's office. A light knock on the office door preceded the arrival of the green tea lady. Mitchell now knew the drill. An attractive young lady minced into the office carrying a tray of freshly made green tea. Her bright floral silk kimono contrasted sharply with the otherwise muted and subdued tones of the office. Expertly, she kneeled before the low table and with exquisitely delicate movements carefully placed the cup in position, before him, rotating it so that the pattern would face him precisely. She then bowed low to him, carefully avoiding any eye contact, and backed out through the open door.

Mitchell lifted the cup, scanning the many pictures of airplanes on the walls. The ceremonial sword was displayed in its case on the burled walnut credenza. Diplomas, awards, and medals hung neatly, symmetrically arranged among the wall hangings and antique scrolls with their undecipherable Kanji characters. At precisely nine A.M., General Yasumitsu would enter with his staff and delegation following. They would bow to him before taking their appointed seats. Yasumitsu would inquire of his health and his wife's and how the Mitchells had spent the days between their last meetings. The small talk would go on for perhaps thirty minutes after which, almost as an afterthought, the negotiations would begin. In the land of cherry blossoms, there was no black or white, no firm "yes" or "no," only shades of the gray, "maybe." But today had to be different. Time had run out. Only "yes" or "no" could survive.

The request for his intercession and assistance in the negotiations with the Japanese caught up with the Mitchells after they had toured Guam and during their visit with Billy's old friend, Douglas MacArthur, in the Philippines. MacArthur's new wife, Louise Cromwell Brooks, complained loudly of being "banished" to those forsaken islands as punishment for spurning the advances of General Pershing and marrying the younger MacArthur.

The former Mrs. Brooks, as wealthy as she was attractive, was not used to being treated that way. She resented Pershing's vindictive behavior and urged Mitchell to tear up the telegram and return it to him in pieces. After all, it was Pershing's directive that he have nothing to do with the world flight, and now they were "begging him to save it."

"Tell them to go to hell," she said.

Mitchell explained to her that he would not be acting for Pershing, but for the good of the United States. This was his flight and these were his pilots he would be helping. He could do no less for himself or his beloved aviation. After completing his review of Philippine defenses with MacArthur and taking his old adversary, Aguinaldo, up for his first airplane ride, the Mitchells departed for Japan.

To the impatient Mitchell, negotiations in Japan seemed endless. For almost two months, the weekly meetings reached few firm conclusions. They would neither affirm nor deny the flight permission to land on Japanese territory. Yasumitsu remained convinced that Mitchell's original military objectives for the world flight of developing defensive and offensive aerial strategies against Japan were unchanged despite Patrick's assertion of its solely peaceful and commercial intent.

Mitchell knew Yasumitsu was right. His objectives for the flight never wavered. Despite what the politicians or even the general staff asserted, the experience and knowledge gained on his world flight combined with his own observations would form a comprehensive Pacific defense strategy. A successful flight would assure the creation of new U.S. air bases and the expanded defense of existing ones, making them impenetrable by any foreign air or sea forces.

The slow pace of weekly meetings gave Mitchell some opportunity to travel and observe Japan's considerable military preparedness. Although encumbered by the military nature of his visit, and the continuing accompaniment of watchful hosts, the growing military strength of Japan was evident. After the world flight negotiations were concluded he planned to continue his Pacific trip and return later as an innocuous, and hopefully anonymous, "tourist couple" to gather additional intelligence.

Before the office clock completed its nine chimes, General Yasumitsu, Chief of the Oversight Committee entered with Admiral Yamamoto, Assistant Chief of the Oversight Committee and the man who would later orchestrate the attack on Pearl Harbor in 1941. Mr. G. Katsuda, an official observer of Mitchell's ship bombing tests and now a member of parliament, entered with them. Mitchell rose with Lt. Nutt and politely returned the welcoming bows. After the usual exchange of pleasantries and recounting the delightful shopping and culinary experiences of he and his wife, Mitchell reopened the negotiations.

"Gentlemen, it has been five weeks and still you have not granted landing rights for our world flight. President Coolidge can give us no additional time. Our flight is poised to bridge the Pacific Ocean to Japan for the first time. As we speak the ships of both our navies are steaming to greet our fliers in the Kurile Islands. If I cannot receive permission from you today, our president must inform the world of your decision and order the flight to return home. History will judge our actions."

Katsuda interpreted Mitchell's remarks into Japanese, and looking anguished, replied, "Billy-san, please understand we need more time. Our Diplomatic Corps already approved your flight. Our Navy remains undecided and only our Army opposes the landing of your army aircraft on our shores."

General Yasumitsu waved his arm to interrupt Katsuda, "The Americans exclude us. Why should we not exclude them?"

Mitchell replied, "Our immigration policy is more open than your own."

Yasumitsu countered, his voice rising angrily. "Not for the Japanese. We cannot become citizens of your country. We cannot own land, property, or businesses. Why? Are we so unworthy? Are we not human beings also?"

Mitchell waited for tempers to cool before answering in low tones, "Politics are beyond my control. Politicians come and go. Policies will change. Advances in aviation will continue long into the future."

Admiral Yamamoto turned to face Mitchell. "Precisely so. The true purpose of your world flight is to strengthen your military aviation. We are already strong. Therefore your world flight is in your interest, not ours."

"Isn't the growth of aviation, and the commerce it will bring, in every country's interest?" Mitchell asked.

"As you have written, aviation is a double-edged sword. Commerce is one edge, military domination the other." Yamamoto replied.

"Our flight comes in peace. We wish to dominate no other country," Mitchell insisted.

Yasumitsu broke in. "Hah! From the time Commodore Perry sailed his four warships into Japan seventy years ago, the West has been trying to dominate us. President Monroe annexed the entire Western hemisphere. You have taken Hawaii, Guam, Wake Island, and the Philippines in a bloody war. The British have taken India, Burma, Singapore, China, Australia, New Zealand, Egypt, and most of the Middle East. The Dutch have taken the East Indies and French Indochina, and the Russians have stolen our own northern territories."

"Yes," Mitchell responded "and Japan has troops in Manchuria, Siberia, and Korea."

Yasumitsu continued, "Japan is a small country, Mitchell-san. We have few natural resources and a large population. We cannot survive without oil, steel, coal, lumber, and food. You want us to stay locked within our tiny island and come to you like a beggar with our tin cup. To survive, we must expand as you have done. Are we any less worthy than you? If you want to expand your military aviation, do not ask us to assist you in that task."

The growing tone of hostility threatened to sink the negotiations. Lt. Cliff Nutt opened his briefcase and withdrew several neatly typed pages. Offering them to Yasumitsu, he said, "Gentlemen, General Pershing has requested I remind you of these sixty enclosed accommodations General Mitchell and others have extended to your army and naval general staff as well as your diplomatic corps. As our trusted ally in the World War, we have shared with you all of the valuable information from our naval bombing tests. When the great earthquake in Tokyo killed one hundred thousand of your citizens six months ago and injured a half million more, it was the United States that came to your aid and is helping you to rebuild. Now we are asking you for a very small favor: permission for four of our aircraft to land in your territory, refuel, and depart. Is that really so difficult for you to give?"

After several long minutes of silence, Yasumitsu turned to his delegation and spoke quietly in Japanese, then looked at his watch before turning again to Mitchell and replying. "Please take lunch with Commander Hara and Colonel Obata. We will continue our discussion among ourselves and try to have answers for you upon your return."

After an extended lunch hour, the meeting reconvened. A "Memorandum of Understanding" had been typed with several copies, one of which was handed to Mitchell:

1. U.S. naval ships must have two Japanese Naval Observers onboard while in Japanese waters and must be accompanied and follow the instructions of our Japanese naval vessel.

2. All U.S. personnel will turn over to us all cameras while in Japan and take no photographs.

3. All guns and ammunition will be locked and secured.

4. From the time of touchdown in Japanese waters, there will be no radio or telephone communication

to any government or news service for thirty
minutes.

5. All flights must be conducted at least five miles
   from shoreline.

6. All military personnel coming ashore must have
   physical examinations and authorization from
   Japanese doctors.

7. The U.S. to provide list of names, addresses, and
   backgrounds of all personnel entering Japanese
   waters.

8. The U.S. to provide a set of plans and specifications for each aircraft and engine so we may
   judge its safety.

9. Prepayment must be received for all expenses
   including berthing, docking, mooring, guarding,
   protecting, fueling, provisioning, etc.

10. A Japanese pilot and navigator must be on each
    airplane.

Mitchell and Nutt looked over the list. Most of the points had
been previously agreed.

Item 10 was impossible. Mitchell explained there was no room in
the planes for any additional crew. Nutt put the plans of the World
Cruiser on the table to prove his point. Mitchell suggested a
Japanese plane lead them, but they had none with sufficient range
and were reluctant to reveal that shortcoming.

After four hours of discussion, General Yasumitsu ceremonious-
ly crossed out Item 10. Mitchell cabled Patrick that evening, "Japan
landing clearance received."

TUESDAY, APRIL 15, 1924
SEWARD TO CHIGNIK

I got the men up at 5:00 A.M. I told them we'd have to push. We
were already ten days behind schedule. After sending our crews
to prepare the planes, Lowell, Leigh, Erik, and I got the weather on the radio. "Clear as a bell," they said.

We took off at 9:45. I asked Erik to lead and watched the three of them get safely off the water before gunning the *Seattle* and joining them. By 10:05 we headed down the fjord at Resurrection Bay.

About a hundred miles out from Seward, near Chugach Island, we passed a lighthouse and then the *S.S. Star*, slowly picking its way between the ice flows. It was good to see Captain Johannsen and our old friends on the *Star* waving up at us. They have a radio onboard and will surely pass a position report on to our Navy.

The weather continued to be quite good except for some light snow squalls. Off the right wing of our ship, we clearly saw Mount Katmai, the gigantic active volcano, spewing live steam from its enormous crater, eight miles in circumference and thirty-five hundred feet deep. Its eruption on June 6, 1912 ranks as one of the most violent in modern times.

By the late morning, I seemed to need more and more throttle to stay with the other three planes. I increased RPM from 1,500 to 1,650 but still found the *Seattle* having difficulty matching their speed. Oil pressure seemed a bit low as well.

At 2:40 P.M., Sergeant Harvey got my attention by moving the control column and pointing at the oil pressure gauge. It read zero. I estimated the northwest wind velocity at forty miles per hour and the sea looked very rough with whitecaps everywhere. In a few minutes we were over Cape Igvak and the sheltered waters of Portage Bay where I safely landed.

Sergeant Harvey investigated and reported a hole in the left side of the crankcase under number 5 cylinder measuring three inches in diameter. We had no alternative but to anchor our ship and hope help would come soon. Fortunately the bay was calm that evening. After consuming our few malted milk tablets, we divided the night into four-hour watches and settled in, resigned to a cold night.

It was too cold in our cockpits for either of us to get any sleep. By 4:55 Harvey noticed a thin wisp of smoke coming from the southeast near Kodiak Island. Through my field glasses, I saw the welcome sight of a U.S. Naval destroyer steaming at full speed toward us. I fired rockets at one minute intervals from my Very pistol. At 5:30 A.M. they anchored at the entrance to Portage Bay, lowered a launch, and soon had us in tow. Within a short time, Lt.

Commander J.C. Hilliard welcomed us aboard the *U.S.S. Hull.* I've seldom been happier to meet up with our navy.

After a hearty breakfast, they towed us to the little village of Kanatak. All forty residents turned out to see their first airplane and told us the previous evening was their first calm day in eight months. That being the case, we took advantage of the next high tide to float the *Seattle* down a creek and into a small pond some two hundred yards from shore where we would await repairs.

Signed F. L. Martin

Saturday, April 19, 1924 Dutch Harbor, Unalaska

Dear Diary

Arrived Dutch Harbor from Chignik at 6:05 P.M. 65 mph headwinds. 390 miles took 7 hrs. 26 mins. Blizzards, squalls, and ice cold Willie-was. Moorings anchored for us by U.S. Coast Guard Cutter Haida. Crew all wet, cold, hungry, shivering, dog-tired, and disagreeable. New engine, gas, and oil shipped from spare cache yesterday on U.S.C.G. Cutter Algonquin. Delivering tomorrow to Major Martin at Kanatak. Boston also needs new Engine. Will check Chicago and New Orleans. Anxiously awaiting arrival of Martin, Harvey, and Seattle.

Signed, Les Arnold

April 25, 1924

Dear Diary,

Now six bitter cold days in Dutch Harbor. Changed engine on Boston. Willie-was blew New Orleans adrift on 4/16. Haida crew helped tow back. Constant snow. Freezing rain. Mornings spent chipping ice from cruisers. Severe Arctic gale through Dutch Harbor last night. 75 mph winds. Tore moorings loose on cruisers and Haida. All ships almost sunk. Both crews waded in icy seas until 4:00 A.M. to secure ships. Badly frostbitten.

Algonquin radioed delayed engine swap now completed on Seattle.
Major Martin now recovered from severe cold and flying to Chignik today.
Everyone here anxious to leave. Hope Seattle can join us soon.

Signed, Les Arnold

```
APRIL 28 1924 RADIOGRAM TO WORLD FLIGHT DUTCH HARBOR

ARRIVED CHIGNIK 550 PM APRIL 25 AFTER HARROWING

FLIGHT STOP ATTEMPTING TO JOIN YOU EARLIEST BUT

WEATHER TOO BAD FOR FLIGHT STOP PLEASE BE PATIENT

STOP MAJOR MARTIN


APRIL 30 1924 RADIOGRAM TO WORLD FLIGHT DUTCH HARBOR

SLIGHT WEATHER IMPROVEMENT TODAY STOP MAJOR MARTIN

AND SERGEANT HARVEY DEPARTED CHIGNIK 11 AM STOP

ESTIMATING HIS ARRIVAL DUTCH HARBOR PROX 5 PM
```

The pontoons of the *Seattle* skimmed faster and faster over the water, its heavy ice-coating pushing it down into the white-capped seas. Each time Major Martin pulled the nose up, she'd rise slightly, and then settle down into the water again. The rock jetty marking the entrance to the harbor came rushing at them, closer and closer. The *Liberty* engine bellowed and strained to lift the heavy airplane with its thickening coat of ice clear of the water. If they hit the rocks of the jetty at this speed there would be little left but splinters and torn fabric. With a silent prayer, Martin pulled the wooden wheel into his stomach at the last moment and closed his eyes.

They were flying. Just a foot or two over the water perhaps, but they were flying. From the rear cockpit, Sergeant Alva Harvey breathed a deep sigh of relief. Ever so slowly, the airspeed increased and Major Martin gingerly applied back pressure once again. With the engine screaming at full power and running full rich, the burned fuel eventually lightened the load enough to start a slow ascent from the wet white fingers of the windblown spray reaching up to pull them into their bosom again.

Ever so slowly, the altimeter needle came to life. Ten feet . . . twenty feet . . . thirty feet . . . forty feet . . . fifty feet. Now Martin could breathe a little easier. For the first time, he felt the damp cold sweat under the fur of his flying helmet and his heart pounding rapidly within his chest. Ever so gently, he banked into a turn toward the west and the rest of his crew anxiously awaiting his arrival at Dutch Harbor.

Martin jiggled the wooden wheel, signaling Harvey to take control of the airplane. Harvey put his fingers lightly around the massive rim and jiggled it back. Martin raised both hands out of the cockpit where Harvey could see them. "You've got it" the motion said. Martin pulled the chart from his inside jacket pocket and studied the route. Mr. Osborne, superintendent of the cannery at Chignik, had drawn a shortcut over the portage to the west. It cut off thirty miles from the 390 flying miles to Dutch Harbor. Osborne assured him the others had flown over that same shortcut.

Martin weighed the options. On pontoons, it was much safer to fly over the shoreline with the seas within gliding distance in the event of engine failure. But with these strong headwinds, saving thirty miles meant saving thirty minutes—and he'd be flying only for a short time through a low pass in the mountains. Martin signaled Harvey, took back control of the *Seattle*, and turned left toward the southwest and the pass through the mountains to Dutch Harbor.

The dark blue waters under him turned to a sea of white snow as he crossed the shoreline. Lighter now, the *Seattle* was climbing, 200, 300, 400, 500, 600, and then, suddenly, they were in thickening snow showers. Everything was white—the sky, the mountains, the pass—all a sea of white. They strained to make out the outlines of the pass under them. The minutes seemed like hours. Martin and Harvey were now standing up in their cockpits, squinting through the snow-encrusted lenses of their flying goggles for some clue as to which way the pass continued.

A huge mountain loomed up through the snow in front of them. Martin, still standing, swung the wheel hard right and the *Seattle* passed scant feet over the trees. The compass swung wildly, offering little guidance. Martin looked anxiously over at Harvey—could his younger eyes make out the way through the pass? Harvey shrugged his shoulders. He didn't know either. *Level the wings, Frederick*, came the voice of his first flying instructor. *Keep the wings level or you'll spiral into a spin.*

But which way was level? Was that the horizon peeking faintly through the snow or was that the profile of the mountain? Was that the sky or the ground? Which way was down? Which way was up?

Where had the pass gone? He had no idea—and neither did Harvey! The snow thickened and the winds howled menacingly around them. Martin held the wheel tightly in his left hand and wiped the snow from his goggles using the chamois on the back of his right glove. Through the cleared lenses, the outline of the mountain immediately in front of the *Seattle* horrified him.

The right pontoon hit first, striking the mountain's incline on the top ledge of a thousand-foot precipice. The pontoon's struts splintered, instantly ripping away great chunks from the lower wing's supporting spars. The right wingtip dug into the frozen ground tumbling the huge biplane over and over, its wings, stabilizers, and fuselage breaking, cracking, and tearing before the twisted wreckage finally came to a stop half-buried in the freshly fallen snow. Suddenly, all was quiet. The *Seattle* had crashed.

The sun at Dutch Harbor was setting. The six remaining crewmen sat on an upturned skiff on the frozen, barren, hostile shore. Lowell Smith scanned the eastern sky with his binoculars. Erik Nelson did the same. "Any sign of the Major, Smitty?" asked Les Arnold. Smith shook his head slowly. This was not a good sign. Even allowing for headwinds, they should have been here by now.

Lowell handed the binoculars to Les Arnold and silently left for the radio shack. When he opened the door, the radio operator took off his headset and looked grimly at him, shaking his head. "No word?" asked Lowell. "No word," was the reply. The radio operator had checked all the wireless stations along the flight route. No one had seen or heard the *Seattle* fly overhead. By this time, the 200 gallons of fuel loaded by Martin would be gone. Silently he left the radio shack.

At 7:10 P.M., the crew of the *U.S.C.G. Haida* returned to their ship, started their engines, unshackled the mooring chains, and sailed eastward out of Dutch Harbor in search of Major Martin and Sergeant Harvey.

By 7:30, Lowell Smith and Erik Nelson had made radio contact with all vessels in the vicinity, asking them to join the search. The *Algonquin* started out from False Point; the *Pioneer* from Shumagan Island; the *Redwood, Modoc,* and *Redondo* from King Cove; the *Unga* from Chignik; and the *Warrior* from Squaw Harbor. Countless small fishing vessels and native kayaks joined the search. Dogsled teams organized by trappers and native Indians started out in search of the interior areas.

At ten P.M., the wireless operator at nearby King Cove fired up his "Big rig" and sent the following message to the Associated Press:

"Fears are expressed here for the safety of Major F.L. Martin, who left Chignik at 11:10 A.M. for Dutch Harbor, and who was not reported passing any points up to six o'clock tonight. Residents at the small tannery station here have just passed through the worst five days known for this period of the year. The North Pacific Ocean has been lashed by terrific gales, the wind frequently reaching one hundred miles per hour . . ."

THURSDAY, MAY 1, 1924
8:00 A.M.
THE HOME OF MAJOR FREDERICK MARTIN

The jangling doorbell was an unwelcome intrusion for Mrs. Martin. She and her six-year-old son had just finished their breakfast and she had to get her little boy bundled off to school. As she continued buttoning his jacket, it rang again. *Who is that*, she thought. She had left the milkman his money last night. Perhaps it was incorrect. She kissed her son and opened the door. The boy recognized General Patrick, saluted him and his aide smartly, then skipped off to school.

Self-consciously closing her house dress and surreptitiously checking her hair, Mrs. Martin was surprised at seeing General Patrick and the unknown aide accompanying him. She said, "General Patrick, what a pleasant surprise. Nice to see you. Do come in and I'll get us a nice cup of coffee and some freshly baked cookies."

Patrick politely introduced his aide, Lt. Crumrine, then entered. They sat on the overstuffed floral couch in the living room while Mrs. Martin went into the kitchen. *How nice*, she thought, *they've come to see how I'm doing in Frederick's absence.* As she prepared three cups and saucers, she recalled the expression on Patrick's face. He wasn't smiling. He looked very serious. It was as she reached for the cookies and arranged them on the platter that she realized there might be another purpose to this visit. A more sinister one. Could something have happened? Could Frederick—her husband, her child's father—be sick or . . . injured . . . or worse?

As she carried the tray from the kitchen, her legs felt weak, rubbery—her knees started to buckle. Lt. Crumrine flew across the room to her side, taking the tray and holding her arm, escorting her over to the large easy chair and helping her sit down. General Patrick sat stiffly, his lips curled down slightly, and his eyes told the story.

"It's Frederick, isn't it?" she said, fighting to hold back the panic creeping up from her stomach into her throat. "Something's happened to Frederick. What is it? Have they crashed? Are they okay? Are they alive? For God's sake—tell me!"

Patrick put his thoughts together before replying. Somehow this was more difficult than he imagined it would be. "Mrs. Martin," he started, "we just don't know. He was separated from the flight with an engine problem and flew to Chignik alone. He left yesterday to catch up with the flight at Dutch Harbor but never arrived. There were some bad storms in the area. He may have made a precautionary landing."

She couldn't stop them. The sobs and tears just welled up and overflowed from her lips and her eyes. She felt self conscious. Frederick would be ashamed of her. She was the wife of a soldier, and must start acting like it. Patrick waited for her to compose herself before continuing.

"I assure you we're doing everything we can. The Navy and Coast Guard have joined the search. We've got every man, woman, and child up there looking for them. I've even ordered a Curtiss flying boat boxed up and sent to Alaska. I'm transferring Lt. Earle Tonkin from Crissy Field in San Francisco up there to fly it. It's a vast area, Mrs. Martin. You must be patient."

MAY 1, 1924
5:25 A.M. THURSDAY
CRASH SITE OF THE *SEATTLE*

The wings lay in a crumpled heap several yards from the main wreckage of the fuselage, hardly recognizable under the blanket of freshly fallen snow. The scene appeared devoid of life with only the sickly sweet smell of high octane aviation fuel dribbling from the ruptured fuel tanks and lingering as mute testimony to the recent crash. As the sky lightened, the outline of the cockpit module revealed its surprising integrity. Just as he had said, Donald Douglas had built a strong airplane.

"Major Martin—Major Martin, are you all right?"

"I think so. Got the wind knocked out of me. I've got some cuts and bruises but I don't think I've broken any bones. How about you, Harvey?"

"I think I'm okay too. We're very lucky, Major. Snow cushioned the impact."

"If you call crashing and failing our mission lucky. Looks like I've gotten us into a fine pickle, Harvey."

"Don't worry about that, sir. You did the best you can."

Harvey climbed out first, then helped Martin out of his cockpit. He went to the baggage compartment and sorted through the gear, finding some survival rations.

"I'm sure glad we didn't get rid of all our survival gear. We've got food for at least three days, maybe four. Wish I had my rifle back. Can't hunt much with a forty-five. Harvey loaded up a large empty knapsack with possibly helpful items. Martin filled a smaller one. Martin found a map and started to study it while Harvey struggled to get out of his flight suit. "Any idea where we are?" he asked.

Martin brought the map over to Harvey and started to retrace their route. "We were flying just over two hours when we crashed. With the headwinds we had, that would put us one hundred to one hundred fifty miles southwest of Chignik but with that storm blowin' us around and all the zigging and zagging we did, we could be anyplace within this area." Martin circled a large area on the map with his finger.

"Major, if we don't know where we are, they're certainly not going to know where to look for us. We'll have to try and hike out."

"In this deep snow? Over those mountains? I don't think we'd make it."

"Only other choice is to stay here and die, Major. Don't think I want to do that." Harvey broke two branches from a dead tree. With his pocket knife he cut off the branches before handing one to the major. They put their knapsacks on their backs and started hiking through the waist-deep snow. It was slow going, each step an effort. As the day wore on, Martin's stops became more frequent. Once, Harvey looked back and found that Martin was gone. Harvey started retracing his steps. After a short distance, he could see the Major. His head was down. He looked tired.

"I . . . I'm sorry. I'm exhausted, Harvey. We've been going six hours. I've got to rest again. Not as young as I used to be."

"Just a little further, Major. I see something up ahead."

They continued hiking. Slowly the dark outlines lying in the snow revealed themselves. It was the wreckage of the *Seattle*. They had spent six hours going in a big circle. Shocked, then resigned, the Major said, "Guess the man upstairs wants us to spend another night right here, Harvey. Let's get some sleep and try again tomorrow."

FRIDAY, MAY 2, 1924
8:00 A.M.
DUTCH HARBOR

L owell and Erik finished their breakfast and walked through the heavy snow driven in horizontal sheets by the Willie-was toward the radio shack. They walked bent over against the strong winds and frozen hail. The illumination coming through the windows and the hum of the adjacent large transformer told them of the activity inside. Their pace quickened as they approached the door. Perhaps some news of Major Martin?

The radio operator looked at them in the doorway. Their eyes asked the question before they closed the door. He shook his head sadly, then handed them the radiogram.

```
TO LIEUT. LOWELL SMITH COMMANDER WORLD FLIGHT

FROM GENERAL PATRICK CHIEF U.S. AIR SERVICE

URGENT YOU DO NOT DELAY ANY LONGER WAITING FOR
MAJOR MARTIN STOP SEE THAT EVERYTHING POSSIBLE
DONE TO FIND HIM STOP PLANES 2-3-4 PROCEED TO
JAPAN AT EARLIEST POSSIBLE MOMENT STOP PATRICK
```

"Erik, I can't just leave them here. We should at least go up and look for them."

"You're in command now, Smitty, but you know as well as I do, they can be anywhere within ten thousand square miles. The chances of finding them alive in this Arctic wilderness is somewhere between slim and none."

"I know that, Erik. But why not at least go up and give it a try?"

"Because if one of those storms catches up with us, we can lose the whole flight. You know the Major would want us to get on with the mission. We all knew before we left that some of us might not come back. But it's your call now, Smitty."

The burden of command lay heavy on Lowell Smith's shoulders. He had never abandoned a downed airman before. He wished someone else had been put in charge. His heart was telling him to try, take his cruiser up, return to Chignik, retrace Martin's route, find them, save them. His head told him Erik was right. The mission had to go forward. It was more important than the Major, than Harvey, than any of them.

The radioman interrupted. "Got a call from the Bureau of Fisheries ship, the *Eider*. Major Blair's aboard. They're anchored at Atka, three hundred sixty-five miles west of here, waiting for you guys. Want to know when you're coming. What do you want me to tell them?"

Erik looked questioningly at Lowell. He seemed lost in thought. "Smitty?" The wheels had stopped turning inside Lowell Smith's head. He knew Erik was right. As commander of the flight, there was only one thing he could do. Follow orders and complete the mission. There was no other way. His heart's personal preference didn't count. He looked at Erik, then turned to the radioman.

"Advise Major Blair we're hoping this blizzard will move out this evening and plan to depart tomorrow morning. Ask him to radio the weather at Atka to us tomorrow."

The radioman gave Lowell a smile and quick salute, "Aye aye, Commander."

SATURDAY, MAY 3, 1924
2:10 P.M.
ATKA, ALEUTIAN ISLANDS

Flying conditions had been peculiar all day. The low ceiling forced the formation of three World Cruisers to fly under one thousand feet. Under the gray overcast sky, the visibility had been quite good, a welcome relief from the fog and snow that followed them through Alaska. Playfully, Leigh Wade had dropped out of the three-ship formation to give an inquisitive herd of reindeer a thrill, flying just feet over their antlers. Now, less than one hour out of Atka, they were again enveloped in a heavy driving rain mixed with snow and sleet. The weather Gods were not going to let them off that easy. They would have to pay the day's dues before being allowed to complete their flight.

Lowell led the flight lower and lower, attempting to maintain visual contact with the barren shoreline. In the descending darkness, Lowell turned on his formation flying lights, the red, green, and white streaks cutting through the driving rain. Leigh and Erik tightened up on Lowell, their full attention on his lighted wingtips now only inches from theirs. The carefree stunting of only a few minutes before became a distant memory as the pilots struggled to maintain formation in the diminished visibility. Suddenly, directly ahead of them, looming up like a black wall, lay the Island of Atka.

At first, there was no sign of the *Eider*, but as they skirted the high cliffs and passed over a protruding neck of land, suddenly it came into view, anchored in a sheltered bay next to a small village. As they circled for their approach, the *Eider* launched its tender and the rowing crewmen waved and pointed to the four neat yellow mooring buoys they had set for their arrival.

The crew of the *Eider* soon had the cruisers safely moored in the growing winds, with the *Chicago* nearest shore, then the *Boston* and furthest out, the *New Orleans*. Needless to say, the fourth mooring was, unfortunately, not necessary. With the mooring completed, the *Eider's* crew reboarded and the *Eider* departed to prepare for their next arrival at Chicagoff on the Island of Attu, lying 555 miles to the west. They now had 2,737 miles behind them. 23,000 to go.

May 6, 1924
5:15 p.m. Tuesday
Somewhere in the Alaskan wilderness

Major Martin loosened the line that tied the two men together, leaned backward against the dead tree to take some of the weight off his shoulders, then painfully pulled one arm and then the other from the straps holding the pack frame he had made from branches. The noise of the pack falling into the snow made Alva Harvey turn around just as Martin eased himself down into a sitting position in the snow, using his walking stick to check his fall.

Harvey turned around and trudged back through the snow to his fallen leader. Martin looked up as Harvey approached. "I'm done in Harvey. My feet are gone. You go on. Save yourself."

Harvey kneeled down next to Martin and gingerly removed the older man's boots and then carefully peeled off the bloodstained socks. The skin on Martin's feet was raw and bleeding. His shoulders sagged, his head hung dejectedly. The pain of even the smallest movement was reflected on his face. The Major looked twenty years older than he did just a few days before.

It had not been easy for either of them. After the first day and their fruitless six hour hike which led them back to their starting point, the path had not been easy. The second day's hike similarly ended in failure. After three hours of fighting their way through waist-deep snows, thick fog forced them to turn back again to the *Seattle*. The third day, snow blindness caused Harvey to fall into a deep crevasse—to be saved only by the line around his waist and the diminishing strength of the Major.

By the fourth day their meager rations were gone and both men had insufficient strength to continue. It was two lucky pistol shots killing two hapless pigeons that had come too close which saved them from starvation. This was now their sixth day, and as Harvey looked down at Martin, he saw a man that was beaten up too badly to go on.

The leaden sky was rapidly darkening, clouds building in intensity that would soon bring another storm down on them. Without shelter, they had no chance to survive. Harvey had to do something. "How old is your son, Major?"

"You know how old he is, Harvey. John is six."

"John's not going to be too happy when I tell him his dad gave up, is he? . . . or your wife, sir. She's not going to be too happy either, will she? . . . . Sir."

Grimly and with great pain, Martin struggled to put his bleeding, blistered feet back into his socks and then his boots. "You're a hard-driving son of a bitch, Sergeant. I'll give you one more hour." Harvey smiled, discarded his own pack, and helped the older man to his feet.

With Martin's arm around Harvey for support, the two men left their improvised backpacks, carrying only their flight suits and walking sticks.

U nited States newspapers carried daily stories of the lack of progress in the search for Martin and Harvey. The pundits were convinced that the *Seattle* lay under the frozen northern seas with their brave crew victims of bad weather, mechanical failure, or both. On May 6, two trappers reported that a biplane flew low over their heads in a blizzard near Port Moller on April 30. The "experts" considered this unlikely. Dutch Harbor lay west-southwest of Chignik, and Port Moller lay almost due north. The search continued to the west and south.

On May 8 the American Newspaper Alliance posted a reward of one thousand dollars for the safe return of the missing flyers. This generated enthusiasm among the Port Moller inhabitants and additional dog-sled teams joined the hunt. On May 9, crewmen of the U.S. C. G. Cutter *Bear* loaded the crated army airplane onto its deck to be used in the search. Lt. Earle Tonkin, the intended search pilot, had arrived in San Francisco and planned to continue his flight the next morning nonstop to Sand Point. The *Bear* prepared to depart the following morning.

By May 10, most newspapers had given up hope of finding them alive. Mrs. Luther Harvey, mother of Alva, tearfully showed his last letter which she had just received. It said, "I think God is watching over us and will carry us safely around to our dear ones in the States." She doubted it was true. Mrs. Nancy K. Martin, Frederick's mother, had also given up hope and was already in mourning for her son. Mrs. Frederick Martin had no doubts. She had taken her young son, John, and had gone to live with her sister. Despite all the unsolicited condolences on the death of her husband from reporters, she assured them that her Frederick would come back within a few days, alive and well. They pitied her and quietly scoffed.

O n the morning of May 6, Harvey noticed a dry stream bed leading to a far off lake. He steered them toward it. It had less snow and was easier walking. Martin's eyes were closed.

He mechanically lifted one foot and then the other through the pain. After several hours, Harvey suddenly stopped and looked up. He couldn't believe what he was seeing outlined in the darkness. It was a trapper's cabin.

Harvey turned to Martin who was now oblivious to anything else but the ritual of lifting one foot and then the other. He was only half conscious. "Major, hey, Major, Major Martin. Wake up! I've just found us a room at the Waldorf Astoria Hotel."

The trapper's cabin was amply equipped with flour, salted salmon, bacon fat, dried peaches, baking powder, condensed milk, syrup, and coffee. Martin laid down on the floor, with his shoes off at last, too exhausted to move. Harvey put the firewood, which had been neatly cut and stacked, into the small pot-bellied stove, lit the fire, and the cabin soon glowed with warmth. Outside, one of the season's worst blizzards which would last for days, had just begun.

On May 9, Harvey shot two horseshoe rabbits with their unknown host's rifle. The condensed milk box had the label of "Port Moller Cannery." They knew civilization must be very close. By May 10, the weather improved and they felt rejuvenated after three days of rest and feeding. Martin and Harvey finished a hearty breakfast of rabbit, pancakes, and hot gravy, restored the cabin to its original condition, and set out toward Port Moller. A smiling group of Indians greeted them. They had just won one thousand dollars, and the newspapers of the world scrambled to reset their headlines.

MAY 8, 1924
THURSDAY, 9:15 P.M.
ATKA, ALEUTIAN ISLANDS

Dear Diary,

Stuck here now for five days. Every day the same. Rain, sleet, hail and Willie-was to 60 knots. Staying in the store of Mr. Goss, the trader from Dutch Harbor. Smitty has the only bedroom. Rest of us sleep on folding bunks in the attic. Lots of rats there. Goss only comes one day a year. We can see why. I asked Goss when winter ends and spring begins here. He replied the only two seasons they had in these parts were this winter and next winter. I believe him.

Smitty cooks Eggs Vienna for us—every day. We wash it down with Eagle Brand condensed milk. Boring diet. The Aleut chief here has a bunch of chickens but refused to sell us any. Yesterday I crossed the ignition wires on his outboard motor. When he came begging us to fix it, we forced him to make a deal with us for some chickens. His motor motes again and we all finally had a good chicken dinner.

Jack and Hank usually wash the dishes. Wade, Erik, and I row out and secure the ship's moorings 2–3 times each day. Last night's blizzard got us all out doubling up the mooring lines. Got soaking wet. We all nearly froze. Didn't get to sleep until dawn. Tonight winds seem to be subsiding. Weather forecasted to improve.

Major Blair at Attu Island advises weather tomorrow expected to be flyable into Chicagoff. All of us going to sleep early. Plan to be up at dawn for early departure. All very anxious to leave.

Signed, Les Arnold.

MAY 15, 1924
9:15 A.M., THURSDAY
CHICAGOFF, ATTU ISLAND, ALEUTIANS

Today was the big day. Everything that had gone before would be only a footnote in the book of aviation history. This was the day that each of their names would be inscribed in bold headlines. The flight from Atka to Attu had gone well. They had left at 9:09 A.M., flown two seventy-five-mile legs over open ocean and, at five P.M., flew over the ring of dormant volcanoes sheltering the harbor of Chicagoff. The little ship *Eider* lying in wait next to the three yellow moorings was a welcome sight.

As the flight flew westward, the villages they landed at became progressively smaller. Chicagoff, with its population of fifty-nine had only three wooden buildings which included a Russian church and two warehouses. The native Aleutians lived in groups of six to eight in barrabora, single room small storm cellars burrowed from the ground with dome-shaped sod roofs and a window.

Attu Island looks like what it is; the end of North America and the end of everything American. Beyond Attu lies the Bering Sea, guardian of Asia. Among mariners, the Bering Sea is considered one of, if not the most hostile and formidable, steeped in mystery and foreboding with dangerous and unpredictable sea and weather conditions.

Colonel Broome, advance officer for McLaren's attempted world flight from England, left a note for them indicating the location of his cache of supplies and inviting the U.S. flight to use whatever they needed from it. Similar notes by Broome had been left for them in almost all of the places they visited.

After the crew of the *Eider* helped moor the three remaining World Cruisers, three of the officers, including Captain Beck, turned over their bunks to Smith, Wade and Nelson. The remaining flight crew made themselves cozy in the fo'csle. On May 11, the *Haida* arrived, bringing the good news received on her long range radio of the miraculous rescue of Major Martin and Sergeant Harvey from the Port Moller Cannery.

Spontaneous cheers from everyone on the *Eider* followed. Les Arnold spun Lowell Smith around in a wild dance of joy planting unwelcome kisses on everyone within grasp. With the arrival of the larger U.S.C.G. *Haida*, the *Eider's* work there was done. After the flyers returned to shore transferring their quarters to one of the warehouses, the *Eider* hoisted anchor to continue her mission. On May 13 a powerful storm hit Chicagoff blowing the *Haida* out to sea and necessitating another cold, wet, and sleepless night reinforcing the cruiser's moorings.

The *Eider* fought her way hundreds of miles through the stormy Bering Sea to the midway point of their flight to Asia. Major Blair sent back the first weather reports by radio to Chicagoff indicating that on May 15, flight to Asia might be possible. The flight plan called for a direct flight to Paramushiru which lay 870 miles away. This would bypass the Russian Komandorski Islands but lay at the limits of the cruiser's range. It would require good weather, good navigation and good luck.

As a precaution, Lowell sent the *Eider* to lie just off the three mile international limit of Russia's Bering Island where it could service and refuel them should an intermediate stop be necessary. At 11:35 A.M., May 15, the flight of three World Cruisers flew over the last bit of American soil.

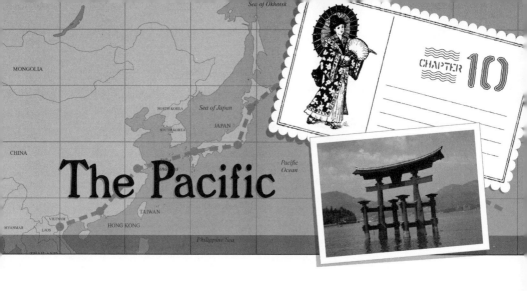

CHAPTER 10

The Pacific

L ost in the crash of the *Seattle* was a delicately hand-tooled leather case containing a very special message intended to "establish permanent international relations between the women of the world." Mrs. Charles H. Toll, representing the Los Angeles district of the California Federation of Women's Clubs, and Mrs. Chester C. Ashley of the Young Women's Christian Association had drafted the document which was to be presented on their behalf by Major Martin in the cause of world peace to all the women of the countries they landed in.

Special permission to carry and present this document had been granted reluctantly by General Pershing, Secretary of War Weeks, and President Coolidge after all references to "disarmament" had been removed. Arrangements had been made to have the document printed upon presentation in the newspapers of each nation visited. The document read:

> "To the women of the whole world, greetings! The government of the United States is sending the American air fleet to establish an airway around the globe which shall be a highway of peace. Twenty-two countries have given friendly cooperation for this flight. The starting point, and likewise the return point, is Southern California. Therefore the directors of the Young Women's Christian Association of Los Angeles seize the opportunity to send from America greetings and a message of friendship and peace to the women of all nations.

We pray to God, our common father, that this airway may be a band of friendship encircling the world, binding all nations of the earth in permanent bonds of peace. And since truth and justice are the only permanent foundation for the peace of the world, we, the mothers of men, voice the plea that all women, everywhere, use their influence to the end that the principles of truth and justice may prevail and govern all our relationships, both as individuals and as governments.

In the love of God, we salute you."

MAY 15, 1924
12:20 P.M.
SIXTY-FIVE MILES SW OF ATTU ISLAND.

When the *Chicago* passed over the *Haida*, Smitty and I waved at its crew struggling through mountainous seas. I looked back. The last vestiges of the outline of Attu Island had disappeared. All contact with land was gone and, in a few minutes, so was the ship. We were now totally alone and praying that our engines would continue singing their sweet song. Howling winds blew the tops of thirty foot high waves into white-capped giant plumes of spray. Flying only four hundred feet above them, the wet salt air permeated every nook and cranny of the cockpit with its lingering cold dampness. The lenses of my flying goggles required constant wiping of the crystalline salt residues.

The *Boston* flew ten feet low and twenty feet behind my right wing. Leigh's lips smiled each time I made eye contact with him. The *New Orleans* bobbed up and down twenty to thirty feet off my left wing. From the altitude excursions I knew Erik was letting Jack Harding fly from the rear cockpit. With Erik and Leigh flying, there were no altitude excursions. They anticipated our every movement and corrected for it better than anyone I had ever flown formation with before. It was as if our three airplanes were tied together with invisible wires, rising and falling in perfect harmony with each other, never deviating from the established separation—an aerial ballet, exquisitely timed to the changing winds and air currents.

I reflected briefly on our rafts, radios, and life jackets left behind in Seattle, but logic told me they would be of little help in the frigid waters of the Bering Sea. If any of our engines quit, our planes would quickly capsize under the monstrous waves. We would lose the ability to swim or even move within ten minutes, consciousness within thirty minutes, and death would mercifully come before an hour had passed.

When a pilot flies far out over the ocean, the engine goes on "automatic rough," and I knew that Leigh and Erik were both listening and feeling the same subtle strange sounds and tingling vibrations I was. To the airman far out at sea, the mind plays tricks. The normal clatter and bang of valves, pistons, and exhaust noises become ominous messengers of impending failure and doom. To give in to them is to let panic into the cockpit and chase reason away, so you put them out of your mind and concentrate on the mechanical aspects of navigating and aviating. If it was simple, someone would have already done it. To be the first, we had to pioneer, blaze the trail, conquer the unknown. Fear comes with the territory and the task.

By 1:30 P.M. the wind-whipped waves were growing in intensity and the sky to the southwest had darkened to an ominous brown with no horizon line. Paramushiru was becoming increasingly unlikely. I turned toward Erik. He shrugged his shoulders and held his palms up. Of course, it was Smitty's call. Some choice. Do we try going through an approaching storm or turn toward the north and take a chance on becoming permanent residents of a Siberian prison? Another look to the southwest and a sky now black with ice-laden storm clouds made the decision for him. Reluctantly, he held his right arm outstretched, pointed toward the north, and rolled the *Chicago* into a standard rate turn toward Bering Island in the Komandorskis, 270 miles away. He signaled to me sitting in the rear cockpit to take the controls by rotating the wooden control wheel rapidly side to side and holding both his arms in the air where I could see them. With me flying, Smitty drew the new route on his chart, north to Copper Island, then northwest to Palatka Point and a final five degree course correction to Nikolski Harbor on Bering Island, the largest of the group.

By 2:30 P.M. we could make out the welcome outline of our first landfall and by 3:05 P.M. I turned northwest over Copper Island.

Russian territory or not, it was good to see land under us again. The engine's "automatic rough" gremlins soon disappeared, and the old Liberty started purring like it would run forever. According to our charts, these outlying islands didn't have much by way of human habitation and our eyes confirmed just that. We were thankful that the only welcome committee anywhere near that barren rocky coastline were a few whales and seagulls scrambling to avoid colliding with the largest birds they'd ever seen.

The charts showed Nikolski to be not only inhabited but a remote military outpost, so we knew our stealthy intrusion was bound to be observed by somebody. I chuckled thinking about the ruckus our State Department would be making if they only knew where we were. I still remember how petrified they were of our Alaskan flight creating an international incident years ago by stopping on Russian territory. Well, Mr. Secretary of State, I sure didn't plan it this way, but man proposes and God disposes, so like it or not, here we are. I just pray it's not here we stay.

"It was just before five P.M. that I spotted a cut in the coastline which looked like it might be Nikolski Harbor. As I flew closer I could see two tall radio transmitting towers and what looked like a pretty good sized outpost with real wooden houses, storage buildings, and a radio transmitting shack. There were some fishing boats anchored in the harbor and some more pulled up on the beach.

A group of Russian fishermen working on their beached boats heard the sounds of our engines and were staring up at us as if we were spaceships from another planet. I laughed when one of them took a look at us and promptly fell off his ladder then scrambled up as fast as he could to get another look. It was apparent they didn't know whether to shoot at us or wave to us. We waved at them to make their decision a little easier but they didn't wave back.

I turned control of the *Chicago* back over to Smitty. I could see the *Eider* lying about five miles offshore in international waters well beyond the three mile limit. She couldn't anchor our moorings in water over sixty feet deep so she had come in toward shore at night under cover of darkness and dropped them for us then. I could see the three yellow buoys bobbing up and down about one mile offshore. We flew over them outbound, banked low around the *Eider*, waved at the crew on the rail, and started our approach inbound. As he cut the engine to begin our landing glide, I could see a large crowd gathering on the beach to watch our approach. A smaller group was launching a longboat into the swells. It did not look good.

As we taxied to our mooring buoys, three longboats were headed for us. Two were coming from the *Eider* to help us and the other came from the beach with two men in uniforms and three in civilian clothes. They all had long shaggy beards and approached us menacingly, shouting questions in what we guessed was Russian. They had several rifles and a machine gun with them but weren't pointing them at us—yet! Judging from the crowd now on the beach, they would have no trouble overpowering any feeble resistance we were capable of, so we all smiled sweetly, spoke in soothing tones, and continued the mooring process until all three ships were securely moored.

They didn't speak a word of English and of course, we didn't speak a word of Russian. For one of the few times in my life, I was speechless. We indicated to them as best we could that we meant no harm and would soon be on our way and that they should follow us out to the *Eider* for a full explanation. They looked suspicious, not knowing what to believe. To allay their fears, I got into their boat with Smitty and directed them to follow the two other boats from the *Eider*.

All three boats motored over to the *Eider*. Fortunately the Fisheries Board had hired a Lithuanian crewmember from Chicago. We called him into the crew room and he interpreted for us. He explained who we were, where we had come from, and the chance encounter with the storm which forced us to land in their waters. Once they realized we were not invading their island, they relaxed noticeably, took their weapons off their laps, and slung them on the backs of their chairs. The idea of playing a small unexpected role in the first flight around the world filled them with delight. The leader of the group described how they would all tell their grandsons of this day, and excused himself to return temporarily to his motor launch.

In a few moments he was back with a bottle of Russian vodka, filling our glasses and toasting our success. One of the *Eider's* crewmen appeared with some homemade "White Lightning." The Russians couldn't understand why our drink had such a funny name—until they tried it! Far from the constraints of our new prohibition laws, we all indulged tasting the delights of each country's version of an alcoholic beverage. If our's wasn't better, it was certainly stronger.

Within an hour, we were all fast friends, learning each other's bawdy songs, toasting each other's health, exchanging cigarettes, and feeling quite amiable. Eventually their leader looked at his watch, excused himself, and asked, almost apologetically, if we had permission from Moscow to land here. We explained we had requested permission but weren't certain if it came through. We advised we would be staying onboard and leaving at dawn tomorrow anyway. With a wink and a nod, he "ordered" us not to set foot on the island until Comrade Trotsky advised we were welcome. He would radio Moscow, return, and advise us tomorrow morning of their decision. We waved them a cheery "Good-bye."

Not wanting to stretch our luck any further, as soon as they had gone, we lowered drums of aviation gasoline and oil into the *Eider's* tenders and completed refueling and servicing of all three cruisers by ten P.M. so we would be ready for an early morning departure. As insurance, Captain Beck wired the larger and far more heavily armed U.S.C.G. *Haida* of our position. She immediately started steaming at full speed toward us just in case some "persuasion" from her deck guns were necessary to rescue us and secure our departure.

Crossing the international dateline the previous day, it was now May 17, 1924. Daylight came early in that part of the world. By 4:30 A.M. we were in the motor launch skimming over the waves toward our waiting cruisers. As we made our planes ready to fly, our Russian friends returned, advising us sadly that Moscow had rejected our request and we must leave immediately. We saluted and nodded our compliance with great vigor and joy at having escaped the clutches of the great Russian bear.

Before I could climb into the cockpit, I noticed another launch from the *Eider* traveling at top speed toward us. I recognized the radioman standing in the bow, holding on for dear life with one hand and frantically waving a piece of paper at us with the other. He handed Smitty a radiogram from the destroyer waiting for us at Paramushiru. It was not good news. "Commander Lowell Smith, Urgent you do not attempt crossing today. Blizzards, heavy icing and fog at Paramushiru. Ceiling zero. Visibility zero."

This was a fine pickle. We couldn't stay and we shouldn't go. We spoke about discussing it with the others but decided there was no point in worrying them also. We had to leave or risk internment or a really nasty international incident. The likelihood of conditions improving were a lot better at our landing site than they were here. Hopefully the ceiling would lift and visibility would improve before we got there. Smitty motioned all the boats out of our path and indicated to Leigh and Erik that he would lead. We climbed into the cockpit, started our engines, and taxied away from the moorings to start our takeoff run. This leg would be a calculated risk, but then again, most legs were and I knew if anyone could get us through, it would be Smitty.

On leaving Nikolski Harbor, we turned to fly over the *Eider* one last time, waving our appreciation to the crew who had done so much for us. Turning toward the southwest, we could see the smoke coming from the *Haida's* stacks as she steamed at full speed to help us. We circled her once and waved another appreciative good-bye before climbing to altitude to complete the first flight ever from North America to Japan.

By 9:30 A.M. we covered the distance of 150 miles over the open water of the Gulf of Kronotski and were over the headland jutting out into the ocean where Cape Shipunski started the continent of Asia. Even if we had all crashed into the sea at that moment, technically the first flight from North America to Asia would have been completed. Erik, Leigh, and I exchanged smiles and a joyous "thumbs up." Next stop; Paramushiru, Japan.

MAY 17, 1924
SATURDAY, 11:20 A.M.
PARAMUSHIRU, JAPAN

Linton Wells, ace aviation reporter for the Associated Press was not a happy man. Neither was his boss. Wells had been on this assignment for two months now with very little to show for it. After renting an airplane and accompanying the world fliers to Seattle, he had hitched a series of rides on U.S. naval and merchant ships to Yokohama. He joined up with Lt. Cliff Nutt, the flight's advance man, in the expectation of accompanying him to Paramushiru in the Kurile Islands. They were disappointed to find the local boat owners considered the run to Paramushiru that early in the season too dangerous and demanded the full cost of their boats to attempt the trip.

The U.S. Navy came to their rescue and sent the U.S. destroyers *Pope* and *Ford* from the U.S. Asiatic fleet at Manila. The destroyers arrived at Yokohama on April 6th and the *Ford* loaded up with spare parts, aviation gasoline, and provisions for two weeks. Captain Halloway H. Frost welcomed Wells, Nutt, and the Japanese officers Mitchell had agreed to onboard. The *Ford* sailed for Paramushiru in the Kuriles on April 10th, expecting the U.S. flight to arrive within one week. The *Pope* sailed with her, also with Japanese officers on-board, for the flyer's next stop at Bettobu Bay, 510 miles south of Paramushiru and also in the Kuriles.

The voyage north to the Kurile Islands was extremely hazardous for both ships with huge ice floes, storms, blizzards, and gale force winds. The Japanese destroyer *Tokitsukaze* followed the *Ford* and anchored close by. On April 15, three additional American destroyers, the *Pillsbury*, the *Paul Jones* and the *Truxton* arrived in Yokohama to support the flight with a sixth, the U.S.S. *Peary* expected shortly.

After two weeks, the *Ford* ran out of food, and the Japanese crew invited the U.S. crew to dine with them. With the Japanese crew supplying the food and the U.S. crew supplying endless Hollywood movies and games, the two crews got along just fine. Friendships were formed, gifts exchanged, and each picked up some of the other's language.

On April 30th an old 125-foot coal-burning Canadian steamship, *Thiepval* anchored close by carrying Colonel Broome, the advance man for Major MacLaren's British Flight, which was also expected shortly. On May 3rd the *Pope* arrived to relieve the *Ford*, which started its nine hundred mile journey to rendezvous with the U.S. destroyers *Truxton* and *Peary* at Hakodate and resupply. Wells transferred to the *Pope* and the hospitality of its Captain McClaren.

All the ships waiting in the Kuriles were being hammered by storms, gales, and hurricane-force winds, dragging their anchors, and under constant threat of broaching or being thrown onto the rocks. To pass the time, Wells started a ship's newspaper—printing the latest dispatches received on the destroyer's powerful radio from Associated Press.

The Teapot Dome investigations expanded daily and their ever-widening ripples reached deeper and deeper within the government. Assistant Secretary of the Navy Roosevelt defended himself against charges of complicity in the tainted oil leases, having secured a job for his brother, Archie, with the Sinclair Oil Company. The director of the Veteran's Bureau, Charles R. Forbes and his chief of the supply division, Charles R. O'Leary were indicted on charges of selling $3,313,250 worth of government sheets, pillowcases, and supplies for $598,159 to Nathan Thomson of Thomson & Kelly Company, Boston. They stood accused of misrepresenting the material sold as obsolete and unserviceable while buying the same material at a far higher cost to the government from November 15 of 1922 to January 28 of 1923.

The attorney general appointed by Harding, Harry M. Daugherty, was accused of profiting from the sale of fight film rights, liquor licensing, and the sale of alien property and depositing funds into a bank controlled by his brother. Cash payments of $100,000 on Nov. 30, 1921 from Edward Doheny to Albert Fall for government oil leases were being investigated.

A new U.S. government air mail service using U.S. Army pilots would start July 1, 1924 and replace the private contractors now flying the mail. One thousand miles of airway using giant lighted beacons visible from one hundred fifty miles away and airports every twenty-five miles were supposed to make the route easy to fly. With the payment of eight cents postage, a letter would be carried via air from New York City to Chicago. Sixteen cents would fly it to Cheyenne, and twenty-four cents would take it all the way to San Francisco using eleven airplanes. The army pilots, flying poorly instrumented obsolete aircraft without cockpit or landing lights, and with little training in flying the route at night and in bad weather, would suffer enormous casualties and air mail would revert back to private contractors.

On April 15, Republican Senator Reed of Pennsylvania, waiting until late in the day when U.S. Senate attendance was sparse, requested and received unanimous consent to vote the Japanese

Exclusion Act "out of order". American policy and attitudes toward Japan, our ally during the war, were strongly divided.

On the one hand, the U.S. supplied more aid to Japan during their previous year's earthquake than any other country. Congress authorized, without objection, the largest loan since the war, $150 million to Japan. Diplomatic and commercial relationships were expanding. Tourism, cultural, and student exchanges were growing.

On the other hand, influential Western interests, the Hearst newspapers, and other media regaled daily against the "Yellow Peril" and actively promoted anti-Japanese sentiments. Over the objections of the Japanese government, ambassadors of both countries, and even President Coolidge, the Senate voted to exclude anyone born in Japan from ever holding U.S. citizenship. U.S. Ambassador Woods resigned in protest. Embarrassingly, President Coolidge did not exercise his veto and the Johnson Immigration Act would become law during the arrival of the U.S. World Flight in Japan.

Despite the brewing geopolitical storm, Lt. Commander Wada, captain of the *Tokitsukaze* toasted and encouraged the growing bonds of friendship between his sailors and their newly-found American brothers of the sea on the nearby *Ford* and *Pope*. These ships would meet again eighteen years later in the Macassar Straits with guns blazing. The *Ford* would prevail and become the first U.S. vessel since the Battle of Manila to send an enemy ship and all of its sailors to a watery grave.

Of most interest in Wells's little newspaper was the progress of the round-the-world fliers. While the Americans had now fallen over a month behind their original schedule struggling with bad weather, mechanical failures, and the loss of their flight leader, the European fliers were making rapid progress.

On March 20 at 12:10 P.M., Major Stuart MacLaren and Sergeant Andrews had started their flight from Southampton, England in his specially-built Vickers Vulture Amphibian. MacLaren, the R.A.F.'s most decorated British pilot, had flown the first British plane into Egypt, and later led the first flight into India. By March 31, he passed through France, Italy, and Greece before making a forced landing on Lake St. Matthew on the Island of Corfu. American Colonel Stephen E. Lowe, director of the Near East Relief Orphanage, came to his aid. With Lowe's help, repairs were completed to his airplane and by April 5 and he was again underway. By April 18 he had made it to Cairo. By the 19th he was in Palestine and by the 20th, Baghdad. On the 22nd, he landed in Bushire, Persia and by the 23rd, landing in Karachi, India, he had covered over five thousand miles in just over one month.

On April 24th, Lt. Pelletier D'Oisy and his mechanic Bernard Vesin took off from Paris in a fast Breguet military biplane powered by a 370 HP Lorraine-Dietrich engine. D'Oisy, with the fastest airplane, made a furious pace covering the distance of 2,800 miles to Basra in Iraq within three days. By May 3rd, D'Oisy caught up and passed MacLaren who had stopped with engine problems three hours out of Karachi. On May 7th he reached Calcutta then Rangoon on May 8 where he paused to nurse an overheating engine. He had covered over eight thousand miles in two weeks, an average of over 570 miles per day while the Americans were averaging only seventy miles per day.

The Portuguese flight of Captain Brito Paes and Lieutenant Sarmento Beiros in their Breguet airplane named *Patria* also was making excellent progress. By April 30 they had reached Bushire in Persia and were winging their way to Bandar Abbas.

On May 11th the *Ford* returned to the barren anchorage at Paramushiru. The crew of the *Pope* cheered their arrival. They could now leave this dreary barren place. The Japanese crew on the *Tokitsukaze* welcomed their old friends' return and many American crewmembers brought small gifts with them for their friends. Wells transferred back to his old bunk on the *Ford*, wondering when his epic wait would be over. He now held the dubious title of the island's oldest Westerner.

Wells's editor grew more impatient with him each day. The slow-paced fits and starts of the American flight made it difficult to sustain the initial public enthusiasm. The flight had been pushed off the front pages of the newspapers. Interest had waned and Wells's time for his assignment had expired. The editor wanted him back and the expenses of his traveling to stop.

Linton Wells sat in the radio room sending a message to his office advising them yet again that the weather today made the arrival of the American flight all but impossible when he heard a commotion on deck. Stopping in mid-sentence, he looked through the porthole in the radio room. He couldn't believe what he was seeing.

From out of the heavy snow, an airplane emerged, then a second and almost at the same time, a third. "They made it," he shouted as he ran out to watch them circling the ship. Remembering his unsent message and the Japanese requirement to close down transmitting for thirty minutes following the crew's landing, he rushed back to the radio room to hurriedly complete his transmission. "Urgent. Associated Press, San Francisco. Fliers arrived Kashiwabara Bay, Paramushiru, 17th, at 11:35." At 11:37, the flight touched down on the waters of Japan. By the time the Japanese destroyers notified their waiting war department, Wells had finally gotten his scoop.

MONDAY, MAY 26, 1924
10:30 P.M.,
TOKYO, JAPAN

Dear Diary:

Writing this in the warm luxury of a beautiful hotel room in Tokyo, the frostbitten hours in the cockpit and the bleak, cold, barren desolation of the Aleutians seems like something from another lifetime. We all felt very badly about keeping the destroyer crews waiting for us so long at Paramushiru. We've been pushing as hard as we could but the weather was just terrible.

After landing at Paramushiru Saturday, May 17th, the winds threw around the cruisers and the destroyers something fierce. The winds blew up to eighty mph and whipped the seas up to thirty foot waves. We had to replace the steel mooring cables twice on Sunday. It's a good thing we checked them because the ones on the Boston and the New Orleans had almost broken. Of nine steel strands, only a single one was left.

2:00 A.M. Monday morning we finally were able to start getting ready. By 7:00 A.M. we were all in the air and flying to Hitokappu Bay on Yeterofu Island 595 miles away. That was the coldest flight of the trip, in and out of snow squalls and freezing rains over hundreds of deserted islands with huge mountains and volcanoes.

At 2:15 we landed and the crew of the Pope helped us moor our ships. Several hundred school children, the boys neatly dressed in black caps and kimonos, the girls in trousers and carrying parasols waited on the shore. They had walked the nine miles to the lake with their teacher for the past three days expecting our arrival. They were all very respectful and cheered us as soon as we stepped foot on shore.

The youngsters had walked fifty-four miles in wooden shoes over the past three days and were obviously in marvelous physical condition. The boys learn jujitsu, long-distance swimming, fencing, and hiking under military discipline before they even enter high school. Then they are all taught the same subjects we learn including English speaking and writing. They really take their schoolwork seriously here. They prepared a show for us but we were all so tired from the long flight, we fell asleep.

The next two mornings we awoke at 2:00 A.M. and went down to our ships but the fog never lifted. We gave up about noon time and spent the days exploring the town. Everything here seems to be in miniature. The people are a good head under our height, the trees are squatty and stunted with cut-off tops, and even the horses are no larger than our own Shetland ponies. We kept hitting our heads walking into homes or stores. Taking off our shoes, as is their custom upon entering a room, presented another challenge. They sit neatly upright on straw mats on the floor with their feet somewhere under them. We can never get our big feet out of sight no matter how hard we try. They seem to bend a lot easier than we do.

We're always being introduced as fliers and the youngsters always ask us to flap our arms and fly around for them. They seem pretty disappointed when we tell them we can't do that. The older ones laugh at that and seem to know as much about flying as we do. Everything here is very neat and very clean. Everyone on the island invited us to visit their home. We did visit several and were treated like royalty. They even put on their Sumo wrestling fights for us. Finally, on May 22nd, our 2 A.M. vigils were rewarded. The fog lifted and we hopped off for Minato 485 miles distant at 5:30 A.M.

Smitty wired ahead to Minato asking that no reception for us be planned but as we approached the landing we could see the beach teeming with thirty thousand spectators, huge welcome signs, reception tents, and rows of dignitaries. Against a backdrop of firecrackers and skyrockets being fired in our honor from the beach, Lt. Cliff Nutt led a small fleet of sampans filled with gasoline and oil out to us and we secured the ships to the moorings.

Minato harbor is open to the sea with little protection and the wind was rising. Not a good place to spend the night. We had another 350 miles to go to reach Tokyo. Wanting to get there in daylight, we gave Cliff the thankless job of making apologies for our not landing. We lifted into balmy skies and landed at the Japanese naval air base at Lake Kasumigaura, forty-five miles north of Tokyo just after 5:00 P.M. Thursday, May 22. We had covered 5,657 miles since Seattle and logged seventy-five hours and fifty-five minutes in the air. Just over twenty thousand miles left to go.

Three stone ramps, each with an attending motor launch had been prepared for us. Upon landing, a motor launch took each of our ships carefully in tow and over to the pier. Tens of thousands of Japanese waved American flags, slapped us on the back, and shouted "Banzai." Photographers from every newspaper in the world snapped pictures of us while reporters eagerly scribbled down each word that dropped out of our mouths as if it were a pronouncement from the heavens.

The "gentlemen of the press" all seemed to have their own national costume. All of the French correspondents had full beards, the Englishmen monocles, the Americans straw hats, and the Japanese cardigan sweaters, ties, and tiny eyeglasses.

After we arrived they took us to the Naval Air Service Club and gave us our own separate room and an orderly. Special cooks prepared American dishes for us and a bunch of entertainment was scheduled. After flying nine hundred miles in ten hours and not having slept for almost twenty-four hours, we were all dog tired and excused ourselves to get some sleep before the entertainment started.

Coming down from the Arctic to Japan was like what I imagine a cat feels coming out of the snow on a winter's day into a warm room, finding a dish of cream by the fireplace, and then stretching out and going to sleep.

Much as we all wanted to see Tokyo, we spent that whole day getting the planes ready for overhaul. It was a good thing we had new pontoons waiting here because a curious boatman got too close, pushed himself off with an oar, and made a big hole in the thin wooden pontoon. One thing we learned this flight: never use wood for pontoons. They always break, get holed, or leak.

The Japanese had two weeks of receptions, banquets, parties, and gala events planned to celebrate the first aerial crossing of the Pacific but we told them we had too much work to do and could only give them two days. They picked us up Friday night from the naval club in two limousines and told us they were taking us to a teahouse in Tsuchimira for a geisha party. We had no idea what that was and felt it would be rude to ask. So we just sat back and waited. Figured geisha wouldn't hurt us anyway. Our dress uniforms hadn't arrived yet so we were in borrowed clothes which really didn't fit too well. The only other clothes we had were our flight suits which were ready to do their own marching. At least we had time to take showers before we left.

When we stepped from our limousines to the veranda of the teahouse, checked our shoes, and were welcomed by a crowd of Japanese maids in flowered kimonos, it seemed as though we had stepped into the pages of a storybook.

We entered a room with a floor covered with straw mats and walls that were mere screens made of wood and paper. The Admiral invited us all to kneel on silk cushions. Then a tiny lacquered table was placed in front of each of us by the pretty geisha girls who were there to serve and entertain us—demure, delightful, laughing-eyed, sixteen year olds. Each time one of them brought in another course she would kneel and touch her forehead to the matting. Each geisha devotes herself exclusively to the man she is waiting on, removes the various courses, brings others, lights his cigarettes as he reclines on his cushions, fills his little cup with warm sake, and initiates him into the mystery of using chopsticks.

The Admiral had ordered nothing but Japanese food, but we were too busy fighting with our chopsticks to care much about what we were eating. Just try eating rice with two knitting needles and you will know what it's like. I had it in my eyes, my ears, and even in my hair. The others didn't do much better either. The hot sake flowed like water and after a short while none of us cared where the rice or anything else we were eating went.

After we had dined, the geishas danced and sang to weird music. But the dancing was incredibly artistic and the polar opposite to our American jazz. In bright silks, with dainty fans, the geisha simply postured before gold and silver screens. It all seemed in exquisite taste. It was the evening of a lifetime for all of us and like a dream.

The next morning, Saturday, May 24th, our dress uniforms arrived so we changed into Army Air Service dress for the first time since Seattle. Japanese naval officers picked us up and drove us in automobiles with a full naval escort to the train station. A special train, just for us, with separate coaches for our naval and military escorts, photographers, reporters, and VIPs was waiting. When we got off the train, a reception committee of high Japanese officials and all the members of the Imperial Aviation Association were waiting for us with a crowd of at least one hundred thousand people.

Lt. General Gaishi Negoaka delivered an address of welcome and his tiny granddaughter addressed us in English and gave Smitty a bouquet. It was a dull day so thousands of flashbulbs were popping off all around us making it seem like a Fourth of July celebration.

With one of the most terrible disasters of modern times having taken place here just over six months ago, we expected to see a city in ruins. But as we sat in the back of the limousines on the way to the Imperial Hotel, there was surprisingly little evidence of the calamitous earthquake which had claimed hundreds of thousands of casualties. The Prince Regent's Palace showed great cracks in the walls and places where even the massive stones had been blistered by the tremendous heat of the fire. Already the debris had been cleaned away in most of the city and temporary structures erected over the ruins. They plan to build a new Tokyo more beautiful than any city in the world.

The Imperial Hotel in which we were staying was the only building in downtown Tokyo that had survived intact. Frank Lloyd Wright, the American who designed it, must be a pretty good architect and will probably be very famous someday.

Our Ambassador to Japan, Cyrus Woods, met with us that evening. He wasn't too happy about the Japanese Exclusion Act being passed by Congress. He feared it would lead to increasing conflict between our two countries in the future and make his job almost impossible. He felt so strongly about it he turned in his letter of resignation to President Coolidge. We feel caught in the middle and hoped the nasty game of politics wouldn't interfere with our flight.

Sunday, May 25 was a busy day for us with some big surprises. Colonel Broome, the advance officer for the British flight, came to our room to join us for breakfast. We were all running a bit late when he arrived and I let him in while several of us were just finishing dressing. He was a good sport and pretended not to notice our flying around the hotel suite looking for last night's jackets, shoes, and belts.

After about an hour, the doorbell rang and a bellman handed him a telegram. He read it, and with a devastated look, handed it to me. It read:

MACLAREN CRASHED AT AKYAB. PLANE COMPLETELY
WRECKED. CONTINUANCE OF FLIGHT DOUBTFUL.

I handed it to Smitty. We all knew MacLaren's spare airplane had just gotten unloaded the previous day at Hakodate, five hundred miles north of Tokyo. As we passed around the telegram, Broome went over to the window and looked down on the streets of Tokyo. He tried to hide it but we could see the silent tears coming down his cheeks in the reflection of the glass. He had spent every day for the past two years planning, traveling, and laying in caches of supplies for this flight. We knew better than anyone else what a devastating blow that telegram was to him. We wanted to win—but not this way.

Smitty looked at me first. I knew what he was thinking. I nodded my agreement. Every one of us did the same. Smitty excused himself and left the room. We all knew where he was going.

When Smitty came back to the room he was smiling and we knew the Navy had come through for us again. Smitty explained to Broome that he had gone to the room of Commander Abbot immediately above ours and explained his predicament. Abbot agreed, on his own responsibility, to send our destroyer, John Paul Jones, to Hakodate, load the cases containing MacLaren's spare plane and carry them to Nagasaki which was at the end of his assigned territory. If necessary, he would cable his "boss," Admiral Washington, commanding the American Asiatic fleet, for permission to carry them all the way to the British fleet at Hong Kong where they could be transferred to a British vessel for the ten-day voyage to Akyab in India.

Broome acted like a man who had just received a last minute reprieve from death and embraced Smitty, crying for joy. After thanking us profusely, Broome left to send a cable to the British Commander-in-Chief of the China Station to make the arrangements for pick up and hand-off to a British vessel.

That afternoon we were the guests of honor at a huge banquet arranged by Field Marshall Kawamura and his aide, Major Watari. We met great numbers of statesmen, military and naval leaders, educators, including the president of Tokyo University, and even most of the Imperial Cabinet. Everyone was most gracious and hospitable. That afternoon, General Ugaki, the Minister of War, honored us with six beautiful silver sake cups engraved with the Douglas World Cruisers.

That evening another reception in our honor was held in the Imperial Hotel organized by Major Faymonville of the American Embassy and the residents of Tokyo. The entire Japanese Diplomatic Corps attended and we blushed with all the nice things everyone said about us and our first crossing of the Pacific.

Prince Kuni, brother of the Prince Regent and head of the Imperial Aeronautical Society, presented each one of us with medals the following morning followed by a visit to the very beautiful home of Soichiro Ansano, owner of their largest shipping lines. Here we briefly met the most gracious Madame Ansano and her lovely daughters before joining many of their most successful business leaders at a wonderful tea party.

Each of the geisha serving us our tea had an American flag fluttering from the back of her flowered kimono. During the tea, Mr. Ansano presented each of us with a silver pepper shaker in the form of the Oriental God of Laughter with a weighted round bottom. He said, "I have made and lost several fortunes, but like this image I have always managed to come up smiling. On this first flight around the world you are sure to encounter many obstacles, some no doubt seemingly insuperable ones. As this doll always stands up after being knocked down, so must you to reach your goal. From old Japan, these Darma dolls remind us, as they must you, you can't keep a good man down."

Of all the wonderful warm welcoming ceremonies given to us in Japan, none touched us so deeply as that of the president of Tokyo University, Dr. Yoshinao Kozai speaking for the faculty and members of the Aeronautical Research Institute of Japan.

"Officers of the Army Air Service of the United States, It is an honor and great delight to us to welcome you to our university—you, who have come to our shores over the seas, through the air. All here assembled, both the faculty and the members of the Aeronautical Research

Institute of Japan, cannot but admire your dauntless spirit and congratulate you on the success you have achieved. At the same time we envy you, for your daring is backed by science. Indeed it is the happy union of courage and knowledge that has gained you your success and this honor of being the first of men to connect the two shores of the Pacific Ocean through the sky. This same spirit and skill, I am sure, will soon make you the pioneers of aerial flight around the globe.

"Looking a little into the past, it is to your nation that the honor is due for having produced the pioneers of aviation, Langley and the Wright Brothers, and during the two decades that have followed their first successes in the air, the progress of aviation accelerated by your fellow citizens has been simply marvelous. Your pioneership is a manifestation of your valor which implies daring and tirelessness in conjunction with deliberation and endurance. Your success is not merely a result of adventure, but is the fruit of study and research in the wide and complicated domain of physics, chemistry, mechanics, and meteorology.

"Gentlemen! Your honor is, of course, the pride of your nation; but the honor and pride are to be shared by all mankind, because they are a manifest expression of moral and intellectual powers in the human race—the will, ability, means, and methods, all illustrate through your success man's control over nature.

"More than four hundred years ago, slow sailing vessels carried Christopher Columbus across the Atlantic. Two centuries later, your pioneers crossed the Rockies with weary horses and carts. Nearly half a century elapsed before the two oceans, the Atlantic and Pacific, were connected by rail. And now you are encircling the earth by machines flying through the sky.

"Again I say, we admire and envy you. Again I say that your honor is to be shared by all mankind.

"Wing westward, farther and farther to your home! Then start anew toward the west and come again to our shores, then on to our neighbors and to yours, and through all the continents of the world! Thus through your efforts and successes will the nations of the earth be made closer friends and neighbors.

"To the west, east, north, and south, we shall everywhere follow your journeys with admiration and congratulation! We bid you God-Speed!"

Lt. General Irasumitsu hosted us at the Maple Club during our last night in Tokyo. Ambassador Woods joined us on the straw tatami mats as the geisha did their usual job of making us feel like kings. After the requisite amount of sake and raw fish had been consumed, the evening moved on to some fascinating games which vacillated from extremely child-like to extremely adult oriented. Dancing around in our stockinged feet, all pretense of dignity left us and we eagerly participated with relish in the night's activities, the details of which shall remain forever sealed within my most memorable reminisces.

Waiting for us in the lobby hotel when we returned was a most dejected Colonel Broome. Without comment he handed Smitty the reply he had received from the British naval commander-in-chief, "Greatly regret we have no vessel available for this purpose."

We took Broome with us and went again to see Commander Abbot. He had anticipated the problem and already prepared a plan and secured the necessary permission of his superiors to implement it. He had the dimensions of all three boxes containing MacLaren's airplane and spare parts. To accommodate them aboard, he had authorized the dismantling of his destroyer's deck equipment, pipes, and radio apparatus.

The *John Paul Jones* was already enroute to Hakodate at full speed to pick up MacLaren's spare amphibian. After loading the aircraft, it would proceed directly to Hong Kong where it would be transferred to the U.S.S. *William B. Preston*, commanded by Lt. Commander Willis A. Lee, Jr. who would carry it to Akyab.

"You may assure Major MacLaren he will have his replacement aircraft at Akyab no later than the thirteenth of June," said Abbot to Broome. Broome again looked reprieved and, with tears in his eyes, said, "I can find no words to express my gratitude. You are neither our rivals nor our opponents but our great-hearted gallant friends and competitors. Thank you . . . thank you . . . thank you."

After Broome left, we all questioned the Admiralty's lack of support for their own flight. Commander Abbot recalled that their greatest sea-borne adventurers, Drake and Raleigh, had similar difficulties obtaining supplies, provisions or even assistance. Upon receiving Broome's cable advising our navy's largesse, MacLaren replied simply, "Well done."

With MacLaren back in the race, D'Oisy breaking records for France, and with both Portugal and Argentina making rapid progress, the record is still very much up for grabs. We are all anxious to get back to our cruisers at Kasumigaura and get going on the overhauls.

THURSDAY, JUNE 5, 1924
10:15 P.M.
SHANGHAI, CHINA

Starting May 24 at Kasumigaura, we all worked like a flock of devils exchanging pontoons, stripping and replacing flying wires, patching fabric, replacing corroded fittings, lubricating flight controls, fixing recalcitrant instruments, tightening all the nuts and bolts, and safety wiring everything. We disassembled, checked, fixed, and reassembled the engines waiting for us. We removed the old engines and installed the new ones, and adjusted all the linkages and flight controls. By May 31st we were ready to go and had a wonderful final dinner at the home of Commander Yaragushi, the hospitable naval officer in charge of the base at Kasumigaura.

At 3 A.M. on Sunday, June 1 we were all assembled at the lake ready to start out for China. A special train packed with the Chief of the Japanese Air Service and a whole bunch of officials arrived at dawn to see us off. We were surprised to see so much brass up at that hour but they said our flight would usher in a new era of air travel and commerce and they fully expected their country to play a leading role.

We shook hands all around and thanked them for their kind hospitality. They bowed low to us and we tried our best to be courteous and bow even lower to them. As we climbed back into our cockpits, they warned us to keep a sharp lookout for Fujiyama off to our right. We assured them we would. All our lives we had heard of the sacred mountain of Japan and seen thousands of pictures of its symmetrical snow- capped cone. We really looked forward to seeing this majestic mountain in all its glory.

The sun was just coming up as we lifted off the waters of Kasumigaura and headed toward the southern end of the main island of Hondo. Just ahead of us on the left was the active volcano O-

Shima belching her clouds of smoke and steam. We knew that Fuji-san was somewhere on our right but clouds obscured her from us.

Suddenly as we flew across the entrance to Yokohama Harbor, the clouds parted as if old Fuji had rolled aside two cosmic curtains and revealed its majesty to encourage and inspire us. Fuji is twelve thousand, four hundred feet high, eighty miles in circumference at the base, and two and a half miles around at the crater. With its snow-white summit rising high into the cobalt sky, Fuji was breathtakingly beautiful. No wonder this is a sacred mountain! No wonder that from the earliest times Japanese poets have sung of Fujiyama's beauty and charm! No wonder the people of these islands are nature worshipers, with this dazzling, snow-capped volcano ever before them!

Fuji was the most lovely sight any of us had ever seen and no words could convey the thrill we felt on seeing it from our airplanes. All of us were stunned by its magnificence but as quickly as those cosmic curtains were opened to us, they closed and we plunged into a bank of rain and fog which held its grip on us for the next two hours.

When we finally arrived over Kushimoto to refuel, the winds were up to gale force kicking up high waves and forcing us to make six tries before finally getting our airplanes down onto the water's surface safely.

After an hour of trying, none of us could capture our moorings. I lay flat on the pontoon while Lowell kept taxiing around in circles. Several times I was almost washed off. The mooring shot up from ten feet below me to ten feet over my head and there was simply no way to catch it.

Finally we had to give up. We taxied into the lee of a small island about half a mile away, dropped our sixty-pound emergency anchors and waited for the destroyer *Pope* to bring our moorings to us. The *New Orleans* and the *Boston* were in the same predicament. The light storm anchors couldn't hold us and we kept getting blown dangerously close to the rocks. It was only the quick action of the pilots in starting the engines and taxiing against the wind that kept the airplanes off the rocks until the sailors of the *Pope* finally got our ships moored.

Smitty and I spent a sleepless night reinforcing the anchors holding the *Chicago* which the storm kept pushing closer and closer to the rocks. The next morning, June 2, the storm finally subsided and we all went ashore for another round of speeches, received three medals and six beautiful Japanese dolls. Nearly every city in Japan had shipped something of value to us in Tokyo including gorgeous paintings on hand-lettered panels. We were all very touched by the kind hospitality of the Japanese people and most grateful for their well wishes.

Lowell begged them to make another three medals for Jack, Hank, and myself explaining we were all equal. He even cabled General Patrick requesting Hank Ogden be promoted from Sergeant to Lieutenant like the rest of us, so from here on, Smitty says we are all the same rank.

About 1:00 P.M. the weather cleared and the sea laid down enough for us to attempt our takeoff for Kagoshima. The weather wasn't bad but a stiff head wind held our ground speed down to forty miles per hour. We flew over flooded paddy fields glistening in the sunlight chasing our shadows far below us.

Over the long water jumps we frequently passed steamers, junks, fishing craft, and even spotted two of our destroyers, the *Perry* and *Stewart*, out patrolling for us. We flew down to deck level and gave the cheering sailors on deck a wave. Wade had a problem with an overheating engine shortly after that and had to put down on the waves to add some sea water to his radiator but he soon took off again and joined up with both of us circling overhead.

The sun had already gone down when we got to the mountains near Kagoshima Bay. If we detoured around them we would have to land in total darkness so Lowell signaled the others to climb over them. Fortunately we had no further engine problems and put down safely on the waters of Kagoshima Bay in the last vestiges of the waning light.

The shore was covered with at least fifty thousand people waiting for us—of which at least twenty thousand were school children. When we got on shore the band from the U.S.S. *Black Hawk* played "My country 'Tis of Thee," and all those twenty thousand school children sang the song in English to us while waving Japanese and American flags. We were so moved by the spectacle we all cried like children and were deeply ashamed of what our Congress had done passing the Japanese Exclusion Act just a few days before. Politicians can sure mess up good relationships.

Kagoshima is the southernmost city of Japan and sits on a bay guarded by the very impressive volcano of Sakurajima. It is one of the finest harbors in the Orient. We dined with the officers of the U.S.S. *Black Hawk* that evening and got a lesson in Japanese history from them.

Japan actually opened up pretty early to foreigners. First to come were the missionary priests from Spain and Portugal and after that a vigorous English evangelist led the Protestant Dutch into the country. In a short time the various Christian sects started fighting among themselves and the Japanese were totally bewildered by this strange expression of "brotherly love."

They sent their most learned men as representatives to Europe to find out more about the principles of Western religions. After seven years they returned with the conclusion that Western nations were hopelessly corrupt, mean-spirited, barbaric, unclean, poorly educated, and intent on fighting wars with each other for dominance.

The Shogun of those days ordered all Westerners to leave Japan or be sentenced to death. Only a few Dutch traders were allowed to remain, virtually as prisoners, to act as intermediaries with the outside world. Japan closed their doors to foreigners for the next two hundred years until the arrival of Commodore Perry and his American fleet on July 8, 1853 pried the doors open again.

The following day, June 4th, we got into the ships again and taxied out just after 8 A.M. The *New Orleans* and *Boston* lifted off after we rippled up the water for them but we couldn't break the suction on our pontoons and gave up after half a dozen runs.

We signaled the others to continue the trip on to China while we got into bathing suits to dive under and inspect our pontoons. We found a metal strip had been torn off by the force of the water and provided just enough resistance to keep us from lifting off. We fixed it and lifted off the next morning, finally departing the land of the Mikado and the warm, gracious and industrious people that inhabit it.

The trip we made today between Japan and China was our longest crossing over water to date. There is no more ideal place in the world for meditation than the cockpit of an airplane flying high above the surface of the earth. The engine ran so smoothly as we clipped off mile after mile across the sea toward China that we both were lost in our own reveries. I felt great satisfaction that our flight would be only the first of many to bridge the nations of the world.

Faster and more efficient planes will follow and in their wake, commerce, understanding, and compassion. Giant ships of the air will make weekend runs between continents bringing brotherhood and love from shore to distant shore. War will become as inconceivable between nations as it is now between our states. If our flight helps in any way to hasten this era, we shall be repaid a million times over for our efforts.

As we flew over the mouth of the Yangtze River nearing Shanghai, we were amazed at the tens of thousands of junks, sampans, and steamers awaiting our arrival. Fortunately the harbormaster had cleared several miles of river for our landing as he had the day before for Erik and Leigh, to spare us the fate of D'Oisy, the French world flier, who had crashed a few days before on the outskirts of Shanghai.

Captain Eisler, the Shanghai representative of the United States Shipping Board, had an excursion boat and several motor launches waiting for us with Erik, Jack, Leigh, and Hank aboard. They helped us moor the *Chicago* after which we went aboard the excursion boat for an official welcome and some dinner.

Shanghai declared a holiday for our arrival. It was the first flight by air from America and Japan. Erik told us of an incredible reception we missed the night before. They were all taken from their hotel to the home of a merchant prince and made to stand in front of two huge closed wooden doors. When the doors opened, a waiting orchestra struck up our national anthem. Thousands of men in tuxedos and the uniforms of dozens of nations festooned with medals and accompanied by an equal number of gorgeous women in Paris evening gowns and tiaras dripping with large pearls, rubies, and diamonds applauded their arrival. They were pushed inside and had to run a gauntlet of roses strewn by dozens of flower girls in sweet little pink dresses and endless toasts to their flying skills. Smitty was grateful to have missed it.

Erik had problems on the flight over with his exhaust pipes overheating and almost burning up the ignition wiring so they removed the exhaust headers and were making up shorter ones at a Shanghai machine shop. Leigh stayed with me to remove the headers from the

Chicago while the rest of the crew returned to the plush Hotel Astor where we were staying.

When Leigh and I finally got to our very fancy hotel, the doorman took one look at our oil-stained mechanic's overalls, tools, and headers we carried, and then scolded us both for attempting to pass through their front door and main lobby.

He told us with great pride his posh hotel had been honored to host the around-the-world fliers and sorry looking riff-raff like us would not be tolerated in their newly decorated front lobby.

Rather than explain and risk embarrassing the hotel, Leigh led me to our rooms through the servant's entrance. The rest of our crew agreed our appearance certainly did not live up to their dapper "Beau Brummel" image and had a good laugh at our expense. When we got our own look at our oil-stained, greasy, disheveled selves in a mirror, we also laughed and heartily agreed with them.

After wrecking his airplane attempting to land on a golf course only thirty miles from here on May 20th, D'Oisy has been given a replacement airplane by the Chinese and is continuing his flight. He departed Shanghai at 5:00 A.M. on May 29th and flew to Peking. He departed Nanyuan air field at 5:15 A.M. on June 1st and arrived at Mukden, Manchuria at 11:00 A.M. enroute to Japan. We'll have to watch his progress very closely.

Tomorrow night the machine shop should finish up our new short exhaust headers so we plan to service up with the help of the Navy and depart the next day, on June 7th. General Li, one of China's aviation heads, will be hosting a departure dinner for us in the evening. Our whole crew have been made honorary life members in the Thieves' Union of Shanghai, a recognized profession in both China and India. I'm not sure what is expected of our union membership nor do we have any intention of exercising our new privileges.

Signed, Les Arnold

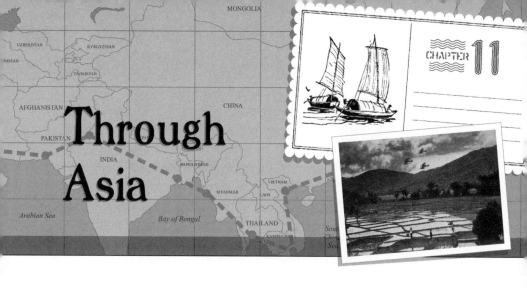

CHAPTER 11

Through Asia

WEDNESDAY, JUNE 11, 1924
2:00 P.M.
OVER INDOCHINA

So far so good. Only one more hour and they would be through the jungle and safely over the shoreline prior to landing at Tourane. There they would refuel and continue on to Saigon where a large cache of spare parts and naval assistance awaited them.

They had started out that morning just before dawn when the quiet of the Haiphong River exploded into a cacophony of sound as each of the three cruisers started their engines. The bellowing exhaust stacks split the air with the noise of a thousand horses and pushed aside the mists rising from the still waters. Again and again each cruiser's engine strained in vain to separate the pontoons from the water's surface but the flat water sucked them relentlessly down.

Wade continued one of his high-speed runs at fifty-five miles per hour, missing junks and sampans by only a few feet. Twelve miles downriver he crossed the mouth of the Gulf of Tonkin. The confluence of the two currents created the ripples necessary to release the river's grip on the pontoons and the *Boston* rose into the air. Wade flew back and waved triumphantly at his hapless companions who soon followed his example with similarly gratifying results. They had lost three hours in the frustrating takeoff attempts but at last they were airborne.

To reach Saigon that day, they would need to make up time. They could do that only by taking a shortcut over the jungle where a safe landing with pontoons would be almost impossible. It would be a calculated risk.

Lowell checked his instruments. All indications were normal. The engine sounded sweet and reassuring. He pointed toward the jungle. Leigh Wade on his right wing nodded his assent. Erik Nelson on his left did the same. Lowell left the safety of the shoreline and turned westward toward the thick jungle, climbing to give himself and the others a cushion of time if disaster should befall them.

Without power, the heavily laden cruisers encumbered with the drag of pontoons, flying wires, struts, propellers, and multiple wings had a glide ratio not unlike that of a brick. To sustain the airspeed required for controlled flight without power the airplane's nose would have to be pushed steeply down toward the ground. The descent rate would vary from two thousand five hundred to three thousand feet per minute depending on the fuel load carried. The airplane would fall toward the earth half a mile within each minute.

In the heat of the noon sun their climb rate slowed and finally stopped. Just a few knots above stall speed he dared not attempt to climb any higher. The airplane could suddenly stall, fall off on one wing, and go into a spin. This was as high as he could go. Lowell lowered the nose and checked his altimeter. They were at six thousand feet. If an engine quit, they would have less than two minutes to locate a landing site, and glide to it before impact.

For the last week the trip had gone well. They had departed Shanghai on June 7 as planned and averted disaster weaving between the countless junks and sampans that seemed intent on colliding with them. They had repeated the hazardous act successfully again the next day in the harbor at Amoy with heroic efforts by the crew of the motor launch from the U.S. destroyer *Preble* which had been required to sink several intrusive sampans to give the cruisers enough room to maneuver for take-off.

They had survived the typhoon that blocked their entrance to Hong Kong harbor and, with the help of heliographs and flares fired from the U.S. destroyer *John Paul Jones*, navigated through its blinding fog, wind, and heavy rain to locate their moorings and land safely. They had repaired the damage done to all three airplanes—replacing propellers and pontoons with the help of the good folks of Standard Oil Company.

Protected by the U.S. Navy's big guns, they had gotten through the maze of China's lawless fiefdoms whose pirates and warlords extracted tribute from all hapless travelers. Their competitors were also going full speed ahead.

At Haiphong the French had boasted of D'Oisy's arrival at Hiroshima, Japan, the day before in the plane loaned to him by the Chinese. They also learned of the Portuguese surviving their crash landing in India and continuing on to Rangoon, Burma in a new plane given to them by the British Royal Air Force. McLaren's replacement airplane would be delivered to him at Akyab by the U.S. Navy within a day or two and he too would be continuing his world flight shortly.

With competitive flights from France, England, and Portugal threatening to overtake them and new flights from Italy, Argentina, and Spain poised to start, the American crew excused themselves from the welcoming ceremonies at Haiphong in French Indo-China in favor of completing refueling and servicing chores, a good night's sleep, and an early start the next morning.

The French Governor-General had the chore of explaining to his elegantly clad guests the mystifying preference of Americans for mechanical devices over the charms of lovely ladies with open arms and their gourmet dinner waiting uneaten for them at their formal welcome reception and gala ball.

From the cockpits the hours passed slowly and the Libertys continued to sing their song of power. Only one more hour to go. They were starting to relax at last. From the rear cockpit of the *Chicago*, Les flashed a "thumbs-up" and a big grin at the others flying just behind his wings. They answered with smiles holding their thumbs high. Soon they would be over the safety of the shoreline.

Sitting in front, Lowell saw it first. It started as a few drops of moisture on the windshield. Lowell looked up. The blueness of the sky precluded any moisture coming from the heavens. *It's just a few drops, nothing to worry about . . . yet!* thought Lowell. He checked his watch. Fifty-two minutes to go. *Surely we can make that,* he thought.

Les noticed the drops on his windshield also. He stood up and reached over the low windshield to tap Lowell's shoulder. Lowell nodded to indicate to Les that he'd already seen it. Forty-eight minutes to go. The leak increased. The water temperature started climbing. Lowell turned the wheel from side to side signaling Les to take control of the *Chicago*. Lowell stood and stretched himself over the top of the windshield to try and see where the water was coming from. He couldn't tell. He leaned all the way out the right side of the cockpit and then to the left. He still couldn't tell. The boiling water droplets stung his face and moistened his helmet.

Sitting down again, Lowell checked his watch. 2:16 P.M. Forty-four minutes to go. The water was now streaming off the windshield. The temperature gauge had pegged in the red zone. The oil pressure was falling. Dark streaks of oil stained the cowling, windshield, and fuselage. Erik and Leigh watched the drama unfolding apprehensively. They knew only too well what the oil streaks meant.

Lowell throttled the engine back and signaled the others he was slowing. Perhaps he could coax it to continue under reduced power. Erik and Leigh slowed also to match his speed. 2:20 P.M. A rhythmic vibration shook the *Chicago*. From deep within the cowling the banging of metal against metal could be clearly heard.

2:22 P.M. A loud explosion from the engine compartment, the sudden appearance of a jagged hole in the cowling, and a large reduction in power told the story. A cylinder had exploded, throwing its connecting rod through the sheet metal. The engine still ran but with gallons of oil streaming out through the hole in the crankcase, Lowell knew the *Chicago* was doomed. Desperately he scanned the tops of the trees for someplace to land. Luck was smiling at him. Four miles ahead lay a lagoon fed by a large stream. Les Arnold banked the airplane and headed for it. Lowell adjusted the throttle to maintain minimum power and took the controls.

Lowell lowered the nose to maintain sixty miles per hour flying speed accepting a sink rate of one thousand feet per minute under partial power. They might just make it. At 2:28 Lowell skimmed over the tops of the palm trees slipping to lose the last fifty feet.

Relieved, he felt one pontoon touch the surface and gingerly set the other one down, maintaining a straight path using large rudder inputs. They were down.

While the airplane coasted to a stop, Lowell cut off the fuel and ignition switches. Les jumped from the rear cockpit with his fire extinguisher and worked his way forward on the lower wing toward the large hole in the cowl. He braced his back on the wing struts and held the fire extinguisher with both hands aimed and ready to trigger it at the first sign of fire. Their luck continued. Despite the popping, hissing, and wheezing of overheated engine parts, there was no sign of fire.

Over the tops of the trees Lowell spotted the other cruisers landing in a trail behind him. They didn't dare shut off their engines on landing but taxied over. Lowell pointed to the large hole in the cowling. Above the din of the idling Libertys Lowell indicated they were to go for help. A new engine was obviously needed. Jack and Hank passed the canteens of drinking water to Les, shouted some words of encouragement, and taxied to the end of the lagoon for takeoff. Within a few minutes the *Chicago* sat alone in the lagoon with few signs of human habitation.

For the first thirty minutes crocodiles, birds, and chattering monkeys were the only signs of life but Lowell and Les felt they were being watched by unseen eyes. This was confirmed when a dugout canoe with a single native paddled silently up to the side of the airplane. They had tied a mooring line onto a bamboo post sticking up from the mud bottom and this was apparently his fish trap. Berating them nonstop in some obscure dialect, the native attempted to release their mooring line from his fish trap. Lowell checked the wind and, after satisfying himself that he would be blown into deeper water toward the center of the lagoon, he released his mooring line and gestured for the native to help them drop their own sixty-pound anchor.

Seeing their companion had not met some dire fate, other dugout canoes paddled out from their hiding places on the lagoon and within a few minutes dozens of natives, clad only in skimpy breech-cloths were climbing onto the pontoons to get a better look at the huge flying monster that had dropped from the skies. Fortunately their feet were bare so no damage was done to the thin wooden floating hulls but the imbalance threatened to capsize the cruiser and they were summarily shooed back onto their own conveyances.

After an hour of broiling in the hot sun, they saw another dugout being rowed toward them by a hollow-cheeked light-skinned man clad in white robes, sandals, and a soiled sun helmet. Their spirits soared with thoughts of rescue, water, a good meal, and a comfortable bed waiting for them somewhere in the wilderness of the jungle. They sat on the lower wing eagerly awaiting their benefactor, anticipating the many questions he would ask.

Closing within a few feet of the *Chicago* the man asked them a question in French which Lowell did not understand. Looking toward Les for an interpretation, Lowell was startled by the answer. "He wants to know how many cartons of cigarettes we have brought and says he'll only pay two cents for each carton." Les advised the man in his best pigeon French that they were not aerial tobacco salesmen. The man indicated his disgust at their uselessness, turned his boat, and paddled away in the direction from which he had come, leaving them both amazed and speechless.

The first native who had assisted them in anchoring returned with a bunch of bananas and split coconuts from which they drank the milk. Les offered some of his cigarettes for his kindness and the use of his dugout. The native eagerly accepted, offering one of the precious cigarettes to a fellow tribesman in another dugout in exchange for a ride back home.

Lowell was left to guard the *Chicago* while Les paddled the dugout in pursuit of their recent white-robed visitor. Spotting the man's dugout a mile upriver, Les came ashore and followed a narrow path which led to a tiny church beside a small stream. Les knelt to fill the small bottle he carried with water from the stream when the white robed figure reappeared, identified himself as the missionary and owner of that church and the stream, and demanded Les leave immediately, launching a most irreverent tirade of French curses.

Les concluded that this man had been out in the sun for too many years. He rose from his knees and lifted him off the ground by his white robe, then hung him harmlessly onto the branch of a tree while he continued filling his water bottle. Returning to the *Chicago*, Les and Lowell finished their dinner of coconuts and bananas, washing it down with the bottled water before stretching out on the lower wing to get some needed sleep.

While Smith and Arnold sat marooned in their lagoon, the *New Orleans* and *Boston* arrived at Tourane landing next to the American destroyer sent to assist them. Lt. Lawton had arranged for M. Chevalier, Standard Oil's local agent, to assist the flight and he was aboard the destroyer when they landed. They arranged for Jack and Hank to service the two cruisers. With Chevalier's assistance, Erik would return with help for Smith and Arnold. Leigh would pursue getting a new engine to them from Saigon.

At that time, Indo-China was larger than France itself and populated by 17 million people. Poring over maps aided by Nelson's description, Chevalier concluded the only roads which existed anywhere close to the lagoon holding the *Chicago* was the city of Hue. Together they started out immediately for Hue.

After three hours of driving over gravel roads through mountain passes, over high peaks, low valleys, dense tamarind forests, and numerous ferry crossings, Erik and Chevalier reached the city of Hue. The French officials confirmed that from Hue few roads existed and those went only a few miles into the jungle. From there on they must travel by sampan or dugout canoes. A friend of Chevalier's owned a rice plantation on a river which ran into the lagoon holding the *Chicago*. They would make that their first stop.

It was now 11:00 P.M. Banging on the door of a nearby hotel to wake the sleeping innkeeper, they bought milk, sandwiches, soda, and drinking water to carry with them to Smith and Arnold. They then drove toward the plantation. Two miles from the plantation the road ended. It was now well past midnight. The night was devoid of moon and stars, pitch black and foreboding. The sampan owners were not happy being wakened and even less enthusiastic about navigating the treacherous river with its rocks and rapids in the dark, the favorite hunting times for the abundant crocodiles and tigers.

After much arguing and an exorbitant cash settlement, one sampan driver finally accepted the challenge. Concluding a ceremony offering prayers and sacrifices of rice to protect them from the dangers of the night, they boarded and the journey continued.

Their arrival was heralded by the loud barking of the plantation's dogs. Chevalier shouted to his friend who had been awakened by the barking and was standing guard at the river's edge holding a large shotgun and a hand torch. Pleasantries were exchanged and they soon sat in the large plantation kitchen poring over regional maps while the coffee pot simmered.

The plantation owner had heard nothing of an aircraft but suggested they visit the home of a native priest who lived several miles into the jungle and toward the direction of the lagoon. If anyone knew of the landing, it would be the priest. He wakened five of his native help and again lengthy negotiations ensued with considerable bargaining to agree on suitable compensation for carrying the supplies and leading everyone safely through the dangers of the jungle at night.

They hiked single file for what seemed like hours. On both sides of the narrow trail was thick jungle with small shrines every five minutes for prayers and offerings which would protect the traveler from "Master Stripes" and his friends. Occasionally they would pass a good-sized temple, quiet and foreboding in the darkness. Eventually they arrived at the thatched house of the priest.

He was of good spirits, considering his slumber had been disturbed, and invited us in while our five native companions remained outside. Unfortunately he had not seen or heard of any aircraft but agreed to send for several natives who were fishing that day. Those natives confirmed they had seen two monsters flying overhead but knew nothing of any in a lagoon. The priest then suggested that the mandarin of that area, who lived about a mile away, be spoken with.

Again they had to reopen negotiations with the five bearers from the plantation to extend their mission to the home of the mandarin, and again an exorbitant fee was extracted from them.

The mandarin's home was impressive and their knock on the large door brought a gaggle of lovely female servants. They were ushered into a large exquisitely decorated room with elaborately cast bronze figures, ivory carvings, and hunting trophies. Eventually a smiling man emerged in gorgeous hand-embroidered silk robes. He also had heard nothing of our lost companions or any flying monsters but would be pleased to help in whatever way he could. He suggested we take three of his sampans and the requisite native crew members, proceed down the river, and inquire in each village as we pass through it of the fate of the *Chicago*. We agreed instantly to his kind offer.

They set off down the river again. Every half hour or so they shone their flashlights on the huts of each new village. Voices from the shore hailed our party and our paddlers inquired as to any flying monsters that might have been seen that day. Again and again the responses were not encouraging. Erik fell into an exhausted sleep on the floor of the sampan.

It was just before three in the morning when Erik was awakened. The last village indicated there was a flying monster floating in the next lagoon. With a loud "Yippee," Erik awakened and threw some water on his face to break the bonds of sleep. Around the very next bend in the river, in the faint beam of their hand torches, was the unmistakable profile of the *Chicago*.

It was the "Yippee" that Lowell heard first. He knew that voice. Even before he saw the two yellow lights pointing at him, he knew the cavalry had arrived to rescue them. He checked his watch. Just after 3:00 A.M. To find them in just over twelve hours was a sensational job. He was deeply grateful as the dugout circled carefully to avoid damaging the airplane.

Smith and Arnold climbed aboard one of the other canoes and followed Erik's boat over to the shore. Lowell put his arms gratefully around Erik and said quietly, "Happy Birthday, Erik." With the events of the day, Erik had totally forgotten. This was June 12th. It was his birthday. "Thank you. Let's celebrate."

Erik opened the box of food. The ice he had packed the drinks in had still not totally melted. Les and Lowell devoured the sandwiches and the cold drinks. "Boy, does this taste good," Les said. After the brief party they went to the nearest village to arrange for native canoes to tow the *Chicago* twenty-five miles upriver to Hue where a new engine could be fitted.

Erik and Chevalier picked up their car and arrived at Hue to warn the local river traffic of the coming of the *Chicago* and to arrange guards for the airplane. Few inhabitants had ever seen an airplane before and had no idea what to expect. The word spread quickly to the entire town and soon thousands lined the sides of the river expectantly awaiting its arrival.

The arrival of the *Chicago* was heard before it was seen. The trip had taken over ten straight hours. Three large sampans, each holding ten native paddlers were tied to the *Chicago* like tugboats. A fleet of

other sampans followed containing the wives of the paddlers who periodically fed their husbands food and drink. The patriarch of the village
sat on his throne on the leading royal sampan being attended by his
harem of attractive young females. His junior wives paddled while
others fanned him with large feathered fans and chased mosquitoes.
Still others offered him drinks, fruit, and exotic native dishes.

His favorite concubine sat beside him rolling his cigarettes and
cigars before lighting them and offering them to him. In the rear of
the royal sampan, a muscular native drummed cadence for the oars-
men, striking a large wooden club onto an animal skin stretched over
the open end of a huge log. The rhythmic *BOOM BOOM BOOM*
could be heard for miles.

Les Arnold and Lowell Smith sat comfortably in the shade
between the wings of the biplane on the cushions they had removed
from the cockpits, and waved self-consciously at the crowds lining
the riverbank. Each bend in the river presented another scene of
beauty and their only regret was that they had no camera to record
it with. Small children ran along for miles on either side to keep
sight of the airplane. This would be a day none would ever forget.

Lowell directed the sampans to tow the *Chicago* under a bridge
near the center of Hue. The plan was to use the structure of the
bridge. As soon as the ship had been moored securely under the bridge
and guards placed around it, Erik, Lowell, and Les went to work dis-
connecting fuel and oil lines, control linkages, and removing its
propeller. The exhausted trio continued working until darkness fell.

The next morning Nelson and Chevalier left to return to Tourane
leaving Smith and Arnold to complete the removal of the defective
engine. By 11:00 A.M. the heat became unbearable. Tools became too
hot to hold and both men grew dizzy. The work stopped and an invitation to lunch at a local French professor's house was accepted.

Nelson and Chevalier returned to Tourane just in time for the
arrival of the American destroyer from Saigon carrying the precious
spare Liberty-12 engine. Arrangements with a local truck driver
were made immediately to transport the engine, Hank Ogden as its
guardian, and four American sailors as additional manpower to Hue.
Leigh Wade would stay behind to guard the *Boston* and *New Orleans*,
while Nelson, Harding, and Chevalier would return to Hue to assist
in the exchange.

While loading the heavy engine crate and tools on the truck, Ogden circled it warily. Its condition was not encouraging. The body was extensively rusted and damage from numerous collisions with objects unknown were evident. The engine sounded as if it were on its last legs and it leaked copious fluids from numerous places. The brakes squealed in protest after the most minute of efforts and the windshield was caked in grime.

The driver seemed totally nonchalant and reluctant to even go through the effort of tying down the heavy cargo. The sailors brought lines from the ship, cleaned the cargo floor of years of accumulated refuse, and secured the crate and tool boxes. Hank cleaned the windshield, refilled the engine's oil and water radiators, and adjusted the mechanical brakes. The driver observed the unusual proceedings contemptuously complaining of the delay such unnecessary precautions were causing and its huge negative impact upon his livelihood.

The truck left Tourane after dark. Ogden sat next to the driver trying in vain to discern the narrow jungle road illuminated only by a single weak and yellowed headlamp. The truck bounced along from rut to rut at what Ogden estimated was over thirty miles per hour. The sailors in back struggled to keep their rear ends in contact with the truck's bed as the suspension creaked and groaned, bucking, bouncing, and bobbing up and down violently. Each attempt by Hank to slow the driver succeeded for only a minute or two before his maniacal pace resumed.

Thankfully, after almost an hour of misery, the road climbed steeply, the engine strained but could not sustain its speed, the driver shifted down a gear and soon a second one. Hank estimated they had slowed to perhaps twenty miles per hour. For the next thirty minutes the road became a narrow switchback climbing steeply over a mountain, one hairpin turn after the next. Hank noted the complete lack of any guard rails. The edges of the road dropped precipitously first hundreds and then thousands of feet straight down to rocks below. Hank was grateful the engine wasn't any stronger since even at that slow speed it was a terrifying drive.

Eventually the summit was reached and the switchbacks continued down the other side. Much to Hank's displeasure, the driver changed gears and sped up in the descent. The truck tilted from side to side, lifting two wheels off the ground, careening around each hair-pin turn. The tires slid on the small rocks, gravel, and mud within inches of the yawning precipice. All attempts to slow the driver by restraining his arms were futile. Hank braced himself and hung on, convinced they would all be launched over the side at the next turn. He regretted he had inadvertently sacrificed the four sailors' lives as well.

After what seemed like hours of sheer terror, the road leveled and the switchbacks disappeared. Hank couldn't believe they had made it down the mountain alive and seriously considered smashing the driver in the face and taking over the truck. Realizing he had no idea where to go or how to get there, he contented himself with urging him in his most authoritarian voice to, "SLOW DOWN!"

Just as the words came out of his mouth, the bouncing stopped. They were airborne, having missed a sharp turn in the feeble glow of the single headlight. Their flight ended abruptly with the nose of the truck burying itself into the mud with a sickening crunch. Hank's head hit the windshield post leaving a small cut. He wondered if the sailors in the back were as fortunate.

Other than some bumps, bruises, and minor cuts they had all averted serious injury. The sailors extricated themselves from the lines crisscrossing the cargo bed and, with the help of several cigarette lighters and a flashlight from the tool kit, surveyed the damage. The radiator had been pushed into the fan but was apparently still holding water and the fenders had been pushed against the tires. With the six of them and an hour of pulling, hauling, pushing, and twisting, they had the damage repaired and the truck back on the road. One of the sailors holding a large pipe wrench squeezed into the front seat next to the driver. Under the threat of imminent bodily harm and the loss of his truck if not his life, the driver finally slowed down.

This was most fortuitous. A second mountain pass lay ahead and a brake band failed in the descent. The driver panicked. Only our slow speed and urging him into a lower gear saved us, although not before another time consuming off-road excursion.

Several miles past the second mountain range, the road ended at a large lagoon. Ferry barges waited for travelers and cautiously the truck drove onto one of the barges. The crossing normally takes thirty minutes if all goes well. This one did not. As they approached the halfway point, Hank noticed the barge was leaking and they were sinking. He alerted one of the natives poling the raft who promptly grew wide-eyed with fright. He said something to the other six natives and all seven started poling the barge frantically back to the starting point. Hank, the sailors, and the truck driver grabbed some extra poles and all of them poled back with all their strength. When the barge finally reached shore, its decks were solidly awash. Another minute and the Liberty-12 would have been residing at the bottom of the lagoon.

A larger barge came to their rescue and made the crossing safely. They reached Hue at dawn. Although exhausted, after completing a brief breakfast, they joined with the others working on the *Chicago.* Within four hours, a new record, they had the old engine out and the new one hoisted into place, installed, and ready for testing. It fired up immediately and after some brief high-speed taxi runs, Lowell and Les were winging their way on the forty-minute flight to Tourane where they refueled and moored next to the other cruisers that night.

Only seventy-one hours had passed since their forced jungle landing. In this short time they gotten the new engine shipped five hundred miles, towed eight thousand pounds of airplane twenty-five miles upstream, transported a thousand pounds of engine, tools, and helpers sixty miles through two mountain ranges, a lagoon, and thick jungle at night, installed the new engine, and had the *Chicago* flying again.

TUESDAY, JUNE 17, 1924
SAIGON, INDO-CHINA

Dear Diary:

Yesterday we hopped off from Tourane for Saigon just after 5 A.M. and arrived at the mouth of the Mekong River at 1:30 P.M. We moored in front of the city which everyone calls "The Paris of the Orient." We spent the afternoon and most of last night servicing the ships and replacing some worn parts with the spares carried by the U.S. destroyer Noah.

Today we borrowed clean white shirts and trousers from our sailor friends and went out to see the sights of this beautiful city. We sat down at a table in an outdoor cafe which reminded us of our days in Paris dur-

ing the war. We waited over an hour for service but the waiter seemed intent on taking care of everybody but us. We called him over a few times but he just gave us dirty looks and turned away. Finally I called the head-waiter over. He ambled over to us with a scowl on his face. When I started giving him our order he stopped me and told us he couldn't serve us and we would have to leave.

Now we know the French can be a little strange sometimes but we had no idea what we had done that had those people so riled up at us. I asked him why the cold shoulder? He lifted his chin up to the sky as if we were the most stupid morons he had ever met. As if explaining to a child he said, "Monsieur, you are not wearing jackets."

We all stared at each other in disbelief. I asked him if he knew who we were. He replied he certainly did. I explained that flying around the world didn't leave much room for formal clothing and we even had to borrow the neatly pressed white dress shirts and trousers we were wearing. He replied, "Then you should have borrowed jackets as well."

I explained that we were all Army Air Corps pilots and are forbidden by regulation to wear full naval uniforms since that was not our branch. He said these were our problems and not his. We would have to leave immediately or he would call the police and have us thrown out. To make the matter even more unpleasant, as we were leaving, the Frenchmen at the adjoining tables applauded their approval of the headwaiter's actions. Seems to me we got a much warmer welcome in France when we came over there and saved their country from being overrun by Germany.

We've been sleeping at the home of the manager of Standard Oil Company and are planning to depart at first light for the 585 mile flight to Bangkok in Siam.

Signed, Les Arnold

BANGKOK, SIAM, JUNE 18, 1924 VIA CABLE AND ASSOCIATED PRESS:

The United States Army aviators engaged in a flight around the world, arriving here at 3:15 P.M. from Saigon, French Indo-China. They made one refueling stop on the way assisted by the U.S. destroyer *Hulbert* before continuing their flight over the thick jungles of the kingdom of Cambodia. They expect to make some minor repairs to their aircraft and depart for Rangoon, Burma on Friday, June 20th headed by Lieutenant Lowell Smith.

AKYAB, BURMA, JUNE 19, 1924 VIA CABLE AND EXCLUSIVE DISPATCH:

Stuart MacLaren, the British round-the-world flyer, has received his replacement aircraft delivered to him by the U.S. Navy. He has given the following statement to the press: "Hats off to the Stars and Stripes. The Americans, the Air Branch and the U.S. Navy have, as we say in England, played excellent cricket." Captain MacLaren plans to depart Akyab for Rangoon tomorrow.

HONG KONG, JUNE 20, 1924 VIA CABLE AND ASSOCIATED PRESS:

The Portuguese Aviators, Lieuts. Beiros and Paes, virtually completed their Lisbon to Macao flight this afternoon when they left Hanoi at 9:00 A.M. and passed over Macao at 12:50 P.M. and landed at Shamshun at 3 P.M. The landing was a forced one, Lieut. Paes being bruised and their machine slightly damaged. The aviators, finding a landing at Macao impractical because of bad weather, had intended to continue on to Canton, following the line of the Kowloon-Canton Railway. Ignition trouble required a sudden landing at Shamshun. The airmen caught a train for Kowloon arriving at 7:15 P.M. this evening. They were showered with congratulations by representatives of Portuguese officials and their ladies.

RANGOON, BRITISH INDIA, JUNE 21, 1924 VIA CABLE AND ASSOCIATED PRESS:

A cargo boat last night collided with one of the United States Army's round-the-world airplanes, badly damaging the bottom left wing of the *New Orleans*. Needed repairs will take at least five days after which the fliers will depart for Calcutta. Their leader, Lieutenant Lowell Smith, has been suffering from dysentery contracted by drinking contaminated water during a forced landing in a jungle lagoon near Hue, French Indo-China. He has been confined to bed but is expected to recover fully before repairs have been completed.

HONG KONG, JUNE 21, 1924 VIA CABLE AND ASSOCIATED PRESS:

The Portuguese aviators Lieuts. Beiros and Paes have returned to their airplane which was damaged in a forced landing at Shamchun. They have concluded the damage caused in the landing and the handiwork of local Chinese vandals and souvenir hunters have made repairs necessary before it can be flown again. The Portuguese government has dispatched their gunboats *Patria* and *Macao* to support the efforts of the local Chinese district commandant and the fifty armed Chinese soldiers he has assigned to guard the aircraft.

Lisbon celebrated their flyer's achievements in completing the route which flew from Lisbon over Vienna, Bucharest, Aleppo, Baghdad, Karachi, Allahabad, Calcutta, Akyab, Rangoon, Bangkok, Saigon, Haiphong, Hong Kong, and Macao.

SUNDAY, JUNE 22, 1924
10:15 A.M. NAGASAKI, JAPAN

Betty Mitchell fidgeted nervously with the locks on her packed steamer trunks, waiting for them to be picked up. Billy sat calmly reading the English language newspaper thoughtfully placed under his door. Betty couldn't help worrying if their spying had been observed. This would be the most logical time to apprehend them. In a few hours they would be safely aboard a steamer sailing for San Francisco.

It had been a long trip. After weeks of negotiating passage for their world flight in Kobe, they had returned to the Philippines and Billy had completed his inspection of its defenses. He had even taken his old adversary Aguinaldo up for his first airplane flight and watched him delightedly dropping hundreds of his calling cards to his earthbound friends while flying over his home village.

While in Manila, Billy had sent a cable to General Patrick requesting permission to visit Korea and return to Japan for the gathering of additional intelligence. Betty had seen the reply before they boarded.

STATE DEPARTMENT ADVISES YOUR PRESENCE AT THIS
TIME IN JAPAN OR KOREA LIABLE TO MISCONSTRUCTION
BY JAPANESE STOP DO NOT ATTEMPT TO VISIT EITHER
JAPAN OR KOREA UNTIL WAR DEPARTMENT ADVISES SAME.

Fuming, Billy had torn it into pieces and thrown it away. "We're just tourists now and no one tells American tourists where they can and cannot go," he replied angrily to Betty.

They joined an innocuous group of tourists taking a world cruise on the liner *Franconia*. Betty liked the ship and its interesting passengers, among which were the famous Spanish novelist Blasco Ibanez. Ibanez marveled at the perfection of Billy Mitchell's Spanish and his incredible predictions of aircraft that would change the face of warfare forever and circle the globe within days flying faster than the speed of sound and never being overtaken by night.

The Mitchells visited Java, Singapore, and India. They were guests of the king of Siam and hunted with him, killing a dozen tigers. Billy inspected his air force of 260 planes noting ruefully that even tiny Siam had an air force larger than America's.

They visited China where Mitchell noted that they possessed all of the attributes necessary to become a world power—with the ability to dominate all of Asia in the future. After taking the Blue Express from Shanghai to Peking, Mitchell held news conferences and delighted reporters with his visions of the future might of air power on the conduct of war. A former officer of Mitchell's was the chief instructor for the Chinese Air Force and let him fly a British bomber on an air tour of China's defenses and its Great Wall. In Mukden, Manchuria, the warlord, Marshal Chang Tso-lin, loaned him a French Nieuport biplane for aerial photography.

At their last meeting a decade ago, Marshall Chang had asked Mitchell to prove his wisdom by advising him how he could prevent flies and mosquitoes from attacking the top of his bald head. Without hesitating, Mitchell replied, "That's easy. Simply tattoo a spider's web on the top." Marshall Chang showed Mitchell he had taken his advice and had no further problems.

From Manchuria the Mitchells traveled to Korea. Then, shipping all of his uniforms and indications of military rank home, Mitchell assumed the guise of naturalist that had served him so well on previous spying missions decades ago and returned to Japan. For the next three weeks, the Mitchells toured Japan. Close to military installations and aircraft factories, Betty posed for pictures. To the casual Japanese observer, another foreign tourist was simply taking his wife's picture. Just before the shutter clicked, however Billy swung the camera around and in a fleeting moment recorded the significant military details in the background.

Billy Mitchell spent most of the day on June 17 observing a Japanese naval fleet in the harbor. The battleships *Nagato* and *Mutsu* with the battle cruisers *Kongo* and *Kirishima*, eighteen destroyers, eight submarines, supply ships, and tenders were preparing to leave for maneuvers. Mitchell watched admiringly as the operation proceeded smoothly and with the highest degree of precision and skill. Starting with the arrival of several squadrons of Sopwith pursuit planes and two-seater observation aircraft, each ship took up its exact position at precisely the correct time. Mitchell noted that each sailor knew his job and performed it flawlessly with no wasted effort or mistakes.

Using information given him by British aeronautical engineers and airmen, formerly with the R.A.F. now instructing the Japanese in the manufacturing of airframes, engines, and flying skills, and personal observations made in their travels, the Mitchells were returning with hundreds of pages of notes. To the casual customs inspector, they were the notes of a naturalist, describing the flora and fauna of Japan but in the coded entries each species represented a different aircraft and engine, each "bird count" a production rate, each "bird sighting location" a manufacturing or training facility. Mitchell had read and committed to memory U.S. intelligence estimates of the military potential of Japan. Through his extensive Pacific observations he realized these intelligence reports totally underestimated Japan's military resources. These resources, as with the training and discipline of Japanese soldiers, sailors, and airmen, casually dismissed as inferior to their Western counterparts, were, in Mitchell's opinion, equal or superior to any in the world.

The knock on the door startled Betty. Would this be the feared Japanese police coming to arrest them? She looked over at Billy. He calmly put down his newspaper, rose, and opened the door. Relieved, she saw two bellhops who had come for their luggage. After a short taxi ride they arrived at the pier. The American steamship, *Thomas* had just completed loading its supply of coal under the protection of armed guards. Anti-American actions had been spawned throughout Japan after the passage of the Japanese Exclusion Act.

Shortly the *Thomas* would be sailing. Billy Mitchell requested several hundred sheets of writing paper from the ship's purser. During the voyage to San Francisco he would complete his report which would alert the general staff to the simmering military eruption in the Pacific. He was certain his report and the actions that he recommended could avert any future conflict with Japan. Betty resigned herself to a very lonely trip.

BANGKOK (SIAM) JUNE 23, 1924 BY CABLE—EXCLUSIVE DISPATCH

BRITISH FLYERS ARRIVE AT BANGKOK

After a terrific two hour battle with the worst storms of the present season, Squadron Leader A. Stuart MacLaren of the British round-the-world flight arrived here from Tavoy.

The crossing of the Malay Peninsula, with its treacherous mountain peaks obscured in masses of low hanging clouds, nearly spelled disaster for the expedition.

The fliers expect to leave tomorrow for Haiphong by way of Vinh, although reports received here today state that treacherous weather conditions are certain along the entire east coast of Indo-China.

CALCUTTA, INDIA, JUNE 24, 1924 BY CABLE—EXCLUSIVE DISPATCH BY A. ELLINGS

AMERICAN FLYERS AT CALCUTTA

The American Army round-the-world flyers headed by Lieut. Lowell M. Smith alighted on the sacred river Ganges at a beautiful rural spot sixteen miles from Calcutta at 3:00 P.M. today after their flight from Akyab.

The flight caused enormous interest among the Indians who lined the picturesque banks of the river at an early hour in the sweltering heat. The scene was like that of a regatta, except a long stretch was kept clear for their landing.

The American airmen departed Rangoon for what was supposed to be a brief refueling stop at Akyab. Their flight passed directly over Major MacLaren and the British world flight which had landed in a small bay waiting for the weather to improve. Due to difficulty making mooring arrangements at Chittagong, the Americans were forced to remain overnight in Akyab risking infection with cholera and malaria epidemics rampaging this unfortunate city.

They left early in the morning flying ten miles to the east to avoid a storm. They reached picturesque Chittagong (also known as Islamabad) in two hours halting for breakfast and refueling. They flew 170 miles over the world's most forbidding jungle swamps, the Ganges delta. Their total flying time to Calcutta was more than five hours. The Americans flew at an altitude of fifteen hundred feet and avoided the monsoon rains.

THURSDAY, JUNE 26, 1924
CALCUTTA, BRITISH INDIA

After landing for refueling at Chittagong, the Americans continued on to Calcutta, arriving late that afternoon and mooring fifteen miles upriver from the city. British river police were given the assignment of guarding the cruisers while the crew boarded the launch of the governor of Bengal for the trip downriver to the center of the city.

The original plans were for the world cruisers to be dismantled and trucked overland to the British airfield at Dum Dum, some twenty miles from the center of Calcutta. There they would be totally overhauled, given new engines, and changed from pontoons over to wheels for the flight over the Middle East and on to Europe.

Basking in the luxury of the bridal suite at the Great Eastern Hotel, Lowell Smith estimated that dismantling and reassembly of the cruisers would cost them at least one month if everything went perfectly and possibly as many as six months if it did not. Discussing alternatives with the rest of the crew, and British and Indian officials, a new plan was developed. They flew the cruisers downriver to the center of the city and adjacent to Maidan Park. Here a crane lifted each airplane from the water and onto the park's lawn where the crew could inspect each ship, install new engines, repair or replace any parts necessary, and change from pontoons to wheels.

Working in sweltering heat from early dawn to well past midnight amid frequent visits from wandering "holy" cows and numerous ash-covered fakirs smeared head to toe with "sacred cow dung" and with withered arms and legs, the crew raced to complete the servicing. In the darkness of night, returning to his hotel on June 29th, Smith fell into a deep hole breaking his rib on timbers which were below ground.

Seeing him in great pain, Les Arnold insisted on calling a doctor. The doctor confirmed that Lowell Smith had at least one broken rib. Refusing to stay in bed more than a single day, Smith had his ribcage taped and despite the pain rejoined his companions to put the last finishing touches on servicing the cruisers.

Caught up in the decade's rush to conquer new frontiers was a very attractive sixteen-year-old girl from England. Aloha Baker was attempting to be the first to drive an automobile around the world. Prevailing over the lack of roads, service stations, innumerable mechanical and tire failures, she had been eagerly rushing to rendezvous with the American world flight and its handsome leader, Lowell Smith in Calcutta. Brandishing the revolver she carried holstered on her belt, she had survived numerous encounters with bandits and threatening natives.

Pushing hard through long days and endless nights, Aloha reached Calcutta the day before the American flight was scheduled to leave. Finding Lowell every bit as handsome as he was depicted in newspaper and newsreel accounts, Aloha embraced a surprised Lowell Smith and kissed him warmly. The strong muscles she developed through months of driving and pushing her automobile through mud, sand, dirt, and heavy jungle made for a very painful embrace. Lowell winced and explained his injuries. Aloha apologized profusely for the pain she had caused and Lowell let her sit in his cockpit before spending some time alone with her.

Sixty years later, during a television interview, Aloha revealed the moments with Lowell were among the most memorable of her life and she remained infatuated for many years with the handsome aviator.

TUESDAY, JULY 1, 1924
6:00 A.M.
MAIDAN PARK, CALCUTTA, INDIA

The three world cruisers squatted on the wet grass of Maidan Park, silhouetted against the first rays of the emerging sun. With wheels in place of pontoons, the ships were lower and seemed to have grown smaller, slightly less imposing, less clumsy. Their pre-flight inspection would be completed shortly and they would soon accelerate down the improvised grass runway protected from intruders by uniformed Indian policemen.

Several reporters and photographers had arrived shortly after they did and busied themselves making notes and taking pictures, the popping flashlamps momentarily illuminating the area with a ghastly white light. Lowell Smith looked around for Linton Wells but he was nowhere to be seen. The previous evening Wells, on the verge of tears, had shown them the cable from his chief at Associated Press ordering him back home immediately.

The crew liked Wells. He had almost become one of them, suffered with them through the frozen north, hopping rides on one boat after another to keep up with them. He had begged, pleaded, cajoled, bartered, and even paid for passage on ships ranging from derelict freighters to sleek naval warships. He had often gone without sleeping, eating, or bathing for days, hurrying to keep up with his heroes and his story. He passed through the same icy cold blizzards and sweltering jungle heat they did. Just when they thought they had finally outdistanced him, arriving at some obscure remote place, Wells would appear. He had paid his dues and become part of their family, part of the adventure they shared.

They all knew Wells was on borrowed time. The sixty days he had been given to cover their flight had come and gone, all used up—and over half the trip still lay ahead. Each of the crew had become fond of Linton Wells, his clowning around, his encouragement when all seemed bleak, his help and willingness to do the most menial task, his gratitude at just being allowed to play a tiny part of their great adventure. They would miss him.

Lowell Smith, always the pragmatist, felt that perhaps it was all for the best. With wheels, more numerous airports over land and shorter distances between fuel stops, their ships would be much lighter and faster. They would make much more rapid progress. From here on it would be almost impossible for Wells to catch up with them anyway. Still, it would have been nice to see him just one more time, to say good-bye, to wish him well and deliver to him the "honorary aviator commission" they had all signed for him on the back of a postcard. But Wells was nowhere to be seen. With a shrug, Lowell turned to completing the last few tasks before take-off time came.

As the sun rose, glowing gold against a pale blue sky, and the air filled with the pungent smells and smoke of untold millions of cooking stoves being lighted, the call to morning prayer echoed over the city's mosques. The roar of first one, then a second, and finally a third Liberty V-12 engine bellowed and rumbled into life. Slowly the three world cruisers taxied, nose to tail, to the end of the improvised grass runway. Within the space of a few minutes, each rose majestically and headed north over the Hoogli River before turning westward toward Allahabad, 450 miles in the distance.

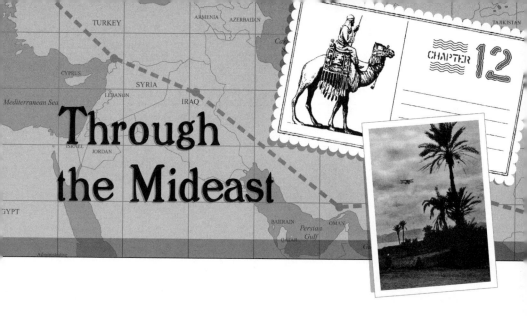

CHAPTER 12

Through the Mideast

TUESDAY, JULY 1, 1924
ENROUTE TO ALLAHABAD, INDIA

F reed of the heavy weight and high aerodynamic drag of the pontoons, the three cruisers flew rapidly following the East Indian Railway across the plains of Bengal, Bihar, and Orissa toward their destination of Allahabad. Heavy rain showers heralding the approach of the monsoon season occasionally pelted their windshields with huge wet droplets which streamed over the edge, wetting their goggles, faces, and clothing.

As the railroad tracks made a great bend to avoid the encroaching Ganges River, the ancient holy city of Benares came into view. Circling low the crews witnessed countless Brahmin priests at worship in elaborate temples which were old thousands of years before western Europeans built their first primitive rock shelters. The crew waved at the curious faces looking upward at them.

A few hours later, the spires of Allahabad came into view. Locating the railway station, the flight flew six miles further west and over the sunbaked field which was to be their home for the evening. After six and a half hours of flying, Lowell closed his throttles, checked the smoke drifting upward from thousands of cooking fires, and led his flight to a graceful landing into the wind.

As Leigh Wade and Hank Ogden climbed from the *Boston* and started to walk away from the airplane, they heard a strange banging from the baggage compartment. Returning to the airplane and cau-

289

tiously opening the baggage compartment, they were greeted by a sweating and smiling Linton Wells curled up in a fetal position. Wade and Ogden, although startled by their uninvited guest, extended helping hands to assist Wells in extricating himself from his confinement. The crew's surprise soon turned to joy as they welcomed Wells again into their fold. With the rest of the crew gathering around him, Wells explained how, after overhearing them speak of the weight saved by changing from pontoons to wheels, he had hatched his plan to sequester himself and follow them into Europe if possible.

After the backslapping and general joviality subsided, the stowaway was handed a gasoline bucket to assist them in refueling the aircraft and was notified he would have all the most menial tasks assigned to him as the most junior of the aircrew. Wells accepted his lowly status with great relish and Smith sent a cable to General Patrick requesting permission to take him with them as the official reporter on their trip.

As they serviced the airplanes, a long line of camels were being driven across the airfield. Leigh Wade and Erik Nelson bet their mechanics they would not have the courage to ride one of the beasts. When they rose to the challenge, Erik Nelson signaled the camel drivers to bring one camel over to Jack Harding and another to Hank Ogden. Within a few minutes they were surrounded by numerous laughing spectators.

Jack Harding stood looking up at the camel selected for him. Standing next to the huge beast, the camel loomed far above his head, being far larger than it appeared from the distance. The drover signaled the camels to kneel down so they could climb aboard. Fighting the panic welling up from within, Harding considered canceling the unwelcome ride, but knowing the endless ridicule that would certainly follow if he did, he reluctantly mounted the camel's back with a forced smile.

When both men were in position, the drover gave a command and the camel unfolded its legs. The jerky fore and aft motion threw them both off balance and left them clinging precariously to the neck of the beast high above the ground in a state of near panic. Another command from the drover and the camels started galloping around the airfield at what felt like an unbelievable rate of speed.

Hanging on for dear life, Jack and Hank were thrown high into the air, coming down just as the beast's humps were coming up to launch them into the air again. Both men shouted at the camel to stop but that simply accelerated its progress across the ground and increased their vertical excursions with painful landings on their private parts.

Spectators, drovers, and the crew were rolling on the ground laughing hysterically. Wells tried to photograph the racing camels and their terrified riders but was laughing too hard to control the camera. Lowell Smith, fearful of injuries to his crew, insisted the drovers stop the camels immediately. Upon hearing the signal, the camels stopped where they were. A second signal had them lowering themselves to the ground where Hank and Jack dismounted and beat a hasty retreat. Both said they would rather do fifty Immelmann turns in an airplane than ride the most docile, best trained camel in the world.

WEDNESDAY, JULY 2, 1924
3:30 P.M
AMBALA, INDIA

Hank Ogden, recovered from his harrowing camel ride and sympathetic to Linton Wells's enthusiasm for covering their flight, had sat uncomfortably in the rear cockpit of the *Boston* for the entire flight. He had graciously offered to share his narrow seat with Wells and both men were stuffed into the space built only for one. The tight quarters made it impossible for either man to move as they counted off each and every mile of the 480 mile flight from Allahabad to Ambala, the main British Royal Air Force field in India and near the Himalayas.

Both men were stiff and, feeling the painful effects of their cramped quarters on the six hour flight, had to be helped from their cockpit by their companions. On the flight Erik Nelson was hard pressed to keep up with the other aircraft and an unwelcome wheezing sound intruded upon the exhaust sounds of the *Boston*. His inspection of his engine upon landing confirmed his fears that the *New Orleans* Liberty-12 engine had developed a leaky cylinder.

The British commander assured them that there were many Liberty engines being used by the R.A.F. in India and he would telephone his machine shops at Lahore, only a few hundred miles away, to request a replacement cylinder be flown to them immediately.

At Lahore later that same evening, an enthusiastic young R.A.F. lieutenant carefully lashed down a new Liberty cylinder in the small baggage compartment of his Sopwith Camel Biplane and took off into the last vestiges of daylight. As the lights of the city of Amritsar came into view, the Sopwith's engine started vibrating badly.

The vibrations increased, culminating in a loud bang and a stopped propeller. Guiding his stricken craft by the last rays of the sun, the lieutenant narrowly missed several large trees before touching down. The Sopwith went up on its nose as the wheels started to bury themselves in the soft sand and for a long moment teetered precariously with its tail high up in the air and its propeller in the sand.

With his face contorted in panic and his eyes closed, the lieutenant held onto the cockpit coaming, waiting for the Sopwith to turn over onto its back. Excruciatingly slowly, its forward momentum stopped and the tail fell back with a dull thud onto its tailskid. The lieutenant cautiously opened one eye and then the other. He was upright and, except for a cut on his forehead caused by striking the leather-covered front cockpit coaming, was unhurt. He sat composing himself as the rush of adrenaline subsided.

His reverie was disturbed by a young boy with a goat-driven cart who came over to the side of the Sopwith. "That was wonderful. Can you do that again, sir?" asked the boy. "Not tonight I can't," the Lieutenant replied. Remembering his important mission he scrambled from the cockpit and was relieved to find the cylinder undamaged. He removed it from the Sopwith, retied its wrapping, and turned to his young admirer.

"I've got to get to a train station, is there one nearby?" he asked. "Yes sir," said the boy. "Can you take me there? I will pay you," the Lieutenant said. "Yes sir, I will take you." The boy emptied the cart of its cargo to give the lieutenant room to ride in it and mounted the goat. They arrived at the train station in Amritsar an hour later. A train to Ambala was scheduled to depart a few hours later.

THURSDAY, JULY 3, 1924
2:20 P.M
ENROUTE TO MULDAN, INDIA

The flight was flying at an altitude of six thousand feet where the lower air temperature gave them some relief from the oppressive heat on the ground. Erik Nelson and Jack Harding had been awake since 3:30 that morning when the young lieutenant arrived with their precious cylinder. Although exhausted himself by his travel and near-brush with death, the lieutenant insisted on helping them install the cylinder onto the engine in the *Boston*, asking no further reward than being allowed to sit in the cockpit of the globe-girdling airplane. By 6:30 that morning the installation was completed, the crew had a hurried breakfast, profusely thanked their R.A.F. hosts, and insisted the young lieutenant accept an engraved silver cigarette lighter given to them by the Japanese for his efforts.

As Lowell Smith had climbed into his cockpit, the airbase commander advised him they had received confirmation that morning that Major MacLaren had successfully flown through Burma, Thailand, Indochina, and China, and was that very day speeding on to Kagoshima in Japan. Smith was profusely thanked for the good sportsmanship shown by the American team and their navy in getting MacLaren's spare airplane to him.

As he settled into his cockpit and completed the takeoff checklist, Smith computed the distances remaining for MacLaren and his own flight. With MacLaren at Kagoshima, the British flight had only 12,000 miles to go. They had 14,000 miles remaining on their flight. The race had again tightened and the British were two thousand miles ahead of them. Smith resolved to pick up their pace.

The blue skies devoid of clouds, excellent visibility, and the simplified navigation provided by the railroad tracks far beneath them leading straight to Muldan filled them all with a sense of complacency. This would be an easy flight—or so they thought.

It came without warning. From the distance in front of them a dark cloud, tiny at first but then growing alarmingly to fill their windscreen, appeared seemingly from nowhere. Suddenly the flight was in the center of a maelstrom with the airplanes being pelted by stones from every direction. In a single heartbeat, the smooth placid air with unlimited visibility became a tornado in which they were being thrown around like little paper planes in a black cutting cloud of sand driven by hurricane force winds. The violence was indescribable, with the sounds of a million machine gun bullets hitting the fabric, sheet metal, and glass windshields of their airplanes. From the cockpits, even the outer wingtips could not be discerned.

With the flight flying in close formation and visibility suddenly reduced to zero, top priority became the avoidance of colliding with each other. Each knew what to do and took the appropriate action. Lowell, leading the flight, attempted to maintain his altitude and heading as best he could. Erik, flying on his left wing, dove sharply downward and turned to the left. Leigh pushed in full throttle and climbed steeply while turning to the right. Within a few seconds the aircraft had safely separated and each could cope with the violence of the sandstorm within their own block of airspace. Next they reduced their throttle opening to slow their aircraft and minimize impact damage as much as possible. Eventually the sandstorm subsided. Visibility improved slightly and the flight rejoined, descending to within fifty feet of the railroad tracks.

At Multan, the commander knew the flight would have a very difficult time finding the airfield with the reduced visibility of the sandstorm. He stationed thousands of troops shoulder to shoulder all around the landing area to make it more prominent, but with visibility severely limited, the flight overflew the field, the soldiers straining to see the aircraft they could hear flying low over their heads.

Smith caught sight of the railroad station through a break in the storm and, realizing he had overflown the airfield, turned his flight back and descended even further. The soldiers heard the flight returning toward them and scattered lest they be sliced by the propellers spinning just feet above the ground. Smith led the flight in, making perfect landings to the cheers and relief of the waiting troops.

As the crew climbed from their cockpits, Colonel Butler, the commanding officer, gave each a tall glass of ice cold lemonade before even introducing himself. The ground temperature was 120 degrees in the shade and Colonel Butler welcomed the crew to the "hottest place in all of India." The ice cold drinks would be remembered as the most delicious and welcome beverages each man ever tasted—and Multan itself remembered as "Molten."

A regimental band had waited five days to play at a gala welcome party for the crew that evening but Lowell, Erik, and Leigh excused themselves to go to sleep early to be in better shape to fly in the morning. Les Arnold inducted Linton Wells, Hank Ogden, and Jack Harding to more than compensate for any deficiencies caused by the absence of the primary pilots. Freed of any restraints, the party enthusiastically celebrated U.S. Independence Day, boisterously continuing long into the night.

FRIDAY, JULY 4, 1924
3:10 P.M.
ENROUTE TO KARACHI, INDIA

For almost four hours the flight continued without incident on the 455 mile flight to Karachi at an altitude of six thousand feet. Without warning, Erik's engine suddenly exploded shedding white-hot molten pieces of metal which made several holes in the wings and damaged the struts of the *New Orleans.*

Smith and Wade saw the white puffs of smoke coming from Nelson's stricken airplane as it slowed markedly. They throttled back and flew around the *New Orleans.* Increasingly large dark streaks of oil stained the fuselage. Nelson looked around for a suitable landing place but the ground beneath them was baked mud with huge cracks, some several feet wide and deep. A landing would certainly destroy the airplane and probably kill them in the process.

They didn't know it at the time but a piston had disintegrated and both exhaust springs were hurled out of the exhaust stacks. The unrestrained exhaust valve was ingested into the cylinder. It combined with pieces of cracked piston causing the connecting rod and wrist pin to break and hurling those parts out through the bottom of the crankcase. With chunks of white hot metal being flung in all directions and highly flammable lubricating oil being pumped through the cracked walls of the engine, the situation looked very grave. Several chunks sliced through the cowling, wing, and strut, narrowly missing decapitating Erik Nelson as he stood in the cockpit to watch for the first signs of fire.

The crews of the other cruisers stood by and watched helplessly as their stricken companions fought to keep the *New Orleans* in the air. Normally the propellers of the cruisers rotated at 1,640 revolutions per minute. Erik's engine was shaking violently and any attempt to increase its speed over 1,100 RPM was met with a volley of banging and crashing and a fusillade of hot metal pieces coming out the exhaust. This was barely enough to sustain the airplane in level flight and the airspeed decayed to just above the stall speed of the *New Orleans*.

The temperature gauge of the stricken ship climbed as the oil pressure dropped. Jack reached a piece of cheesecloth, wiped the oil as best he could from his goggles, hair, and face, and passed the cloth to Erik to do the same. Erik removed his gloves and controlled the aircraft with only the tips of his bare fingers. Any large deflection of the aircraft's control surfaces could reduce its speed precipitating a fatal stall and spin. The overheated engine occasionally locked solid, the propeller stopping suddenly. Nelson lowered the nose of the airplane, diving it down to within inches of the ground. In the dive the increased airspeed cooled the engine down sufficiently for the airblast to cause the propeller to rotate again and with a mighty backfire, the Liberty would start running again. Erik would then struggle to coax the dying engine into pulling the flying machine back up to a higher altitude.

As long as the engine continued rotating, the other cylinders of the damage-tolerant Liberty-12 might get them to safety. Erik knew the critical factor would be oil. When all the oil in the tank had been pumped overboard, all the bearings throughout the engine would disintegrate. The engine would seize within seconds and no amount of cooling would help. The inhospitable terrain would rip and tear at the soft belly of the *New Orleans* until a wheel caught in one of the myriad cracks and crevices below. The airplane would cartwheel, turning over on its back, crumpling wings, fuselage, and tail surfaces. He'd seen it many times before—and had buried most of the pilots. Even if they were lucky enough to survive the crash, for them the flight would be over.

Smith signaled Arnold to take control of the *Chicago* while he measured the distance on his chart to Karachi and calculated the time remaining. They would need forty more minutes. Lowell pointed at his watch and held up ten fingers four times to Erik. Could he keep his stricken ship flying for another forty minutes? Would the oil last?

To Erik Nelson, each minute seemed like an eternity. The oil was still staining the windshield and fuselage. Now the stains were his friends. When they stopped he would know the oil was gone and the engine would soon overheat and seize. The water temperature gauge was pegged in the danger area as the diminishing water and oil reservoirs overheated with the task of cooling.

Lowell signaled to Erik when thirty minutes remained, then twenty and finally ten as Karachi came into view. Lowell signaled to Leigh Wade to stay with Erik while he accelerated and sped on ahead to locate the airfield so Erik would not have to do any unnecessary maneuvering. The oil leaking from the *New Orleans* slowed to a trickle. Soon it would stop—and so would the engine. Erik pulled the throttle back further and put the airplane into a slow descent to further cool the overheated engine.

Within a few minutes he spotted Lowell's airplane circling and saw Karachi's airfield. As Erik's altimeter unwound he calculated that the margin between salvation and destruction was razor thin. If he could hold the *New Orleans* to its present descent rate, he should touch down just as the airfield border passed under his wheels.

At the threshold of the airfield, the Liberty-12 breathed its last and with a final bang and whimper the propeller stopped for the last time just before the wheels lightly brushed the ground. Erik instantly shut off the fuel to the overheated engine to prevent a fire from starting. With the propeller stopped he rolled toward a large crowd waiting to welcome them.

Major-General Cook, the commander of the Karachi base, sat calmly in the rear of his chauffeur-driven Rolls Royce nearby, watching the proceedings. As Erik's plane rolled to a stop, his chauffeur drove him over to the *New Orleans* where his footman alighted to open his car's door for him. The fuselage was oil-stained and wisps of black smoke were rising from the cowling amid sizzling and crackling noises. Cook got out and casually walked around the cruiser, stopping at the cockpit as Erik emerged. "I see you've had a spot of trouble, old boy," he observed, with typical British understatement.

Smith and Wade, greatly relieved by the flight's miraculous safe arrival, landed shortly after Nelson. Among the spectators was the American consul who handed Smith a cable from General Patrick which replied to Smith's request for Linton Wells to fly with them. Its message was short: "Request denied." A second cable was handed to Linton Wells from Associated Press. It too was short, "You're fired."

Fortunately for the flight, Karachi had been assigned as a major refurbishment point and large quantities of spare parts, including three fresh Liberty engines and propellers, had arrived shortly before the flight landed. After brief formalities and a thankfully short speech of welcome, Smith requested the aircraft be towed immediately to the well-equipped maintenance hangars on the airfield staffed by enthusiastic and helpful mechanics of the Royal Air Force. The R.A.F. airfield at Karachi had played host to many previous round-the-world flight attempts by the British, French, Italians, Portuguese, and Argentineans. They were quite knowledgeable of the requirements and disappointed that each flight had failed and dozens of aircraft had been lost through the years in the process. They were especially grateful for the assistance given the British flight by the American Navy.

Within an hour of landing, each plane had the ministrations of half a dozen mechanics who eagerly assisted the American crews with maintenance and repair of the airframes. By eight o'clock that evening, removal of the old propellers and engines had started.

When General Cook's Rolls Royce arrived at the hangar to pick up the crew and bring them to a gala welcome party, they were at a critical point in the disassembly process and wanted to continue working. Les Arnold, the least mechanically proficient among them, was chosen to express their regrets and represent them at the party, a task he accepted with great relish.

Arnold wrote in his diary that evening:

"I was so smeared from head to foot with oil and grease that when General Cook's Rolls Royce, complete with chauffeur and footman, took me to his big white mansion I felt like the ragged urchin in the storybooks who dreams that he is a prince. As I whirled up the driveway through an avenue of palms, I could see a crowd of men and women in spotless white

sitting on the lawn. I was in my one and only suit of grimy overalls, so as soon as the car stopped I ran up the steps in order not to be seen. But with my face black from smoke and dirt and my overalls coated with grease, the general insisted that I must come right out to meet the assembled company. They were so charming, treating me as though I were a knight of the Garter instead of a mere unwashed lieutenant, that I soon felt quite at ease."

Repairs, maintenance, propeller and engine replacement took the next several days. The three pilots stayed with the chief commissioner of Sind who had hosted the pilots of previous flights including MacLaren, D'Oisy, Ross Smith, and many others. Harding and Ogden were guests of the Collector of Karachi while Les Arnold remained with General Cook.

After a weekend filled with work starting at dawn and continuing long into the night. The crew arose at 3:30 A.M. to have their last breakfast at Karachi, bid a fond good-bye to Linton Wells, and depart for the 410-mile flight to Chahbar in Persia. They had flown 178 hours and 7 minutes covering 12,577 miles since leaving Seattle, but still had nearly 14,000 miles before their mission would be completed.

MONDAY MORNING, JULY 7, 1924
4:30 A.M
KARACHI, INDIA

General Cook sat across the table from Lowell Smith. As Cook raised his cup of strong morning tea, he looked over the rim, discreetly observing the quiet young man he had come to admire over the past three days. He had seen all the previous pilots of attempted world flights. Many were overbearing and pompous, puffed up with their own prodigious aerial abilities, contemptuously dismissing the challenges mother nature or just bad luck might hold in store for them. Others seemed almost too cautious, somber, and serious, hesitant to climb again into their cockpits and put their lives on the line for a venture that had proven far more difficult than they had anticipated and which stretched endlessly yet before them.

Previous British, French, Italian, and Portuguese attempts had all ended with broken airplanes, bodies, and spirits. Dead airmen lay in unmarked graves while crash survivors limped home, chastened but grateful to be spared. New expeditions still flew into Karachi airfield to refuel and breathe new life into their worn engines and airframes. But this American flight was different. All the others flew in from the west and continued toward the east. These Americans were the first to fly in from the east and were neither boastful nor timid. Their good-humored jokes and playful stunts concealed a quiet self-assured competence and an eagerness to work from dawn to long after midnight to complete servicing and maintenance of their aircraft. No detail was too small, no task too great to escape their diligence. As the first hesitant rays of sunlight filtered into the mess hall, one by one each American aviator rose, warmly shook General Cook's hand, and eagerly departed to resume their flight.

MONDAY, JULY 11, 1924,
MIDNIGHT
CONSTANTINOPLE, TURKEY

Sleep evaded Lowell Smith as he tossed restlessly on the smooth soft silk sheets on his luxurious bed. He swung his long legs over the side, poured a glass of water from the pitcher that had been thoughtfully left for him, and lit a cigarette.

Lying down again, he blew round smoke rings, watching them spiral lazily up into the darkened ornate tapestries that hung above his bed. Their schedule had called for four days in Constantinople. His hospitable Turkish hosts had planned a full week's schedule for them but Lowell had other plans. In three days, the French would celebrate Bastille Day. It would be a fantastic accomplishment if they could fly over the millions of Parisians filling the streets around their Eiffel Tower and Arch de Triumph on their national holiday. The spectacle would be memorable and all the world's newspapers would headline their arrival. Aviation would receive enormous publicity and support.

The flight from Karachi had gone well. Racing through Persia with a brief refueling stop at Chahbar on the Gulf of Oman, they had spent a wary night at Bandar Abbas where a cholera epidemic raged. The next morning they flew over the harsh barren deserts toward Bushire. Arriving at 11:00 A.M. after a five hour flight, they refueled again and, eager to depart, took off without waiting for their sandwiches to arrive from the city. At Baghdad that evening, the hungry crew eagerly devoured the dinner prepared for them by pilots of the Royal Air Force before starting the grueling process of "servicing up" their trusty cruisers. Two days later they had passed through Aleppo in Syria and were in Constantinople, Turkey, and on the threshold of Europe.

Europe

CHAPTER 13

SATURDAY, JULY 12, 1924
11:15 A.M.
ENROUTE TO BUCHAREST, ROUMANIA

Even the cold crisp air of the early morning could not subdue the ebullient spirits of the American crew. The takeoff at dawn from the San Stefano airfield in Turkey had gone without a hitch. In the first rays of the early morning sun they flew over the crumbling ruins of old Byzantium and its long-forgotten battlefields of ruined villages. Abandoned trenches cut into unkempt fields littered with barbed wire and shell holes gave mute testimony to the macabre and savage battles which raged on for centuries. Residents of Constantinople told of seeing the ghosts of thousands of mutilated soldiers from a dozen different countries who had fought and died to conquer this strategic port city by the Bosphorous.

As the hours passed, the land under them rose as they entered the foreboding Transylvanian Alps. This was the land of werewolves, vampires, and dark-haired gypsy girls who danced with seductive passion to a music free and untamed, without constraint nor shame, filled with the joy of life and the promise of unimagined sensual delights.

Their spirits soared as Bucharest drew closer. Soon they would be in the civilized world again, over lush green valleys and neatly aligned streets, in a world where the airplane was known and accepted as a part of modern life. Most important, mechanical help in the event of an emergency could be easily found. They had come over fifteen thousand miles and their flight had become a return journey with "only" eleven thousand miles remaining. They were now totally focused on their triumphant entry into Paris on Bastille Day even if they had to carry their cruisers on their backs to make it.

The landing at the airfield of the Franco-Roumanian Aero Company in Dobrudja near Bucharest was without ceremony. Although they had sent word of their planned arrival, the telegram had not gotten to Colonel Foy, the American consul in Roumania. Relieved at the lack of crowds to impede their progress, the crew began refueling and servicing the airplanes while Les Arnold telephoned their arrival to an embarrassed Colonel Foy who had believed they were still thousands of miles away in southern Asia.

Later that afternoon, the chief of the Roumanian Air Service arranged an inspection of his air forces noting, with pride, that it was larger, more modern and better equipped than the United States. The same could not be said of their plumbing. Turning on the faucets in their hotel rooms, no water came out through any of them. Erik Nelson inadvertently left the faucet open in Leigh Wade's room. As Leigh slept, the water suddenly started gushing from the open faucet, filling the entire hotel room and dripping onto the bed of Lowell Smith, who occupied the room directly under.

When Lowell went up to investigate the sudden deluge, they found Leigh Wade happily snoring on his bed which was tenuously floating in a sea of water and on the verge of sinking and thereby drowning the sleeping Wade. Lowell shut off the faucet and called the night attendants, who formed a bucket brigade to empty the room of its liquid content. Through it all Wade continued to sleep, oblivious to his timely rescue. The next morning he couldn't understand how everything, including his bedclothes, had gotten so damp.

MONDAY, JULY 14, 1924
4:20 P.M.
LE BOURGET AIRFIELD NEAR PARIS, FRANCE

The crowd had started forming shortly after dawn and the numbers swelled as the morning surrendered to the afternoon. On this Bastille Day, in this place, all were gathered—waiting—Generals, politicians, ambassadors, cabinet ministers, fellow aviators, and countless others, all there, all waiting.

The arrival of the American world fliers had been watched with increasing interest by the French. The arrival on their national holiday was almost too good to be true. Bastille Day became "Aviation Day" in France and the newspaper headlines covering the flight became larger and bolder as the day approached, most recently relegating the day's other news and even the outcome of the Olympic Games being conducted nearby to second-class status.

France recently celebrated the record-setting speed of the flight by Lieutenant D'Oisy from Paris to Tokyo with great national pride, expecting it to stand for a long time. Today the Americans would shatter this record by two full days, an undeniable tribute to American ingenuity, technology, and persistence.

In the cockpits of the world cruisers, each of the pilots were being moved by wide ranging and deep emotions which welled up unbidden, and brought tears into their eyes. The 465-mile flight from Bucharest to Budapest the prior day was without incident and, after refueling and a brief lunch, they continued on another 113 miles into Vienna. There a crowd of well-wishing American tourists buoyed their spirits while they again "serviced up" the airplanes, then posed for pictures.

After a comfortable night in huge suites at Austria's super-posh Imperial Hotel, the fliers breakfasted from large bowls filled with raspberries and cream which Les Arnold described as almost delicious enough to make all the tribulations of the flight worthwhile. They took-off from Vienna at 5:50 A.M. and within thirty minutes were fighting their way through high mountain passes engulfed by heavy rains with dark, gloomy skies, menacing low clouds, and heavy fog which obscured the ridge lines and made the flight extremely hazardous.

For several hours they flew scant feet over the Danube River, fighting strong headwinds and barely avoiding collisions with bridges and castles which popped out at them from the fog-shrouded banks. After six and a half hours of flight and with the last few drops of fuel remaining in their tanks, they finally sighted the slender spire of Strasbourg Cathedral, their reference point for locating the grass airfield from which they could refuel and service the ships.

After a brief stop, they were again airborne in improving weather to start the final leg of their flight into Paris. It was the familiar profiles of the lovely churches, gardens, parks, and "Hotel de Ville" of the city of Nancy which brought back the long-forgotten nightmares of their wartime experiences. Their ears filled with the engine sounds of the German Gotha bombers dropping their lethal cargo of death and destruction, and the sounds of bullets, mortar, and artillery shells snuffing out the lives of hapless victims— many of whom were close friends and fellow airmen. Below them lay the battlefields of St. Mihiel where the First American Army fought under its own leaders for the first time and countless fallen comrades earned their eternal reputation for bravery and self-sacrifice in the pursuit of freedom for unknown friends and allies.

As the flight passed Verdun, flying over the pockmarked fields of bomb craters, trenches, and rusting barbed wire, and over the Argonne Forest, each of the crew felt the presence in their cockpits of those Ace airmen who had flown into battle with them and against them—and changed the face of war forever. The fields below them, even disguised with a new mantle of green, evoked the great air battles of years gone by. In each cloud, their minds' eye could clearly see the Allied Spads and Nieuports of Billy Mitchell, Eddie Rickenbacker, Raoul Lufbery, and Frank Luke locked in mortal combat with the Iron Cross-marked Albatrosses and Fokkers of Manfred von Richthofen, Ernst Udet, Erich Loewenhardt, and Werner Voss.

As they approached the outskirts of Paris, their reveries appeared to come to life. Closing on them rapidly from the front was a military formation of eight biplanes. Instinctively Smith signaled the arrival of the unknown airplanes to Wade and Nelson and pointed to the nearest cloud formation into which they could take shelter. Fighting against the impulse to break formation, and noting no hostile intent from the growing images in his windscreen, Lowell recognized them as French airplanes sent to escort them to Paris.

The *Chicago* led the growing V formation in a large circle over the Eiffel Tower, the spires of Notre Dame, the impressive buildings on the left bank of the Seine River, the dome of the Opera, and the vast wings of the Louvre. Descending over the Garden of the Tuileries, Lowell continued at rooftop level up the Champs Elysees, dipping his wings in salute when he passed just above the Arc de

Triumph. Millions of Parisians tightly packed in the streets below waved delightedly at the flight. Lowell made a climbing turn for their landing at Le Bourget.

Noting the huge crowds awaiting his arrival, Lowell was thankful that no one ran into the path of the planes as they landed. It was just 5:15 P.M. when the three world cruisers parked in front of the waiting hangars at Le Bourget. It took a full hour before the fliers could finish shaking the hands of the vast array of high officials that had come to greet them and begin the job of "servicing up" the airplanes.

Most of the dignitaries waited for them patiently until well after nine o'clock when the work finally finished. Exhausted, they climbed into waiting limousines and were taken to their hotel rooms where a specially prepared French version of a typical American dinner awaited them. With great effort, they showered, cleaned off most of the grease, and looked forward to nothing more than a good night's sleep. That was not to be.

They had no sooner gotten into bed than the door opened and a delegation including most of the French cabinet ministers entered explaining they had prepared a magnificent evening in honor of their American airmen guests. Not wishing to offend their kind hosts, Lowell reluctantly accepted on behalf of the crew and they all wearily dressed again for what they hoped would be a very short evening. It was now almost midnight and they were all dead tired.

Entering a specially prepared box at the Folies Bergeres, they were startled to hear each of their names called by the dazzlingly beautiful showgirls who promised them the best performance of their lives to the suggestive envious snickers of the audience. In groups and singly, the amply-endowed showgirls pranced and danced next to them, sensuously revealing charms usually hidden from view.

In the darkened theater, lighted only by the spotlights on the showgirls, one by one the weary crew . . . fell fast asleep. The lack of sleep of the previous week—followed by ten hours of flying that day before five additional hours servicing the planes—had taken its toll. As the spotlight was turned on the Americans, the surprised French hosts found themselves among loudly snoring Americans totally oblivious to the charms paraded before them. Despite sharp nudges in their ribs from their hosts each time a beguiling spectacle began, they would awaken startled momentarily and then relapse into a deep sleep.

The French audience could hardly comprehend the American reaction to what they found to be an enormously interesting and compelling show. An enterprising reporter took several photographs of the Americans soundly sleeping at the feet of their stunning showgirls and the Paris newspaper headlines the next day questioned, "If the Folies Bergeres won't keep these American airmen awake, we wonder what will?" The masculinity of the crew and Americans in general were called into question. They became the butt of jokes in most of the world's newspapers, which they took with good humor. An unexpected result was that tens of thousands of women the world over became anxious to prove that their charms could certainly overcome the diffidence of the Americans. Les Arnold offered to give each of them a chance.

When the crew finally returned to their hotel late that evening, they wrote the following notice and put one on each of their doors:

> PLEASE DO NOT WAKE US
> UNTIL NINE O'CLOCK TOMORROW MORNING
> UNLESS THE HOTEL IS ON FIRE;
> AND NOT EVEN THEN
> UNLESS THE FIREMEN HAVE GIVEN UP ALL HOPE!!

TUESDAY, JULY 15, 1924
PARIS, FRANCE

Dear Diary:

This has been an unbelievable day for us. At ten o'clock we visited the Arc de Triumph and laid a wreath on the tomb of the unknown soldier. We then visited cabinet officials who fortunately forgave us for our lack of etiquette in falling asleep amid their most beautiful ladies last night. I can hardly believe we did that, but I intend to make up for our indiscretion at my earliest opportunity.

We attended a luncheon in our honor hosted by General Pershing. As lieutenants in the Army he had seemed about as far from us as the Dalai Lama of Tibet. But there in Paris he put his arm around us, told us funny stories, and seemed like a regular fellow!

President Doumergue invited us to the Elysee Palace. We expected our visit with him to take only a few minutes but he kept us an hour,

*and just when we were getting ready to leave, he invited us to join him
to meet the athletes and delegates of the Olympic Games, which we did
with great pride.*

*The president wanted to decorate us with the medal of the Legion of
Honor but Smitty explained we couldn't accept foreign decorations without getting the permission of Congress first, so the president gave us
autographed pictures of himself instead.*

WEDNESDAY, JULY 16, 1924
1:07 P.M.
ENROUTE TO LONDON, ENGLAND

The steady staccato roar coming from the three Liberty
engines was reassuring. Lowell led the familiar V formation
flying over the English Channel at an altitude of seven thousand feet. Thirty minutes earlier the pilots of the three French
military escorts and the Pathe cameraman's ship had bidden them a
cheery "thumbs up" and given a crisp salute before turning their
planes back toward France.

They had departed LeBourget precisely at 11:00 A.M. Earlier
they had observed tourists departing on daily flights to London,
Brussels, Lyons, Marseilles, and Amsterdam. No such scheduled air
service existed anywhere in the United States. They marveled at this
glimpse into the future of air travel and became convinced that
someday their own country must follow suit.

As Lowell led his three-ship formation in the familiar V formation toward the shoreline of England, a multi-engined passenger
airliner climbed to their altitude. The pilot slowed to keep pace with
them a short distance off Lowell's right wing. The tourists waved
excitedly through the windows of the large plane. An attractive
"flapper" displayed a shapely leg and attempted to carry on a pan-
tomimed exchange which Les eagerly encouraged until the pilot
finally gave a cheery wave and accelerated away.

Today was another very special day for them. Within the next
hour they would be landing at the Croyden Aerodrome near
London where a luncheon had been prepared for them by their fellow aviators of the Royal Air Force. The wife of Stuart MacLaren

also awaited their arrival, anxious to express her gratitude for the help they had rendered her husband.

That same morning, her husband had taken off from Toshimoye Lake, on the Japanese Island of Yeterofu, for the long flight northward to the frigid waters of Paramushiru. Aware of the frequent blizzards and freezing cold temperatures his flight would encounter, she confided to the Americans her fears for her husband's safety. They did their best to reassure her despite their knowledge that her concerns were well founded.

WEDNESDAY, JULY 16, 1924
6:30 P.M.
BLACKBURN AIRFIELD, BROUGH, ENGLAND

At last, all of the bolts, wires, hoses, fittings, and generators had been removed from the three engines. Tomorrow morning they would hoist the engines from their mounts in preparation for replacing them with new ones. Now they could go to dinner.

It had been a long day. Starting at dawn from Croyden it had taken them two hours and ten minutes to cover the 165 miles north to Brough. This would be their last extensive refit and thorough service for their airplanes before attempting the most dangerous part of their trip. All of the other pilots who had been tempted to fly the shorter route across the North Atlantic had been lost at sea, never to be heard from again. No detail could be overlooked, nothing on the airplanes could be left to chance if they were to have any hope of surviving.

The Blackburn Aviation Company had offered their airfield and hangar facilities for refitting and servicing the flight. Here they would change again from wheels back to pontoons. New engines would replace the old ones and each component, however small, would be minutely inspected and replaced if necessary. Months before the flight started, four spare engines and four sets of components, pontoons, and tools had been shipped from the United States to Blackburn Aviation.

At the airfield in Brough several cables were waiting for them. Billy Mitchell, having completed his ten-day leave after arriving in

San Francisco, wished them well and would be in Washington D.C. that day to assist them if necessary.

They were also advised that MacLaren's airplane had never completed the four hundred and fifty mile flight to Paramushiru. The Japanese destroyer *Isokaze* was steaming at full speed toward Broughton Bay on Shimushiru Island. This island lay about halfway between Yeterofu and Paramushiru. Colonel Broome, who accompanied MacLaren and laid out the route for his flight, had cached provisions for the flight at Broughton Bay and it was hoped they might have made a precautionary landing there. A second destroyer, the *Hamakaze*, which had been waiting to assist MacLaren, left its post at Paramushiru and started searching other nearby islands in the Kurile group.

Another cable from Admiral Magruder advised that his cruiser, the *U.S.S. Richmond* would rendezvous with them at Kirkwall in the Orkney Islands just north of Scotland, their final stop before their attempted North Atlantic crossing.

BY CABLE AND ASSOCIATED PRESS—CHARTRES, FRANCE, JULY 17, 1924

The French aviators Coupet and Droupin today broke the world's record for a duration flight, remaining in the air 38 hours. The previous record of 37 hours, 15 minutes, 48.8 seconds was made by Lieutenant Lowell H. Smith, leader of the American round-the-world flight, and Lieutenant J.R. Richter at San Diego, August 27–28, 1923 when the American airmen used a DH-4 plane and refueled for the first time in the air.

BY CABLE AND ASSOCIATED PRESS—TOKYO, JAPAN, JULY 18, 1924

Major A. Stuart MacLaren, the British aviator on a flight around the world who has been missing since he left Yeterofu Island for Paramushiru, Kurile Islands, early Wednesday morning, has been found. The aircraft, MacLaren, and his three companions were found safe in a bay on the southwest shore of Uruppu Island, the island adjoining Yeterofu Island. Dense fog forced the MacLaren party to land soon after taking flight. MacLaren plans to continue his journey to Paramushiru tomorrow.

BY CABLE AND THE *LOS ANGELES TIMES*—AMSTERDAM, HOLLAND, JULY 18, 1924

Major Pedro Zanni, the Argentine aviator who plans to start a world flight next Tuesday, intends to follow the route of Major Stuart MacLaren, the British flyer. The Argentine anticipates that the superior speed of his machine will enable him to overtake his rivals in the globe-encircling contest. Major Zanni purchased three Fokker airplanes and for the first stages of the flight the regulation landing gear will be used. The second stage will be flown with another plane having pontoons, and for the last stage across the Atlantic a third special seaplane is being built.

By July 22nd the work on the world cruisers should have been completed. New engines, generators, and smaller radiators had been installed, all tears in the fabric had been repaired, worn areas had been recovered, cables had been tensioned, and fittings inspected and replaced where necessary. The replacement wings that had been shipped to them were found to be unnecessary.

Just before noon, Lowell and Erik were working underneath the *Chicago* securing the bolts which completed the conversion from wheels to pontoons. The 5,000-pound empty airplane was suspended by a crane (with a marked capacity of 12,000 pounds) several feet over their heads. Erik suggested they take a short break for lunch and they rolled out from under the airplane. Just as they cleared the pontoons, the chain broke and 5,000 pounds of airplane crashed onto the concrete floor—the pontoons brushing by both of them before smashing into pieces. If it had happened a single second earlier they both would have been killed.

Fortunately an extra set of pontoons had been shipped for the *Seattle* and could be used as replacements. Several additional days would be needed for repairs, but with delays in getting the naval ships on station, no time was lost by the accident. The work schedule of the Americans which continued from dawn to dusk amazed the management and British workers at the Blackburn Aircraft Company which were used to a far shorter and more casual workday. The "Brough Evening News" quoted G. Bentley, manager, as follows: "We simply admire and admire and admire these Americans. Their thoroughness and the fierce manner in which they attack the dirty work which they know must be done in connection with the refitting and adjusting of their machines are wonderful."

The accompanying naval flotilla did not expect the world flight to make the rapid progress they did. In pushing themselves to the limits of their endurance they had arrived far in advance of the predicted schedule and General Patrick ordered Lowell Smith to delay the flight until all the naval ships had arrived on station.

The cruiser *U.S.S. Richmond*, flagship of Rear Admiral Thomas Magruder, departed from Newport, R.I. on July 21. The cruiser *Raleigh* and two destroyers from the European fleet left that same day to take up stations in the North Atlantic on the route to Iceland. On July 24 the destroyers *Lawrence, Coghland, Barry*, and *MacFarland* left Newport for the North Atlantic, stopping at Boston to be joined by the destroyer *Charles Ashburn* and at Halifax, Nova Scotia to be joined by the cruiser *Milwaukee*. With the whole world's attention on the flight, every effort was going to be made to bring the men back alive no matter what happened along the route.

By July 24 the airplanes and crew were ready to leave but under orders to stand down until the end of the month when all ships would be on station. On July 25th they received the news that MacLaren's flight had arrived safely in Kamchatka on the Bering Sea from Paramushiru and was poised to enter North America.

These were difficult days for the crew. All joy for the flight had gone. They were physically and emotionally drained. Their usual good humor had gone and the strains of six men living in close proximity to each other for the past six months was evident. Tempers were short and small incidents precipitated harsh words. The energies channeled into overcoming the challenges of the flight were now being directed to less productive ends.

Excerpts from the diaries of Lowell Smith:

"Wednesday morning, July 30th, we were up at four o'clock, launched the planes down the runway into the Humber, and took a load of gas and oil. There was a low fog hanging over the coast, so it was not until ten-fifteen that we got away. With the Boston and New Orleans close behind, I headed the Chicago out over the North Sea.

North of Montrose, the clouds kept forcing us down until we could go no farther, so we climbed up over them and for an hour we flew without

*so much as seeing a glimpse of heather or the bank and braes of bonny
Scotland. But I did see a Scottish castle that caught my fancy. It was built
on a promontory jutting right out into the sea. On three sides were sheer
cliffs with the waves from the North Sea pounding against them, and on
the land side was a high wall. When I'm a millionaire, I shall buy it.*

*Our longest water hop on this flight was for eighty miles to
Dunkensberry Point. From there we flew onto Scapa Flow, where the
Germans surrendered, and then scuttled their fleet. We were now in the
Orkney Islands, the place where some of the British and American fleets
were based throughout the final years of the World War. At the northern
edge of Scapa Flow is Houten Bay, where the British had a wartime air-
plane base, near the city of Kirkwall, which we decided to use. The U.S.S.
Richmond waited for us just outside the little bay.*

*At last we were on the edge of the North Atlantic, all set for the
adventure ahead.*

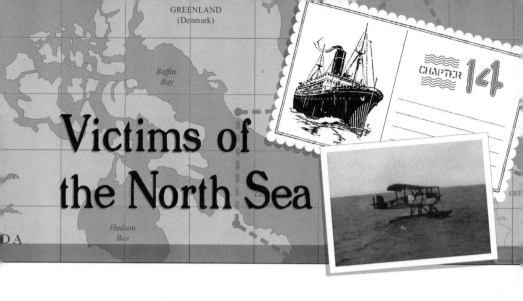

Victims of the North Sea

CHAPTER 14

THURSDAY, JULY 31, 1924
SCAPA FLOW AIRBASE, KIRKWALL, ORKNEY ISLANDS

The day started badly. If anyone harbored the hope of an easy crossing in the morning, it was certainly changed as the day wore on. The flight route across the North Atlantic had been chosen very reluctantly by the American team. Everyone knew it was fraught with danger and had never been successfully flown before. It would take them over ice-laden seas and the frozen wastelands of Iceland, Greenland, Labrador, Newfoundland, and Nova Scotia before finally arriving back over U.S. soil.

The more benign southern route across the Atlantic with its better weather had been successfully flown in 1919 by the multi-engined U.S. naval flying boats, but the required distance of 1,400 miles between the Faeroe Islands and Labrador or the 2,100 miles to Bermuda were beyond the range of the single-engined Douglas Cruisers. The single Liberty engine lacked the power to lift the heavy airplane from the grasp of the seas with pontoons and filled fuel tanks.

Despite the certainty of bountiful hunts, even the bold captains of the whaling ships avoided these treacherous seas of dense fog and lethal floating mountains of ice. The American team was ready to resume the flight but the naval destroyers on station were sending back gloomy weather reports of dense fog, high winds, huge waves, and blizzards. While the American team waited, a cable from

315

General Patrick advised of still another complication. The Italian government requested assistance for their own world flight led by Lt. Antonio Locatelli. He planned to catch up with them in Iceland and join in the dangerous crossing to Newfoundland and requested access to any unused caches of supplies. Patrick agreed on the condition that there would be no interference with the U.S. flight.

8:44 A.M.
SATURDAY, AUGUST 2, 1924

They had taken off only ten minutes ago under clear blue skies. The hearty fishermen of Kirkwall had helped with the lines and wished them well. One of them had climbed up to the cockpit and pressed his wrinkled weatherbeaten face close to Lowell's, saying, "Keep a sharp eye out, gonna be in fog soon for sure." In the bright sunlight and clear air it didn't seem possible. But these descendants of the Vikings, eking out subsistence on that barren island, devoid of trees, by catching herring, cod, and lobsters knew well the ways of the Northern seas.

The fog came at them like a blanket. They hurriedly lit the formation flying lights, the dim glow barely seen through the impenetrable sea of white surrounding them. Lowell signaled them to follow him down. Now they were in heavy rains, the droplets hitting the taut fabric of their wings and fuselage, sounding like machine gun fire and drowning out the sounds of their engines. The altimeters unwound until they were barely above the waves. The rain stopped as suddenly as it started and the streaks on their windshields gave way to mist which required constant wiping to see through. The fog thickened. With visibility down to scant inches they were in danger of colliding with each other. Lowell again signaled and they started separating and climbing up through the veil of fog desperately looking for clear air.

At 2,500 feet the *Chicago* suddenly popped out of the undercast. The rain had stopped and the fog was below them. Scanning the horizon, Lowell spotted Leigh Wade in the *Boston*. They joined up and circled searching in vain for Erik Nelson and the *New Orleans*. Had they crashed or gone on to Iceland? There was no way to know. Reluctantly both ships turned back toward Kirkwall.

Erik Nelson had his hands full. Climbing to follow the other cruisers up through the fog, he had hit their propwash and wingtip vortices. The miniature tornadoes struck his plane as it slowed close to stall speed in the climb and was highly vulnerable to upset. Instantly the right wing dropped and the aircraft was flipped on its back in an inverted high-speed "Split S" maneuver. The wind shrieked through the flying wires as Erik pulled the throttle back, stopped the turn with rudder and, intently watching the turn indicator for gyro guidance, he gingerly raised the nose, ever so gently, as the airspeed slowed and the shrieking diminished. The wing spars creaked and groaned as they absorbed the unaccustomed G forces of leveling off just as the waves started lapping at the pontoons.

After regaining control of the *New Orleans*, Erik and Jack started climbing back up through the fog. In the area they were in, the fog extended up through 3,500 feet. Erik searched for the *Boston* and *Chicago* with no success. Through a break in the clouds he spotted the U.S. destroyer, *Billingsby*. Circling low over the ship they dropped a message bag asking if the other planes had passed, and requesting the ship point the way toward Iceland. Flying a few feet off the bow of the destroyer, the crew signaled no other planes had passed and confirmed the same bearing to Iceland which Erik had deduced with his sextant and celestial navigation.

Knowing the destroyer would radio the others, Erik headed for Iceland, passing the cruiser *Raleigh* enroute. Despite losing oil pressure, they landed at Hornafjord, Iceland at 5:37 P.M. and became the first airplane to ever visit that country. Several naval crew from the *Raleigh* had been dropped off to set up radio communications and they joined the throngs of well wishers to help them moor their plane.

SATURDAY, AUGUST 2, 1924
4:35 P.M.
BERING ISLAND, KOMANDORSKI ISLANDS

Major MacLaren stared intently out of his windshield into a sea of white. They were flying less than one hundred feet over the sea which broiled and raged underneath them. Again and again he pulled the pocket chronograph from his pocket and checked the time. Sea Lion Rock should have been passed thirty minutes earlier but it was nowhere to be seen. Just a sea of white with visibility that he estimated at less than one hundred yards. They were lost.

Removing the 250 pounds of wheeled landing gear several days ago had permitted Colonel Broome to join the flight and together they poured over the charts to find out where they had gone wrong. McLaren silently regretted his decision to take Colonel Broome with him in place of increasing his supply of reserve fuel. He also regretted that, unlike the American aircraft, they did not have dual controls and he could not relieve his pilot.

In keeping with long-held naval traditions, the commander would never lower himself to the mechanical chore of steering but instead devote his efforts to the more challenging tasks of navigating and directing the course of the flight. Flying Officer Plenderleith had flown the large amphibian six hundred miles since they had left Paramushiru. After six hours he was exhausted, his flying increasingly imprecise. But there was no way to relieve him.

They had switched to their reserve fuel tanks some time ago and very soon that fuel too would be exhausted and the engine would stop. MacLaren made the decision to land the airplane close to shore as best they could, while they had power, and then attempt to taxi to safety on to the beach.

Plenderleith flew over the beach, observing the direction in which the sand was being blown. He lined up the big amphibian parallel to the beach and into the wind but that direction would force the nose of the amphibian into the largest swells and would likely swamp the plane. He turned 30 degrees away from the shoreline as a compromise heading between and wind and wave, pulled the throttle back, and held the nose of the amphibian high into the air. The big plane struck belly first, bounced, and struck again. The nose came down and the amphibian buried itself into a wall of water damaging both wingtips before coming to rest.

All attempts to taxi the large plane through the surf and onto the beach failed. First the starboard wing would slide underwater, damaging it and turning the plane to the right, and then the port wing would be inundated, turning it to the left. Through it all the airplane rocked violently from side to side. Broome and MacLaren climbed outside and ran from side to side on the upper wing in a vain attempt to keep it level in the relentless swells.

After several hours of fruitless efforts with winds and waves increasing, the aircraft sustained substantial damage and started to break up, threatening to capsize at any moment. MacLaren reluctantly removed survival gear and maps and ordered his crew to swim to shore. Devastated, he watched in silence from the beach until the large amphibian sank under the waves. Examining his charts in better weather the next day, MacLaren found that he had crashed less than twenty miles from the place that Vitus Bering, explorer and discoverer of the sea bearing his name had been shipwrecked. At least he was in good company. He would recall years later that August 2, 1924 was the blackest day of his life.

SUNDAY, AUGUST 3, 1924
10:55 A.M.
ENROUTE TO HORNAFJORD, ICELAND

The crews of the *Chicago* and *Boston* were sorely disappointed that losing contact with the *New Orleans* the day before forced them to return to Kirkwall. They had departed again at 9:30 A.M. hoping today would be a better day. It would not.

In improving weather and a brisk tailwind, the two-ship-formation-flight sped toward Iceland averaging over one hundred miles per hour at an altitude of five hundred feet. All had gone well for the first hour and a half but now, as Les Arnold turned to confirm that the *Boston* was safely tucked into its usual position on the right side of the *Chicago*, slightly aft and lower, it was nowhere to be seen. Looking on the other side of the airplane, Lowell and Les saw Leigh Wade descending and lining up into the wind preparatory to landing on the rough seas.

Without warning, the oil pressure aboard the *Boston* had dropped to zero. Wade had no alternative but to make an immediate landing before his engine seized. Only Wade's incredible skill enabled the *Boston* to land in the heavy swells without damage. The rough seas caused two of the vertical wires supporting the wings to break. The *Chicago*, circling, clearly saw the trail of oil stains on the fuselage and in the waters around the *Boston*. Wade, fearful that

Smith might try to land and thereby put the *Chicago* into jeopardy, frantically waved them off. Lowell, seeing the wave-off and realizing there was little he could do beyond notifying the Navy as quickly as possible of the *Boston's* predicament, gave a final wave to Wade and continued on to Iceland in search of a naval vessel.

Aboard the *Boston* the situation was deteriorating. They hoped that the problem would be a leaking oil tank which might be repaired at sea, but the tank was full. That meant that the oil pump itself had failed—which they could not fix at sea. The ship was taking a brutal punishment from the waves hitting her broadside, and the broken wires had left her very vulnerable to further damage. Reluctantly they crawled out onto the wings which were rising and falling violently. After several hours of work under the most difficult of circumstances, they managed to repair the wires and, exhausted, crawled back into the cockpit to await assistance. They had minimal survival rations and neither life rafts, nor life jackets.

They calculated their position as midway between the *Billingsby* and the *Richmond.* The earliest help that could be expected would be late that afternoon or evening, and then only if the weather remained good. They had touched down at 10:56 A.M. After two hours with no signs of life, their spirits were buoyed when a friendly seagull "adopted" them, settling down beside the *Boston* as if recognizing that it too was a creature of the skies.

At 2 P.M. the telltale smoke of a distant ship could be seen, but despite firing flares from their Very pistol and signaling with mirrors and waving sheets of canvas from the top wing, the ship steamed steadily over the horizon and out of sight. Soon the waves increased from ten to twenty feet as the temperature started dropping and a drizzly rain accompanied by fog set in and damped their spirits. Their craft was fragile and no match for the towering seas. Human survival in those frigid waters was measured in minutes, not hours. Rescue became more questionable as the hours passed.

As the day grew darker, another wisp of smoke appeared on the horizon. Out came the flares again and Hank Ogden climbed on the upper wing with one of the wooden supports from the rear of the fuselage onto which a lighter piece of canvas had been attached. This time the wisp of smoke continued in their direction. A fishing trawler, the *Rugby-Ramsey,* came alongside at 3:30 P.M.

"Do you want any help?" the Captain asked.

"Well, I should say we do!" Wade replied.

"What kind of help?" asked the Captain.

"Throw us a tow line," said Wade.

That was more easily said than done. Again and again the trawler tried to approach the *Boston* to throw them a line without success in the high winds and mountainous seas. A collision between the two seemed inevitable if they continued. Wade finally had the captain attach a float to the tow line and circle the *Chicago* until the float was close enough to be reached. Finally the line was retrieved, secured, and the tow started.

The tow went poorly, the rising waves causing the line to become slack and allowing the *Chicago* to weathervane into the wind and broadside to the towing direction. As the line became taut again, it would yank the *Chicago* hard enough to cause structural damage and frequently submerge her pontoons. After half an hour with no headway and further damage likely, Wade requested the trawler discontinue towing efforts and remain tied to them until a U.S. naval ship arrived.

They didn't have long to wait. Steaming toward them at top speed the U.S.S. *Billingsby* arrived a few minutes later, the tow transferred, and the trawler departed. Soon afterward, the cruiser, *Richmond* arrived and the tow was again transferred to the larger vessel. As the transfer was being made, one of the *Boston's* wings dipped below the waves and the ribs of the trailing edge broke, "like the crackle of a machine gun." Towing in those seas presented formidable problems and the likelihood of further damage. It was decided to lift the *Boston* clear of the water and put it onto the deck of the *Richmond* using the ship's crane. Wade and Ogden drained the fuel and oil tanks to lighten the load and secured the crane's hook to the lifting eyes of the *Boston*.

As the ship rose from the water, Wade and Ogden were overjoyed and giddy watching their precious ship rising to the safety of the cruiser's main deck. Just a few more feet and all would be well. And then it happened. With a mighty crash, the crane's tackle broke from the main mast and the *Boston* fell heavily back into the sea, breaking the pontoons and narrowly missing the sailors holding stabilizing lines from the ship's launch.

Wade and Ogden were horrified to see the *Boston* again in danger of sinking and quickly scampered down the ship's ladder to help their stricken craft. With many willing hands, the remaining baggage, tools, and spare parts were removed to further lighten the cruiser while a bilge pump was lowered to remove the water rapidly accumulating in the broken pontoons. Repair materials including veneer, fabric, and "dope" were used in a further attempt to repair the damage and keep the "Boston" afloat. The wings were being pummeled by the ship's hull and suffering additional damage. Wade decided the best chance remaining to save their plane was to saw off the wings and pontoons and attempt to raise all the parts onto the deck.

With the winds increasing to gale force, the *Boston* was being thrown violently against the hull of the *Richmond* in the huge waves now developing. Both crews were having great difficulty just holding on to the wet, slick fabric of the cruiser. One of the sailors was washed overboard and saved at the last moment only by the valiant efforts of two fellow sailors who risked their own lives to rescue him.

The huge seas and raging gale made any further attempts to dismantle the *Boston* impossible and a tow line was attached. The *Boston* would have to fight for her life alone. In the darkness, the ship's spotlight remained focused on the *Boston* as she struggled to remain afloat through the heavy rains and developing fog. Leigh Wade and Hank Ogden watched silently at the stern rail, refusing the crew's pleadings to go below, warm up, and have some food. They were grateful the heavy rains concealed their own tears rolling down their cheeks as they watched their beloved *Boston* struggle for life against the relentless seas. It was a feeling of helplessness and despair they had never felt at any time during their trip. Occasionally a sailor would bring them a cup of hot coffee, see the expressions on their faces, and leave silently, understanding and respecting what each man felt.

Ever so slowly the *Richmond* continued toward the Faroe Islands, her speed reduced to just a few knots to avoid swamping the cruiser. Just past midnight Captain Cotton pleaded with the exhausted men to go below and get some sleep, promising he would notify them of any change in the condition of the *Boston*. Reluctantly they went below, changed into dry clothing, and went to sleep.

Being the flagship of the supporting fleet in the North Atlantic and having the best radio communication equipment, the *Richmond* carried dozens of reporters from newspapers around the world. Wade was grateful that they respected their feelings and left them to their solitude.

Shortly after 5 A.M. Captain Cotton knocked on the door of Wade's cabin. The spreader bar holding the pontoons in place which had been damaged during the fall from the crane had finally broken completely. The *Boston* had capsized and, with the tanks left open by Wade to prevent his floating plane from becoming a hazard to shipping, the *Boston* was sinking.

Leigh and Hank rushed onto the deck of the cruiser. Photographers, snapping photos of the death throes of the valiant cruiser, self consciously averted their gaze and silently yielded their position at the stern rail. Inverted, the cockpits and engine were already underwater. Only the rear of the fuselage and the pontoons remained above the water. In the background, the islands of the Azores loomed scarcely a mile away. So near—and yet so far.

Towing the swamped *Boston* any closer to the uncharted shoreline in these freezing waters would risk losing the ship and all the men who sailed on it. Submerged rocks could easily tear open the hull. The captain explained the situation and told Wade he would let him make the decision. With a heavy heart, at 5:30 A.M. Leigh Wade ordered the tow line cut, turning his back so he wouldn't see the final death throes of his loyal, trusted, and beloved old friend. As the *Boston* sank, the *Richmond* turned toward the safety of deeper waters and in the direction of Iceland.

THURSDAY, AUGUST 21, 1924
6:55 A.M.
REYKJAVIK, ICELAND

After three weeks which seemed an eternity in Iceland, Lowell Smith and Erik Nelson sat in the cockpits of their world cruisers warming up their engines. In a few minutes they would taxi out and start their takeoff run across the waters of Reykjavik Bay and into the unknown. Neither was under any illusion that this would be an easy trip. This would be the longest and most difficult flight over hostile seas. Although upbeat and confident to the reporter's incessant questioning, inwardly each knew that the new challenges they faced on this flight would require every ounce of their piloting skills and the outcome was far from assured.

Behind them, Lieutenants Locatelli and Crozio and their two assistants waited patiently in the Dornier-Wal flying boat. Even to the untrained observer the sleek, streamlined aluminum Dornier-Wal, with its single high wing and pylon mounted twin engines, was clearly the future of aviation and made the boxy, ungainly open cockpit world cruisers of fabric and flying wires look like relics from the past, a bygone era, the designs of yesterday. The Dornier-Wal could fly higher, faster, and farther than the Douglas World Cruisers while pampering a larger crew in a heated enclosed cabin protected from the elements. It represented the pride of advanced Italian design. Premier Mussolini himself encouraged its construction and requested President Coolidge to assist its world premiere flight.

Lieutenant Locatelli brought the rear-facing engine to life and, after waiting a few moments for the battery to recharge, the front engine. When they were running smoothly, he signaled his readiness to Lowell Smith to fly with them to Greenland.

Their stay in Iceland seemed to go on forever. On August 4 they completed the 290-mile flight east from Hornafjord to Reykjavik flying over neat farms, grazing cattle, glaciers, steaming volcanoes, and a rugged shoreline. In Reykjavik they were dazzled by the beauty of the statuesque blond women, their tall handsome male companions, the neat streets with modern shops and hotels, the superb local seafood, and agreeable moderate outside temperatures.

For the period of time the flight was in Iceland, it looked like nature might win after all and frustrate all of the attempts at world flight. MacLaren had crashed and, with his aircraft a total loss, had given up the idea of world flight. He and his crew had boarded the *Thiepval*, a Canadian trawler, and were now enroute to Dutch Harbor. The Argentinean flyer, Major Zanni, had crashed on take-off to Canton and his aircraft was a total loss. D'Oisy had crashed near Shanghai and now the *Boston* was lost at sea. Leigh Wade, to avoid delaying his comrades, unselfishly turned down the offer by General Patrick to ship the remaining prototype world cruiser to him in Iceland to continue the flight.

Lieutenant Schultze on the Danish boat he chartered, the *Gertrude Rask*, was embedded in seventy miles of pack ice which was unseasonably thick. Making only fifteen miles in four days toward the intended refueling base at Angmasalik lying tantalizingly forty miles distant, the U.S. destroyer *Raleigh* was ordered by Admiral Magruder to assist them and departed with Leigh Wade onboard to evaluate the landing site.

The *Raleigh* encountered gale force winds and heavy seas which slowed their progress considerably. Upon reaching the pack ice, the powerful engines of the *Raleigh* broke a path for both boats. They reached an area close to Angmasalik on August 5. Wade confirmed that the numerous floating icebergs made landing safely with their fragile thin-walled pontoons impossible.

The *Raleigh* remained with the *Gertrude Rask* and sent back hourly weather reports to Iceland where Smith, Nelson, and Lt. Crumrine, their advance officer, plotted each report on a large map hoping for an improvement in the weather and meanwhile doing everything possible to lighten the cruisers to make it possible to carry more fuel. The ice and bad weather remained stubbornly entrenched.

The only port now open to them and free of ice lay at the southern tip of Greenland at Fredericksdal, 835 miles from Iceland on Davis Strait facing Labrador. This distance was 335 miles further than the original plan and almost 200 miles further than the pontoon-equipped cruisers had ever flown before. It was barely within fuel range, a poor and highly risky alternate, but the only choice left to them if the flight were to continue.

The days passed with little improvement and a week later the *Raleigh* started a five hundred mile journey through ice-laden seas to explore the alternate site. During the exploration, the heavy pack ice damaged the two starboard propellers of the *Raleigh*, reducing its power just when it was needed most.

On August 11th the advance agent for the Italian flight arrived. By August 17th, the ships had taken up stations for the flight from Reykjavik to Fredericksdal. The Americans prepared to leave the next morning.

That same day, Lieutenants Antonio Locatelli and Tullio Crosio, war hero pilots of the Royal Italian Air Service, arrived with their new, streamlined, modern, all-metal airplane. With them were two mechanics, Giovanni Branni and Bruno Farcinelli.

On August 18th, Lowell and Erik were up at dawn analyzing weather reports which showed some improvement as the hours passed. By 10:15 A.M. both planes, loaded heavily with fuel, taxied out for take-off. With no wind to help them, the large swells launched them prematurely in the air only to fall heavily back down into the waves. Try as they might, becoming airborne eluded them until finally the propeller on Erik Nelson's airplane broke into pieces and the spreader bar on Lowell Smith's met a similar fate. The pounding seas had loosened many of the flying wires on both airplanes. Dejectedly, they had no alternative but to be towed back to their moorings. They radioed the *Richmond*, which had departed for Greenland with all of their spares aboard, requesting it return to Iceland as soon as possible so repairs could be made.

The next few days, waiting for the arrival of the *Richmond*, they spent much time with the dashing Locatelli and his merry crew who had requested and received permission to join them on the attempted flight to Greenland. All were anxious to leave but without the needed spare parts carried on the ship, they impatiently passed the time catching up with world news from Iceland's newspapers.

I n America, fear of the Japanese was growing as Japan announced a new modernization program for their army, navy and air forces. A high-level delegation of capitalists visiting Mexico City from Japan, led by M. Yamaguchi, a former general and now director of a Japanese oil company, requested permission to colonize areas of Mexico for rice growing, cotton plantations, and oil exploration. This reignited American pre-war fears of a hostile alliance of Mexico and Japan on the American border. The Ku Klux Klan, emboldened by the Japanese Exclusion Act and the American Supreme Court decision upholding the diminished status of Asians, were using guns to terrorize Japanese farmers into leaving their farms in California, raising strong anti-American feelings throughout Japan.

The murder of Vice Consul Robert W. Imbris and attacks on his wife at the hands of a fanatical religious mob in Persia gave rise to U.S. State Department protests and demands for local consulate protection of U.S. diplomats in Teheran.

The American Petroleum Institute reported that 90 percent of the oil used within the U.S. came from domestic production which reached two million barrels daily during August of 1924 and was selling for three dollars per barrel.

The Italian aviator Leandro Passalova set a new world speed record in Rome of 188 miles per hour in a seaplane. Deep-sea diver C.A. Jackson gave the first broadcast to the world from the bottom of the ocean, exploring a shipwreck off Atlantic City on radio station WIP.

A spirited debate raged between Santa Monica and Seattle over the Army's decision to make Seattle the official starting and ending point for the world flight. Governor Richardson and Commerce Secretary Herbert Hoover were appealing directly to President Coolidge to intervene in the decision of General Patrick.

Mrs. Jasper Smith and Mrs. Roberta Harding, the mothers of Lowell and Jack, were making newspaper headlines and delighting readers by giving joint press conferences providing insights into the childhood endeavors of their sons and debating who was the more handsome. Lowell's sister Frances, a teacher, married her high school sweetheart, Lewis Bolander in Los Angeles during their Iceland stay.

The first installment on the investment made by Donald Douglas was returned in Santa Monica as the flight waited in Iceland. Lieutenant Lutsow-Holm, flying ace and procurement officer in the Norwegian Air Force, arrived at the Douglas plant on August 12. Norway, for the first time, came with an order in hand for a non-European airplane. They concluded, as would the many customers that followed, that any airplane which could survive the stresses of a world flight would be a proven reliable addition to their fleet. Four aircraft were ordered at $21,500 each.

By the time the middle of August passed, most of the reporters covering the world flight left Iceland convinced the flight to Greenland could not be successfully made and the flight would be terminated there. Historically the ice-laden seaports of Greenland close to sea traffic by late August and the weather that year was exceptionally bad. Billy Mitchell had sent several cables to Lowell Smith warning of the increasing pressure from within the government for the Army to call off the world flight rather than risk the lives of the young men the whole world had come to know and admire.

In the early morning of August 20, just as the *Richmond* was arriving back in Reykjavik, Lowell received word that President

Coolidge, recently renominated by the Republican Party to run for president, had requested General Patrick to cancel the flight as too dangerous. Patrick was appealing the decision but did not expect to prevail. They knew that unless they left immediately, there would be no hope of saving the flight. Within minutes of the arrival of the *Richmond*, the whole crew went to work repairing the damage suffered by the cruisers during their abortive takeoff attempt. Working feverishly without pausing through that day and long into the night, repairs were completed at 2:30 A.M. the next morning.

Without sleeping, the American crew wakened Lieutenant Locatelli and his crew, devoured their first food in almost twenty-four hours, and made the ships ready for launching at dawn.

L owell Smith, sitting in the cockpit of the *Chicago* watched the Liberty engine slowly come up to operating temperature. He rubbed the sleep from his eyes and looked to his right side for a signal from Erik Nelson that he too was ready. When he saw Erik's smiling salute, he looked to the left. Locatelli signaled through his windshield that they too were ready. It was now or never, success or failure, life or death. The politicians were out of it now. His fate was in his own hands. They came too far, suffered too much, worked too hard, to have it end here. Failure was not an option. Without hesitating he opened the throttle on the *Chicago*, accelerating faster and faster into the wind, feeling the chop of the seas splashing against the thin skins of his pontoons. Through the corners of his eyes, he saw the noses of the *New Orleans* and the sleek Dornier-Wal rising as they accelerated to maintain position with the *Chicago*.

This time the strong headwinds and light chop that followed the passing front were helping the takeoff. The Liberties screamed their defiance of capture by the sea and finally broke loose from the suction that pulled them down. The lapping waves were felt no more—they were airborne at last. Lowell checked his compass, and dipped his wings to salute the waiting prime minister of Iceland and the thousands of his citizens now waving enthusiastically after having given so generously of their assistance and hospitality. He recorded the time and set course for Fredericksdal 835 miles away.

Aboard the Dornier-Wal, Locatelli was finding it difficult to fly slowly enough to stay with the lumbering world cruisers. With both his engines at minimum flight power to maintain their slow pace, the nose of the Dornier-Wal rose uncomfortably, obscuring his forward vision. After trundling along for some miles at an awkward nose-high angle, he lowered the nose and increased power to his engines, flying lazy circles around the cruisers to keep them in sight. It was apparent that his advanced airplane was at least forty to fifty miles an hour faster than the cruisers. Tiring of the dawdling pace, Locatelli circled for the last time in front of Lowell and Erik and waved a cheery good-bye. Within a few minutes they had lost sight of his rapidly disappearing profile.

Between Iceland and Greenland five American ships were in a line under their projected flight path. The cruisers *Richmond* and *Raleigh*, and the destroyers *Reid*, *Barry* and *Billingsby* were aligned approximately 125 miles apart. Due to the unexpected delays, the ships were running low on supplies and fuel.

As they flew over the *Richmond*, Captain Lyman A. Cotton looked up and recorded his impressions: " . . . it made a lump come in one's throat to realize how fragile were these man-made ships of the air and how many miles of restless waters lay ahead of them before they reached Fredericksdal."

As they passed over the *Billingsby* they knew this would be the last time they would see those sailors that had shared their sacrifices to assist them. They flew low over the destroyer to wave a heartfelt "thank you and good-bye." On the deck of the ship the sailors had painted "GOOD LUCK" in large letters. The well-wishes of the crew brought tears to the eyes of the airmen and a renewed resolve not to let them down.

An hour and a half later the *Barry*, enroute to Pictou, Nova Scotia and carrying Wade and Ogden, came into view. Two flags flew from her staff. They indicated dangerous weather lay ahead. Grimly Lowell looked over to Erik and pointed to the flags. Erik shrugged his shoulders and pointed straight ahead. They both knew they were past the point of no return. They lacked both the fuel and the inclination to turn back now. Their fate lay in the hands of Providence, their flying skills, and the Liberty engines that pulled them ever closer to destiny.

As the flight passed through the five hundredth mile, the weather changed dramatically. The light mist surrounding them developed into a light rain which increased in intensity until they were being inundated, water streaming over the low windshield, drenching their cockpits and flying suits. The headwinds increased, slowing their progress toward their goal. The fog thickened, reducing visibility until the glow of their own wing mounted formation flying lights disappeared in the gloom.

With no outside references and primitive flight instruments, keeping the cruiser's wings level became increasingly difficult. Lowell started descending in the hope that Erik would be able to follow him down through the heavy fog. According to Lowell's timepiece, the *Raleigh* should be just beneath them, but the fog obscured their view and the ship couldn't be seen. The altimeter unwound until they were just feet over the ocean. Still no sign of the *Raleigh*.

Seventy-five miles out from Greenland the flight started encountering floating icebergs which suddenly loomed out of the water in front of them. Small at first, they increased in size and number until the gray ghosts hidden in the gray fog rose to hundreds and then thousands of feet high. These floating mountains were impossible to climb over. Only the quick reflexes of the pilots averted disaster as they banked and weaved at the last second, often missing an iceberg by inches. Each pilot would recall this flight as the most terrifying experience of their flying career.

One particularly large "growler" separated the two airplanes. Lowell banked hard to the left while Erik banked hard to the right. In the thick fog it would have been suicidal to try to find each other so Lowell proceeded on his own toward Fredericksdal. Erik Nelson, lacking Lowell's innate sense of direction, headed in the wrong direction for thirty miles before recognizing his error and turning toward what he hoped and prayed was Fredericksdal.

Lowell used full power to climb out of the fog bank which lay like a blanket within inches of the ocean's surface. Finally topping the fog, the mountain peaks of Greenland rose through it like silent sentinels pointing for him the direction home.

After eleven hours of flight, Lowell calculated he was above his landing area. He circled slowly to try to find a break in the fog through which he could descend. Miraculously an opening appeared just over the Danish coast guard cutter *Island Falk* which, upon hearing the bellow of the Liberty engine, was making smoke, sounding her whistles and firing her guns in an effort to help Lowell locate the ship. His engine drowned out the guns and whistles, but the smoke was easily seen.

Lowell put the *Chicago* into a tight spiral and descended over the ship. At 5:30 P.M. of that day, Lowell completed the first flight ever from Iceland to Greenland and became the first airman to cross both the Atlantic and Pacific oceans. As he secured his airplane to the mooring prepared for him, a launch from the *Island Falk* approached. A Danish officer asked anxiously, "Where are the airplanes of Erik Nelson and Lieutenant Locatelli?"

Lowell exchanged apprehensive looks with Les Arnold before replying; "I don't know. We became separated in the fog." With tight pursed lips they continued tying up with the cruiser. With what they had been through it seemed too much to hope that the *New Orleans* could have had the same many miraculous escapes from death that they had experienced. Sadly, they finished tying the *Chicago* to its mooring and stepped into the waiting launch. As they climbed the ladder onto the deck of the cutter, Lowell checked his watch. Forty minutes had passed. Lowell knew they had only a forty-five minute fuel reserve. In a few minutes, if it hadn't crashed, the *New Orleans* would run out of fuel and, wherever it was, plunge into the icy seas. Within a few minutes, both of their dear friends and fellow airmen would most likely be gone forever.

Turning to shake the hands of the ship's captain, Lowell heard a familiar faint sound. He pushed the captain aside to rush to the rail of the ship peering anxiously at the small patch of sky visible through the fog. The sound grew louder. Les Arnold clutched Lowell's sleeve tightly. He knew that sound also. It was the throaty bellow of a Liberty-12 and it was growing louder. Lowell whispered, "Thank you, God, thank you, thank you, thank you." It seemed impossible, but the *New Orleans* had found her way home.

The crew, startled at first, stared at the approaching speck silhouetted against the sky. The Captain barked orders for smoke to be made immediately. The *New Orleans* made a tight circle high over the opening in the fog above the ship, banking sharply to identify it before starting its tight landing spiral. Tears of joy and relief flowed freely down the cheeks of Lowell and Les while they climbed down into the waiting launch to join the Danish sailors who had broken into a Viking song of triumph.

SUNDAY, AUGUST 24, 1924
11:24 P.M.
SEAS OFF CAPE FAREWELL, GREENLAND

Captain Cotton, skipper of the U.S.S. *Richmond*, anxiously peered out into the starless night through the windows of the darkened bridge. He and his crew were hungry, exhausted, wet, and tired, but not a single man had complained during the entire search. Since Lowell Smith had sent the news of Lieutenant Locatelli's disappearance the evening of August 21, they had been part of the U.S. naval fleet searching the ice-laden, hostile waters of the North Atlantic for him.

On the captain's right side stood Seaman First Class Willis T. Pinkston. Since reporting for duty on the bridge at 8 P.M. he swept the seas through high-powered binoculars, his sharp young eyes eager to pick up some sign of the lost airplane before the fast approaching deadline of midnight when all search efforts would be discontinued. Captain Cotton checked the ship's chronometer. In thirty-six minutes he would order the helmsman to steer a course for Ivigtut enroute to a refueling and resupply stop at Labrador. In thirty-six minutes the search for the Italian crew would officially end.

They had little to go on when the search started. The last sighting of the Dornier-Wal amphibian was by the U.S. destroyer *Barry* at longitude 39 degrees west so that it became the eastern limit for the search. The western limit had no definition other than the considerable fuel range of the airplane. That could have put them well over the high mountains of Greenland and far inland. The strong winds that prevailed during their flight could have blown them hundreds of miles off course.

The search area extended over hundreds of thousands of square miles of both land and sea. Knowing the airplane could easily have sunk beneath the sea or lie buried under many feet of freshly fallen snow, the search parties held out little hope.

The loss of two war heroes and intrepid aviators of the highly esteemed Royal Italian Air Service, along with two likable crew members who had been popularized in the Italian press, came as a great shock to Italians. The good-natured international competition to be the first flight around the world was suddenly transformed in the eyes of many Italians into a foolhardy risky duel in which death awaited the loser and a trail of broken-hearted wives, children, friends, and family were the unwilling victims. Premier Mussolini appealed to President Coolidge to spare no efforts to locate his lost fliers, but even he despaired of finding them alive.

The American flight crew were no less saddened by the loss of Locatelli and his crew. In Iceland they had bonded in a fellowship of the air and now felt the same "there, but for the grace of God, go I" that all pilots feel toward a fallen fellow airman. In those who challenge the sea and the sky, the bonds of kinship are strong no matter where each may call home.

Lowell Smith also requested the help of the Danish Coast Guard in organizing fleets of natives in their kayaks. By the hundreds they paddled into countless nooks and crannies extending from the many fjords stretching from Cape Farewell north to Angmasalik. Despite going without sleep for forty-two hours, Nelson and Smith helped organize the search vessels and one of them remained at the radio station aboard the Danish ship at all times to help coordinate the search efforts.

The five American ships crashed through rough seas with heavy fog and blizzard-like conditions. The crews were on reduced rations and were cold and wet under the assault of the relentless wind-driven frigid walls of water coming across the bow. The pitching and rolling of the ships made sleep elusive and moving about on the slick ice-encrusted decks difficult and dangerous. Time and time again they had to take immediate evasive action to avoid colliding with one of the thousands of icebergs floating menacingly in their path and just beneath the surface. A collision with any one of them would likely sink the ship and yield a painful death in icy waters for all hands.

As the days of searching continued, the American ships were running very low on fuel and supplies. One by one, they were forced to discontinue the search. First the *Billingsby* and then the *Reid* dropped out with barely enough fuel to return to their stations in Europe. The next day the *Barry* reached the limits of its fuel endurance and turned for home. By the evening of August 24th, only the *Raleigh* and *Richmond* remained. Each carried a tiny scout plane aboard. During the short intervals of acceptable weather, they launched their small planes in the futile search. The pilots scanned the seas from their high vantage point using high-powered binoculars and found—nothing.

After four and a half days of searching, not a clue had been found. Most of the world, including their families, had given up all hope of ever seeing them alive again. The Italian press speculated that no sign of the Dornier-Wal would ever be found and obituaries were prepared for publication in the newspapers.

I n thirty-six minutes, it would be midnight. Seaman Pinkston would stand down, lower his binoculars and end his watch. Captain Cotton would order the helmsman to steer a new course for home. The ship would turn south and the search would end—forever.

He had done everything he could to complete his mission successfully but finding a tiny object, that may or may not exist at all anymore, with four puny humans who may or may not still be clinging to it, in the vast wastelands of the North Atlantic, seemed doomed from the start. They had finished their mission, covered all but a few miles of the vast area they were given. Captain Cotton was disappointed but not surprised. He knew intellectually, mathematically, and statistically, that there was no hope. He, his men, and his ship, did the best they could on a mission that was all but impossible to begin with. Now, it was over.

"Flare sighted, sir!" Pinkston's voice was shrill, rising an octave as young men's voices often do when they are excited. Captain Cotton turned incredulously to face the young seaman, then turned and stared out into the darkness. Seeing nothing he turned back angrily toward him. "What are you talking about, Pinkston? There is nothing out there," he said.

"I-I-I saw a white s-s-streak of light, C-c-captain. I swear I did, it-it-it looked like it might have been a f-f-flare s-s-sir, thirty degrees off the starboard bow," said Pinkston, stuttering and nervous under the steely, reproachful gaze of his captain.

Captain Cotton took the binoculars out of Pinkston's hands and focused on the bearing he indicated. He saw nothing. He panned 60 degrees right—nothing, 60 degrees left—nothing. Disgustedly he returned the binoculars to the young seaman. "You saw a shooting star, Pinkston, and when you get to be my age you'll have seen a bunch of them."

Pinkston took the binoculars back and focused them on the area of the sighting. He too could see nothing but the occasional star. Under his breath and to no one in particular, he muttered, "It sure looked like a flare to me."

Captain Cotton heard the tone of rejection which whispered defiance and belief. He looked at Seaman Pinkston and felt the hair on the back of his neck rising. "What if . . . " The thought went unfinished before the words came unbidden from his mouth, "Helmsman, steer thirty degrees starboard,"

"Aye aye, sir," said the helmsman as the large wooden wheel spun in his hands. Slowly the ship turned and Seaman Pinkston concealed the smile on his face under the binoculars. He continued to focus on the area from which the streak of light appeared. Captain Cotton took his own binoculars from their rack and stared through them at the spot Pinkston indicated. Four minutes passed agonizingly slowly with nothing but the inky blackness in view, and then it came. A luminescent white streak rose from the sea and then exploded into a shower of green streaks of light.

The helmsman recoiled reflexively at the dazzling display twelve miles in the distance. Captain Cotton ordered, "Full speed ahead" and the ship surged forward under the pull of one hundred thousand horses accelerating the ship well past their slow fuel-saving pace of the last few days. Seaman First Class Willis T. Pinkston smiled and muttered under his breath, "I *told* him it was a flare!"

MONDAY, AUGUST 24, 1924
12:03 A.M.
SEAS OFF CAPE FAREWELL, GREENLAND

Aboard the Dornier-Wal, the crew had resigned themselves to dying at sea. They had landed four and a half days ago "temporarily" when the fog had gotten too thick to continue. They too had been forced lower and lower by the descending fog, but their faster speed had made evasion of the looming icebergs almost impossible. After brushing several with the tips of their wings and surviving, they knew they had already pushed their luck further than they deserved. Rather than risk the collision they felt was imminent, they found a small patch of ocean clear of ice and landed, planning to takeoff when the fog had lifted.

After landing, the weather had become even worse. As the crew huddled together for warmth during the frigid night temperatures, gale force winds churned the sea into a maelstrom. All during the long night the seaplane had been thrown around violently, tossing, turning, pitching, and rolling in the heavy seas that pounded it. With the dawn came the realization that the engine pylons had buckled, the ailerons had been torn from the wings, the elevators were bent and twisted, and the horizontal stabilizer lay broken at the attachment points. The Dornier-Wal would never fly again, nor could the engines be started that might taxi the hull closer to Greenland.

There was nothing they could do but wait for rescue and they were under no illusions of the extremely small likelihood of that. For the first three days each of them had taken turns keeping watch through the small escape hatch over the pilot's seats for a ship that never came.

Their meager survival rations were now gone. Cold, hungry, and exhausted, unable to sleep during the last four days, none had the strength to keep watch any longer. They lay together in a heap on the floor of their once-magnificent flying machine, feeling as broken in spirit and body as it was. All hope was now gone and they were resigned to a death at sea. Twenty-five minutes earlier their Very pistol had fired the last of their flares. Each man had written a final letter to his most loved ones in the event their bodies were ever found. When they could find the strength to speak, it was to discuss the most merciful way to end their agony.

The Aurora Borealis plays its tricks in that area of the world. The strange glow lit the cabin of the seaplane each night making strange shadows dance across the inside of the hull and giving false promise of rescuers at hand. Now they would not be fooled and remained huddled on the floor without moving as the large spotlight on the *Richmond* played its beam on the hull of the flying boat. Then the sound of the ship's horn split the night, the blast vibrating the thin hull of the Dornier-Wal.

At first the crew thought that they had gone mad, their stressed brains playing cruel tricks, seeing and hearing that which was not there. But each man saw the wide eyes of the other. They had all heard the same horn, seen the same powerful light playing on the windows, felt the same vibration in the fuselage.

Lieutenant Locatelli was the first to reach the hatch. He flung it open. High above them towered the gray hull of the *Richmond*, her huge propellers thrashing at the seas to hold her position as the ship's launch was being lowered. He rubbed his eyes. The "mirage" was still there. "Thank God," he said to his men. "We are saved."

Aboard the *Richmond*, bedlam had broken loose. Photographers and reporters, many still in their bedclothes oblivious to the frigid night air, pushed and elbowed the ship's crew to gain enough room at the rail of the ship to take photographs, make movies, and scribble notes on the unlikely rescue. The ship had come alive. Every light was on in every cabin and corridor. Sailors raced to the upper decks to view the hull of the Dornier-Wal proudly carrying the red, white, and green colors of the Italian flag on its rudder.

Locatelli and his crew were carried up to the deck of the *Richmond* by many willing hands. All were eager to touch the four flyers, embrace them, comfort them. Many of the sailors went down on one knee and gave thanks to the Almighty for the salvation of the flyers and the privilege of playing a role in the rescue. Under the glare of the unique northern lights, the sailors seemed as happy to see the flyers as the flyers were to see them. They competed with each other to offer their bunk, their clothing, their comfort. Grown men were teary-eyed with joy and relief.

Locatelli requested the damaged Dornier-Wal be hoisted onto the deck of the *Richmond*, but the sixteen thousand pound seaplane was too heavy for the cranes of the ship. A group of sailors returned to the airplane and removed all personal effects. They solemnly folded the Italian flag the ship carried. Captain Cotton explained the necessity of preventing the ship from becoming a hazard to any future shipping. Locatelli had the choice of sinking or burning the Dornier Wal. In these waters, a Viking's funeral seemed appropriate to him. Sadly the sailors punched holes in the gasoline tanks and, as the fuel ran down the fuselage, threw a torch onto the ship. Locatelli and his crew watched in tears as their ship was consumed by the flames.

Admiral Magruder, usually even-tempered and measured, had a difficult time restraining the joy he felt personally in the successful rescue. He had never failed to complete a mission and felt being ordered to assist the flight was one of the most difficult missions he had ever been assigned. The mission to rescue Locatelli he felt was almost impossible. With unaccustomed relish, he dictated the cable to be sent via short wave radio advising his superiors, the *Raleigh*, and the cruiser *Milwaukee* now at Ivigtut, "MISSION ACCOMPLISHED—FLYERS SAFELY ABOARD."

Lieutenant Clayton Bissell, long-time friend and aide of Billy Mitchell and now advance officer for the flight, received the news of Locatelli's miraculous rescue on the *Milwaukee*. He immediately woke the sleeping Lowell Smith and Erik Nelson. They had completed the 165-mile flight from Fredericksdal, uneventfully landing beside the cruiser twelve hours earlier. They were overjoyed and the usually retiring and taciturn Smith grabbed Nelson, Harding, and Ogden in a spirited jig. They were far too excited to go back to sleep and went to the ship's mess hall to share the good news with the other sailors. They celebrated far into the evening, filching the alcohol in the ship's infirmary for an illegal but delicious libation.

Before starting the 560-mile flight to Icy Tickle on Labrador, they decided it would be prudent to install the new Liberty engines carried for them on the *Milwaukee*. The cruisers had been hauled up on the beach to protect them from the floating ice using a ramp prepared by the sailors. Despite the hangovers induced by the indulgences and celebrations of the previous evening, the happy if subdued crew of the world flight started working on the cruisers the next morning. While they worked, Erik Nelson related to his fellow Vikings of the air the original history of the area.

I celand was colonized a thousand years before the visit of our intrepid airmen by a group of fifty thousand Norsemen rebelling against paying taxes to their king, Harold Fairhair. Risking the terrors of the sea and an unknown land, they found fertile fields on which grass could grow, sheep and cattle could flourish, and a surrounding sea filled with an endless bounty of nature's treasures. The pleasant temperate climate and earth from which continuous hot water and steam rose as if by magic from fissures to heat their homes, were much to their liking. A brisk commercial trade developed between the colony and Norway, Denmark, and the British Islands.

In 875 A.D. a severe storm blew one of the crews of the large dragon-prowed fishing vessels across to Greenland where they survived the winter before being able to return home the following spring. A hundred years later, Erik the Red set out to explore this new land on which his forefathers had wintered. He spent three years exploring the fjords and coastline of the western land before returning to his established colony. Being one of the earliest real estate promoters with the scruples of which they are endowed, he named his new land "Greenland" and offered his fellow citizens large tracts of "his" Greenland at far lower prices than prevailed at home, promising all of the advantages they now enjoyed, multiplied a hundredfold.

The scheme worked and he was soon inundated by settlers from Iceland and Scandinavia, all eager to purchase their piece of the promised paradise. The following season he embarked with twenty-five shiploads of settlers. Eleven of the ships struck icebergs and sank, saving the occupants from the shock of reality. History did not record the comments or profanity of the ones that did arrive at their "Greenland" or whether Erik the Red escaped retribution.

A chip off the old block, Erik's son Leif left years later on an exploratory trip to find a suitable piece of real estate so that he too could equal or even surpass his father's real estate prowess. Sailing southwest from the southern end of Greenland, Leif eventually landed on the continent of North America, which he found very suitable.

Preliminary exploration revealed its great potential and Leif hurried back to Greenland to launch his new real estate bonanza. With his genetically inherited public relations instincts, he named his new continent "Vineland," taking advantage of his countrymen's fondness for its fruit. Despite his reputation as "Leif the Lucky," Leif Eriksson died before he could implement his scheme—forever changing America's history.

The work on the cruisers was completed just in time for Les Arnold's birthday bash on August 28. Les had become an accomplished master at locating, "liberating," and blending the alcohol supply of the ship's dispensary into the ship's "punch," making certain it lived up to its name. The entire Danish population of Ivigtut was invited onboard the *Milwaukee* to celebrate the miracle of Les's birth. A huge movie screen was improvised on the forward bow of the cruiser on which the antics of Charlie Chaplin were displayed. With a dazzling display from the northern lights, the surrealistic scene of celebration aboard the huge ship contrasted with the thousands of miles of hostile, desolate isolation and the floating icebergs that surrounded it.

The next few days were spent in the ship's radio room anxiously monitoring the gloomy hourly weather reports coming from Labrador. Finally, on the night of August 30th they received reports of improving weather and prepared to begin their flight.

SUNDAY, AUGUST 31, 1924
3:20 P.M.
ICY TICKLE, LABRADOR

Admiral Magruder and Captain Cotton waited patiently on the rocky landing area at Icy Tickle. Their long double-breasted dark blue woolen coats protected them from the raw cold air of the waning Labrador summer. The throng of reporters, kept at a respectful distance, rubbed their hands together to keep warm and wiped the accumulating frost from their still and motion picture cameras. Most of them had prepared three articles in advance for their newspapers which had been set into type awaiting only the call from their reporter on which to use and the time of landing.

The first story told of a successful landing by both aircraft. The second told of one aircraft landing and the other being lost to dreadful weather. The third sadly reported the loss of both airplanes in a valiant but vain attempt to survive an arctic storm. Fortunately for the world fliers, the reporters radioed the first account as being accurate. The welcoming committee was unaware of the headwinds and the mechanical problems the flight had encountered during the 560 mile crossing of Davis Strait and had expected them earlier.

The *Milwaukee* had radioed the flight's departure at 8:25 A.M. from Ivigtut to the waiting *Richmond* and estimated their arrival at 2:30 P.M. The flight started off in good weather. On the shoreline below, the clouds hovered at six hundred feet over the sea, the visibility was excellent. When they were five miles offshore the clouds extended down to the ocean's surface and they were forced to fly for thirty minutes in heavy fog with visibility barely beyond their wingtips. Erik fought hard to stay focused on the formation flying lights of the *Chicago* but time and time again he lost sight of them in the thickening fog. Each time he carefully maintained his exact speed, heading, and altitude until the lights again came into view. He pushed thoughts of colliding with the *Chicago*, and losing both planes after all of their efforts, out of his mind.

After what seemed an eternity, the fog dissipated suddenly and they were flying in clear air. With spirits buoyed by the break in the weather and the knowledge that visibility and ceiling were excellent at their destination, success seemed assured—until fate stepped in again. Two hundred miles out of Icy Tickle, the Liberty engine on the *Chicago* stopped with no warning, the propeller windmilling in front of the windshield. Fortunately, with the improved weather, Lowell had climbed up to four thousand feet. He instinctively lowered the nose to maintain flying speed. He quickly scanned his instruments. He was losing fifteen hundred feet per minute. In less than three minutes, they would be swimming.

The electric fuel pump had failed. The spinning hand of the altimeter went through three thousand feet. Moving as fast as he could, he reached down for the cable which lowered a small wind-driven back-up fuel pump. Belching clouds of white smoke, the big Liberty-12 struggled to come to life. With a few cylinders chugging into life, Lowell manipulated the throttle, timing, and mixture controls. One cylinder at a time, the firing spread until all cylinders were finally firing smoothly. They were down to one thousand feet. Cautiously he adjusted the engine's controls and increased the throttle opening. With tremendous relief he leveled the nose, then gently pulled back until the altimeter stopped its downward spiral, paused, and then reversed direction. Lowell looked over at the panicked face of Erik who had followed him down. He gave him a smiling "thumbs up" and continued climbing.

Lowell's relief was short lived. He had just reached 3,500 feet when the back-up fuel pump failed and the engine sputtered and gasped for fuel. This time Lowell immediately switched to the reserve fuel tank in the upper wing center section which did not require any pump pressure but drained by gravity down to the engine below. He estimated with the strong headwinds, they had three hours left to go. The reserve fuel tank carried only two hours of fuel. In the rear cockpit, a lever handle controlled a manual fuel pump which transferred fuel from the lower tanks into the upper reserve tank and functioned as an additional back-up to the wind-driven pump.

Les Arnold recognized immediately what was happening. He had practiced transferring fuel from the lower tanks into the upper reserve tank with the manual pump during training flights. It was extremely tiring and required almost all of his considerable strength. In anticipation of the grueling chore, Les had stripped to the waist in the frigid air. He knew what he had to do. He left his flying gloves on to prevent blistering his skin and seized the handle with both hands.

Lowell could do nothing to help him. He had his own problems up front. Erik Nelson flew close to him and pointed at the right side of the fuselage. Lowell rose and looked over the cockpit coaming. Rivulets of dark oil poured from the engine cowling louvers, staining the sides of the fuselage and the right horizontal stabilizer. He prayed that the large oil tank would not run dry before they reached Icy Tickle. After two hours, Lowell heard the pumping stop. He turned and saw Les, covered with sweat despite the freezing cold, lying over the pump too exhausted to go on. "I can't pump any more, Smitty," he said. Wordlessly Lowell shrugged his shoulders and pointed down at the icy waves below them. Les went back to pumping.

As they approached the coast of Labrador they encountered the strange phenomenon local sailors had warned them of, the dreaded "looms." These strange mirages are seen from twenty to five miles out from the coastline and have baffled and terrorized mariners for centuries. Walls of granite appear to conceal the entrance to inlets, huge mountains arise from ice flows, lighthouses appear where their are none, columns of granite rise high into the heavens, and safe havens beckon victims onto concealed rocks. Lowell and Erik had been warned. When the looms appeared they held their course. Eventually the mirages faded into the true visage of the coastline.

When they finally landed at Icy Tickle, Les was exhausted and had to be helped from the cockpit by the sailors that had come to moor the planes. Lowell checked the large oil tank of the world cruiser. Of the ten gallons it held, only a few ounces remained. They had barely made it.

The eight sailors on the thirty-two-foot open motorboat had the planes quickly tied safely to the moorings and the four aviators stepped into the launch for the trip ashore. Lowell was the first to step to shore. Admiral Magruder stepped forward to take his hand saying, "Welcome to America, Lieutenant." Lowell had only two words, "Thank God,"

That evening, after the celebrations had run their course and congratulatory messages from President Coolidge, Secretary of War Weeks, and General Patrick had been read publicly on the deck of the *Richmond*, the adrenaline subsided. Les Arnold collapsed and required medical treatment with severe muscle and chest pains as well as an irregular heartbeat. These symptoms were diagnosed as arising from the extreme stress on those muscles during the pumping that day. He was put to sleep and awoke the next morning feeling much better and insistent upon joining the rest of his crew in the replacement of the fuel pumps and the repair of the oil leak which had nearly doomed the *Chicago*.

Tuesday morning, September 2, the flight left the Labrador coast behind them and flew four hours and fifty-six minutes, most of it through heavy fog, down the west coast of Newfoundland 315 miles to Hawkes Bay. Several near-misses with commercial steamships kept them from getting bored and severely tested their flying reflexes. A waiting destroyer's crew helped them secure the airplanes to the moorings the sailors had prepared for them. After the ships were safely tied down for the night, the sailors helped them refuel and service the cruisers. After a hearty meal they retired to a comfortable berth aboard the ship.

The following day they took off on the 430-mile flight for Pictou, Nova Scotia arriving at 5:40 P.M. Waiting for them was the prototype world cruiser, now renamed the *Boston II*, with Leigh Wade and Hank Ogden. Lieutenants Bertrandias and MacDonald, one of Les Arnold's best friends from the wartime days, had ferried the *Boston II* from Virginia so that Wade and Ogden could join the flight and participate in it to the finish.

After servicing the aircraft and refueling, they joined a caravan of automobiles in an impromptu parade which carried them, with honking horns, through the town. A band of highlanders preceded them piping noisily, their plaid skirts swishing to the rhythm of the bagpipes. Crossed Canadian and American flags flew on each corner, thousands of schoolchildren cheered and a large sign read, *Welcome World Fliers*.

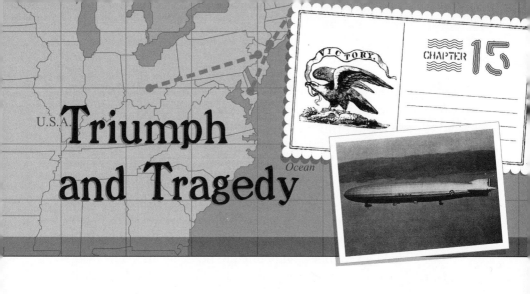

CHAPTER 15

Triumph and Tragedy

U.S.A.

Ocean

he round-the-world flight intended to leave Pictou, Nova
Scotia the morning after they arrived but the weather was
not cooperative. The morning of September 4, 1924,
dawned bleakly with high winds, thick fog, and heavy rain. During
their enforced day of rest, the aviators went shopping. The most
amazing bargains they found were the local lobsters, a dozen of
which could be purchased for fifty cents. With a dollar's worth of
lobster that afternoon all the aviators stuffed themselves, devouring
twenty-four lobsters for lunch. That evening they were invited to a
splendid banquet aboard the Canadian destroyer, *Patriot*, at which
the main course was—lobster!

At 11:15 the next morning, joined by the *Boston II*, they departed south toward Boston, but again the weather intervened.
Increasing fog forced them to fly lower and lower. By the time they
passed over the Canadian border into the United States, they were
skimming the tops of the waves. After a few miles and with the fog
getting worse, Lowell turned the flight back to the north, landing at
Casco Bay in Maine. The wealthy residents, enjoying their summer
homes in the area, were delighted by their now-famous uninvited
guests and met them with motor launches competing for the honor
of providing hospitality, dinner and lodging.

Early the next day, Saturday, September 6, the fliers were again
ready to depart but the brisk head winds that cleared most of the fog
away would considerably extend their flying time to Boston.

Additional fuel would be required and this had to be brought in from the nearby town of Brunswick. The kindly residents organized a caravan of vehicles to bring the needed fuel to them. Meanwhile the fliers waited nearby with their airplanes.

Just before noon, a formation flight of ten DeHaviland DH-4s led by General Patrick, and including Billy Mitchell and Lieutenants Streett and Brown of the World Flight Committee located the world cruisers. They had come to escort the world flight aircraft to Boston. Diving steeply, they passed just a few feet over the heads of the fliers.

Lowell held up a funnel and pointed to the fuel tanks. The escorts immediately understood the situation and flew on, landing on the beach at Old Orchard, Maine to wait for their comrades to refuel. Shortly after noon, the procession of local residents returned with their cars filled with fuel cans. After refueling, the three world cruisers departed and, joined by the ten escorts, continued the flight to Boston.

The American public previously lacked interest in aviation in general and previous record flights in particular. The first crossing of the Atlantic by the Navy, the first flight to Alaska and the first nonstop crossing of the U.S. by the Army all failed to create widespread enthusiasm. Lowell Smith and his crew hardly expected the huge welcome that awaited them in Boston.

When the flight and their escorts flew over Boston Harbor in preparation for landing, it seemed the whole city had turned out to greet them. Naval ships fired 21-gun salutes, fire boats sent streams of water cascading high in the air, ocean liners, tugs, ferries, and private yachts blew their whistles. After the fliers secured the cruisers to their moorings, they stepped into a naval launch for the short ride over to the airfield bedecked with ribbons, flags, marching bands, a speaker's platform, local and national politicians, and military leaders from every branch of the service.

General Patrick led a reluctant Lowell Smith up to the speaker's platform looking as if he would have preferred a gallows. When Patrick handed him the microphone, the crowd, now hushed and silent awaiting a memorable speech, heard "What am I supposed to do with this." After everyone stopped laughing, Patrick explained that the whole nation was listening for his pearls of wisdom including family and friends in the audience. Lowell stared at the open microphone as if it was going to come to life and bite his head off.

Finally, he spoke into it, "Hello, folks; I'm glad to be home," and then handed the microphone back to General Patrick.

After lengthy speeches of welcome by the governor, the mayor, Secretary of War, and various other politicians, a slender, ramrod-straight young man in the uniform of a major in the Royal Air Force stepped up to him from out of the crowd. He extended his hand to Lowell Smith saying; "Well done, Lieutenant. I'm Stuart MacLaren. You have my eternal gratitude for your unselfishness assistance to my flight and the high standards of good sportsmanship you and your crew displayed. Thank you, sir."

Relatives and friends of the fliers came forward with tears of joy to welcome and embrace the fliers. They then boarded the waiting caravan of Rickenbacker Automobiles which took them to the Boston Commons. After a second round of speeches of welcome, they were showered with the keys to the city, sabers, silver wings, watches, and large silk American Flags. Erik Nelson, the lone naturalized American, deeply moved, tearfully fell to one knee and kissed the folds of his adopted country's flag. Despite the accolades of an adoring public, the fliers knew they had four thousand miles ahead of them and tried, with some success, to avoid the well-meaning social activities until they completed the flight.

September 7, 1924 in Boston was spent exchanging the pontoons for wheels. At 12:02 P.M. on Sunday, September 8, the flight resumed accompanied by General Patrick, Assistant Secretary of War Davis, their liaison, Lt. Burdette Wright, Erik's brother, Gunnar, Senator James T. Williams of N.Y., Boston editor, James Wadsworth, and Captain Billy Streett. Lt. Wright had the thankless job of making excuses for the pilots being late or not being able to participate in the many events prepared for them.

From Boston the flight made triumphant entries into the cities of New York; Aberdeen, Maryland; Washington, D.C.; Dayton, Ohio; Chicago, Illinois; Omaha, Nebraska; St. Joseph, Missouri; Muscogee, Oklahoma; Dallas, Sweetwater, and El Paso, Texas; Tucson, Arizona; San Diego, Los Angeles, and San Francisco, California; Eugene and Portland, Oregon; and, finally, Seattle, Washington.

Each city tried to outdo the other in staging celebratory events and the fliers were inundated with gifts of gold, jewelry, cigarette cases, commemorative plates, medals, and keys to the cities which received them. In Washington D.C., President Calvin Coolidge, in contrast to his perfunctory departure ceremony for the world flight, waited for four hours in the rain to greet the homecoming triumphant aviators. Many attributed his newfound enthusiasm for aviation mainly to his reelection efforts. The continuing celebratory events combined with some mechanical problems resulting in unscheduled landings, delayed the completion of the flight and its return to Seattle until September 28, 1924. After years of planning and preparation, they had endured almost six months of incredible adversity, flown 26,445 miles in 363 hours and 7 minutes and given to their country forever the honor of being the first to fly around the world. They were anointed by books and newspapers as, "The Magellans of the Air."

W ith the successful completion of his round-the-world flight, Billy Mitchell fully expected that his most vocal critics within the government would be silenced and aviation would flourish with an increased budget and elevated status. The reports he returned with, of U.S. vulnerability in the Pacific region and the rapid modernization and expansion of Japan's aviation strength, in his eyes constituted irrefutable truth of the military holocaust toward which his country was headed.

Mitchell's original Pacific report, most of which had been written on the journey home, consumed over one thousand pages filled with specific and exquisite details of exactly how the Japanese attack would begin and the military effects of that attack. At the urging of his wife, he reluctantly condensed it to "only" 323 pages.

His late 1924 report described, with incredible accuracy, the weaknesses of Hawaiian defenses and the coming attack on Pearl Harbor as follows: "Air forces in Hawaii were by far the poorest I inspected in any country."

He then detailed the many weaknesses;

> . . . obsolete aircraft, too few planes, too few pilots, a lack of bombing equipment, no machine guns, no reserve supplies or pilots, no intelligence or reconnaissance systems, no centralized command or even control of defense activities, no communication or coordination between army and naval personnel, ineffective anti-aircraft

emplacements, rampant complacency and denial of any credible external military threat, inadequate defensive training of both naval and army officers, infrequent and inadequate air raid drills, and a lack of proficiency training and military discipline in both sailors and soldiers stationed in Hawaii.

Mitchell's report detailed exactly how the Japanese attack would proceed;

> . . . Two airplane transports would be provided, each loaded with fifty bombardment planes. These ships could be equipped with a flying-off deck . . . The objectives for attack are: 1. Ford Island (in the middle of Pearl Harbor) airdrome, hangars, storehouses, and ammunition dumps; 2. Navy fuel oil tanks; 3. Water supply of Honolulu; 4. Water supply of Schofield; 5. Schofield Barracks airdrome and troop establishments; 6. Naval submarine station; 7. City and wharves of Honolulu.
>
> "Attack will be launched as follows: bombardment, attack to be made on Ford Island at 7:30 A.M. . . . Group to move in column of flights in V. Each ship will drop . . . projectiles on the targets . . . nothing can stop it except air power.

Mitchell then accurately predicted the attack on the Philippines and many other Pacific islands which would follow the attack on Pearl Harbor.

> Attack will be launched as follows: Attack to be made on Clark Field at 10:40 A.M. . . . Group to move in columns of flights in V formation over Clark Field, proceeding by squadrons, one at three thousand feet to Clark Field from the southeast and with the sun at their back, one at five thousand feet from the north and one at ten thousand feet from the west . . . airdrome would be attacked with machine guns . . . ground forces will subjugate the island of Luzon. The air force would then carry out a systematic siege against Corregidor and other Pacific islands prior to their capture as remote air bases.

In addition to U.S. defensive weaknesses, Mitchell's report included the output of many of Japan's largest military factories, learned through his lengthy "spying" activities, and the strong anti-American feelings which were emerging.

Mitchell's report on Japan's military factories included the Tokorosawa factory, nine miles from Tokyo making Salmson airplanes and engines using high quality U.S. machine tools, the Heika and Kiki aircraft plants at Nagoya, the naval seaplane factories at Yokuska and Nagoya, the Mitsubishi airplane engine factory making powerful Hispano-Suiza aircraft engines, Sopwith airplanes and submarines in Kobe and Nagoya, the Kowasaki plant at Kobe also making Salmson engines, and the Nakajima works at Ota making Nieuport-29 pursuit planes.

Mitchell's report listed the number of employees in each factory, the number of shifts worked, the factory's present monthly output of engines and aircraft and their maximum monthly capacity. It also listed many civilian sub-contractor plants that had been converted from bicycle wheels to aircraft landing gears, from musical instruments to propellers, from linens for household use to fuselage coverings, etc. His report concluded Japan's aircraft production was at least three times as large as America's, and had the capacity to easily double or even triple its output of modern, militarily effective aircraft and engines, virtually overnight if needed.

Mitchell included in his report an extensive analysis of the political climate in Japan and its recognition that a future struggle for dominance in Asia between the U.S. and Japan was inevitable. He believed Japan's preparations were already underway and called for a lengthy list of immediate actions the U.S. must take to counteract them.

Mitchell's explosive report, despite its accompanying facts, figures, illustrations, and detailed analysis, did not meet with the universal acceptance that he had naively expected. General Summerall, the Army's commander at Pearl Harbor, felt deceived and was furious that the warm hospitality and trust he had shown to Billy and Betty Mitchell had been abused, and considered Mitchell's criticism to be a personal attack upon his competence and judgment. Other Pacific commanders, even his old friend Douglas MacArthur in the Philippines, were similarly angered and hostile.

The Intelligence Division (G2) took issue with all of Mitchell's figures on Japan's military output, believing them to be grossly exaggerated and inaccurate when compared to their own. Operations (G3) and Supply Divisions (G4) dismissed Mitchell's views as being old ideas of Mitchells being presented in a self-serving and deceitful product of his fertile imagination. The War Plans Division reviled it as being; "based upon the author's exaggerated ideas of the powers and importance of air power, and are therefore unsound." General Patrick, fending off an avalanche of harsh criticism of Mitchell, discreetly avoided commenting on the report with the excuse that he had been too busy to read it but would later, "in due time."

The timing of Mitchell's report in October of 1924 could hardly have been worse. Calvin Coolidge was running for reelection on a platform of having reduced government spending almost 50 percent and income taxes by 25 percent. His policy of keeping the U.S. out of costly foreign wars, reducing defense expenditures, and stimulating the rapidly growing domestic economy had widespread support. A contented electorate eventually gave him the largest majority in U.S. election history, almost sixteen million votes.

A lifelong democrat, Mitchell was out of step with the Republican administration. He had supported Senator Bob LaFollette, a democrat of Wisconsin, to challenge Coolidge. He wanted to increase military expenditures and risk confrontation with Japan which the administration and public opinion opposed. He had broken the unwritten military code by getting involved in politics, criticizing his superiors, his fellow officers, and the policies of both the War Department and the State Department.

Mitchell saw himself as the last hope for military aviation. During his nine month absence, General Patrick had been trying to get additional funding for his Air Corps his way, through diplomacy and tact. He had as little success as Mitchell did using defiance and confrontation. In Mitchell's absence one entire air group had all but disappeared, two squadrons had been inactivated and the remaining 60th squadron was pared back to forty-two men with only ten officers. The world flight, as successful as it was, didn't seem to be having the impact he had hoped for. Aviation was dying.

Since the bombing tests of 1921, Mitchell had been under strict orders from Secretary of War Weeks not to publish anything without his specific approval and authorization. Although chafing at the restriction, he had generally complied, being content to "leak" whatever information was necessary to the public under the promise of anonymity. In October of 1924, he was approached by the editor of the *Saturday Evening Post*, Thomas Costain, to write a series of aviation articles which would eventually be extracted into a book to be published by George P. Putnam. Mitchell, seeing this as a way to circumvent Weeks' scrutiny, agreed provided that they could go together and get the permission of President Coolidge.

Not wishing to turn down the editor of an influential magazine at the height of his reelection campaign, Coolidge agreed to give Mitchell his permission in the interest of furthering the science of aeronautics, provided he obtained the permission of his superior officer, the Chief of the Air Service. Knowing Mitchell's talents in stirring up controversy and promoting his ideas, as soon as Mitchell and the reporter left, Coolidge penned the following letter of clarification and had it delivered to Mitchell:

> Confirming my conversation with you this morning, I do not know of any objection to your preparing some articles so far as I am concerned, but of course I cannot speak for your superior officers. The matter should be taken up with them and their decision in relation to the articles followed.

Visiting General Patrick the next morning, Mitchell advised he had received the permission of the president to write the articles and now required only Patrick's approval. With the president's approval already in hand, Patrick quickly acquiesced.

Mitchell's first article appeared in December, 1924 and the series of five articles concluded in March of 1925. The articles described a future war of massive air attacks on an enemy's industrial base which would destroy its war-making capability. The articles strongly advocated the supremacy of air power over sea and land forces and the establishment of an independent air force, all anathema to current military doctrine.

At the time the articles appeared, the Navy was conducting bomb tests on a newly finished ship, the U.S.S. *Washington*, scheduled to be scrapped under the arms limitation treaty. As with previous tests, the Navy was using sand-filled bombs released from four thousand feet, and dropped onto the decks of the ship. TNT charges were then set off underwater at varying distances to the hull. The ship incurred substantial damage but before it could sink the Navy finished the ship off with the deck guns of a nearby warship. The story released by the Navy to the newspapers reported that the

U.S.S. *Washington* had withstood both bombs and depth charges and could be sunk only by naval gunfire from another ship.

Mitchell had observed the rigged tests and was angered at the erroneous conclusion. Offering to testify before a House committee of inquiry headed by Julian Lampert of Michigan, he reported that, "no bombs were used in any shape, form, or fashion." He accused the Navy of subterfuge, deceit, and the rigging of the tests to reach the conclusion they desired. Admiral Sims broke with his superiors to support Mitchell's testimony. Frank R. Reid of Illinois, another member of the committee sympathetic to Mitchell's views, led him through a questioning during which he vociferously expressed his vision of the future of American air power and the vulnerability of U.S. military bases throughout the Pacific. The magazine articles and committee appearance marked a new defiant change in the rhetoric and tactics of Mitchell. Hap Arnold, now director of information under General Patrick, joined many of Mitchell's friends in urging caution, discretion, and a more conciliatory approach in his public speech and writing.

Mitchell believed his world flight firmly established the importance of aviation internationally in both military and commercial roles. Through the winter of 1924 and the early spring of 1925, he became increasingly outspoken in its advocacy.

Mitchell's congressional appearances and magazine articles once again awakened public interest in him. Newspapers wrote stories of his wartime heroism and reminded the public of his legendary accomplishments and many successes earlier in his military career. In the political world of double-speak and the military realm of discreet silence without criticism, public sympathy grew for Mitchell's outspoken style, his enthusiasm, and his candor.

By January of 1925 open warfare raged between pro and anti-aviation forces. Mitchell spearheaded the attack against conventional and outmoded concepts of defense within both the Army and Navy. Arrayed against Mitchell were General Pershing, Secretary Weeks, and most of the military's older admirals and generals. General Patrick supported most of Mitchell's views as did Congressmen Fiorello La Guardia and Charles Curry. Admiral William Moffett, chief of the Navy's Bureau of Aeronautics, although he opposed a unified air force, admitted that most of the Navy's airplanes were obsolete and unfit for service. He also admitted that, contrary to naval doctrine, aircraft could sink surface vessels unaided by naval firepower.

As the conflict between the "old" and "new" military viewpoints grew, naval Secretary Wilbur publicly announced that the renewal of Admiral Moffett's status as Chief of Aeronautics was in question. This overt pressure being brought to silence Moffett backfired when Admirals Sims, Fiske, and Fullam came to his aid. Fullam stated, "The Navy has never feared the truth; it has always stood for truth and honor, and it must stand the test in this case. General Mitchell has done more to demonstrate the power of air attack against the forces of our possible enemies than the general board of the Navy and all the admirals of the Navy combined."

Secretary Weeks, piqued at Mitchell's successful efforts to circumscribe his "gag order," and President Coolidge, angered at being duped into authorizing Mitchell's controversial magazine articles, decided that Mitchell had to be silenced.

Mitchell's four-year appointment as Assistant Chief of the Air Service and his temporary rank of brigadier general was coming up for renewal in March of 1925. Weeks visited with Patrick early in March to discuss Mitchell's renewal. Patrick acknowledged the difficulty of controlling Mitchell but recommended renewal based upon his unquestioned competence and enthusiasm.

During February and early March, the controversy grew. Thousands of telegrams supporting Mitchell poured in daily from aviation and veteran's organizations as well as an adoring public in awe of his status as war hero and courageous aviator. Emboldened by the outpouring of support, he disregarded the advice of his friends who counseled discretion and renewed his attacks upon the foes of aviation with unbridled passion. His testimony before the Lampert committee became more direct, charging that the U.S. had only nineteen aircraft "fit for war." He accused the military of trying to muzzle their officers when they appeared before Congress and advised that he too fully expected to be punished for his testimony. As evidence of intimidation he pointed to the high ranking officers accompanying all witnesses advising them of the "correct" answers to the committee's questions.

New Jersey Representative Randolph Perkins, chief examiner for the Lampert committee, informed the *New York Times* of the impending disciplinary action being planned for Mitchell and Moffett for their testimony supporting air power.

The headlines the next day, "Foes May Force Mitchell Out," required Weeks to appear before the Senate Military Affairs Committee to explain his position. Weeks admitted having muzzled Mitchell since 1921 and requiring any public statements receive his personal approval after receiving "constant complaints from the Navy Department" and "to live in peace with other departments in the government."

The *New York Times*, critical of Mitchell in the past, now leapt to his defense editorializing, "General Mitchell has done more by example and initiative to advance military aviation than any other officer in either the Army or the Navy. To get rid of him by demotion or exile would be a scandalous misuse of authority."

As the days wore on the rhetoric became increasingly inflammatory and accusatory. Secretaries Weeks and Wilbur went to Coolidge with the support of General Pershing and threatened to resign unless Mitchell were disciplined and sent away—far away, and silenced forever. Congressman Fiorello LaGuardia, a decorated pilot himself during the war, came to Mitchell's defense and introduced a bill that protected army and navy officers that testified before congressional committees against demotion or transfer. LaGuardia also introduced a joint resolution;

> . . . that we hereby compliment Brigadier General Mitchell and commend his position in this matter . . . and severely condemn the evident purpose of the national administration in its attempt to punish and discredit him. We believe in his courage and in his devotion to the nation . . .

Mitchell's influential enemies in government and the military far outnumbered and outranked his friends. This bill, like many other attempts to save him, was soundly defeated in committee.

On March 5, 1925, Secretary Weeks concluded his recommendation of punishment and demotion for Mitchell which he presented to President Coolidge as follows;

> General Mitchell's whole course has been so lawless, so contrary to the building up of an efficient organization, so lacking in reasonable team-work, so indicative of a personal desire for publicity at the

expense of everyone with whom he is associated, that his actions render him unfit for a high administrative position . . . .

An elated Weeks left the president's office with permission to dispose of the matter as he saw fit. On returning to his office, Weeks had the letter of demotion typed, signed it, and returned home for a celebratory dinner. The next day he would not only hand Mitchell the letter which would devastate him, but, through tests he had arranged, prove to the world that Mitchell was dead wrong in dismissing with contempt naval attempts to protect their ships with anti-aircraft fire.

Mitchell received word of his impending punishment from a supporter in the White House soon after Weeks departed. That evening he composed a statement to be issued as soon as he received the official rebuke. It read, in part; "The question of my reappointment as Assistant Chief of the Air Service is a small matter. The question of reorganization of our system of national defense is a big matter . . . " He pleaded once again for the creation of an integrated Defense Department, reasserted his belief in the supremacy of air power, and pledged to continue his struggle to awaken a military steeped in the outmoded traditions and weaponry of a bygone era.

March 6 dawned bright and clear. The gun emplacements at Fort Monroe were neatly arranged in multiple rows pointing toward the sea. The skilled gunners, hand-picked from the most accurate group, carefully adjusted the sights of their anti-aircraft guns. Neat stacks of ammunition were placed beside each gun. Against the clear sky, they expected they would need little of the ammunition before establishing the deadly accuracy and efficiency of their modern guns. Surely no incoming aircraft could ever get through the withering fire to launch an attack on U.S. soil and today Secretary Weeks would dispel all the nonsense coming from General Mitchell and his contemptuous dismissal of the effectiveness of anti-aircraft guns.

In anticipation of his moment of triumph, Weeks had invited a large contingent of congressmen, reporters, and military officers including Billy Mitchell. After the targets, ten feet long by four feet in diameter, towed by slow moving aircraft, had been shredded by his gunners, he would confront an embarrassed and chastened

Mitchell to deliver the "coup de grace," the letter of demotion in full view of the many photographers and reporters.

Exactly on schedule, three DeHaviland DH-4s appeared from the northwest. Their engines struggled at full power to overcome the drag of the long tow lines and huge targets they were towing. One by one they slowly circled the gunners at an altitude of three thousand feet and less than half a mile from the firing guns. After thirty-nine rounds had been fired, not a single hit had been made. Weeks signaled the aircraft to come closer and fly lower. They descended to two thousand feet and came within one quarter mile of the firing guns. Again no hits were registered. Laughter now started among the reporters. Frustration and anger boiled within the General Staff.

Weeks signaled again for the aircraft to drop down to just one thousand feet over the heads of the gunners, the minimum safe towing altitude. Weeks ordered now that all guns be fired including banks of machine guns which were pressed into service. The noise was deafening as a virtual rain of bullets and cannon shells filled the air. After the fusillade had ended and all the ammunition had been expended, the targets were examined. Two had not been hit at all and a third showed only a single small hole.

Billy Mitchell found it very difficult to conceal his smile as a frustrated and furious Secretary Weeks approached him to deliver his letter of demotion. Mitchell took it silently, saluted, and then walked over to one of his favorite reporters to deliver his prepared statement responding to it. The next morning's newspapers carried the headlines; "MITCHELL OUSTED . . . BLOW TO MITCHELL SHOCKS CONGRESS . . . AIR TARGETS DEFY WEEKS' GUNNERS."

General Patrick tearfully watched Billy Mitchell packing the mementos of twenty years' service with the Army. Dozens of photographs of bomb tests, maps, charts, blueprints of new airplanes yet to be built, fragments of the two thousand-pound bombs used in the tests, pieces of the Nieuport he flew against the Germans in France, the steering wheel of the Zeppelin shot down in France, the brass shield of the U.S.S. *Alabama* his pilots had sunk, his hunting trophies, his fishing boots, and his buckskin shoes were all put into cardboard boxes. Patrick said he had done his best to save Billy from demotion and reassignment but he was overruled. Billy put his arms around the older man's shoulders. "I know you did," he said quietly. "Thank you."

Mitchell had only one request; to be transferred to Chicago where he could continue working closely with the aeronautical engineers at McCook Field and contribute to the development of new aircraft. Patrick recommended the reassignment he had requested, but a vindictive War Department turned it down, instead transferring him to one of the most remote and isolated posts at Fort Sam Houston, on the outskirts of San Antonio, Texas.

Twenty-five of Mitchell's aviators made a surprise farewell luncheon for him at Bolling Field. The younger pilots idolized Mitchell and the courage he had shown as their champion and protector. Individually each one of them had been eager to give testimony to Congress supporting the positions he had taken which were being attacked as false and misleading. Mitchell had forbidden them from coming to his aid and risk ruining their careers. Waiting for their honored guest, the mood was somber, angry, and incredulous that their hero was being sidelined and "put out to pasture." Meeting among themselves the previous evening, they had decided to request transfer en masse to serve with him in Texas and, if that were denied, they would all turn in their resignations.

Mitchell walked into the room, deeply moved at the teary-eyed young aviators standing to applaud him. A spokesman stepped forward and told him of their plans. Mitchell's smile changed to an angry frown. He faced them sternly and said, "Sit down, every damned one of you. This is insurrection. Not one of you will resign. Not a one. And that's an order." There was a long silence, and the young men bowed their heads, chastened by the angry tone of their leader's voice. Mitchell immediately regretted the harsh tones he had used. These were his children of the sky, and he would lead them no more. His lofty rank would soon be gone and the orders of an isolated colonel at a remote airbase could hardly be binding on them. His tone softened, "Who will carry on . . . when I'm gone?"

A long silence followed the unanswered question. The young airmen present never forgot that day. One recalled many years later; "We obeyed him. We obeyed him the rest of our lives. And long after he was dead."

If the War Department really believed the newspaper editorials which mourned the loss of Mitchell and expected him to fade silently into obscurity in exile, he quickly disabused them of that idea. Relieved of most command responsibilities, his quiet post provided the perfect environment from which to continue and expand his writings which he combined in a new book he had published called *Winged Defense.*

The new book became a bestseller and soon Mitchell's doctrine of America's military and commercial strength requiring the expansion of aviation became well known and accepted throughout much of the country. On July 14 he delivered a public address in San Diego at which he charged that "the air force in this country is almost extinct now." He described the United States as vulnerable and exposed, its security dependent on obsolete surface ships and coastal fortifications that had been proved conclusively were useless in defending an attack from the air. He decried the waste and inefficiency of competing military branches of government and called for the establishment of a unified Department of Defense. A modern, powerful, rapidly deployable Air Force would be its largest and most effective branch and the recipient of most of the funding.

Betty Mitchell had moved into her parent's home near Detroit to await the birth of their first child. Billy joined Betty in August for the birth of his daughter, Lucy. While visiting Detroit, Billy met with Henry Ford who made him a lucrative offer to become the director of his Aviation Division. Billy thanked his old friend, but declined explaining he had to remain in the Army until the defense of his country could be assured.

After seeing the new aircraft and engines being produced by Ford, Mitchell gave a news conference to reporters at which he predicted a nonstop thirty-seven-hour flight could now be flown from New York to Paris and would eventually become routine. He would request the Army to immediately make that flight upon his return to beat any French attempt at it. His request was denied. It was left to Charles Lindbergh two years later to fulfill the prophesy in thirty-three hours and thirty-nine minutes.

That same month, *Liberty* magazine published a major article by Mitchell in which he reasserted the premise that battleships were totally obsolete, enormously costly to build and maintain, and provided negligible defensive capability. He concluded the article by writing, "What is keeping them up as much as anything else and largely preventing open and free discussion of their uses are the propaganda agencies maintained by navies for perpetuating existing systems."

With Mitchell's exile hardly slowing his one-man public relations assault on the Navy, Secretary of War Weeks, a graduate of the Naval Academy, and Secretary of the Navy Wilbur launched a major effort to prove Mitchell's charges of inadequate aviation capability were untrue. They would make a nonstop flight to Hawaii.

The Hawaiian flight was planned in great haste to silence criticism and balance the Army's successful world flight. Three radio-equipped type PN-9 seaplanes would be used, with ships of the Pacific fleet stationed below them to assist. With favorable winds and accurate navigation the pilots would have adequate fuel and safe reserves.

Commander John Rodgers was chosen to lead the flight. Rodgers was from a long and distinguished line of naval captains. They traced their roots back to the birth of the American Navy. "There has never been a U.S. Navy without a John Rodgers, and never a John Rodgers that has not served proudly in the U.S. Navy," said the newspapers. On August 31, meteorologists confirmed favorable winds and forecast them to continue over the next few days. The flight planned to depart the next day.

On the morning of September 1, 1925, amid much fanfare with politicians, photographers, and reporters watching, the flight was poised to start across the Pacific. To the surprise of the meteorologists, the winds had changed direction and were now not nearly as favorable. If the flight left that day, the fuel would probably be adequate but there would be precious little reserve fuel available. The meteorologists advised postponement in the interests of safety. Anxious for the favorable publicity, the Navy launched the flight despite the decreased safety margins.

Things went badly from the start. One plane could not break free from the sea that held it and taxied helplessly around in large circles without becoming airborne. The second plane rose in the air only to be brought down by an engine problem in view of the spectators a short distance from the shoreline. Only the third seaplane carrying Commander Rodgers finally got airborne and started the long flight to Hawaii.

Rodgers's calculated arrival time came and went on Hawaii with no sign of the PN-9 or its crew. A few minutes later a naval ship stationed three hundred miles off the coast of Hawaii picked up a series of plaintive messages from Rodgers and his crew of four: "Plane very low on gasoline . . . Gas is about all gone . . . Running out of gas . . . "

The signals were very weak, barely readable aboard the ships. It was obvious that the flight crew was very far off course, but how far and in what direction remained unknown. All attempts to contact Rodgers were in vain and no further messages were received. A search of the area was immediately started but as the hours passed with no trace of the PN-9, Commander Rodgers, or his crew, prospects of ever finding them alive again were growing very dim.

WEDNESDAY, SEPTEMBER 2, 1925
6:30 A.M.
FORT SAM HOUSTON, TEXAS

The soft knock on the door seemed to come from far away. Despite his efforts to stay awake, Billy Mitchell had finally succumbed. He sat slumped over an old oak table with his head resting on his right forearm. Hearing the knock he had opened his eyes and struggled to comprehend where he was. Was he in Washington, at his familiar airfield, dozing as he had done so many times before after an all-nighter, planning the day's missions, analyzing the squadron's performance? His eyes took in the desktop in front of him. Something was wrong. He wasn't at his expensive mahogany desk, with its leather inlay and wooden framed photographs. He was at an old, stained, weather-beaten oak table with a drawer, the many cracks and crevices on its worn top outlined with the spilled ink of a thousand unknown writers.

A second soft knock. Billy snapped upright and closed the top button on his uniform shirt. He was in the boondocks of Texas, exiled. He answered the unknown visitor, "Come in!"

The door opened slowly. A young lieutenant entered carrying a breakfast tray and several radiograms. "Begging your pardon, General Mitchell. I've been monitoring the short wave bands from Hawaii this morning. Sorry to say, sir, still no trace of Commander Rodgers or his crew. I've brought you the latest cables, also some breakfast for the general."

Mitchell looked over the young lieutenant with the silver wings proudly worn on a freshly starched uniform shirt, standing stiffly at attention. He looked so young. Mitchell recalled how much he reminded him of himself, so many years ago. It was simple then, before the complexities, intrigues, and back-stabbing politics of the general staff. He knew who the enemies were then, and how to fight them. Now he wasn't so sure. They were every place and no place at all. They struck mortal blows with pens and paper and vile speech filled with ignorance and hurtful lies. They were deceitful and dishonest in a way that he could never be. His knowledge of trench warfare, of bombs and bullets and barbed wire was of no use in these wars. For all his fighting skills, he was totally defenseless against the onslaught of power politics. He was one man fighting the world and anyone he allowed to join his struggle would be stripped bare and have burned into their skin forever the cruel mark from which their could be no escape. "At ease, lieutenant," he finally said, "and I appreciate your thoughtfulness, but I'm a colonel. The general was from another time."

The young lieutenant saluted and turned to leave, then, hesitating, turned back to Mitchell. "Begging your pardon, sir, but you'll always be a general to us, sir. We know what a step down for you it is, sir, to be at this tiny patch of scrub grass, rattlesnakes, and sand gophers. You certainly deserve a lot better, sir, but we want you to know, sir, that every man here is plumb busting out with pride to have you here, sir. We know that without you, sir, their wouldn't be any aviation in the Army. You took a bullet for us, sir, and we owe you a debt we can never repay. You make us all mighty proud to serve under you, sir."

Mitchell listened in silence. The young pilot came to attention again, saluted, turned, and left. Mitchell stared at the door for a long time before starting on the breakfast cooling on his desk. He was lost in reverie, longing for what might have been. That evening he traveled to San Antonio and gave a speech on the radio asking the people of Texas to pray with him for the safe return of Commander Rodgers and his crew. It wasn't until well after midnight that he finally was able to return to his quarters, mercifully unaware of the deadly drama unfolding in the northern skies as he slept.

THURSDAY, SEPTEMBER 3, 1925
3:30 A.M.
2,100 FEET OVER BYESVILLE, OHIO

In the darkened control room of the airship, *Shenandoah*, Commander Zachary Lansdowne peered out anxiously through the large windows. Tall, slender, and handsome, he could have been the poster model for naval recruiting. His square chin and rugged good looks were softened by an easy smile. Mischievous eyes twinkled with hidden laughter. On the ground he was the joke-teller, the jovial new friend whose embrace cast a spell on men and women alike. At home he was the consummate husband and father, caring and compassionate. In the air, the good-humored easy-going demeanor disappeared and Commander Lansdowne emerged, ramrod straight, by-the-book, brilliant, a gifted and courageous pilot.

He was also one of Billy Mitchell's oldest and best friends. They had played together, flying naval and army aircraft to neutral fields, challenging each other's aerobatic skills, swooping, zooming, and diving in mock combat until the setting sun called them home. They had comforted each other when the inevitable losses came to those they held dear, those who chose the sky and eventually ran out of skill—or luck—and joined the airmen of immortality.

The dim lights faintly illuminating the instrument boards blended eerily with the phosphorescent glow of the radium dials. The elevatorman struggled with his large metal wheel to keep the nose of the huge behemoth level. Across the gondola, suspended by struts and cables from the airbag enclosure above, his counterpart, the rudderman, rotated a matching wheel hard left and then hard right to maintain the course westward to their next waypoint, Zanesville, Ohio.

Lieutenant-Commander C.E. Rosendahl, still rubbing the sleep from his eyes, had just reported for his watch relieving Lieutenant-Commander Hancock. From the increasing swaying motion he felt in his bunk, Rosendahl felt something was wrong. Looking over at the worried expressions on the dimly lit faces of Commander Lansdowne, the elevatorman, and the rudderman, his fears were confirmed. This was going to be a night that he and the entire nation would never forget.

Shenandoah is an Indian word meaning, "Daughter of the Stars." Most found it particularly fitting for one of the most imposing objects ever sent toward the heavens by man. It was a rigid airship longer than two football fields laid end to end. It contained a huge metal skeleton which included walkways, crews quarters, mess halls, fuel tanks, and gas bags enclosed by an outer aluminized cotton fabric covering. At her birth, on September 4th, 1923, she first rose from the ground majestically at the Lakehurst Naval Air station as the ZR-1, the first airship to join the Navy's aerial armada. The birthing process of the ZR-1 had not been easy.

It was early in 1916, with the mighty Zeppelin airships of Germany dropping bombs on and striking fear into the hearts of the Allies during the First World War, that the idea of building a U.S. airship was born. The U.S. Congress authorized and provided funding for airship construction. Naval Admiral D.W. Taylor assigned the task of investigation and implementation to Lieutenant Jerome C. Hunsaker while Major General G.O. Squier, Chief Signal Officer of the U.S. Army, joined the effort and in October of 1916 a Joint Airship Board was formed.

On February 26, 1917, the Joint Board assigned responsibility for construction formally to Hunsaker and Army Captain C. deF Chandler. Engineering expertise had to be developed and that task fell to Lieutenant Garland Fulton, U.S.N. and Mr. Starr Truscott, a naval architect with experience ranging from large vessels to the Panama Canal. The War and Navy departments gave the green light to the project the next month and a technical committee was sent to England to investigate construction details of the German airship L-33 forced down in England the previous year. In October of 1917, the German airship L-49 also fell and was captured intact before her crew could destroy it at Bourbonne les Bains in France.

The committee returned to the U.S. and recommended two airships be purchased from England and then two others duplicated in the U.S. With the armistice, funds were cut and in July, 1919 Congress approved funds for one airship and the purchase of a second in England. The English copied the fallen L-33 and constructed their R-38 which, unfortunately, soon suffered a massive structural failure and was destroyed. When this occurred, the U.S. decided to base its design and construction on the L-49 and designated the new airship, "Fleet Airship Number One" or ZR-1.

In consideration of the R-38 disaster in England, the National Advisory Committee for Aeronautics made improvements to the ZR-1 inserting a ten-meter section into the body to accommodate the additional gas required when changed from the highly flammable hydrogen of its original design to the nonflammable but heavier helium. They also strengthened the bow, provided mooring gear, redesigned the fins and rudders, fitted a top walkway to facilitate servicing, and added more powerful engines.

With competition between the services slowing development, the Navy was assigned full responsibility for construction, maintenance, and deployment of airships. The Army turned over to the Navy the abandoned site of Camp Kendrick near Lakehurst and a huge hangar was erected to begin construction. Parts were fabricated by the naval factory at Philadelphia and shipped by rail to Lakehurst. The ZR-1 was an enormous undertaking. It stretched 680 feet long with a diameter of 78.7 feet and towered to a height of over 90 feet. It used six 300-horsepower engines totaling 1,800 horsepower. It had a range of 2,250 nautical miles at its maximum speed of 50 knots without refueling and carried a crew of 43 lifted aloft by over two million cubic feet of helium.

Shortly after her birth on September 4, 1923, the ZR-1 made increasingly longer flights culminating with Admiral Moffett, to show his confidence in airships, stepping aboard for its first flight over the Allegheny Mountains on October 1, landing at Lambert Field in St. Louis to attend the Pulitzer Air Races. On its return to Lakehurst, on October 10th, the wife of Naval Secretary Denby christened the ship. The ZR-1 became the U.S.S. *Shenandoah* and the "Daughter of the Stars" was put under the command of Commander F.R. McCrary.

For the airship to visit outlying airfields lacking huge hangars, a docking system using easily erected mooring masts had to be developed. Despite a harsh winter season, outside mooring masts and techniques were practiced seeking a perfection of that method. On January 16, 1924 a fast moving winter storm caught the *Shenandoah* outside secured to an experimental mooring mast. The crew fought hard through the entire day to save their ship, battling wind gusts which reached 63 miles per hour. By 6:00 P.M. tears in the fabric developed which made the ship vulnerable to further damage.

At 6:44 P.M. a violent gust of 74 miles per hour rolled the ship around its horizontal axis and tore the nose off the ship and blowing it backward toward certain destruction in the electrical wires, high ridges, and tall trees that surrounded the flying field. With the wind howling through the gaping hole in the nose of the ship, the crew, still aboard, frantically started dropping water ballast and jettisoning fuel tanks, tools, and anything else they could in an attempt to get the ship to rise above the terrain.

Other crew members started all of the engines on the ship and brought them to full throttle attempting to slow the rapidly increasing backward motion. The next few hours were spent by the crew trying to seal the rips and tears against the onrushing wind threatening to destroy the ship's fuel and gas cells, and bring the ship, which had now assumed an upwards stern angle of 30 degrees, under some semblance of control. The battle went on all night with the great ship thrown around by the storm with violent gyrations in altitude and direction. Lost and out of contact with anyone, the world expected that was the end of the *Shenandoah* and her brave crew. Notification and condolences were sent to families and friends by the Navy.

Through the entire ordeal, the ship's radioman worked calmly and deliberately, despite being thrown violently around the tiny radio room, to repair the radios onboard and reestablish communications. Finally he was able to transmit and establish communications with radio station WOR in Newark, N.J. which shut down its regular programming to assist and broadcast the ship's condition and status. To everyone's relief, the storm abated as dawn neared and the exhausted crew of twenty-one officers and men aboard were able to bring the ship under control and return it to Lakehurst for repairs at 3:30 A.M.

A positive result of that frightening experience was that, at the time the storm hit the ship, Aeronautics Professor C.P. Burgess, one of the designers of the ship, was onboard with measuring instruments to record mooring mast stress levels. The information he obtained during his wild ride made it possible to design improved mooring masts and mounting fittings aboard the airship which could withstand high wind levels by yielding to them gradually without damage. Improved mooring masts were installed across the continent and up to the Pacific Coast of Alaska to accommodate transcontinental airship journeys. Several oil tankers were also equipped with seagoing masts to serve as floating servicing bases for the expected large fleet of naval airships.

On February 16, 1924, while the ship was still undergoing repairs, Commander Zachary Lansdowne was put in charge of the *Shenandoah*. Repairs finished on May 22, 1924 and Lansdowne again resumed far-reaching flights using land and sea based mooring masts. On October 7, the *Shenandoah* left Lakehurst and completed the first transcontinental airship crossing, arriving in San Diego on October 10, 1924.

While the *Shenandoah* roamed up and down the West Coast delighting the numerous taxpayers that had funded its development, the Navy basked in its reflected glory. A sister ship was already enroute. October 15th marked the arrival of the ZR-3, built, revered, and remembered in Germany as the LZ-126. The wife of President Calvin Coolidge hastily rechristened the ship *Los Angeles* to insulate it from criticism arising out of the hard feelings many Americans still held for their enemy from the not-too-distant past.

When the *Shenandoah* returned to Lakehurst, the *Los Angeles* lay comfortably ensconced in her hangar, emptied, for safety reasons, of the hydrogen gas installed in Germany. With helium in short supply, the *Shenandoah* suffered the indignity of having her helium transfused into the new arrival. She lay in enforced retirement until the following summer while her young sister ship frolicked to new destinations including record-setting flights to Bermuda and Puerto Rico.

Revenge came sweetly to the crew of the *Shenandoah* in June of 1925. The keel structure and gas cells of the *Los Angeles* had been corroded by a poorly chosen mixture of antifreeze. Extensive repairs were necessary. With helium still in short supply, the *Shenandoah* was given her own gas back and was once again commissioned into service. After a July 4th flight to the Governors' Convention at Bar Harbor, followed by target sleeve towing for ship's gunnery practice, Admiral Hughes honored the airship by using it as his flagship during naval training exercises.

By August 22nd the *Shenandoah* had made fifty-six flights covering some twenty-five thousand miles. Little did any of its crew imagine that its next flight was to be the last flight for their beloved airship.

I n the fateful pre-dawn hours of September 3, 1925 each of the men in the darkened control room of the *Shenandoah* could sense that something was terribly wrong. Shortly after midnight they were relieved to have come through the dreaded Allegheny Mountains, relieved that the hostile terrain of jutting peaks and the unpredictable wind gusts they generated were at last behind them, relieved that they were, at last, over the flattened countryside of Ohio where an emergency landing could be expected to have a reasonable likelihood of success, even in the dark of night.

The headwinds were weaker than they usually encountered westbound. Even with the airship slowed to a fuel-saving airspeed of thirty-eight knots, the navigator confirmed encouraging progress over the faint lights of the towns passing beneath them. But now the airspeed indicator, usually passive and slow to change, moved rapidly in the swiftly changing, unfamiliar air currents rising and falling by five, then ten, and now fifteen knots. Each time the airspeed needle moved the great airship creaked and groaned in protest, the altimeter rising and then falling, the floor swaying underneath them, pitching and rocking as the helmsmen fought a losing battle to maintain level flight and a constant direction.

The crew braced themselves against the gyrations, grasping the rail running around the control room at waist level with one hand while attempting to perform their duties with the other. The officers peered anxiously through the darkened windows at the thin, black, streaky clouds which were rapidly forming first on their starboard bow and then overhead the great ship. Lieutenant Anderson, the ship's aerologist whose duty it was to interpret and advise the captain of the significance of developing weather patterns, seemed unsure, hesitant, and perplexed.

Commander Lansdowne had seen these clouds before on a transcontinental flight he had made in an airplane. They looked all the world like the roll clouds, violent seething and churning that developed atop great mountains when conflicting masses of air made war on each other for dominance. He recalled being caught up in one once and experiencing the wildest ride of his life as his aircraft tumbled through the sky totally out of control, end over end, first hurtling up thousands of feet before being flung down the mountainside, spat out by some giant force. He remembered regaining control scant feet from the rocks below and limping home with broken flying wires, shattered struts, and torn fabric. But that was on the West Coast and he was still well to the east. He looked to Anderson for some other explanation, but the lieutenant just shrugged his shoulders and opened his hands. He couldn't read the unfamiliar signs.

At that instant his knees buckled as the ship started rising rapidly. He shouted above the shrill noise of the rising wind at Chief Rigger Allen at the elevator controls, "Check that rise Mr. Allen." The helmsman spun the wheel rapidly, lowering the nose of the great ship until the angle reached 18 degrees. The crew fought to maintain their balance as the floor sloped downward away from them.

"I can't check her, sir. She's rising at two meters per second," cried Allen—his voice becoming more urgent. Lansdowne lowered his voice, to avoid alarming the others. Panic was the last thing he needed now. "That's okay Allen, she'll level out eventually. Just don't exceed the present angle. We don't want to stall the ship." Mechanic Bill Russell saw it first. Off in the distance to the northeast, faint jagged lines of white lightning outlined the dense black clouds of a developing squall line. "Could the clouds over the ship be part of that same squall line?" Lansdowne wondered. If they were, it would be very large and possibly dangerous. The situation was deteriorating but still not an emergency—yet.

Lansdowne watched the altimeter intently; 2,100 feet—2,200— 2,300—2,400—2,500—2,600—2,700 . . . The rate of climb needle lay hard against the pin, pegged now at over 1,000 feet per minute—And still the altimeter climbed—2,800—2,900—3,000— 3,100 . . . His easygoing smile was gone—*This can get serious in a hurry*, he thought.

He turned to his left where Lieutenant Joffray was struggling with the large wheel controlling the rudders: " Head Southwest, Joffray. Let's get out of here." "Aye, Aye captain, I'll do my best but she's not responding." Joffray and Allen were the best wheelmen he had. If they couldn't control the huge airship, he knew no one else could. But they were still climbing 3,200—3,300—3,400—3,500 and now the lightning flashes were growing more frequent and intensifying.

An airship rises by reducing its weight by discharging ballast, usually water, from tanks carried for the purpose. It falls by venting its precious supply of buoyant helium gas through a combination of automatic and manual safety valves. It can also be driven downward by lowering the nose and using the power of its engines to drive the ship lower and counteract the lifting effects of the helium.

The *Shenandoah* was designed with eighteen automatic safety valves but, to economize on helium, ten had been removed. She normally carried six 300-HP engines, but one had been removed for maintenance leaving her only five.

Jerome Hunsaker, the designer of the *Shenandoah*, protested the removal of the automatic safety valves before the ship left on her voyage. As an airship rises, the buoyant gas, hydrogen or helium, expands and the pressure within the gas bag increases until "pressure height" is reached. At this altitude, the automatic safety valves open to vent the excess gas before extreme pressures build up and cause the airbags to burst and damage the ship.

Rigger Allen held the wheel hard against its stop. Even with the elevator holding the nose of the ship in the full down position and the engines at full power, they were still rising. Lansdowne cursed the missing engine and ordered emergency power be applied. The mechanics scrambled to their stations in the cars attached to the side of the *Shenandoah* which held the engines. With emergency power, they had to add an "anti-knock" dope to the fuel, add additional cooling water to the radiators, and additional reserve oil to the supply. The noise was deafening but pull as she might, the airship was still rising. Soon they would be at pressure altitude.

One by one the eight remaining safety valves opened but Lansdowne knew at this rate of rise, there were too few valves. "Manually blow all valves," he shouted into the speaking tube. The crew was already awake, alarmed at the unusual motions of the ship and the pressure building up within their own ear drums. Airship crewmen and submariners know well the dangers of rising or diving too fast in their respective chosen mediums. Their stout ships, no matter how well built or designed can explode or implode in an instant if their ships transgress the design envelope, and each man could tell, as if by animal instinct, when they were getting too close for comfort.

The crewmen of the *Shenandoah* raced along the suspended catwalks above the control car, with flashlights and knives, pushing against each airbag with a trained touch, feeling the pressure build and preparing to slit the sides and vent the bag if the efforts of their fellow crewman, now opening the manual valves, should prove too slow or ineffective.

The engines shrieked in protest against the unaccustomed strain, belching clouds of steam and spewing hot black oil over the sides of the ship. The telegraph clanged the urgency of still more power needed. Keel officers ran from one end of the ship to the other making certain the control lines were not being squeezed into submission by the expanding air bags. The violence of the swaying, rocking, pitching, and rapid climb of the darkened *Shenandoah* played against an eerie background of dancing flashlight beams and lightning flashes, brighter and more frequent as the thunderous booms joined with the jagged streaks of hot white light and hail pelted the outside envelope. Despite their best efforts, the ship was now violently out of control.

Commander Lansdowne watched the altimeter climb—4,100—4,200—4,300. Despite the maximum efforts of engines and venting valves, they had now reached pressure altitude and were still rapidly rising. 5,000—5,400—5,600—5,800—6,000. "My God, what's holding this ship together?" Lansdowne spoke out loud, without meaning to. Suddenly the rise stopped and the ship leveled. The whole ship seemed like an overfilled balloon, ready to explode at any moment but it was holding. They had entered the eye of the storm. Then No. 2 engine started knocking furiously, its oil depleted, and had to be shut down. A few minutes later No. 1 engine succumbed to a broken water hose, overheated, and died in a cloud of hot steam.

Now the rise started again; 6,100 feet—6,200—6,300—then all hell broke loose and the ship plummeted at over 1,400 feet per minute towards the ground. The men in the control room dove for the ballast release toggles and thousands of pounds of water poured from the underside, slowing the descent as the ship emerged from the eye and entered again the swirling maelstrom of the storm at an altitude of just under 3,000 feet. With the water ballast and two engines now gone, the crew had few options left to them. The rise started again even more violently than before.

Chief Radioman Schnitzer cupped his headphones against his ears attempting to block out the bedlam filtering into his tiny radio compartment and hear better the weak signal he had detected. Most

radio stations had long been secured, their operators sleeping peace-
fully, unaware of the drama unfolding in the skies. His headphones
picked up a distant signal and he eagerly zeroed his transmitter to its
frequency. He fingered the morse code key, then expertly started his
transmission; "SOS—SOS—SOS—THIS IS THE AIRSHIP
SHENANDOAH CAUGHT IN STORM WEST OF CAM-
BRIDGE OHIO—SOS—SOS—SOS."

As the rise continued unchecked, Commander Lansdowne
ordered Lt. Rosendahl out of the suspended command module and
up into the keel structure above. When the ship fell this time they
would have no ballast to slow its descent or prevent its plunge into
the ground. Rosendahl was ordered to cut loose the middle one of
three aluminum fuel tanks which had been rigged as an emergency
slip tank. The seven hundred-pound filled tank would fall through
the ship's cover and enhance its buoyancy. As Rosendahl climbed up
the ladder through the narrow tube leading up from the command
module and into the ship's main envelope, the nose rose high into
the air.

Instantly the deck angle changed from several degrees nose
down to over thirty degrees nose up. Behind him Rosendahl heard
the sound of snapping wooden struts and breaking cables. He looked
down the narrow tube and unbelievably the entire command room
under him was falling away with all its crew members held only by
the control cables leading from it into the main body of the airship.

For a short while the heavy command room swung in a wide arc,
suspended from the control cables as desperate crew members
attempted to climb out and up into the main body of the airship.
Then the control cables started cutting into the structural skeleton
of the *Shenandoah*, breaking one set of struts after another until the
gigantic backbone of the ship finally snapped and broke, condemn-
ing the command module and all of its human cargo to its death
plunge into the earth below.

Freed of the command module's heavy weight, the main body of
the airship climbed rapidly, the remaining crew grasping the interi-
or framework for dear life. The strain proved too much on the
weakened structure and it broke into two sections, each with airbags
keeping it airborne. The nose section drifted to earth with four survivors, while the tail, with eighteen men, went on a much longer

excursion followed by spectators on the ground not quite believing what their eyes were seeing.

Eventually the crew in the tail section led by Charles Rosendahl, used pocket knives to skillfully vent the helium for a controlled descent from its estimated maximum altitude of ten thousand feet and land successfully. From its original crew of forty-three, fourteen men had lost their lives in the *Shenandoah* including its brilliant young Commander, Zachary Lansdowne. Twenty-nine luckier crew members had survived.

Eventually the damage done to the reputation of the Navy and airships in general caused by the *Shenandoah* tragedy would be over-shadowed by new airship records.

Within a few short years, the German airship *Graf Zeppelin* demonstrated the utility and commercial application of the airship by breaking the fastest steamship's record of sixty-six hours for an Atlantic crossing, completing it on a flight from Lakehurst, New Jersey to Friedrichshafen, Germany in only forty-two hours and forty-two minutes. A few months later it again astounded the world by completing a flight of 21,255 miles, circumnavigating the globe in only 20 days, 4 hours and 14 minutes.

But in the fateful pre-dawn hours of September 3, 1925, the grieving over the tragic death of the Daughter of the Stars, her Commander and her crew, had just begun.

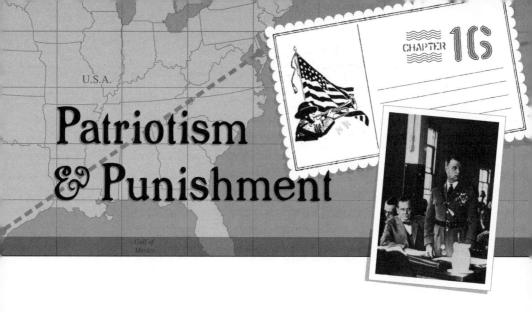

CHAPTER 16

Patriotism
& Punishment

U.S.A.

Gulf of Mexico

THURSDAY, SEPTEMBER 3, 1925
3:30 A.M.
FOR SAM HOUSTON, TEXAS

D espite the joy of his daughter's recent birth, Billy Mitchell hadn't slept well since his visit with Betty at the home of his in-laws near Detroit. They were wonderful people, not much older than he was and with a belief that he was the best man for their daughter which seemed as unjustified as it was unshakeable. His father-in-law had taken him into his home and his heart. He could ask no more of any man. Being a guest in the Miller home sharpened the contrast in their lifestyles. Sidney Miller, Packard Motor Company's attorney, provided all the trappings of success and security while Mitchell was a government employee dependent upon a modest monthly bequest from his grandfather and a parsimonious Congress for sustenance.

No matter that the people of Wisconsin, his home state, wanted him to run for Congress. No matter that Henry Ford and other industrialists begged for him to join their firms at generous salaries. No matter that influential politicians, newspapers, and veteran groups idolized him. The shrinking role of military air power meant that his personal mission in life teetered on the brink of failure. His goal of U.S. strength through aviation seemed as elusive that day as it had been a decade before. The ill-fated Navy flight to Hawaii and its decision to send the *Shenandoah* on a flight he considered reckless and dangerous reinforced his conviction that indeed the inmates were running the asylum while the sane remained silent.

He tossed and turned restlessly that night feeling hot then cold, alternately sweating and trembling, his rheumatism an unwanted souvenir from his youth spent in Alaska. The clock beside his bed had moved at a glacial pace since midnight. Even the shortest interludes of sleep brought nightmares of his brother, his friends, and his fellow airmen dying amidst the horribly twisted flaming wreckage of airplanes.

Lying on the damp sheets, wet with his perspiration, he could feel his pulse racing madly one moment then slowing almost to a stop the next. He had little respect for doctors and tried to avoid them wherever possible, but for him they were a necessary evil. Annual checkups from his flight surgeon were required to maintain his active flight status. He felt angry and rebellious that someday soon, perhaps at his next medical exam, he would not be successful intimidating, cajoling, or begging the flight surgeon into "just one more year." He feared death itself less than the loss of his pilot's license. To be grounded forever . . . nevermore to rise majestically, freed of the earth's bonds to become one with the heavens, nor to chase the birds through the sky, nor fly lazy circles through the clouds was too horrible a fate to contemplate.

The luminous radium-painted hands of the alarm clock moved ever more slowly as its rhythmic *tictac, tictac* grew louder, mocking him as its hands crept around the dial. Depressing thoughts came unbidden, tumbling out of the darkness unstructured and disorganized.

He was forty-five years old and, at an age when most men were basking in the warmth of families grown, his was just beginning. Other men his age had the pinnacle of their careers in sight with elevated staff positions just a few years if not months in front of them. Demoted from his rank of brigadier general, he was no longer welcomed in the weighty Washington centers of gravitas and importance. With the stroke of a pen he had been thrust decades back in his career, an unimportant colonel in a forgotten outpost, irrelevant and immaterial, and, they hoped, soon to be gone and forgotten.

THURSDAY, SEPT. 3, 1925
5:28 A.M.
SAN ANTONIO, TEXAS

At first she thought the raucous noise of the jangling telephone came from her bedside clock. Maydell Blackmon reached over wearily to silence its offending alarm but it stopped before she could touch it . . . and then restarted. Startled, she sat bolt upright in her bed and reached for the telephone. It was still dark and the luminous dial of her clock told her it was very early. As she lifted the receiver to her ear her mind raced through the possibilities. At this hour, they were all bad. She knew something terrible had happened. She caught her breath before speaking tentatively into the mouthpiece, "Hello . . . "

She recognized the high-pitched young voice at the other end . . . it was Jimmy . . . the night radio operator. They called him "Sparks" and he took pride in the name which conveyed maturity and experience beyond his years. The days of the old spark-gap transmitters had long since passed replaced by modern vacuum tubes with glowing incandescent filaments that raised the temperature of the tiny radio room often to unbearable limits. "The *Shenandoah* has . . . has . . . has crashed. You've got to tell the General."

"Were there any survivors?" she asked quietly.

"A few . . . maybe more . . . nobody knows for sure yet," he replied.

She wasn't surprised. She'd been expecting something terrible to happen. Ever since the aborted naval flight to Hawaii and the start of the *Shenandoah's* flight over the Allegheny Mountains, Billy Mitchell had been predicting another debacle. For the past three days she had patiently listened while her boss railed against the stupidity of the War Department in general and the Navy in particular. "I'll be there as quickly as I can," she replied stoically before hanging up the phone.

Passing the main gate of the air base, Mitchell knew something was wrong. Air Cadet Patterson had always saluted him smartly and smiled broadly at his personal idol, his hero, the ultimate aviator he strived to be, "someday." The snappy salute was there but he was obviously avoiding eye contact. The smile was gone and in its place was a look of great sadness.

Maydell waited for him just outside the door but by the time he pulled into his usual parking space and shut down the engine, he already knew what had happened. She started to tell him, but the words just wouldn't come out of her mouth. He put his arm around her shoulders and wiped her tears with his handkerchief. "It's okay, I know," he said, and led her through the door.

Billy spent the next few hours in the hot cramped radio room, young "Sparks" scribbling furiously, decoding for him the rapid dits and dahs streaming into his headset from many transmitters. Mitchell eagerly read each scrap of paper. Slowly the picture was emerging:

> Ship torn to pieces . . . control car plummeted to earth . . . tail struck trees . . . survivors leaped from great height . . . bow rose to ten thousand feet . . . gas cells slashed . . . 15 survivors likely . . .

Then a pause with little news coming. To Sparks, the wait seemed endless. Out of the corner of his eyes, he could see Mitchell's face, implacable, expressionless, only his tightly clenched lips and fists betrayed the anger and hostility building within him. Then, as suddenly as they had stopped, they started again, the merciless dits and dahs with the news he had feared most:

> Lansdowne dead . . . looters stole his wristwatch, wallet, and ripped Annapolis Class ring and wedding band from his fingers . . . now stripping all dead bodies . . . souvenir hunters cutting up wreckage . . . stealing instruments, fabric, logbooks, even clothing and shoes of dead fliers.

Billy's face was ashen, contorted with rage and sorrow. The tears streamed down his cheeks. He rose and silently left the radio room pushing his way through a mob of reporters shouting for his comments. Slamming the door behind him, he slumped into his large upholstered desk chair and covered his face with his hands. Maydell Blackmon made certain no one else got close enough to his office that day to hear the cries of uncontrollable grief coming through the door. For that entire day, Billy Mitchell communicated with no one.

FRIDAY, SEPT. 4, 1925
8:00 A.M.
FORT SAM HOUSTON, TEXAS

As Maydell's car approached the main gate of the air base, she slowed to ask Cadet Patterson, "What time did he leave last night?"

"He didn't, Ma'am. He's still here," he answered. She continued on, resigned to this being a very rough day.

Mitchell saw her car approaching through the window of his office and got to her desk before she did. Uncharacteristically, he hadn't shaved and the open collar of his rumpled shirt was stained with sweat. It was obvious he had slept in his clothes that night. The anger and grief were gone now, channeled into a purposeful resolve to take on the entire War Department or even the entire U.S. Government if necessary. He had made his decision to declare war against the bureaucracy and, with the public's help, he had every expectation of winning. "Miss Blackmon, hold all my calls, bring a dozen pads and pencils and come into my office. We've got a lot of work to do."

Mitchell filled several pads with notes through the night. He started dictating rapidly. The words streamed from his mouth tumbling like missiles from some unseen castle's walls onto the heads of the invading barbarian hordes below. They were filled with vituperation, condemnation, and criticism in a tone so harsh that Maydell would occasionally shudder after writing them. She knew that this was his doomsday message from which recovery would be impossible. She was hoping that after her notes had been transcribed, he would have cleansed his soul and the terrible words would remain in their own secret place where no one else would ever see them. She hoped a good night's sleep would make him reconsider and come to his senses before they exploded into print.

By the time he had finally edited, corrected, changed, and completed his statement, noon had passed. "I must leave for lunch, I don't feel well. I'll be back shortly," she said. "Hurry back. I need that statement for the reporters as soon as possible," he called after her.

After leaving the air base, Maydell rushed to a nearby telephone. Her first call was to a family friend, Dwight Davis, a retired Army attorney now in private practice in San Antonio. After swearing him to confidence, she read selected passages from her shorthand notes and sought his advice. "You're right to call me, Maydell. This is serious . . . very serious. For his sake don't let him talk to anyone until I get there or he's going to wind up in jail. I'm on my way."

She pressed down on the lever which terminated the call, then raised it and dialed another number. This call was to Captain Steve Brown, a fellow aviator and close personal friend of Mitchell's. He was stationed several hundred miles away. After listening to the incendiary language, he begged her to delay the statement until he could fly down and try to talk him out of making it. He would fly out immediately and be there in a few hours.

Returning to the base, Maydell avoided Mitchell's pointed glares and exaggerated stares at his wrist watch. "I need my statement. We can't let that whole pool of reporters go home without it," he said pointing at the growing group of reporters and photographers smelling blood and waiting impatiently for the incendiary statement they knew was coming. She sat down at her desk and slowly inserted a mimeograph sheet, carefully aligning the margins several times before striking the first letter.

Mitchell came out of his office several times whenever he heard the slow rhythmic typing stop. Pretending to have trouble reading her own shorthand, she sought extensive "clarification." After stalling an increasingly frustrated Mitchell for two hours, attorney Dwight Davis finally arrived. Maydell knocked, then opened the door for the visitor. "General Mitchell, I need to speak to you in private." Mitchell looked at the distinguished graying gentlemen standing in his doorway. He had seen Davis several times in Washington and knew who he was. He stared momentarily at the visitor, then at Maydell. He understood instantly why she had been so slow.

Their conversation started in measured tones, Davis summarizing the charges Mitchell's statement exposed him to and the possible punishment each charge could bring. Mitchell admitted he had not considered many of the charges that might be brought but was intent upon going through with it regardless of consequences.

The conversation became more heated as Davis became increasingly frustrated by Mitchell's intransigence. Maydell knocked on Mitchell's door and entered, ushering in fellow pilot Steve Brown and carrying a tray of Mitchell's favorite pastries. With the tension relieved, the conversation continued for several hours but neither man could make Mitchell change his mind.

At eight o'clock Maydell announced she was leaving for the evening. Mitchell insisted she stay and complete typing his statement and then make twenty copies for immediate press distribution. Maydell looked over to Dwight Davis for advice. Davis turned to Mitchell, "General, you have not gotten a good nights sleep in three days. If you agree to go home now and sleep on what we've just told you so you can make a more rational decision in the morning, Maydell will stay late tonight to finish your statement. She'll leave twenty copies on your desk. If you still want to commit suicide in the morning, it will be your call." Davis extended his hand to Billy who carefully considered the offer before slowly extending his own.

Mitchell walked down the hall to the waiting pool of reporters. "Gentlemen, I'll have a statement for you tomorrow morning. You all might as well go home now. I'll say nothing further on the matter today."

A young reporter called from the back of the room, "What time tomorrow, Colonel?" The older reporters glared disapprovingly at the young man. Despite what the desk-bound army chair-polishers decreed, to them, as to everyone on the base, he would always be the rank he earned in battle by putting his life on the line again and again. He would always be *The General*. "I'll be here at 5 A.M." replied Mitchell.

SATURDAY, SEPTEMBER 5, 1925
5:00 A.M.
FORT SAM HOUSTON, TEXAS

H e didn't really expect them to be there that early, but as he rolled into his usual parking space in the early predawn hours, about a dozen other cars were already parked nearby. He entered the reception hallway, strode through the waiting throng silently, and opened the door to his office. As promised, Maydell had left twenty copies of his statement on his desk, the blue mimeographed sheets piled neatly with the original marked and placed in a file folder. He read it, then carried the twenty copies from his office.

Climbing onto a desk in the hallway to address the reporters before giving out the copies of his statement he said, "For the record gentlemen, please note that my statement is being given to you only after mature deliberations." As the statements were handed out, the reporters started reading them and cries of "Wow . . . Can you believe this? . . . Holy mackerel . . . " filled the small room. As if by signal, the reporters hurried off with their treasures scurrying to find a telephone and thus "scoop" their colleagues.

The statement ran 6,080 words, its preface summarized its tone; "My opinion is as follows: these accidents are the result of the incompetency, the criminal negligence, and the almost treasonable negligence of our national defense by the Navy and War Departments." He accused the Army and Navy of collusion to prevent the formation of an independent air force calling airmen "pawns in their hands" to be "bluffed and bulldozed" and "banished to out of the way places" if they told the truth.

He accused the Army of encouraging commanding officers to, "either distort the facts or openly tell falsehoods about aviation to the people and to Congress so disgusting as to make any self respecting person ashamed of the cloth he wears."

He accused the Navy of staging the attempted Hawaiian flight as, "a Pacific Parade to fool the public by untried primitive good-for-nothing big lumbering flying boats" and the support fleet of being too busy, "joy riding around the Antipodes" to effectively help the flight.

The *Shenandoah* crash was characterized as an unnecessary propaganda trip, undertaken in an unsafe and seriously damaged airship whose fate could have been easily predicted using the most basic knowledge of airmanship or common sense. "What business had the Navy over the mountains anyway?" he opined.

Military aircraft were forced to rely on "a weather bureau organized to turn out reports affecting onions, cabbages, and other crops" through unreliable and inaccurate aviation weather forecasting. American bombing capability had been allowed to deteriorate into impotence with, "not one single heavy bomb having been dropped for the past two years, and only four or five modern (bomb) sights available." No more than "two perfectly capable bombing crews could be put together in the event of an attack on the United States."

He went on to state that, "The development of effective weapons such as aircraft and submarines had come to an abrupt halt due to a lack of funding while the Navy squandered hundreds of millions of dollars on useless battleships and other surface ships which had no role in modern warfare other than to transport aircraft to the scene of battle."

Mitchell blamed the deaths of many airmen on "official stupidity, gross incompetence and criminal mistakes" in the handling of its aeronautics and forcing pilots to fly and die in "flaming coffins."

SUNDAY MORNING, SEPTEMBER 6, 1925
DAWN
ACROSS THE UNITED STATES

Almost every major Sunday newspaper featured Mitchell's inflammatory statements in its headlines, its front pages, and its editorial columns. Most praised his candor and bravery in defying his superiors efforts to conceal the truth from the public. Many were not as charitable.

The New York World editorialized, "Permit this violent outburst to go unpunished and every private in the Army and enlisted man in the Navy will feel at liberty to denounce his superior officers. Armies and navies are not made that way."

Charles Rosendahl, the navigator who had survived the crash of the *Shenandoah*, was infuriated by what he perceived as a crass effort by Mitchell to gain support for his cause by slandering the Navy and its officers who had sacrificed their lives. His brother wrote an open letter to Mitchell and sent it for publication to the *Houston Chronicle* saying, "You have no place in the service of your country when you have so little respect for its authority."

The following week's newspapers were filled with editorial comments on Mitchell's original statements. Buoyed by mountains of mail generally sympathetic to his views, he kept the pot boiling by amplifying and extending his comments in language increasingly inflammatory. Readers views were published alongside the newspaper's editorial columns. Sharp divisions between proponents and opponents piqued public interest and newspaper readership soared.

Soon the entire country took interest and the media fanned the flames enjoying the additional readership and the advertising revenue which it created.

The *New York Times* charged Mitchell with "insubordination and folly." The *Herald Tribune* said, "He shockingly violates military standards," and was "opinionated, arrogant and intolerant." The most prophetic editorial was published in the *Kansas City Star:*

> How are we going to punish a man who wants nothing more than to be punished and is deliberately inviting court martial? Mitchell is a zealot, a fanatic, a one-idea man. He will go to any limit to make his case . . . But with all that, he sincerely believes in what he preaches.
>
> If a military court-martial is ordered, no one will be happier than Mitchell . . . If he is made a martyr in the process, no one knows better than Mitchell that there will be a wave of sympathy for him. . . .
>
> Some day Mitchell's dream may come true. He may be a prophet without honor only because he came a decade or two decades ahead of his time.

Reaction from the administration was muted initially but, behind the scenes, President Coolidge fumed at the latest affront from his exiled airman. He requested his old friend Dwight Morrow, a wealthy banker and future father-in-law of Charles Lindbergh, to form an investigatory commission which would bypass any congressional investigation. Morrow chose eight members, most of whom were naval advocates and opposed to a defense strategy dominated by aviation. The Morrow Board attacked the credibility of Mitchell's charges and generally supported the court martial being prepared against him. Admiral Moffett released a statement dismissing Mitchell's charges as "utter untruths" and concluding he was "suffering from delusions of grandeur or mental aberrations."

The Army opened an official investigation into Mitchell's statements and summoned him to Washington to testify. Before departing from San Antonio he defiantly admitted making all of the statements accrued to him and shipped eight hundred pounds of supporting documentation to Washington for use in his trial.

Betty met Billy at the train station in St. Louis and the couple arrived in Washington on the evening of September 25, welcomed by his old friend Hap Arnold leading tens of thousands of cheering supporters. In the late morning of September 29, the Mitchells arrived at the House Office Building to begin testifying before the Morrow Commission and a packed gallery of well-wishing spectators. Typical of Coolidge's penurious allocation of public funds, the commission was denied monies for its expenses or recording its proceedings with the expectation its wealthy members would pay their own expenses.

From the beginning, Mitchell's testimony went poorly. He appeared physically and emotionally exhausted and chose to read long excerpts in a monotone from his recently published book, *Winged Defense*. In place of the fiery oration and emotional heartfelt plausible arguments expected by his supporters and the press, he droned on hour after hour reading from a book which many had already read. When informed that his recitations were providing little if any new information since almost everyone had read his book and many copies were already in the chamber, Mitchell disregarded the criticism and continued reading to his increasingly bored and restive audience.

The *Washington Post* reported the next morning, "The witness does not look you in the eye, his face is down . . . the unexpected never happens . . . you count the pages to see when he will be through." His testimony continued the next day with much the same lack of impact or originality.

Following his testimony before the Morrow Commission, Mitchell spent the first few weeks of October 1925 preparing for his court martial trial. Frank Reid, an attorney who had practiced with the famous Scopes trial attorney Clarence Darrow, and now a freshman congressman from Illinois, offered his services free of charge to represent Billy Mitchell. Reid was a strong supporter of Mitchell and shared his belief in the importance of aviation.

Before the court martial proceedings began, Mitchell was called to testify in the *Shenandoah* hearings being conducted by the Navy. As Mitchell had warned, the board of inquiry was dominated by the same adversaries of air power that had opposed and rigged the aerial bombing tests of ships in 1921.

Reporters covering the inquiry denounced the obvious naval efforts to absolve themselves from any blame for the breakup of the *Shenandoah*. Their image was tarnished when it was revealed that they were refusing to pay any compensation to the crash victims or even any burial expenses to the family, claiming they had already spent the allocated $150 per man preparing the bodies for burial. The public became especially incensed at the Navy's apparent lack of compassion when it was revealed that they planned to spend six million dollars to replace the crashed airship.

Mitchell's testimony before the *Shenandoah* board of inquiry was quite acrimonious and resulted in creating additional support and sympathy for him. The American Legion chose Mitchell to speak at their convention in Omaha. The Army, fearing the consequences, stepped in to block the appointment by placing Mitchell under arrest and forbidding him to leave the city. President Coolidge offered to speak in his place, taking the opportunity to strongly criticize Mitchell saying:

"Any organization of men in the military service bent on inflaming the public mind for the purpose of forcing government action through the pressure of public opinion is an exceedingly dangerous undertaking . . . "

WEDNESDAY, OCTOBER 28, 1925
10:00 A.M.
WASHINGTON, D.C.

The crowds were already waiting when Billy Mitchell's car pulled up in front of the dilapidated Emory Building chosen by the Army for his trial. Flanked by his wife Betty, sister Harriet, and legal team, Billy waved to the cheering crowds, then bounded eagerly up the crumbling steps of the old building leading his entourage through the graying wooden front door.

It wasn't supposed to be like this, but he had no choice. The Army had carefully chosen a warehouse that long ago had fallen into disrepair and had been abandoned many years ago by the Census Bureau. The wooden floors were rotting, splintered, and strewn with garbage. Pools of stagnant water had accumulated through the leaking roof and windows. Many of the panes were missing or broken. Little of the original paint remained on the warped, dirty, cardboard walls. The rotting supporting floor beams creaked and groaned when anyone walked on them, and the ceiling sagged menacingly, threatening to collapse at any moment. The deserted rooms were permeated with the stench of damp decaying wood and cardboard. The rooms were small, dark, and lacked heat.

Mitchell had watched silently the week before as workmen attempted to make a few rooms and corridors in the building temporarily habitable. It was obvious to him the Army was going to great lengths to deny him the large public audience he so desperately wanted at his trial. As expected, they announced—regretfully of course—that due to the condition of the building only a few spectators could be accommodated. The trial of Billy Mitchell would be as quiet and as low key as the Army could make it.

The Navy played its part in preparing for Billy's trial by releasing a new film, *The Eyes of the Fleet* the week before the court martial trial was to begin. A Martin bomber was shown making several bombing runs over the U.S.S. *Alabama*. J.B. Bockhurst, a newsreel cameraman, flew the photo plane over the ship and was tossed into the air violently by the force of the exploding bombs on the superstructure of the ship, recovering in time to record the ship—her decks a shambles—rolling over and sinking.

In an effort to discredit Mitchell's forthcoming testimony on the effectiveness of air power, all bomb hits were carefully edited out of the film and only misses were shown, leaving the audience to conclude that aerial bombing was ineffective against naval vessels.

As Billy Mitchell led the way through the front door of the Emory building to start his trial, he faced twelve judges, all of whom were generals, including his childhood friend, Douglas MacArthur. It was the highest ranking court ever assembled for an American military trial. All had come up through the ranks of the infantry, cavalry, and artillery. None were airmen, nor especially sympathetic to the role of aviation advocated by Mitchell.

Clayton Bissell, his friend and attache in prior years, was assigned as assistant defense council and aviation expert. Joseph Davies volunteered to provide military legal counsel. Betty's father, Sidney Miller, at great personal sacrifice, insisted on paying all of his trial expenses including travel, food, and hotel expenses for the defense team and a lengthy list of witnesses, many from remote locations.

Mitchell had rented two floors of the Anchorage apartments in Washington, which served as his defense headquarters and storage for hundreds of boxes of supporting documents shipped from San Antonio. At a lengthy strategy session several days before the trial opened, there was general agreement that the language Mitchell used both in his original statement to the press on September 5 and his reassertion on September 9 was insubordinate as charged.

A breach developed between Davies and Reid when Davies insisted that, since everyone agreed he was guilty as charged, he should plead guilty and then go into his defense for justification. Reid was dead set against a guilty plea and felt salvation lie in proving everything Mitchell said was in fact true, and therefore covered by the constitutional right of free speech. Davies left and was replaced by William Webb, a young House Committee lawyer who was given the assignment of researching legal precedents for supporting case law.

Shortly after the trial opened, Reid challenged the right of two generals to sit on the court. General Albert Bowley had made a speech the week before ridiculing the idea of a national defense department and critical of Mitchell's exaggerations of the effectiveness of air power to the general public.

General Charles Summerall's Hawaiian defenses had been severely criticized in Mitchell's report as being inefficient, badly organized, with neither coordination nor cooperation between Army and Navy units, and totally inadequate to defend against an air attack from Japan. Both judges were dismissed and not replaced since the court required only six sitting judges.

THURSDAY, DECEMBER 17, 1925
10:15 A.M.
WASHINGTON, D.C.

I t was cold that morning sitting in the unheated makeshift courtroom of the Emory building. Betty Mitchell wrapped her coat tightly around her against the cold which caused her to occasionally tremble. The men's jackets and overcoats insulated them from the frigid damp air of the warehouse. The trial that was expected to last only two weeks had stretched into its seventh week. Public interest had gradually subsided as reporters moved on to more current stories. Repetitive and highly technical testimony bored the average reader and the trial occupied less and less space in the daily newspapers.

For Billy Mitchell, the trial had gone predictably poorly. Under relentless cross examination by the prosecution, Mitchell had admitted many of his press statements were based upon his opinions rather than first hand knowledge or involvement of the matters he criticized. Mitchell was also reluctant to let many of the younger airmen testify on his behalf fearing that their careers would be ruined.

Mitchell's public assertions of the vulnerability of the Pacific Fleet to an attack on Pearl Harbor were strongly denied and ridiculed by both the Army and Navy during the trial and his Pacific Region report, which had languished unread in the "flying trash pile" file cabinet, was suddenly classified "secret" so it could not be used in his defense. Its thousand pages of illustrations, diagrams, facts, and figures which accurately predicted the entire timing and strategic planning of the Japanese air attack on Hawaii and the Philippines using aircraft carriers, and the bloody air and naval battles on the Pacific Islands which would follow, remained apparently unread until finally declassified in 1958, thirty-four years after they were written.

Each side had concluded its presentation and the stern-faced judges filed into the courtroom and mounted their raised dais. General Howze called on Mitchell's defense attorney for summary. Reid gathered his carefully prepared book of summary notes and started to rise. Mitchell reached out and restrained him, rising himself instead. Reid looked questioningly at Mitchell but a sharp glance made him sink down again into his seat. He had seen that look before and knew protest was useless.

As Mitchell rose, silence fell over the entire courtroom and all eyes focused on the handsome lean figure that stood ramrod straight and looked directly into the eyes and souls of each judge. Even in his unremarkable neatly pressed uniform of the Air Service, Sam Brown belt, and silver aviator's wings—disdaining the many medals he had won and was entitled to wear—he looked every bit the war hero that he was. The few reporters that remained scurried to get note pads and paper ready as electricity passed through the courtroom. As he began speaking, his demeanor was unbowed, his voice firm, and his words reflected the deep conviction from whence they came;

"My trial before this court martial is the culmination of the efforts of the General Staff of the Army and the General Board of the Navy to depreciate the value of air power and keep it in the auxiliary position, which absolutely compromises the whole system of national defense.

"These efforts . . . were begun as soon as the sound of the cannon had ceased on the Western Front in 1918. When we sank the battleships off the Virginia Capes in 1921, and again in 1923, and proved to the world that air power had revolutionized all schemes of national defense, these efforts have redoubled and continued to this day.

"The truth of every statement which I have ever made has been proved by good and sufficient evidence before this court, not by men who have gained their knowledge of aviation by staying on the ground and having their statements prepared by numerous staff . . . but by actual fliers . . . To proceed with the case would serve no useful purpose. I have therefore directed my counsel to entirely close out our part of the proceeding without argument."

As Mitchell sat down, all the spectators in the courtroom rose in anticipation of giving him a standing ovation. General Howze, seeing what was happening, stood on the dais and motioned forcefully for everyone to be seated in silence. The prosecution's counsel, Major Gullion, then began his presentation, deriding, scorning, and diminishing each of Mitchell's defense witnesses who bore out the truth of his charges, even hinting they had perjured themselves to help an old friend.

Admiral Sims was characterized as narrow-minded and egotistical. Congressman Fiorello LaGuardia, a decorated world war combat pilot, was inexperienced with only fifteen or twenty hours in the air. Major Gerald Brandt, an ace fighter pilot and hero of the Royal Air Force, and Eddie Rickenbacker, ace of aces, were misdirected and corrupted into his testimony by the evil influence of Mitchell. Other airmen had been bribed by Mitchell with grandiose schemes and promises of rapid promotion. Only the prosecution witnesses were sober, clear-thinking, patriotic men of impeccable credentials and character. Gullion concluded with a vicious attack on the character, truthfulness, and morals of Mitchell, calling him wild-ly imaginative and destructive. He characterized him as a charlatan and demagogue, and likened him to Aaron Burr.

The judges took less than thirty minutes to find Mitchell guilty on all charges. General Howze pronounced sentence, "The Court upon secret written ballot, . . . sentences the accused to be suspend-ed from rank, command, and duty, with the forfeiture of all pay and allowances for five years."

Many if not most of the public expected President Coolidge to show leniency to the heroic and popular war hero, but he gave his full support to the decision of the court, forcing Billy Mitchell to resign from the Army a few days later.

To the aging bureaucrats, generals, and admirals, steeped in the traditions of defense based upon the insulation provided by its two great oceans and content for its defense on its colorful cavalry and trusted naval surface ships, their arch enemy had been defeated. The confusion that Mitchell had fostered among a gullible public and Congress with his radical doctrine of the importance of aviation was at last silenced. What they could not do with exile, he himself had done with his own hand and mouth.

A major nuisance had been extracted, removed from their midst along with his fanciful tales of a coming second world war dominat-ed by aerial bombardment of cities, flying bombs, airplanes traveling hundreds of miles per hour, and aircraft carriers coming from Japan to attack U.S. bases in the Pacific.

With their chief trouble-maker gone, the status quo could now prevail in harmony among the services. Aviation was finally put into its place as an impotent and scarcely necessary adjunct to an Army which ruled the land and a Navy which ruled the seas . . . or was it?

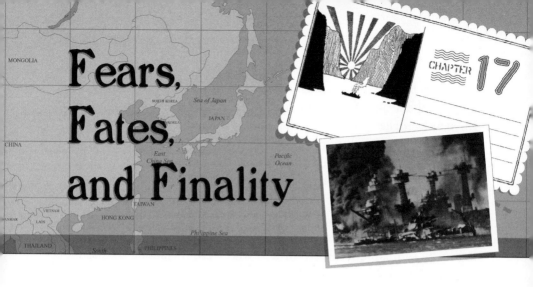

Fears, Fates, and Finality

D espite Mitchell's acknowledgment that his behavior qualified as insubordinate and merited the charges against him, when the actual verdict came from judges that were friends and foes alike, he found the reality deeply discouraging. Outwardly he dismissed it to Betty saying that the judges were under Army orders to reach that verdict. Inwardly he felt abandoned by men who had claimed to be his friends. On his last day of flying in the Air Service, Mitchell made thirty-seven flights to qualify for the flight pay his enforced grounding during the trial had denied him. Observers recalled his obvious enjoyment at skillfully performing the demanding rapid flight sequences.

After his forced resignation from the U.S. Air Service, Billy Mitchell enthusiastically threw himself into a busy schedule of traveling, lecturing, and writing books and magazine articles. The theme remained the same; the need for a separate Air Force, the global vulnerability of U.S. bases, the need to expand aviation research, development and deployment, and the unshakeable belief that the very survival of the United States depended upon the encouragement, support, and nurturing of aviation-minded young men and women upon whom the future depended.

With Betty, he visited Europe in 1927. During the trip he was under constant surveillance by the U.S. Army. Upon his return he warned of the huge German effort to promote aviation among the country's youth through large-scale glider programs, while German engineers bypassed the armistice restrictions on building new military bombers and fighter planes by secretly developing them in Russian factories.

Lacking the bully pulpit of rank and authority, Mitchell's lecturing opportunities declined and, within a few years, his writings became far less popular. Rejected by editors, he tried writing books on other subjects, outdoor life, and the Civil War, but none achieved widespread readership. As his health declined, his personal flying was curtailed and he was relegated to the passenger seat of military flights by sympathetic fellow airmen who were forbidden to discuss military matters with him.

From his home at Boxwood, his most joyous moments were spent teaching his young daughter, Lucy, horseback riding and outdoor skills, lavishing on her the attention that he had denied the children of his first marriage in his younger days.

His last book, *Skyways* was published in 1930 but was not a huge success. His warnings of the war to come with Japan and Germany and the lack of U.S. military preparedness continued relentlessly in numerous articles which he published in magazines and newspapers, but the deepening Depression made larger military budgets politically unacceptable.

Mitchell's star almost rose again in 1934. As a strong supporter of Franklin D. Roosevelt for President, he was considered the logical choice to head a newly formed Federal Aviation Commission in the new administration. He was recommended and supported for the post by several influential congressmen, and his nomination was announced by the newspapers as being all but assured. Bills were introduced in the Senate and House clearing Mitchell of the Court Martial charges and restoring his rank and salary. It looked certain that, at last, his life's dream would be realized and he would assert a major influence on the course of U.S. aviation . . . but it was not to be.

His testimony before a Senate Investigative Committee headed by Hugo L. Black during February of 1934 charged that many of America's largest companies had formed an Aviation Trust. In possession of aircraft patents seized on an emergency basis during World War I, they refused to return them to their original owners and profited excessively from monopolistic practices, denying the original inventors outside the trust the use of their own patents and stifling aircraft development.

Credible support for these charges came from several sources. A Presidential Commission headed by the noted aerodynamic engineer Gutzon Borglum concluded in the *Congressional Record* of April 11, 1922 under the heading of "War Frauds" that a group from Dayton, Ohio, allied with President Harding, had misappropriated $1,650,000 of government aviation funds with little to show for the expenditure. Jimmy Martin, an aircraft designer and manufacturer who had been excluded from the Trust, had forty-seven patented inventions taken from him and never returned. He revealed that two of the companies controlled by Harding's associates had been financed by Mitsui and Company, the fiscal agents of the Japanese Government and paymasters to the German secret service. Carloads of airplanes labeled as "household furniture" had apparently been diverted from the allies during the war and shipped to Japan.

Borglum wrote in the *Congressional Record;*

> There will be no convictions for this gigantic fraud, and we will get nothing but a political burial of a crime of which Republicans and Democrats are equally guilty. . .
>
> There is something profoundly rotten in this (the aircraft scandal) business. It was conceived and carried out with such intent to defraud—it was so bad in its conception and its building, and finally in its production—so vast was the machinery of evil—that I doubt if we should be able to do anything in aeronautics during this present generation because of what exists . . . . There are not five or six public men who have the character to prosecute the Air Trust, in or out of public life. . . . I do not know any who will sacrifice his job or his chance for preferment to speak the truth. The government must completely overhaul its aeronautical salvage, discard practically all the men heretofore connected with it, and put the entire department in the hands of new people . . .

Mitchell believed the slow pace of U.S. aircraft design and development in the 1920s and into the 1930s was caused by the monopoly the Air Trust enjoyed, the lack of competitive bidding on military aircraft acquisition, and the blanket protection given to the Trust against any claims of patent infringement or prior invention.

These charges created powerful enemies who joined with older and more traditional Army and Navy officers in opposing Mitchell's nomination and the clearing of past accusations against him. With Mitchell again enmeshed in controversy, Roosevelt quietly withdrew his name from consideration.

Mitchell considered Charles Lindbergh a pawn of the Air Trust who had done little for aviation. He belittled his first solo flight across the Atlantic in 1927 and felt it unworthy of the enormous attention it received. Lindbergh's failure to publicly support Mitchell's positions and his marriage to Ann Morrow, whose father headed the Morrow Commission and criticized many of Mitchell's goals, did little to endear the two airmen to each other. In later years Lindbergh's admiration of Adolph Hitler, anti-semitic speeches, and attempts to prevent America's preparation and involvement in the war against Nazi Germany, further eroded his popularity among Mitchell's supporters.

With the Depression deepening, Mitchell's pleading for increased expenditures for aviation fell on deaf ears and military morale in the Air Service sank to new lows. Mitchell's charges against the Air Trust caused a lawsuit for libel to be filed against him with a demand for $200,000. Besieged by mounting legal expenses, frequent personal attacks on him by the military, and frustrated by his failure to arouse public support in preparing for the war he was certain was coming, all proved too much of a burden on his weakening heart. His poor health prevented him from flying or even driving himself.

In 1935, just before his fifty-sixth birthday, he wrote to a close friend; "I am suddenly grown old." The newspaper delivered to his home on the morning of January 28th, 1936 proved to be the final blow. The House Committee had overruled their own Chairman and followed the recommendation of the Military Affairs Committee. His appeal from his Court Martial conviction had been denied. Weak and with troubled breathing, Mitchell was admitted to the hospital later that day. On February 19, 1936, with his sister Harriet and wife Betty at his bedside, Billy Mitchell went to sleep . . . and never awoke. His total estate came to less than fifteen thousand dollars.

After testifying on behalf of Billy Mitchell during his court martial, Lowell Smith chose to remain with the Air Service, as did Frederick Martin and Alva Harvey. Their love of flying kept them in during the bleakest of times. Martin rose to the rank of Major General and was in command of the Hawaiian air defenses when the Japanese attacked Pearl Harbor . . . in precisely the same way and with the same results Billy Mitchell had warned in his report seventeen years before.

Joint reports had been sent only months before the attack from all of the Hawaiian commanders warning of inadequate defenses and the fleet's vulnerability. They were ignored by the General Staff in Washington. The huge losses sustained in the attack required scapegoats be found and blame assessed. The inadequate air and ground defenses were blamed on General Martin, Admiral Husband Kimmel of the Navy, and General W.C. Short of the army. Martin was relieved of his command eleven days after the attack and recalled to a lesser post at Spokane, Washington. Court martial charges were considered against the others with military leaders and politicians blaming everyone but themselves.

Alva Harvey had better luck. With a grateful Martin's recommendations, he rose from the rank of sergeant to colonel—commanding a wing of the 20th Bomber Command during World War II—and fulfilled his dream of again flying around the world.

Smith, tainted by his association and strong support of Mitchell's positions, never rose beyond the rank of colonel. In the decade following the first world flight he developed methods of rapid ground force deployment using aircraft which, along with his aerial refueling techniques, were invaluable during the war.

When hostilities started, he was given command of bomber crew training at Davis–Monthan Field in Tucson, Arizona. When many years passed without promotion or recognition of his many aviation accomplishments, his wife urged him to leave the service for greener pastures. He replied, "Oh, I would rather be an old Colonel." Shortly after the war ended, fate stepped in. Smith—the heroic pilot who had prevailed over countless aerial disasters and seemingly impossible odds, cheating death when it seemed most imminent—died in a fall from a horse in 1945.

Hank "Houdini" Ogden left a demoralized Air Service shortly after Billy Mitchell did in 1926 and worked at various aviation related activities until 1938 when he joined Lockheed Aircraft. During the war he volunteered to manage all of their air activities in embattled

England where his knowledge of aircraft and engine systems proved very helpful to the war effort. For his outstanding service during the war he was promoted to Vice President of Lockheed Air Services.

"Smilin' Jack" Harding left the Air Service shortly after the flight to join Lowell Thomas on a lecture tour promoting aviation and the book Thomas wrote about the world flight. When the tour ended, he helped start Florida Airways, one of the first scheduled airlines, before joining the Boeing Aircraft Company as an engineer.

With a clever mind, gifted hands, and strong entrepreneurial spirit, "Smilin' Jack" started Harding Devices Company making solenoid operated aircraft fuel valves of his own design. With the war, his small business grew rapidly and Harding fuel valves were used on a wide variety of large aircraft including most of the B-29s.

Les Arnold remained with the air service until 1928 when he finally gave up all hope for its future. He flew for an aircraft company which eventually became Trans World Airlines but left in 1940 to accept the position of Vice President of Eastern Airlines. When the war started, Arnold took a leave of absence and rejoined the Army Air Corps to fly with the Eighth Air Force in England. Under the threat of constant German bombs and rockets, he often huddled with Hank Ogden downing a pint of bitters and reminiscing about their fantastic adventure two decades before.

Erik Nelson also left shortly after Mitchell resigned in 1926 and became Vice President of Sales for Boeing Aircraft Company. He reenlisted when the war started, first serving as a colonel in the Pacific Region. His organizational, engineering, and flying skills were of great value. He was soon promoted to brigadier general and helped establish an expanded network of air bases in China and many of the Pacific Islands. After the war he retired and, as a consultant to Scandinavian Airlines, helped establish their polar air routes.

Leigh Wade also testified on behalf of Billy Mitchell during his Court Martial trial in 1925 and was outspoken in his support of Mitchell's positions on aviation matters. With little reason to stay on what he considered the sinking ship of military aviation, he resigned from the Air Service. He had formed a close relationship with Linton Wells, the aviation-smitten reporter who had followed the flight for over fifteen thousand miles and flown with Wade across India in the tight cockpit of the *Boston*.

Needing money and seeking a new adventure, the two came up with a plan that would give them both. Wade and Wells decided to attempt the first non-stop motorcar drive across the United States from Los Angeles to New York and break all the existing transcontinental automobile speed records. Roads were primitive, often no more than rutted cow paths or waist-deep mud, gas stations were few and far between, high mountains with ice and snow lay in their path and outside help could not be counted on. They decided the new Packard Straight Eight-cylinder model would have the best possibility of surviving the trip.

They visited Packard to inform them of their good fortune in being selected and to obtain a car and sponsorship funds. The Packard sales department listened politely then informed them that no existing car could be expected to travel 3,800 miles without major service and no existing engine could be expected to run continuously for the 170 hours it would take to make the trip. They were then ushered to the door with the plea to "please go away and ruin the reputation of some other manufacturer."

Not to be deterred, Wade withdrew all of his savings, borrowing from his family the additional funds needed to purchase the Packard outright. Wells, the typical reporter of the time, contributed only his enthusiasm. With the car secured they set about finding the sponsorship funds to cover expenses. The Kelly-Springfield Tire Company agreed to supply tires for the trip and pay a bonus of $5,000 if they succeeded. Pennzoil Company agreed to pay them $2,500 for the exclusive use of its oil and advertising rights. The American Automobile Association agreed to donate an official observer who would accompany them in the car at all times and certify the results. The AAA used their nationwide representatives to facilitate and support them with food, gasoline, oil, and water while clearing the route of any obstructions and even stopping trains long enough for them to pass unimpeded.

Early in July of 1925 the dynamic duo left the Ambassador Hotel in Los Angeles and arrived just 167 hours and 50 minutes later in front of the AAA headquarters at Broadway and 57th Street. In less than one week they covered 3,965 miles. The one flat tire had been changed without stopping by placing a dolly under the car's axle. Wells ran alongside and changed the tire while Wade drove on slowly.

The rewards of the trip exceeded their greatest expectations. With all risk now gone, Packard reconsidered and voted them a handsome sum in exchange for advertising rights. The AAA was also delighted. The record-breaking trip would have a large impact in pushing the road building efforts they supported through Congress. The governors of the states they passed through were very grateful. Federal road building would provide a rich source of state income and generate many new jobs. When the congratulatory telegrams, bonuses, awards, and gifts were finally counted, they shared a profit of $30,500 over their expenses.

Leigh Wade, tiring of his earthbound bondage if not his sudden wealth, traded his car for an airplane and flew to South America as an aircraft broker selling parts and complete airplanes for passenger and farm service. During one of those flights he became the first aviator to fly over the Andes Mountains. During another he met Pedro Zanni, the Argentinean aviator who had attempted to beat him around the world. Despite the language barriers, the two aviators spent many hours swapping tales of their hazardous world flights.

When the war began, Wade reenlisted in the Army Air Corps serving in Cuba. When it ended, he served with the U.S. Military Commission to Brazil before being appointed Air Attache to Greece. He retired as a major general and participated in many reunions of the World Flight crew.

Of all the participants in the First World Flight, Linton Wells— the reporter, eager passenger, and official stowaway—led the most interesting and adventuresome life. After setting the U.S. transcontinental motor car speed record he joined a group of aviators who had reformed the famous Lafayette Escadrille. These American combat pilots had distinguished themselves gallantly during World War I and grown weary of the placid life back home. As soldiers of fortune they offered their services flying and fighting again for the French, this time against insurgent forces in Morocco. Under threat of the loss of their U.S. citizenship and criticism by the U.S. Congress, the French decided the Americans were too controversial, changed their name to the Moroccan Escadrille and transferred them to the Sultan of Morocco.

Wells returned to the United States in the winter of 1925, eager to set his own record for traveling around the world. Ferdinand Magellan, the Portuguese explorer, sailed around the world in three years from 1519 to 1522. Jules Verne wrote of Phileas Fogg's legendary trip in 1872 *Around The World in 80 Days*. Joseph Pulitzer, the New York publisher assigned Nellie Bly the task in 1889. She completed the trip in 72 days, 6 hours and 11 minutes.

In 1890 the record was reduced to 67 days and 12 hours by George Francis Train. In 1901 Charles Fitzmorris, Chicago's Chief of Police reduced it further to 60 days and 13 hours. In 1903 the record fell to Henry Frederick. He completed the trip in 54 days, 7 hours and 2 minutes. Colonel Burnley Campbell next pushed it to forty days and 19 hours in 1907 by using the newly built Trans-Siberian Railway. In 1911 Andre Jaeger-Schmidt brought it further down to 39 days, 19 hours and 42 minutes. In 1913, John Henry Mears, a well known New York Theatrical producer, dashed around the world in 35 days, 21 hours, and 35 minutes.

By 1926, this record had not moved in thirteen years. Wells intended to use airplane travel for the first time to shatter all previous records and prove the utility of commercial airplanes. He presented the idea to Edward S. Evans, a wealthy Detroit businessman with a penchant for exploration and adventure. Convinced that his son would learn more of the world by racing around it with Wells rather than staying in college, he offered to finance the trip if Wells took Edward Evans Jr. with him. Wells agreed and the elder Evans provided $25,000 for trip expenses.

Wells studied and carefully prepared the route making advance preparations through various trip facilitators at strategic locations. Their trip began at 1:30 A.M. on the morning of June 16, 1926. After many harrowing escapes and adventures, duly recorded in his book on the trip, he completed his journey with young Evans. Wells completed the trip with a new record time of 28 days, 14 hours and 36 minutes at a cost of $42,000.

Wells left soon after to report on the growing insurgency in Nicaragua. Constantly dodging bullets from the rear cockpit of an ancient *Standard* biplane flown by an old friend for the Nicaraguan military, after a few months he decided he had stretched his luck as far as possible. He returned home and spent 1927 lecturing and writing, often promoting aviation and the establishment of airports in towns that lacked them. Lindbergh's flight that year made his message much easier to sell.

In 1928 Wells joined Paramount Studios as a screenplay writer. After several months, he demanded a substantial salary increase to extend his contract. David Selznick shook his hand, wished him well, and terminated his employment.

The *International News Service* then hired Wells and sent him to Europe to cover international events. His tenacious aggressiveness and likable demeanor soon had him interviewing and being entertained by many European heads of state. Continuing unrest in the Balkans, the rise of the IRA in Ireland, fascism in Italy, and the economic ills of Germany, provided a rich source for his reports. His interviews with such diverse figures as Mahatma Gandhi of India, President Cosgrave of Ireland, Benito Mussolini of Italy, Kaiser Wilhelm of Germany, and England's Prime Minister, David Lloyd George, were eagerly read by a world-wide audience.

It was the extended assignment to Moscow in 1932 which determined the future of Linton's life. He was the first reporter to break the story to the world that President Roosevelt had agreed to formally recognize the Soviet Union and establish diplomatic relations, the first to break the story of the U.S.S.R. forming a mutual defense pact with France, and the first to discover that Germany, Japan, and Italy had signed a secret agreement to assist each other in military action against the U.S.S.R.

In 1932, during Stalin's second *Five Year Plan* to expand heavy industrial production ahead of consumer goods, J.H. Gillis, a distinguished American mining engineer, successfully constructed several electrolytic zinc plants in the Soviet Union. His extensive efforts earned him the admiration and recognition of the Kremlin and they bestowed upon him their highest medal, the Order of Lenin.

His very attractive and adventurous daughter, Fay Gillis, had fallen passionately in love with flying since starting her flight lessons in 1929 and quickly became the first female member of the Caterpillar Club, fliers whose lives had been saved by parachuting safely to earth.

Forced to follow her father to Moscow, Fay charmed her way into the cockpits of Russian army planes, none of which had ever been flown by a female pilot. She became the first woman aviator permitted by the civil aviation authorities to fly Red Army powered airplanes and the only foreigner allowed to own her own glider. She lectured extensively throughout the Soviet Union on flying and the future of aviation.

Linton met Fay in Moscow and was immediately captivated by her adventuresome spirit and shared love of aviation. After several years of courtship they eloped and were married in New York on April 1, 1935, Linton's birthday. Wiley Post selected Fay as his copilot on his planned flight across Alaska and Siberia to Moscow scheduled to depart a few months after her marriage. She canceled the flight to follow Linton to Ethiopia when war suddenly broke out in East Africa. The well known humorist, Will Rogers, took her place. Their airplane crashed during a takeoff in Alaska and both men died.

Fay was a good friend of Amelia Earhart's and cofounded with her the Ninety-Nines, the largest international organization of female pilots, and the International Forest of Friendship in Atchison, Kansas, Earhart's birthplace. Its trees come from every one of the three dozen countries with a Ninety-Nines Chapter.

Their life was one of shared adventure, reporting together as a team. While making their home on a boat in Fort Lauderdale with their pet leopard, "Snooks," they met the owner of Storer Broadcasting Company vacationing on a larger boat. He needed a White House correspondent. Linton and Fay were hired and spent the next decade covering the administrations of Lyndon Johnson, Richard Nixon, Gerald Ford, and Jimmy Carter. Linton Wells died in 1976. Fay Wells at 92 is still actively traveling and participating in aviation activities from her home in Alexandria, Virginia.

Now we come to the central question, "What effect did the success of the First World Flight have on the future of U.S. aviation?"

From the viewpoint of its progenitor, Billy Mitchell died feeling the greatest achievement of his life was a colossal failure, a wasted effort by brave young airmen who put their lives on the line with little to show for it. Was his drama nothing but a stage play with a cast of hundreds of thousands, a touring road show that had gotten rave reviews in newspapers throughout the world then, when the curtain fell, left little trace?

From the viewpoint of the few remaining airmen of the U.S. Air Service, who continued dying in ancient, obsolete, and dangerous "flying coffins" long after the flight, it changed little. The hoped-for bonanza of new equipment, improved training, and an expanded, energized Air Service never materialized.

The solo flight of the tall, handsome lone eagle across the Atlantic in 1927 provided a new hero to worship. Charles Lindbergh's eminently agreeable, quiet, unassuming demeanor didn't challenge or confront or threaten the political bureaucracy of the time as Mitchell and his supporters did. They could safely promote, publicize and glorify the new event and the man.

The World Flight itself and the young men who made it have long since been forgotten by all but the most dedicated aviation enthusiasts. It is seldom discussed or even mentioned in U.S. aviation history being taught across America. It has been, as many of Mitchell's accurate and brilliant aviation prophesies have been, relegated to the "flying trash pile," languishing in the bottom drawer of the dustbin of history.

Today few know when the first flight around the world was made or who made it. Fewer still could tell you the names of the airmen, the paths they blazed, or describe the planes that prevailed against insurmountable odds. But a look back through the prism of time with the advantage of hindsight, shows us that, far from failure, the First World Flight remains the pivotal, single most important aviation event of the century.

The flight accomplished all six of the original peaceful Army objectives as stated by General Patrick:

1. The feasibility of aerial communication between the countries of the world had been established beyond question.

2. The practicality of travel by air through regions where surface transportation does not exist had been demonstrated.

3. The ability of aircraft to operate under all climactic conditions had been proven.

4. The applicability of aircraft to adapt to the needs of commerce was now evident.

5. The reliability of American produced aircraft had been firmly established.

6. The honor of being the first to fly around the world would belong forever to the United States.

Before the flight most countries believed the United States too backward in its aviation development to be considered as a source for military or commercial aircraft. Donald Douglas proved his World Cruisers could survive forced landings on primitive fields and heavy seas. They could prevail over blizzards, thunderstorms, gale force winds, monsoons, and sandstorms. They could operate in freezing Arctic temperatures down to thirty-five degrees below zero and fiery desert heat up to one hundred thirty-five degrees Fahrenheit. Inquiries came flooding in to his young company. Orders followed and the U.S. aircraft industry was reborn . . . stronger and better than ever.

With scheduled airline service throughout Europe and none in the United States, a vast market opened to U.S. aircraft manufacturers which had been closed before the flight. Domestic military and commercial aircraft demand was very limited but the credibility established by the world flight created foreign markets which eventually led to American aircraft manufacturers' dominance for the balance of the century.

The flight established an air route across the Pacific for the first time from Alaska to Japan and beyond. It pioneered a new, shorter route across the Atlantic from England to Iceland, Greenland, and North America, and made it possible for many types of aircraft to make the crossing. Airplane travel became competitive with steamships.

The military implications of the flight were not lost on Army and Navy officers. The assumption that the oceans provided impenetrable protection from hostile forces, a long established principle of U.S. defense, had been shattered by the world flight. If people and cargo could be delivered by air across the Atlantic and Pacific Oceans, so could the enemy's bombs and bullets. The safety of geographic isolation would never again be accepted as gospel by even the oldest and most backward of the military's General Staff.

Mitchell's concept of the changing face of modern warfare was seen all too clearly by the younger officers. In the next war civilian centers would have to endure massed bombing by raids of hundreds or even thousands of airplanes. Control of the air would be essential for victory by both the Army and the Navy. The world flight proved that the back doors of America, Alaska, and the Aleutians to the west, as well as Greenland and Labrador to the east, could be easily accessed by an adversary and must be reinforced, locked and guarded against any potential enemy.

In a sense, Mitchell lost his battle but won his war. With his departure, the rancorous infighting, animosity and personal resistance to his ideas faded away. Admiral Moffett died in an airship accident. General Pershing and many of the old line Army officers of the General Staff joined the older battleship admirals and sailed into retirement. Their replacements believed, as Mitchell did, that "the war to end all wars" was not the grand finale of man's inhumanity to man, but the opening scene of future wars to come that would be fought in the air with new weapons, coldly efficient killing machines, more terrible and deadlier than the world had ever seen.

In the last book written by Billy Mitchell and published in 1930, the dedication reads;

> I dedicate this book to my two little children, Lucy Trumbull and William, Junior, who in their lifetime will see aeronautics become the greatest and principal means of national defense and rapid transportation all over the world, and possibly beyond our world into interstellar space.

Despite the deepening Depression during the 1930s and a lack of adequate military funding, dedicated pilots such as Curtiss LeMay, Jimmy Doolittle, Hap Arnold, and Tooey Spaatz encouraged America's aircraft manufacturers to develop a new generation of fighting planes.

Among those that flew were the Bell P-39 Airacobra, the Brewster F2A Buffalo, the Curtiss P-40 Warhawk, the Grumman F4F Wildcat, and the P-38 Lightning. The Vought F4U Corsair, Republic P-47 Thunderbolt, and North American's P-51 Mustang were also being built before the decade ended. Despite the Army's reluctance to develop long-range bombers, a group of Mitchell's disciples prevailed upon Boeing to build the model 299 "defensive transport" with private funding. This evolved into the famous B-17 Flying Fortress. Medium bombers such as the B-25 Mitchell by North American, and the B-26 Marauder by Martin, were also designed. Over ten thousand of Douglas Aviation's popular, reliable and highly versatile DC-3 commercial airliner went to war in numerous military designations and configurations for carrying cargo and troops.

Without the impetus and credibility of the First World Flight behind them, U.S. aircraft manufacturing would almost certainly have been on a smaller scale and military aircraft development much further behind. When war finally came in 1941, few if any U.S. fighting airplanes were competitive with the best from Germany or Japan. Encounters with the Fockewulf FW-190, Heinkel's HE-100 and HE-280, Messerschmitt's Bf-109, and Mitsubishi's A6M Zero put the American pilots at a great disadvantage.

America entered World War II as she had the First; poorly prepared and weak militarily. As in World War I, she prevailed only from her incredible industrial capacity, the bravery and sacrifice of her diverse citizenry and eventual air superiority. The enemy's airplanes initially were smaller, lighter, more maneuverable, and up to 100-miles-per-hour faster. It took several years and the deaths of many American pilots before the early American aircraft developed into competitive and eventually superior fighting machines. Considering the years of gestation and development required of new aircraft designs, it is likely that without the kick start of the world flight and the new aircraft models of the 1930s, victory in the 1940s might not have been possible. Eventually, the government concluded Mitchell had been correct and created the strong independent air force and combined Department of Defense that he had given his life to secure.

Billy Mitchell's contribution to the security of the United States was finally recognized after the end of World War II. On August 8, 1946, President Harry Truman posthumously awarded him the Medal of Honor. Through the balance of the Twentieth Century, aviation flourished in the United States nurtured by a vast grass roots community of enthusiasts and a benign government environment.

The innovation, invention, and enthusiasm of this general aviation movement gave birth to new aircraft designs, skilled airmen, mechanics, and engineers. From this pool of talented civilian entrepreneurs, Dick Rutan designed and built the *Voyager*, a radically new aircraft intended to fly around the world without stopping on a single tank of fuel. On December 14, 1986 Rutan and his co-pilot,

Jeanna Yeager, left Edwards Air Force Base in California. After fly-ing 26,358 miles they returned on December 23.

In nine days, three minutes and 44 seconds they completed the first nonstop nonrefueled flight around the world.

In most other countries, the heavy hand of government regula-tion, taxes, and fees effectively strangled widespread grassroots general aviation and with it the source from which trained airmen and support personnel can be drawn in the event of war. America's vast pool of millions of civilian aviation enthusiasts; pilots, mechan-ics, inventors, experimenters, builders, dreamers, and doers, neophytes, and rocket scientists, provide a unique resource from which man's reach into the heavens can equal his grasp and the chal-lenges of the Twenty-First Century, in peace and war, can be met.

Bibliography

Burlingame, Roger. *General Billy Mitchell*. New York: McGraw-Hill Book Company, 1952.

Davis, Burke. *The Billy Mitchell Affair*. New York: Random House, 1967.

Ethell, Jeffrey L. *Frontiers of Flight*. Washington: Smithsonian Books, 1992.

Gathorne-Hardy, G. M. *A Short History Of International Affairs—1920 to 1934*. London: Oxford University Press, 1934.

Gauvreau, Emile and Cohen, Lester. *Billy Mitchell*. New York: E.P Dutton & Co., 1942.

Glines, Caroll V. and Cohen, Stan. *The First Flight Around The World*. Missoula, Montana: Pictorial Histories Publishing Company, Inc., 2000.

Gunston, Bill. *Fighting Aircraft of World War 2*. New York: Prentice Hall Press, 1988.

Hane, Mikiso. *Modern Japan—A Historical Survey*. London: Westview Press, 1986.

Hartney, Harold E. *Up and At 'Em*. Garden City: Doubleday & Company, Inc. 1940.

Johnson, J. H. *1918—The Unexpected Victory*. London: Cassell Group, 1997.

Levine, Isaac Don. *Mitchell—Pioneer of Air Power*. New York: Duell, Sloan & Pearce 1943.

McKay, Ernest A. *A World To Conquer*. New York: Arco Publishing, 1981.

Mitchell, Ruth. *My Brother Bill*. New York: Harcourt, Brace & Company, 1953.

Mitchell, William. *Winged Defense*. New York: G. P. Putnam's Sons, 1926.

Mitchell, William. *Skyways*. Philadelphia: J.B. Lippincott Company, 1930.

Mitchell, W.A. *World's Military History*. Harrisburg: Military Service Publishing Company, 1931.

Platt, Frank C. *Great Battles of World War I*. New York: Weathervane Books, 1966.

Reischauer, Edwin O. *The Japanese*. Cambridge: Harvard University Press, 1977.

Rosendahl, Charles E. *Up Ship*. New York: Dodd, Mead & Company, 1931.

Smythe, Donald. *Pershing*. Bloomington: Indiana University Press, 1986

Thomas, Lowell. *The First World Flight*. Boston: Houghton Mifflin Co., 1925.

Thomas, Lowell and Thomas Jr., Lowell. *Famous Flights that Changed History*. Garden City: Doubleday & Company, 1968.

Wells, Linton. *Blood on the Moon*. Boston: Houghton Mifflin Co., 1937.

Wells, Linton. *Around the World in Twenty Eight Days*. Boston: Houghton Mifflin Co., 1926.

Whitehouse, Arch. *Billy Mitchell*. New York: G.P. Putnam's Sons, 1962.

Woodward, Helen. *General Billy Mitchell*. New York: Duell, Sloan & Pearce, 1959.